CD Cracking Uncovered:
Protection against Unsanctioned CD Copying

CD CRACKING UNCOVERED

PROTECTION AGAINST UNSANCTIONED CD COPYING

KRIS KASPERSKY

a-list

A-LIST, LLC
295 East Swedesford Rd.
PMB #285
Wayne, PA 19087
702-977-5377 (FAX)
mail@alistpublishing.com
http://www.alistpublishing.com

This book is printed on acid-free paper.

CD Cracking Uncovered: Protection against Unsanctioned CD Copying
By Kris Kaspersky

    ISBN 1-931769-33-8

Printed in the United States of America

04 05 7 6 5 4 3 2 1

A-LIST, LLC, titles are available for site license or bulk purchase by institutions, user groups, corporations, etc.

Book Editor: Thomas Rymer

Contents

PREFACE _____ 1

INTRODUCTION _____ 3

   Notation Conventions _____ 4
   Historical Aspect _____ 4
   Thoughts about Hackers, Protection Mechanisms,
   and Programming _____ 10

PART I: CD ANATHOMY _____ 13

CHAPTER 1: CD ORGANIZATION _____ 15

   Pits, Lands, Frames, and Sectors in Brief _____ 16
      Subcode Channels _____ 18
      Sector Addressing _____ 21
      Raw and Cooked Sectors _____ 22
      Sync Groups, Merging Bits, and DSV _____ 25
      Scrambling _____ 29
      F1-, F2-, and F3 Frames and CIRC Encoding _____ 38
   Lead-in Area, Data Area, Lead-out Area, and TOC _____ 46

CHAPTER 2: POWER OF REED-SOLOMON CODES _____ **49**

Basics of Error-Correcting Codes
and Error-Correcting Encoding _____51
Idea of Reed-Solomon Codes _____58
General Concept _____63
Recommended Reading_____63
Polynomial Arithmetic and Galois Fields _____64
  Polynomial Arithmetic_____65
  Galois Fields _____66
    Addition and Subtraction in Galois fields _____68
    Multiplication in Galois Fields _____69
    Division in Galois Fields _____75
    Simplest Practical Implementations _____76
Reed-Solomon Codes in Practical Implementations_____80
  Legend _____80
  Encoder _____81
  Decoder _____85
    Syndrome Decoder _____86
    Error Locator Polynomial_____87
    Polynomial Roots _____89
    Data Recovery _____89
    Source Code of the Decoder _____89
  Interface to the ElByECC.DLL Library_____89
    Linking the ElByECC.DLL Library to Your Programs _____90
    GenECCAndEDC_Mode1 _____91
    CheckSector _____92
    Final _____92

PART II: LOW-LEVEL CONTROL OVER HARDWARE ___ 95

CHAPTER 3: PRACTICAL ADVICE ON URGENT SYSTEM RECOVERY ___ 97

Applications, Illegal Operations, and Everything Else ___ 97
Doctor Watson ___ 99
Microsoft Visual Studio Debugger ___ 106
Inhabitants of the Shadowy Zone, or From Morgue to Reanimation ___ 108
Forcibly Exiting the Function ___ 108
Unwinding the Stack ___ 111
Passing Control to the Message Handler Function ___ 115
How to Process Memory Dump ___ 122
Recovering the System after Critical Failure ___ 130
Loading the Crash Dump ___ 130

CHAPTER 4: INTERFACES FOR INTERACTION WITH THE HARDWARE ___ 137

Access via the CD-ROM Driver ___ 138
Access in the Cooked Mode (Block Reading Mode) ___ 146
Access via SPTI ___ 149
Access via ASPI ___ 169
Access via the SCSI Port ___ 181
Accessing the Drive via SCSI Miniport ___ 185
Communication via Input/Output Ports ___ 194
Access via the MSCDEX Driver ___ 205
Communicating via the Custom Driver ___ 208
Summary Table of Characteristics of Various Interfaces ___ 209

CHAPTER 5: METHODS OF REVEALING PROTECTION MECHANISMS ___ 211

CD Burning: Pros, Cons, and Something about ___ 213
Locking and Unlocking the EJECT Button ___ 217
Hacking Secrets. Brake Fluid for CDs ___ 219

Investigation of Real Programs _____ 220
    Alcohol 120% _____ 220
    Easy CD Creator _____ 221
    Clone CD _____ 221

PART III: PROTECTION AGAINST UNAUTHORIZED COPYING AND DATA RECOVERY _____ 223

CHAPTER 6: ANTI-COPYING MECHANISMS _____ 225

Built-in CD Protection _____ 230
Protection Mechanisms Based on Non-Standard Disc Formats_____ 230
    Incorrect TOC and its Consequences _____ 230
        Incorrect Starting Address for the Track _____ 232
        Fictitious Track in the Genuine Track _____ 258
        Fictitious Track in the Data Area of a Genuine Track _____ 267
        Fictitious Track in the Post-Gap of the Genuine Track _____ 273
        Fictitious Track in the Pre-Gap of a Genuine Track_____ 273
        Fictitious Track in the Lead-Out Area _____ 277
        Fictitious Track Coinciding with the Genuine Track _____ 283
    Invalidating Track Numbering _____ 285
        Incorrect Starting Number for the First Track _____ 287
        Two Identical Tracks_____ 290
        Incorrect Number for the Last Track _____ 293
        Gap in Track Numbering of the First Session_____ 296
        Gap in Track Numbering in the Second Session _____ 299
        Discs That Start from a Track With a Number Other Than One_____ 303
        Disc with Track Number Zero _____ 304
        Track with Non-Standard Number _____ 319
        Data Track Disguised as Audio_____ 327
        Incorrect Run-out as Protection Tool or X-Sector_____ 334

CHAPTER 7: PROTECTION MECHANISMS FOR PREVENTING PLAYBACK

       IN PC CD-ROM _____ **345**

Audio Overlapped by Data _____ 346

Castrated Lead-Out _____ 350

Negative Starting Address of the First Audio Track _____ 350

CHAPTER 8: PROTECTION AGAINST FILE-BY-FILE DISC COPYING _____ **353**

Invalid File Sizes _____ 354

File Encryption _____ 367

CHAPTER 9: PROTECTION MECHANISMS BASED

       ON BINDING TO STORAGE MEDIA _____ **375**

Putting Marks vs. Dynamic Binding _____ 376

Protection Mechanisms Based on Physical Defects _____ 377

Protection Mechanisms Based on the Read Timing Characteristics ___ 381

    Measuring Angles between Sectors _____ 385

Protection Mechanisms Based on Weak Sectors _____ 389

CHAPTER 10: DATA RECOVERY FROM CDS _____ **393**

Restoring Deleted Files from CD-R/CD-RW _____ 394

    Getting Access to Deleted Files _____ 395

    Recovering Entire Sessions _____ 400

    Beginners' Errors, or What You Should Never Do _____ 401

Restoring Cleared CD-RW Discs _____ 401

How to Recover Unreadable CDs? _____ 408

General Recommendations on Recovery _____ 408

The Disc Cannot Be Recognized by the Drive _____ 410

The Disc is Recognized by the Drive, but Not
by the Operating System _____ 412

The Computer Freezes When Inserting the Disc into the Drive _____ 413

The Disc Is Read with Errors _____ 414

ON THE CD _____ _____ 417

INDEX _____ _____ ___ 419

Preface

This book is a practical guide to protecting CDs against unauthorized copying. It is oriented toward a wide reader audience, including advanced users and application and system programmers.

It is not necessary to have expensive specialized equipment or be a security expert to create strong, inexpensive, and reliable protection. All that you need to achieve this is a low-end CD recorder and a couple of evenings free from other work. This book provides a detailed description of CD structure and will let you in to a lot of secrets known only to security experts (and not even they know them all), explaining all this in simple language, without higher mathematics and practically without Assembler language. This is the book's main unique feature!

While reading this book, you will learn how to invalidate the disc format in order to make it readable (that is, playable) on most CD-ROM drives, but practically impossible for any copier to copy, and how to bind to the physical disc structure so that copiers are unable either to reproduce or imitate it. You'll also learn about the physical and technical limitations of low-end recorders and how to use these to achieve your goals.

Also covered will be the control over CD drives and recorders at a low level and how to get the maximum control allowed by specific drive models over CDs. All circumstances being equal, a disc protected using high-tech drive cannot be copied by all other drives. The book provides detailed information on the differences between drive models and which characteristics deserve the most attention when choosing a drive.

The book also discusses practically all commercial CD protection packets available today. It lists their implementation errors, "thanks" to which the copying of protected discs is still possible. The author also suggests several protection mechanisms that take into account his own bitter experience and that of his friends and colleagues. These protection mechanisms cannot be copied using any of the copiers that exist today.

With regard to copiers, here you'll find detailed description of the most popular protected CD copiers: Clone CD and Alcohol 120%, which, according to their developers, "can copy practically any protected disc, provided that the right combination of CD-ROM and CD recorder is chosen." The author demonstrates, using practical examples, that this is not actually the case, and suggests some protection mechanisms that cannot be copied by Clone CD and/or by Alcohol 120%.

Finally, the book explains how to create a protected CD copier on your own, making the replication of protected discs a much easier task.

Introduction

CD protection is important today as never before. The widespread use of low-end re-corders allowed any user to duplicate discs in almost mass-production quantities. The lion's share of existing discs has not been purchased because users simply borrow them from their friends or colleagues. At the same time, most shareware programmers distribute their products on CD-R discs by mail, which considerably complicates the hacker's task. If the program is not freely available, how can it be cracked?

As a result, users are interested in cracking protected discs, while developers have the opposite goal, namely, protecting CDs against cracking. This book satisfies the needs of both groups. It explains how to crack practically any currently existing pro-tection software and suggests a range of new protection mechanisms that virtually cannot be cracked.

CD protection against copying contains a large amount of material that has never been published before. It provides the reader with detailed information on CD struc-ture and discloses lots of secrets known only to professionals (and not even to every professional). At the same time, the author tries to present this material in an accessi-ble form, without excessive use of higher mathematics and practically without the use of Assembler language.

Having read this book, the reader (even with no special training) will learn how to create discs that, in principle, cannot be copied because of the hardware limitations of contemporary CD-R/CD-RW recorders. Besides this, the reader will learn how to avoid conflicts with non-standard equipment, as a result of which protection mecha-nisms refuse to work or, even worse, damage the user's equipment.

The book is oriented to the wide spectrum of readers, so the reader doesn't have to have any previous experience or background knowledge. The reader might even lack knowledge of the sector structure of a CD-ROM (by the way, 99 percent of programmers don't know much about this either). All of the information necessary for understanding the principles of CD operation is provided directly in the book, and references to third-party sources are minimal. The reader doesn't need to be a programmer, because all of the required utilities for the analysis, protection and cracking of CDs are supplied along with the book. These copiers, developed by the author, will make all work automatically for the reader. Thus, the book is worth purchasing, if only for of the contents of the companion CD alone.

At the most, the reader must be familiar with mathematics at the University level, know how to use disassembler, and be able to work with C and Assembler programming languages. Of course, reading this book won't make you a guru, but you'll still acquire almost unlimited power over CDs and be able to do whatever you like with them.

Notation Conventions

To prevent confusion and at the same time avoid unnecessary verbosity, the book will use several notation conventions, which are briefly outlined below:

- ❑ *NEC drive* — _NEC CD-RW NR-9100A, firmware version 1.4
- ❑ *ASUS drive* — ASUS CD-S500/A, firmware version 1.4
- ❑ *TEAC drive* — TEAC CD-W552E, firmware version 1.09
- ❑ *PHILIPS drive* — PHILIPS CDRW2412A, firmware version 1.5

Alcohol 120% — an excellent copier of protected CDs, a shareware version of which can be downloaded from **http://www.alcohol-soft.com/**. This automatically cracks more than half of all currently existing anti-copying mechanisms and allows you to mount images of protected discs dynamically to a virtual CD-ROM drive, which is very convenient for the purpose of experimentation. Unfortunately, only "correct" images can be mounted, and most images in protected discs cannot be classified as such.

Clone CD — a good copier of protected discs, a shareware version of which can be downloaded from **http://www.elby.ch/**. Copying protected discs in completely automatic mode is, of course, not the strongest point of Clone CD. It could be more accurate to say that it copes with this task poorly. However, after manually tweaking the program settings and the image of the protected disc, it also can copy over half of all existing examples of protection mechanisms. But to say that Clone CD can "crack" practically any types of protection would be far from accurate.

Historical Aspect

The first attempts to protect CDs against copying were undertaken in early 1990s. CD recorders didn't exist at that time, and developers mainly had to prevent unauthorized copying of CD contents to hard disk. But what about pirates? you may ask.

Yes, piracy always has been and remains a serious problem. However, attempts at stopping piracy by software protection are, at least, naive. Those who replicate discs in commercial quantities always employ a team of experienced hackers who crack these protection mechanisms without any real effort. The intellectual potential of "cracking" teams in these clandestine enterprises is practically unlimited. They always try to employ the very best (I know this from personal experience, because some years ago, before the adoption of appropriate laws, I also worked on a team like this). The financial factor, by the way, is not the primary one here. Hackers were not paid large money, and had to work like slaves. The work itself was what attracted them. Where else could you get acquainted with such a large number of various protection mechanisms and learn how to crack them?

To be honest, I have exaggerated a bit in discussing the variety of protection mechanisms available. At that time, the "variety" included two main types of protection: LaserLock and "code wheel". With the arrival of CD recorders, the importance of protection against copying grew considerably. As a result, they began to grow like mushrooms after a warm rain. By the beginning of 2003, there were already more than 50 various protection mechanisms available on the market. The majority of these were marketed on the basis of the "know-how" of their developers. However, most hackers, having analyzed one of these protections using a disassembler, began to feel nostalgic for days gone by, when software came on diskettes and one out of every two examples was protected. Contemporary CDs, of course, are different from old-fashioned diskettes. However, the techniques of their protection are, in principle, the same!

Contemporary protection mechanisms use the mainly following methods: *non-standard formatting*, the *introduction of key marks*, *binding to the disc surface*, and *weak sectors*. Let us consider each member of this family in more detail.

Non-standard formatting, in general, consists of intentionally introducing specific errors to prevent the normal processing of information. For example, if we artificially increase the length of every protected file to ~666 GB by correcting the length field, any attempt at copying such a file to a hard disk will fail. At the same time, the protection mechanism that knows exactly where each specific file starts and ends can work with them without any problems. Naturally, such a protection mechanism can be hacked easily by copying the disc at the sector level. However, to do this, the copier must know the exact number of sectors available on the disc. The developer of a protection mechanism can easily tweak the disc structures so that the disc looks either absolutely blank or, on the contrary, grows beyond any conceivable size. Recorders that mechanically read the disc TOC and blindly rely on the correctness of each byte of control data will fail immediately. More advanced examples will manage to determine the actual size of the disc through some implicit indications. Recorders of this type will move the optical head until the sectors under it remain readable while it is being moved. Let's assume that the protection is using a cunning mechanism and "digs a hole" consisting of a bunch of bad sectors near the end of the disc. Some recorders will fall into that pit, thinking that they have reached the end. Some recorders won't be deceived by this trick, because they carefully analyze the information returned by the drive, which should know the cause of the read error — be it the actual end of the disc or simply a bad sector.

Some protection mechanisms play even dirtier tricks, boldly writing irrecoverable errors to the original disc (which means that these errors cannot be eliminated by the special error-correction codes placed on the CD). If this approach is used for protecting an audio CD, this means that its playback will be accompanied by endless clicks. This doesn't happen in practice because the developers of audio players have made the provision of a special filter that discards data that are sure to be erroneous and uses interpolation when necessary (in this case, the current sample is recreated on the basis of the averaged values of those that precede and follow it). Naturally, this degrades the playback quality. Media magnates, however, don't give much of a damn about this, and, realistically, the degradation isn't significant. However, the situation is different with regard to digital playback. Early versions of the standard instructed the drive to report only occasions where one or more irrecoverable errors were encountered, but didn't provide any mechanisms for "marking" the faulty bytes. So the drive has read 2,352 bytes of data and detected that about hundred of them were invalid! What next? Use interpolation? If the answer is yes, what should we interpolate — which byte by which?! Analyze the signal manually, searching for "outbreaks?" This is too difficult and, anyway, the quality of the "restored" audio will be very far from perfect. It is, of course, possible to try grabbing the audio flow from the digital audio output. However, most low-end sound adapters do not support this capability. Even if this kind of support is provided, it is implemented so poorly that music lovers would be better off simply shooting themselves. Put simply, dark clouds without the slightest trace of a sunshine began to gather over hackers. However, everything changed after manufacturers began to offer CD drives capable not only of simply reporting read errors, but also of reporting the positions of erroneous bytes within the sector. Now, fully functional interpolation became possible at the interface level! After this, software grabbers exploiting new possibilities arrived quickly.

Still, we are running ahead of ourselves. Let's return to that distant past when there were no CD drives, even in the project phase. All software was distributed on diskettes (both copyright and copyleft). By that time, everyone who wanted to protect their diskettes scratched them using any means available: those who had the necessary financial resources burnt the magnetic layer using a laser, while others simply scratched it with a needle or rusty nail. All that remained to ensure protection was to check whether the surface defect was present in the predefined position. Copying such a diskette without special equipment was not a realistic task, because no one could place the scratches from the original in the same position on the copy. However, hackers understanding controller ports quickly came up with the idea that, if they modified the checksum of the key sectors, the diskette would be read with errors, despite the fact that its surface was physically intact! CD protection is based on the same method, and CDs can be cracked using the same approach. The manufacturer can stuff the disc with bad sectors and check their presence any time the protected software started. This generated the following problems: first, not every copier would agree to copy a disk bearing physical defects. Even if it agreed to do what you asked it, you would have to wait a very long time for the copying process to be completed (everyone is familiar with the snail's pace of reading defective sectors). Further, the resulting copy would be unusable, because it didn't contain the defects in predefined positions.

Less than intelligent hackers simply invalidate the checksum of the sector, thus making the drive return an error (naturally, the recording drive must allow us to write sectors with a checksum error, which is not always the case). This, however, doesn't solve the problem. After all, the disfigured sector is read practically immediately, and the protection mechanism, provided that it isn't absolutely useless, can detect easily that something is wrong here. Or, as a variant, it can carry out long sector reading, meaning that the sector with modified checksum will become readable.

What should a cunning hacker do? This question can't be answered immediately or in simple language. Simply speaking, the CD format is such that the high-frequency signal that results when reading a sequence of pits and lands under an optical head has no reference level. For the drive to be able to detect where there is a minus and where there is a plus, the number of lands must be approximately equal to the number of pits. If some specific section of a sector contains only pits, it will be catastrophically dark, and an automatic amplifier will try to increase the laser-ray power, erroneously assuming that there is something wrong either with the disc or with the optics. In this case, a number of the pits will be turned into lands and the drive will be confused in every respect. First, it will try to carry out recalibration, drag the optical head for some time, and only then will it sadly report that this sector is unreadable. From the protection mechanism's point of view, this sector will appear to be damaged, although, at the physical level, its surface is intact.

Now, let's return to the main aspect: Because the drive must be able to record any imaginable (and even unimaginable) data correctly, the developers must make provisions for a method that can bypass such unfavorable situations. In fact, such a mechanism does exist! To put it simply, there are several possible methods of encoding the data being written to the disc, and the drive must choose the most favorable options. Fortunately (or unfortunately), not every drive is so scrupulous. Since the possibility of the unintentional occurrence of unfavorable sequences is infinitely small, some (in fact, many) drives encode the data using a single predefined method. Consequently, there is the possibility for simulating faulty sectors that practically do not differ from actual faulty examples.

The protection developers saw this as a gold rush! If they could only specially glean an unfavorable sequence of bytes, then a specialized drive would be required to write it correctly. When copying such discs on a normal low-end drive, the original would be read wonderfully, but there would be a lot of bad sectors on the copy and the duplicated disc would be unusable. Sectors with unfavorable sequences became known as weak sectors. To copy such sectors, it is necessary to have high-end sophisticated drives from well-known brand manufacturers. But what if you don't have such a drive at your disposal? Does this mean that you are unable to copy such a disc? The answer is no! If the protection doesn't take additional measures, the copier can compute error-correcting codes for a true unfavorable sequence and then correct it slightly and write to the disc. At the physical level, such a sector will be readable without any problems. At the logical level, the drive will restore it to its initial form using redundant codes. However, if the protection reads the sector in RAW mode, it will immediately recognize the forgery. Therefore, not every disc can be copied using this method.

To understand the concept behind the next protection mechanism, we must return to diskettes once again. The physical surface of the diskette is divided into concentric rings named cylinders, and cylinders, in turn, are divided into sectors. When the read head moves from the last sector of one cylinder to the first sector of the next cylinder, it is moved some distance away due to diskette rotation. Consequently, the drive must wait for an entire turn to meet that sector again. Those who spent days and nights in computing centers came to the idea that if the sectors of each of the next cylinders were shifted, the speed of the sequential reading would grow considerably, because the required sector would immediately be under the head. On the other hand, by rotating the sectors of different cylinders by certain angles, we would achieve certain fluctuations of the data-exchange speed. According to these fluctuations, the protection mechanism would be able to distinguish a duplicate from the original, because a duplicate wouldn't produce such fluctuations.

Now let's return to CDs. There are, of course, no cylinders, and the sequence of sectors has a spiral form. Head positioning to the sectors of the adjacent spiral track turns is carried out by means of deviating the laser head by a magnetic system (which means that it takes place almost instantly). Positioning to remote sectors involves the mechanism of moving the head along special "sliders," which requires considerable time. Knowing the speed of disc rotation and having measured the time required for positioning the head to the sectors of the adjacent turns of the track, we will be able to find the angle between them, which depends directly on the spiral's swirl. Different types of CD-R/CD-RW discs have different spiral structures. Even worse, this structure is created by the manufacturer, which means that the discs are supplied to the market with preliminary formatting required for orientation of the CD recorder. Copying a disc protected in this manner is unrealistic and, therefore, it is necessary to emulate it. The copier must carefully measure the angles between different sectors and recreate the initial structure of the spiral. The process of scanning the disc requires a monstrous amount of time (sometimes, several days). The result, however, is worth it.

The disc can also have a catastrophically non-standard format. For instance, it can have sectors of variable lengths. As a result, some sectors will be read faster than others. Because every change of the sector length is immediately reflected in the structure of the spiral track, the copier has to deal with two unknown values — the unknown angle of the spiral swirl and an unknown sector length. From the mathematical point of view, this equation can have many possible solutions. Only one of them, however, is correct. The copier can (and must!) present several variants of copies to allow us to decide on our own, which of them cracks the protection and which doesn't. Unfortunately, no copier, of which I am aware, is capable of doing this.

Nevertheless, long sectors represent a stand-alone entity, and some discs use these sectors alone for the protection. The dark side is that no CD burner available on the market allows us to control the lengths of the sectors being written. There is one clue though. Although we cannot increase the sector length, we can still create two sectors with identical headers. Having successfully read the first of the two sectors, we will ignore the second, but the visible sector length will be increased twofold. The weak spot in this technology is that we can only increase the sector length by a value that is a multiple of two. Even worse, not every drive provides this possibility. Some drives simply refuse to write twin sectors.

Now let's discuss key marks. Besides the user data sector area, which is copied by practically all copiers, there are numerous locations on CDs which have been poorly investigated. First, there are subcode channels. There are eight of these channels in total. One stores service information, according to which the laser head is oriented, the second stores information about pauses, and the remaining six channels are free. Standard copiers do not copy them, and not every burner provides the possibility to write them. These channels are exactly where protection mechanisms insert key marks!

By the way, subcode channels are stored independently on the main data channel, and there is no direct correspondence between them. First, when reading the subcode channel of sector X, the drive can return the subchannel data from any of neighboring sectors at its discretion. The second important factor is that most drives have very poor stability characteristics, and, when reading subchannel data from sectors X, Y, and Z, can return the data from X, X, X, or Y, Z, X, or Y, Z, Z, or any other combination. Let's assume that the subcode channel of one of the sectors contains a key mark, and we are trying to read it. Will we succeed? Not necessarily. If service information is modified at least slightly, we won't be able to determine, to which sectors the subchannel data that we have read actually belongs or whether or not our sector belongs to their list. The only way out is to use a high-quality CD-ROM drive that has good stability characteristics when reading subchannel data.

Finally, CD-R/CD-RW discs are significantly different in some characteristics from the replicated mechanically stamped CD-ROM. Is there any need to introduce ATIP? Aside from this, there also is such thing as TDB (Track Descriptor Block), where, among other information, there is laser power and other similar data. Naturally, CD-ROM discs do not contain anything of the sort. It is impossible to falsify the CD-ROM disc nature directly. However, there are many utilities that intercept all attempts at accessing the drive and return exactly what we need instead of the actual information.

At this point, let's complete our brief overview of protection mechanisms. Further on, each of them will be considered and discussed in more detail.

Note that bypassing the protection against CD copying is not the same thing as copyright violation! The laws of many countries explicitly allow the creation of backup copies of licensed media. At the same time, there is no existing law that prohibits the "cracking" of legally purchased software. License agreements can prohibit whatever the manufacturers like. They have, however, no legal status. By violating a license agreement, you automatically cancel the contract with the software vendor, which means that you make void all warranties and privileges that the vendor promised you. This is approximately the same thing that overclockers do when they cut specific processor pins to unlock its frequency multiplier. You won't land in court if your processor dies in clouds of smoke. However, no one is going to replace your burnt-out specimen. You can only be prosecuted by law if you start to distribute the cracked software. This is a risk, therefore, that I don't advise you to take.

Thoughts about Hackers, Protection Mechanisms, and Programming

Hackers and developers of protection mechanisms are not just opponents. They are also colleagues. If we assume that hackers are parasitic for programmers, exploiting their inability to build truly high-quality protection mechanisms, then we have to realize that programmers are parasitic for users, exploiting their inability to write programs!

Hacking and programming actually have very much in common. Creating high-quality and reliable protection mechanisms requires the skills of low-level programming, working with the operating system, drivers and equipment, knowledge of the architecture of contemporary processors, the specific features of code generation typical for specific compilers, and the "biology" of the libraries being used. At this level of programming, the distinction between programming as such and hacking becomes so thin and difficult to differentiate, that I won't even try to draw it.

Let's start by stating the fact that every protection, as is the case with any other software component, requires careful and thorough testing in order to evaluate its usability. In this context, "usability" is interpreted as its ability to withstand attempts at cracking it done by qualified users armed by hacking tools (protected disc copiers, virtual drive emulators, window and message spies, file and registry monitors). Protection quality is not evaluated by its strength, but, instead, by the *relationship* between the man-hours required for its implementation and the man-hours required for its cracking. In the long run, every protection system can be cracked, because cracking is only a matter of time, money, cracker qualification, and efforts. However, expertly designed protection must not provide easy opportunities for this cracking. Here is a practical example illustrating this statement. A protection mechanism that binds to bad sectors (which are actually unique to each storage medium) is practically useless if it cannot recognize their rough emulation by incorrect EDC/ECC fields. Here is another example. Binding to the geometry of the CD spiral track, even if its implementation is bug-free, can be bypassed by means of creating a virtual CD-ROM drive that emulates all of the specific features of the original disc structure. Notice that you don't have to be a hacker to do this, because in this case, it is enough to run Alcohol 120%, which cracks such protection mechanisms automatically.

The design errors of protection mechanisms bear a dear cost for their developers. However, no one is warranted against such errors. Attempts at applying a "scientific" approach to the development of software protection are an absolutely senseless farce. Hackers laugh at academic-style works with names like "Computing trajectory of a spherical cube in vacuum." In fact, practically all of these types of protection can be removed within 15 minutes without any serious mental effort. Here is a rough, but illustrative example. Designing a defensive strategy for a fortress without taking into account air power will allow anyone to occupy it using even the oldest aircraft used in warfare (MS WDB is such an aircraft), let alone modern fighter-bombers (Soft-Ice is a fighter, while IDA Pro is a bomber).

To develop protection mechanisms, the programmer must have at least a general idea about the working methods and technical tools used by his or her opponents. To master this technical arsenal at a level no lower than that of the opponent is even better. Practical experience (actually cracked programs) is highly desirable, since it allows to study the tactics and strategy of the offensive party carefully, thus allowing for the organization of an optimal defense. Simply speaking, it allows us to detect and reinforce the most probable targets against hacker attacks, concentrating on them the maximum available intellectual resources. This means that the developer of protection mechanisms must be inspired by the hacker psychology, and start thinking like a hacker.

Thus, mastering information-protection technology assumes the mastering of cracking technology. If you don't know how protection mechanisms are cracked, what their vulnerabilities are, and have no information about the hacker's arsenal, you won't be able to create a strong protection mechanism that is, at once, inexpensive and easy to implement. The books about security that consider this subject exclusively from the protection point of view have the same drawback as storage devices that can only write information — they have no practical applications.

Part I

CD Anathomy

Chapter 1: CD Organization 15

Chapter 2: Power of Reed-Solomon Codes 49

Chapter 1: CD Organization

In this, mainly theoretical chapter of the book, the reader will become acquainted with CD organization and the principles of optical recording. Without this knowledge, any study of CD-protection principles is simply impossible.

Physically, a CD is a thin plate made of polycarbonate plastic with a thin *reflective* aluminum (or, in some cases, golden) layer. The reflective layer, in turn, is covered by another, special *protective* layer (Fig. 1.1). The reflective layer is imprinted with a chain of microscopic *pits* and *lands*, arranged in a form of a long, continuous spiral track. This track is similar to those that you would see on an old vinyl phonograph record (Fig. 1.2). Unlike the vinyl record, however, the information on a CD winds from the disc's center to its outer edge. CDs, therefore, are similar to sequential access devices with accelerated rewinding.

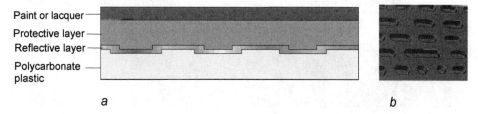

Fig. 1.1. Cross-section of a CD (*a*) and enlarged image of the pits on its surface (*b*)

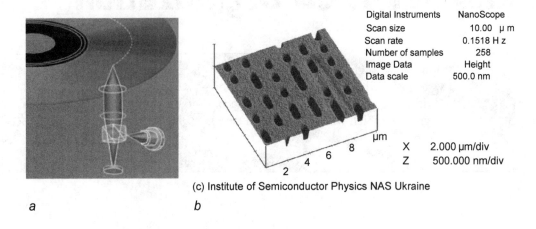

Digital Instruments   NanoScope
Scan size   10.00 μ m
Scan rate   0.1518 H z
Number of samples   258
Image Data   Height
Data scale   500.0 nm

X   2.000 μm/div
Z   500.000 nm/div

(c) Institute of Semiconductor Physics NAS Ukraine

a   b

Fig. 1.2. CD is similar to an old vinyl phonograph record

Pits, Lands, Frames, and Sectors in Brief

Contrary to common belief, pits and lands do not directly correspond to the ones and zeroes of binary code. Information is stored on CDs according to much more sophisticated and advanced principles. The *one of binary code is represented by a change from a pit to a land or from a land to a pit, while the zero of binary code is represented by the lack of a change for the current interval* (Fig. 1.3). At the same time, between two ones there must be no less than two and no more than ten zeroes. The lower limit is a result of technological problems involved in the manufacture of the physical discs manufacturing, while the upper limit is due to the instability of disc rotation speed. For example, if the stability of rotation speed is 3 percent, then, when reading a sequence of ten zeroes, the error will be 1/3 bit, which doesn't pose any problems. However, when reading a sequence of fifteen zeroes, this error grows to 1/2 bit, and the drive will have problems with rounding this error.

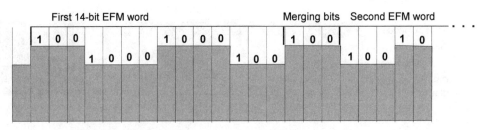

Fig. 1.3. Principle of writing data on a CD

Fourteen bits make up one *EFM-word*, which is encoded into a normal 8-bit byte according to special table. In fact, the abbreviation *EFM* stands for *Eight to Fourteen Modulation*. Every two EFM words are separated by three merging bits, which are intended, first, for resolving situations of encoding conflict (for instance, where one EFM word terminated by the binary value of one is followed by another EFM word that starts with the same binary value), and, second, to prevent the occurrence of erroneous sync groups, which will be covered in detail a little bit later.

A group of 36 bytes makes up an *F1 frame*, which comprises the *sync group* preceding it, a *subcode* byte, and two 12-byte *data groups* supplied with 4-byte *checksum* (or *CRC*) fields.

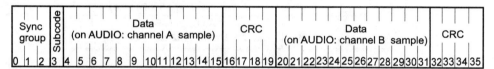

Fig. 1.4. Structure of an F1 frame

Frames are joined to form *sectors*, also called *blocks*. Each sector contains 98 chaotically mixed frames (mixing allows for the reduction of the influence of medium defects, since useful information is spread over the track). At the same time, the first 16 bytes of each sector are occupied by the *header*, which contains a 12-byte *Sync* field, a 3-byte *Address* field, and a 1-byte *Mode* field (Fig. 1.5).

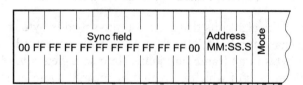

Fig. 1.5. Structure of the sector header

The sector is significant because it is the smallest unit of data that a CD drive can read in raw mode. Note that there are no drives that would allow for the retrieval of the frame contents "as is." On the contrary, all drives forcibly recover frame contents at the hardware level, using CRC fields for this purpose. Details related to error-recovery technique will be provided later. For the moment, it is enough to note that the lack of access to actual "raw" bytes rules out obtaining a bit-by-bit disc copy. This means that the protection mechanism has the principal capability of distinguishing a copy from the original.

Subcode Channels

Along with various auxiliary information, the F1 frame contains one *subchannel byte*, also called the subchannel or control byte (see Fig. 1.7). Subchannel data are entirely isolated from sector contents and, in some ways, behave exactly like multiple data flows in the NTFS file system (see *"Inside Windows NT File System"* by Helen Custer). Fig. 1.6 illustrates this.

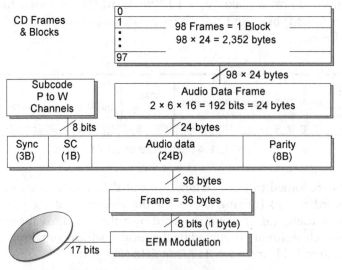

Fig. 1.6. Hierarchy of different data structures

Every one of the eight bits that make up the subcode byte is designated by an upper-case Latin character: P, Q, R, S, T, U, V, and W, respectively. Similarly named bits of subchannel bytes in all frames are joined into so-called *subcode channels*. Channels consist of *sections*, each of which is created by means of joining subchannel data from 98 frames, which equals one sector (see Fig. 1.7). However, section and sector boundaries may not coincide. Consequently, to guarantee the retrieval of one section from a disc, we must read the first two sectors. The first two bytes of the section are used for synchronization, while 96 are dedicated for the storage of actual data. By means of simple calculation, we can discover that for every channel there are exactly 16 bytes of raw, unprocessed data.

Data of P and Q subchannels are supplied in the form of data that are ready for use. The first 12 bytes are the most important, while the others are used for alignment. Data of R-W channels must be specially prepared before used (this process is known as "cooking"). The 96 6-bit *symbols that make up these channels* are divided into 4 groups comprising 24 words. Every group of this type is called a *pack*, and includes

16 symbols of user data and two EDC/ECC fields, one of which contains 2 symbols of correcting codes, and the second of which contains 4 symbols of correcting codes.

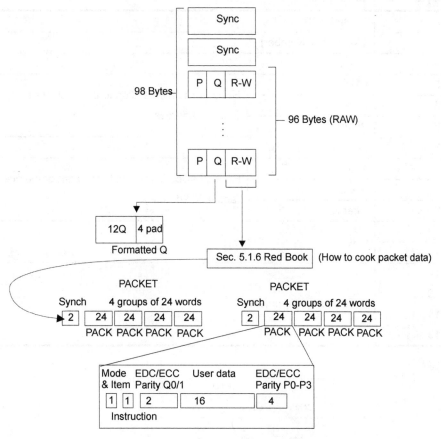

Fig. 1.7. Subchannel data organization

What information is stored in subcode channels? According to the ECMA-130 standard, "normal" CDs use only two subchannels: P and Q.

The *P subchannel* contains the termination marker of the current track and a pointer to the next track, while the *Q subchannel* is used for the storage of service information, which determines the current position of this block on the disc. Of all of the channels, this is the most important.

In its structure, the Q subchannel comprises the following four parts: four control bits corresponding to the *Control* field, four address bits corresponding to the *q-Mode (ADR)* field; 7 bits of Q-data, corresponding to the *q-Data* field, and 16 bits of the checksum, corresponding to the *CRC* field (Fig. 1.8).

Table 1.1. The format of Q-subchannel data

Byte	Description	
0	Control/ADR	
1	TNO (Track Number)	
2	Index	
3	PMin	Head position in relation to the track start (relative address)
4	PSec	
5	PFrame	
6	Zero	
7	Amin	Head position in relation to the start of the disc (absolute address)
8	Asec	
9	Aframe	
10	CRC	
11		
12	Reserved for alignment	
13		
14		
15		

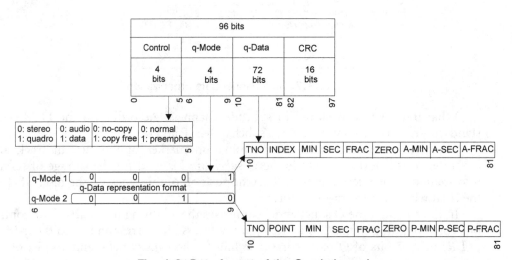

Fig. 1.8. Data format of the Q-subchannel

The *Control* field defines the track contents (audio or data), the number of audio channels (stereo or quadro), and specifies whether the copying of data is permitted. In particular, the sequence "0110" specifies that the user-data part of the sector stores digital data that may be copied. Conversely, the sequence "0100" prohibits data copying from the disc. In other words, if the first bit from the right (numbering starts from 0) is set, then copying is permitted. Curiously, most drives always reset this bit to zero, even if files created by the user are written to the disc. Nevertheless, copiers ignore these absurd prohibitions altogether. Therefore, the end user may be unaware of the problems that could arise!

The *q-Mode* field defines the format of data representation in the *q-Data* field. For most CDs, this is equal to 1.

The *q-Data* field in the `q-Mode == Mode 1` mode comprises nine single-byte fields containing information about the sector (other modes are not considered because of their exotic nature):

❏ *TNO* (Track Number) — contains the number of the current track, receiving values ranging from 01 to 99; the magic value of 0xAA points to the Lead-out track.

❏ *INDEX* — contains the index of the current section within the current track: 00 — specifies pause, while values from 01 to 99 identify sections with useful data. Currently, however, this possibility is not utilized and the section index is either always equal to zero (audio-pause), or to one (actual data); the Lead-out index of the track must be equal to zero.

❏ *MIN, SEC, FRAC* — the time or sector playback, from the starting point, of the current track (minutes: seconds: frames, respectively). Also called the relative playback time.

❏ *ZERO* – this field must always be equal to zero.

❏ *A-MIN, A-SEC, A-FRAC* — the playback time of the disc from the starting point of the data area (`minutes: seconds: frames`, respectively). Also called the absolute replay time.

The **CRC** field contains the checksum of the contents of the Q subcode channel. It is calculated according to the following polynomial: $G(x) = x^{16}+x^{12}+x^5+1$.

Sector Addressing

The addressing of sectors originated with audio discs. It is written in the following format: `Time — mm:ss:ff` (minutes:seconds:fractions fractions of a second range from 0 to 74). Counting starts from the beginning of the program area, i.e., the addresses of the Lead-In area are negative.

To convert MSF address to the LBA format, the following formula can be used:
```
Logical Sector Address = (((Minute*60)+Seconds)*75) - 150
```

Raw and Cooked Sectors

IEC 908 is the standard for audio CDs. Because it was published in 1982 in the form of a book with a red cover, it is officially called the *Red Book*. This standard describes the sector as a logical block *2,352 bytes long* that has no additional fields and represents a continuous audio flow of digitized music. Logical enough, the sectors of all other storage media, including diskettes and hard disks, are organized in a similar way at the logical level. They only differ with regard to the sector length (for instance, the length of a sector for diskettes and hard disks equals to 512 bytes).

Unfortunately, any attempt to use an audio CD for storing data invariably failed. The prohibitively high storage density, along with the technical imperfection of the read mechanism, resulted in persistent errors while attempting to read the disc. The number of these errors for a 10-second interval might reach 200! For audio, this seemed relatively normal, since erroneous bits can easily be corrected by interpolation. Although the reliability of streaming audio is not a guarantee in this case, even the well-trained ear of a musician is unable to notice the difference. Therefore, the increase in storage density for the sake of increasing disc capacity seems justified.

Naturally, for the correction of errors that occur in the course of reading data files, the interpolation approach is not suitable. Consequently, the file being read will be irrecoverably corrupted. To solve this problem, it was necessary to increase the redundancy of the information being written to the CD and to introduce additional error-correction codes. For the purpose of maintaining compatibility with existing equipment (including the existing production capacities), the existing information-storage format was preserved, but with another level of abstraction added.

The *Yellow Book* standard, published in 1983, describes the sector as a complex structure comprising a 12-byte *sync* sequence, a 4-byte *header*, a 2,048-byte *data area*, a 4-byte *Error Correction Code* (ECC) field, an 8-byte *Auxiliary* field, and a 276-byte *Error Detection Code* (EDC) field. This structure is shown in Fig. 1.9.

Naturally, CD-ROM drive hardware hides all of these details and displays the contents of the auxiliary fields only when it receives a special command (which, by the way, is not possible on all models). From the programmer's point of view, 2,048 bytes of user data area is the minimum set of information, with which the standard drive must work. Therefore, it is fine that the length of a logical sector became a multiple of the sector length of all of the other devices as a result of the contraction of the "actual" sector! So, what is the problem? Why should we dig so deep? The answer is obvious: By manipulating with auxiliary fields, you can create discs that cannot be copied with standard tools. Besides, you'll be able to crack protection mechanisms that prevent users from unauthorized copying of protected discs.

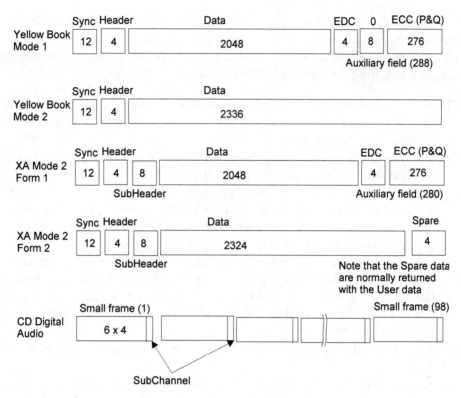

Fig. 1.9. Sectors of different types

	Sector: 2352 bytes						
Sync	Header		User data	EDC	Intermediate	P-Parity	Q-Parity
	Sector address	Mode					
12 bytes	3 bytes	1 (01) byte	2048 bytes	4 bytes	8 bytes	172 bytes	104 bytes

0   11 12   14 15 16   2063 2064 2067 2068   2075 2076   2247 2248   2351

Fig. 1.10. Sector format for the MODE1 mode

Thus, if you are not too bored with the pure theory, let's continue with our efforts. In order to, hopefully, bolster your inspiration, I'll just point out that these theoretical considerations will soon come to an end, and we will embark on the captivating process of investigating the disc "under the microscope."

❑ The *synchronization* field contains the following sequence: 00h FFh FFh FFh FFh FFh FFh FFh FFh FFh FFh 00h, and serves as an indicator of the sector's starting point.

❑ The *Header* field contains four bytes, the first three of which are occupied by the physical address of the current *physical sector address*, specified in the following format: minutes:seconds:frames. The final, fourth, byte determines the format of the remaining part of the sector (*mode*). If mode == 0, then the remainder of the sector if mode == 0 this shall mean that all bytes in positions 16 to 2,351 of the *Sector* are set to 00h and read without any additional processing. If mode == 1, then the remainder of the sector appears as shown in Fig. 1.10 (which we are discussing presently). Naturally, there are also other modes. However, because they are not very common, we won't engage in a discussion of this topic. Interested readers can find all of the required information in the appropriate specifications.

❑ 2,048 bytes of *user data* area, as its name suggests, represent the useful information.

❑ The four-byte *EDC* field contains the sector checksum, calculated according to the following polynomial: $P(x) = (x^{16} + x^{15} + x^2 + 1) \times (x^{16} + x^2 + 1)$. At the same time, the least significant parity bit (x^0) is written into the most significant bit of the checksum, and computation of the checksum starts from the least significant data bit.

❑ The auxiliary *Intermediate* field stores eight bytes filled with zeroes. To be honest, I don't quite understand how it is used (for all appearances, it is not used at all, or, at least, it is clearly not used by protection mechanisms).

❑ *P-parity* and *Q-parity* fields, whose lengths are 172 and 104 bytes, respectively, contain so-called Reed-Solomon error-correction codes. The mathematical principles of their operation are described in detail in ECMA-130. We won't concentrate on these codes here, especially because for the vast majority of problems, there is no need to compute ECC codes. Most frequently, crackers simply fill these fields with random, senseless garbage, thus imitating an irrecoverable sector read error (or, simply speaking, emulating the physical defects of the disc surface by means of creating sectors that cannot be read logically). This approach is the most appropriate for cracking protection mechanisms that rely on physical defects of the discs surface.

Sync Groups, Merging Bits, and DSV

Merging bits solve three important problems, without which it would be impossible to read information from a CD.

First, merging bits prevent conflict situations from arising. These conflict situations can occur at the junction point of two EFM words, the first of which terminates with a one, and the second of which also starts with a one (Fig. 1.11). Because two binary ones (each of which corresponds to the transition from pit to land or from land to pit) must be separated by at least two zeroes, this combination is considered a violation. The drive simply won't notice that something is present here (the length of one pit/land is considerably smaller than the diameter of a focused laser trace). Therefore, to detect this reliably, its length must be increased to at least 3T (see Fig. 1.12 for more details). On the other hand, if the "tail" of one EFM word consists of eight successive binary zeroes, and the following EFM word starts with the same sequence of 8 zeroes, we will have the chain comprising 16 zeroes. When reading such a chain, an error will occur, since according to the standard, there must be no more than eleven zeroes between two binary ones. Otherwise, the length-detection error will become too extreme. If you haven't quite grasped the idea, just take a map and try to measure the distance between two cities using an ordinary ruler. This makes the nature of the problem a bit clearer. Briefly speaking, merging bits are chosen in such a way as to ensure that there are no less than three and no more than eleven zeroes between the two closest neighboring binary ones.

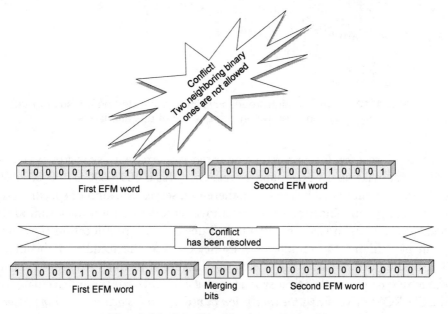

Fig. 1.11. Principle of using merging bits

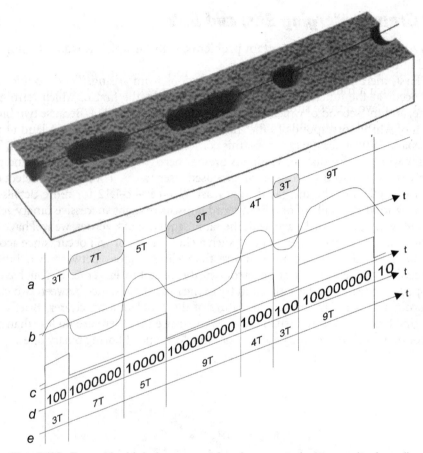

Fig. 1.12. Form of a high-frequency signal generated as a result of reading and interpreting a sequence of pits and lands

Second, merging bits prevent the occurrence of erroneous sync groups. The sequence of bits that make up a sync group (for reference, this is 100000000001000000000010) can only occur in the frame header, and, therefore, serves as a kind of specific indicator of its starting point. When the read head moves across the spiral track to find the specified sector, it has to use some method to detect its current location (i.e., the starting point of a frame, the middle of a frame, or even the middle of the EFM word). The reading device passes the stream of digital data through itself until it encounters the next sync group. When a sync group is encountered, the intellectual circuitry of the CD-ROM drive *draws the conclusion that this point is actually nothing other than the starting point of a new frame!* Just imagine the confusion if false "parasitic" sync groups were allowed to appear in the middle of a frame! In fact, without merging bits, this would occur on a regular basis! For example, consider the following EFM words: 10000000000100 and 00000000100100. If these words are "glued" together, a false "parasitic" sync group appears (the digits forming it are in bold). Any attempt at reading such a frame would cause a crash. Merging bits that connect such EFM words allow us to avoid these situations.

Third, look at the illustration shown in Fig. 1.12 — the CD has no other markings except for the spiral track comprising the sequence of pits and lands. Fast alternation of pits and lands generates a *HF* (*High Frequency*) signal, shown in graph (*b*). This signal is important for holding the read head on the spiral track because there is no other method for distinguishing the track between inter-track intervals. Another complication relates to the lack of a reference signal (or decision signal, as it is called in the standard), without which the read head cannot reliably distinguish dark surface areas from light areas. A precise quotation from the standard is provided below: *"The information contained in the HF signal is extracted in the form of the positions of the crossings of the HF signal with a decision level I_D. This decision level I_D is the level in the middle of the extreme values of I_3 (I_3 is the signal level corresponding to the maximum frequency of pit and land alternation)."*

Now, imagine what will happen if in some section of a spiral track there is a considerable excess of pits in relation to the number of lands, or vice versa. Instead of an alternating high-frequency signal, the drive will produce a direct current of a high or low level. Under conditions where there is no decision signal, the drive will experience considerable difficulties in detecting which is which! In other words, within one frame the number of pits and lands must be approximately equal.

How can this balance be achieved? After all, we cannot write strictly ordered sequences to the disc. Furthermore, even a brief glance at the EFM code table is sufficient to show that the zeroes predominate over the ones. Whatever EFM sequences we write, it is simply impossible to achieve the necessary "quorum" of ones! But there is no direct correspondence between bits and pits (lands). This means that the binary zero can be encoded both by a pit and a land! Assume that we are writing the following EMF sequence to the disc: "10000000100000". Despite the evident excess of binary zeroes, this EMF code contains an approximately equal number of pits and lands (Fig. 1.13, a).

To compute this ratio more precisely, a special value was introduced, known as the *DSV* (*Digital Sum Value*). This value is computed in the following way: initially, the DSV is equal to zero, but each next pit increases it by one, while each land decreases it by one. In particular, for an EFM sequence such as "10000000100000", the DSV value is equal to two (Fig. 1.13, *a*). Note that this is 2 rather than "–2", since we are interested only in the absolute value of the number, while its being positive or negative is of no importance (in fact, if this sequence started from a land rather than a pit, we would get the inverse result — eight "+" and six "–").

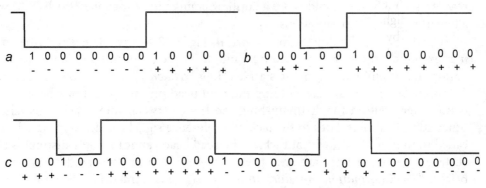

Fig. 1.13. Demonstration of DSV calculation

According to the standard, the DSV computed for the entire frame must fall within the interval from 2 to 10, otherwise, there will be problems in reading the sector (if the read operation were even possible). Note that not all EFM codes are characterized by a low DSV value. For instance, consider the following — "00010010000000", for which the DSV is 8. In fact, although this value formally satisfies the standard requirements, if there are at least ten such sequences on a disc, the DSV value will grow catastrophically to a value of *80*!!!

Decreasing the DSV level to an acceptable minimum is the third task that is carried out by merging bits. How do they do this? Look at the illustration shown in Fig. 1.13, *b*. Here, one EFM word having a large positive DSV is followed by another EFM word with a high DSV. As mentioned above, the DSV is an unsigned value, or, to be more precise, the actual DSV sign (negative or positive) of an EFM word doesn't depend on the word itself, but rather it depends on the word's context! Let us consider the example of the following degenerate sequence: "...00000000...". Since binary zero corresponds to the lack of a change in this location on the disc surface, this sequence can be encoded both by eight lands or by eight pits. Now, let us assume that we are writing two EFM words, both of which have a significant excess of lands. Is it possible to turn the lands of the second word into pits? This is, in fact, possible, provided that at least one of the three merging bits is equal to one. As we know, binary one corresponds to the transition from land to pit (or from pit to land). Therefore, the second EFM word will start from a pit, and its DSV will become strongly negative (in other words, there will be an excess of pits over lands). As a result, the EFM word with a strongly positive

DSV will be, to some extent, compensated for by an EFM word with a strongly negative DSV. Thus, the total DSV will be close to zero (Fig. 1.13).

Do application programmers need to know all of these details of physical encoding, you might ask? The answer is straightforward: The requirements for merging bits are mutually exclusive and can produce very unfavorable EFM sequences with unavoidably high DSVs. Such a sequence is shown in Fig. 1.14. The first EFM word is terminated by 8 zeroes. Since sequences comprising ten or more consecutive zeroes are disallowed, either the first or the second of the merging bits must necessarily be set to 1. However, in this case, the next EFM word will take strongly negative DSV value, for which we cannot compensate. This is because of the fact that between the second and the third EFM words only a single combination of merging bits is possible — "000", while any other combination will violate the rule that no less than two zeroes must be present between two neighboring binary ones. As a result, the third EMF word also has a strongly negative DSV value. If we fill the entire sector with this sequence, its total DSV will be catastrophically negative!

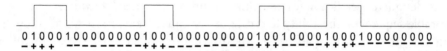

Fig. 1.14. EFM sequence with catastrophic DSV

To prevent the occurrence of such sequences, all data being written to the disc are previously scrambled, i.e., transformed into a pseudo-random sequence that resembles "white noise" in its characteristics. Accordingly, when performing data reading, an inverse operation is carried out. However, if desired, it is possible to bypass the scrambler! Some protection mechanisms do exactly this (see *"Protection Based on Weak Sectors"*).

Scrambling

Before writing the data to the disc, sector contents undergo a *scrambling* operation. Scrambling means that the data is transformed into a pseudo-random sequence that resembles "white noise" in its characteristics. This eliminates the unpremeditated generation of regular sequences with high DSV values, because such sequences are considered unfavorable from the point of view of the read device. As a result, the reading of such sequences is extremely unstable (for more details see *"Sync Groups, Merging Bits, and DSV"*).

Scrambling is applied to all fields of a sector, except for the 12-byte sync group at its start. In fact, if we also scramble the sync group, how would we find it later in the data stream? In total, this operation will produce 2,340 bytes of data (Fig. 1.15).

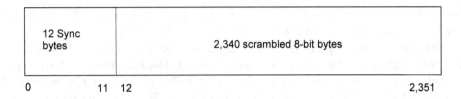

Fig. 1.15. Sector format from the point of view of the scrambler

Scrambling is carried out by the CD-R/CD-RW drive at the hardware level, and is absolutely transparent for the programmer. Accordingly, when reading a sector, an inverse procedure is carried out, i.e., *descrambling*. As a result of this operation, the "white noise" is removed from the sector, which is then converted back to its initial form.

The transparency of the scrambling mechanism creates a false impression, meaning that its algorithm seems absolutely useless for the programmer and only of any interest to hardware designers. In reality, however, this is not the case. Since scrambler was designed specifically for the elimination of *unpremeditated* occurrences of unfavorable sequences, the ability to create these sequences *on purpose* will allow us to create discs that are unreadable at the hardware level. What next? — you might ask. Why choose such a complicated way of creating an unreadable disc? Why not just take a disc, scratch its reflecting layer with a sharp needle, so that it will also be unreadable? After all, it is also possible to smash it with a paperweight or a sledge hammer. All joking aside, there is a point to this. The point is that, as a result of the presence of correcting codes, it is possible to create an unfavorable sequence, compute the correcting codes corresponding to it, and write this sequence to the disc in a slightly modified form in such a way as to ensure that, on one hand, it changes from an unfavorable to a favorable one, and, on the other hand, that after passing through Reed-Solomon decoder, it is restored into its initial (unfavorable) form. Any attempt to copy such a disc using a standard CD-copying program will fail, because the program will write an unfavorable sequence "as is." When an attempt is made to read this sequence, an error will occur! Promising, isn't it? More details on this technique will be provided in *Chapter 6*, which is dedicated to protection mechanisms based on weak sectors. For the moment, let's concentrate on the scrambler.

According to the ECMA-130 standard, the scrambling algorithm appears as follows: *"Each bit in the input stream of the scrambler is added modulo 2 to the least significant bit of a maximum-length register. The least significant bit of each byte comes first in the input stream. The 15-bit register is of the parallel block synchronized type, and is fed back according to polynomial $x^{15} + x + 1$. After the Sync of the Sector, the register is pre-set to the value 0000 0000 0000 0001, where the ONE is the least significant bit"* (Fig. 1.16).

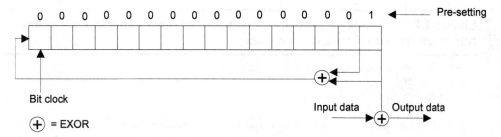

Fig. 1.16. Scrambler flow chart

Listing 1.1. The software implementation of the scrambler shown in Fig. 1.16

```
UpdateShiftRegister()
{
    int i;
    for(i = 0; i < 8;i++)
    {
        int hibit = ((ShiftRegister & 1)^((ShiftRegister & 2)>>1)) << 15;
        ShiftRegister = (hibit | ShiftRegister) >> 1;
    }
}


void Scramble()
{
    int i;
    for (i=12;i<2352;i++)
    {
        Scrambled[i] = Scrambled[i] ^ (ShiftRegister&0xFF);
        UpdateShiftRegister();
    }
}
```

Does this make sense to you? It didn't to me either.... at least until I used disassembler and carried out reverse engineering of the Clone CD program. As a matter of fact, Clone CD is an excellent tool for bypassing protection mechanisms based on weak sectors. Because of this, it must contain its built-in scrambler.

Among the functions exported by the ElbyECC.dll (supplied as part of Clone CD), there is one very interesting function: RawSrcambleSector, the disassembled listing of which appears as shown in Listing 1.2.

Listing 1.2. An example of the implementation of the scrambling algorithm borrowed from the Clone CD program

---

```
.text:100020E0 RawScrambleSector proc near
.text:100020E0
.text:100020E0 arg_0 = dword ptr   4
.text:100020E0
.text:100020E0    mov      eax, [esp+arg_0]       ; Loading the passed argument into EAX
.text:100020E4    mov      ecx, offset ScrmblrTbl ; ECX contains pointer to ScrmblrTbl.
.text:100020E9    add      eax, 0Ch               ; Skipping 12 bytes of sync sequence
.text:100020EC    push     esi                    ; Saving ESI
.text:100020ED    push     edi                    ; Saving EDI
.text:100020EE    sub      ecx, eax               ; Computing delta
.text:100020F0    mov      edx, 249h              ; 2340 / 4 bytes for scrambling
.text:100020F5
.text:100020F5 loc_100020F5:                      ; CODE XREF: RawScrambleSector+22↓j
.text:100020F5    mov      esi, [ecx+eax]         ; Take next DWORD from the table
.text:100020F8    mov      edi, [eax]             ; Next DWORD for scrambling
.text:100020FA    xor      edi, esi               ; XOR'ing
.text:100020FC    mov      [eax], ed              ; Saving the result
.text:100020FE    add      eax, 4                 ; Next DWORD
.text:10002101    dec      edx                    ; De-incrementing the counter
.text:10002102    jnz      short loc_100020F5     ; Looping
.text:10002104    pop      edi                    ; Restoring EDI
.text:10002105    pop      esi                    ; Restoring EDI
.text:10002106    retn                            ; Returning from the function
.text:10002106 RawScrambleSector endp
```

Analysis of the disassembled listing shows that the developers of Clone CD preferred a fast table algorithm to the tedious and resource-consuming fuss of working with a polynomial. This algorithm is reduced to superimposing a pseudo-random sequence over the sector being scrambled, which is carried out by means of the XOR operation. The actual result is nothing other than a disposable Vernam cipher, which has a length of the private key equal to the length of the sector part being scrambled (2,340 bytes). Implementation of this algorithm in a high-level language will appear approximately as follows:

Listing 1.3. An example of the application of the table scrambling algorithm written in C

```c
RawScrambleSector (char *raw_sector)
{
    int a;
    DWORD *p;
    DWORD *MyScramblerTable = (DWORD *) ScramblerTable;
```

```
    p = (DWORD*)(raw_sector + 12);
    for (a = 0; a < 2340 / 4; a++)
    {
        p[a] ^= MyScramblerTable[a];
    }
}
```

Now all that remains is to look into the pseudo-random sequence itself. The first eight members of this sequence (which were retrieved by the disassembler from Clone CD) appear as follows:

Listing 1.4. The first eight members of the pseudo-random sequence used for sector scrambling by Clone CD

```
dd 060008001h
dd 01E002800h
dd 006600880h
dd 081FE02A8h
dd 028606080h
dd 0889E1E28h
dd 0AAAE6668h
dd 0E0017FFCh
```

The full table is too large to be provided in its entirety here. Even printed in the smallest font, it would consume the entire page — more than 4,000 characters). Therefore, it is more interesting to discover the pattern, according to which the members of this sequence are related to one another and recreate the algorithm that computes all of the members of the sequence if we know the first. This small programming puzzle is not as difficult as it might seem at first glance. Sure, a brief glance at the first 8 members of the pseudo-random sequence won't provide any clues to its nature. In fact, the numbers changed chaotically and seem to bear a close resemblance to the "dancing men" mystery solved by Sherlock Holmes. In this case, however, frequency analysis is useless, and this problem cannot be solved by brute force. The good news, however, is that we are not trying to solve this problem from scratch! First, we know for sure that scrambling is carried out by 16-bit words (the width of the scrambling register is exactly 16 bits). Because of this, we must analyze words, and not double words. The fact that XORing is carried out by 32-bit blocks doesn't change anything because XOR is a bitwise operation. Therefore, the bit width of the operands has no influence on the final result! Second, the most convenient way for analyzing patterns is to do so at the bit level, because this level is precisely the one, at which this pseudo-random sequence is generated.

The script shown in Listing 1.5 automatically converts all table elements into 16-bit words displayed in binary format. Start IDA, press <F2>, and load the file containing this script. Then, move the cursor to the first element of the table, press <Shift>+<F2>, and enter the following command: x2bin(ScreenEA(), ScreenEA()+2340, 2). Pressing <Ctrl>+<Enter> (or simply <Enter>, if you have an earlier IDA version) will start the script for execution.

Listing 1.5. The IDA-C script converting table elements into binary code

```
// x_start - the starting address for conversion
// x_len - the number of bytes for conversion
// x_pow - the number of bytes in a single element
static x2bin(x_start, x_end, x_pow)
{
    auto a,p;
    for(p=x_start;;)
    {
        // Converting into the element of the required width
        if (x_pow == 1) MakeByte(p); else if (x_pow == 2) MakeWord(p); else
        if (x_pow == 4) MakeDword(p); else return 0;

        // Converting into binary code
        OpBinary(p, 0);

        // Next element
        p = p + x_pow;

        // Exit, if everything is done.
        if (p>x_end) break;
    }
}
```

The "updated" pseudo-random sequence of the scrambler will appear as follows (Listing 1.6 provides its first 16 elements).

Listing 1.6. A pseudo-random sequence written in the form of 16-bit words displayed in binary format

```
dw 1000000000000001b
dw 0110000000000000b
dw 0010100000000000b
dw 0001111000000000b
dw 0000100010000000b
dw 0000011001100000b
dw 0000001010101000b
```

```
dw 1000000111111110b
dw 0110000010000000b
dw 0010100001100000b
dw 0001111000101000b
dw 1000100010011110b
dw 0110011001101000b
dw 1010101010101110b
dw 0111111111111100b
dw 1110000000000001b
```

Now, the pattern can be detected easily (this shows how important it is to format the listing correctly). The bits of each of the next elements are moved one position to the right, nestling up to the logical "East" and making a kind of bit "stream", which increases its size linearly in its diagonal flow (each next element adds one bit to it). However, at a certain stage, it is suddenly "broken" into a set of smaller "streamlets," interlacing and forming a indecipherable mess. Nevertheless, the "physical" principles forming the foundation of this pattern are still hidden in the darkness and the mist. So, there is nothing left for us to do other than to resort to the blind trial method, hoping for a little intuition and luck.

Now what do we know? Unfortunately, there is not a glut of information... The scrambler XORs the contents of its internal register with the flow of data being scrambled. After each scrambled 16-bit word, it modifies the value of this register... but how? Let's take two adjacent elements of our pseudo-random sequence and try to guess the sequence of operations that generates the next element. There are only a few possible answers: shift, XOR, AND, or OR. It is unlikely that the creators of the CD-ROM would have used anything else in the scrambler.

Let's, therefore, take the starting element (i.e., the number 0110000000000000b) that the scrambler has created from 0010100000000000b in some yet unknown way. Clearly, there has been a shift. To compensate for this, let's shift the next element to the right by one and write the new value under the original (as if were carrying out modulo-2 addition):

```
dw 011000000000000b
dw ?????????????????b XOR
-------------------
dw 010100000000000b
```

All but the most lazy readers will be able to determine the source item here: 011000000000000b XOR 010100000000000b gives us...0011000000000000b. But wait! This is our unknown item shifted one position to the right! Let's consider how the next pair of numbers would behave:

```
dw 010100000000000b
dw ?????????????????b XOR
-------------------
dw 0001111000000000b
```

Well, 010100000000000b XOR 0001111000000000b gives us a value of 001010000000000b. Consequently, we can see that we have chosen the right method! After quickly writing the simplest script computing the next members on the basis of those preceding them, we can determine the correct results for all of the members of the sequence, running from the second member to the seventh, inclusively. After that, however, our theory will cease to work. In fact, the theory and practice will go different ways, like a married couple after a divorce. Quite unexpectedly, the binary one will appear in the most significant bit. In the next iteration, it will generate a parasitic "streamlet." Is it possible that the bit shift in the word takes place cyclically, i.e., that the least significant bit is periodically carried upwards? An attempt to compute the next member refutes this theory.

Having spent a couple of hours trying to find information on polynomials and the specific features of their implementation in the literature available to me, I couldn't find anything out. Having finally decided that, so to speak, hasty climbers have sudden falls, I simply produced a printout of the first hundred members of our pseudo-random sequence and manually computed the next element for each on the basis of the one that preceded it. Having completed this operation, I simply marked all of the exceptions that I detected. It turned out that the 14th and 15th bits (starting from zero) are spontaneously inverted from time to time. All of the other bits behaved in complete accordance with the theory.

Now, all that remained to do was to detect, under which conditions these bit "mutations" take place. I discovered pretty quickly that if the first bit (counting from zero) is set to 1, then 15th bit of the same member is inverted. This was fairly obvious, especially

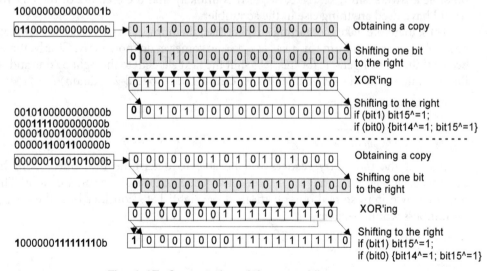

Fig. 1.17. Computation of the scrambling sequence

on the printout. Discovering the second exception from the rule was a little more diffi-cult: if the bit 0 of the computed member is set to 1, then 15th and 14th bits of the same member are inverted. Accordingly, if both the 0th and 1st bits are set to 1, then only 14th bit is inverted, due to the double inversion (Fig. 1.17). That's it! Now we can compute the entire pseudo-random sequence!

    The source code of the program generating the scrambling sequence is provided below. Naturally, it isn't a masterpiece of optimization. It is, however, illustrative enough.

Listing 1.7. [/etc/RawScrambler.c] The program for computing the scrambling sequence

---

```
/*-----------------------------------------------------------------
 *
 *            GENERATES THE SEQUENCE FOR CD SCRAMBLER
 *            ============================================
 *
 * build 0x001 @ 07.06.2003
 -----------------------------------------------------------------*/
#include <stdio.h>

// Check fragment of the real scrambling sequence for checking the program
// -------------------------------------------------------------------------
//0x8001,0x6000,0x2800,0x1e00,0x0880,0x0660,0x02a8,0x81fe,0x6080,0x2860,0x1e28,
//0x889e,0x6668,0xaaae,0x7ffc,0xe001,0x4800,0x3600,0x1680,0x0ee0,0x04c8,0x8356,
//0xe17e,0x48e0,0x3648,0x96b6,0xeef6,0xcccc6,0xd552,0x9ffd,0xa801,0x7e00,0x2080,

printf_bin(int a)
{
    int b;
    for(b = 15; b >= 0; b--) printf("%x",(a & (1<<b))?1:0);printf(" %x\n",a);
}

main()
{
    int a, tmp;
    int reg = 0x8001; // The first element of the scrambling sequence

    for(a = 1; a < 1170/* The scrambled sector part length in words*/; a++)
    {
        // Printing
        printf_bin(reg);
        if ((a % 8) == 0) printf(".............%03d.................\n",a /8);

        // Modulo-2 addition with shift
```

```
tmp = reg >> 1; tmp = reg ^ tmp; reg = tmp >> 1;

// processing polynomial x^15+x+1, e.g., 1<<15 + 1<<1 + 1<<0
if (reg & 1<<1) reg = reg ^  (1<<15);
if (reg & 1<<0) reg = reg ^ ((1<<15) | (1<<14));
    }
}
```

F1-, F2-, and F3 Frames and CIRC Encoding

The next "production cycle" starts with chopping the hurriedly scrambled sector into 24-byte "slices" of data called *F1-frames*. A simple computation shows that one sector with a length of 2,352 bytes can be sliced into exactly *98* F1-frames.

F1-frame. The structure of F1-frames is extremely simple: each frame consists of 24 bytes (12 words), numbered from 0 to 23 and sequentially mapped to the appropriate cells of the sector (Fig. 1.18, *a*). At the same time, the boundaries of frames and sectors do not necessarily have to match. Therefore, the sector can start from any of the following positions of the first frame: 0, 4, 8, 12, 16 or 20 (Fig. 1.18, *b*). The starting position of the sector in the F1-frame isn't stored anywhere (after all, there is no place to store it). Instead, the starting position of the sector is recognized by the presence of a sync group, which is hard not to notice!

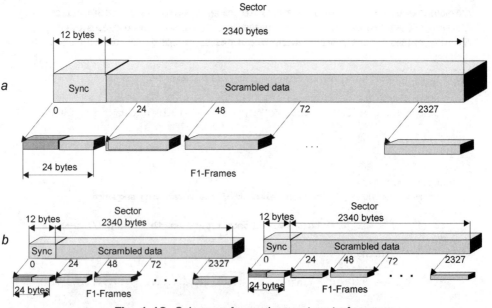

Fig. 1.18. Scheme of mapping sectors to frames

The standard provides a rather vague description of the process for mapping sectors to frames. However, it does tell us that the starting point of the next sector directly follows the end of the previous sector (*Byte 2,351 of a sector is immediately followed by byte 0 of the next sector*). Consequently, the change in the starting position of the sector doesn't "wrap" the sector's tail to the starting point of the first frame. Instead, the sector tail is carried into the next frame. Briefly speaking, if the starting position of the sector is not equal to zero, then each 49th frame simultaneously contains the bits of *two* sectors. As is easy to see, these will be the first and the last frames of the sector, and, since one sector contains 98 frames, 98/2 == 49.

The change of the starting position of the first byte of the sector within a frame results in considerable changes in its DSV (see "*Sync Groups, Merging Bits, and DSV*"). As a result, a CD-R recorder is able to "normalize" sectors that have catastrophically high DSV values. The drive's firmware must choose the starting position with the smallest DSV value or, at least, ensure that the DSV value doesn't exceed the allowed limits. Unfortunately, most low-end CD-R recorders are too simple for coping with this task. They always start the frame from byte 0 of the sector. As a consequence, the disc copy at the frame level can significantly differ significantly from the original. Despite the fact that it is impossible to determine the starting position programmatically (standard CD-ROM drives refuse to disclose this information), nothing is easier for the developers of protection mechanisms than forming a weak sector with a catastrophically high DSV value for the starting position 0, but quite normal for all other starting positions (see "*Protection Mechanisms Based on Weak Sectors*"). After this, it is practically impossible to copy such a sector using standard writing equipment, because few CD-ROM drive models will be able to read the sector with the high DSV. For example, my ASUS-50x seems to be able to do this. However, it doesn't do it reliably, and, of course, it can't do it for every disc. At the same time, none of the recorders, of which I am aware, allows you to choose the starting position manually (this possibility, at least, is not provided for by the standard, and at the same time, CD-RW drives cannot yet operate at a level this low). It is, of course, possible to use a little cunning and to corrupt several bytes of the sector intentionally, without damaging the error-correction codes (even minor changes introduced into the source data will result in monstrous changes to the DSV), so that the drive's firmware will return the corrupted data to its initial state on the fly. However, if the protection mechanism isn't completely stupid, it will easily distinguish this kind of rough imitation from the original. After all, when reading raw sectors, all of the tweaks that have been performed with error-correcting codes will be disclosed immediately!

At the same time, most CD-RW drives (if not all of them) carefully trace the DSV value and correctly choose the starting position. Well, this seems logical enough — the contrast range of the CD-RW media is too low and, therefore, the requirements for DSV value here are considerably more stringent than for CD-R media. Hence, if a protected disc cannot be copied on CD-R, try to copy it into CD-RW. By this

I mean to use the CD-RW drive to copy the protected disc onto a CD-RW disc, because some CD-RW recorders (for example, Plextor, PHILIPS) always start the frame from 0 byte of the sector when writing to CD-R discs, but at the same time, determine the starting position of the sector correctly when writing to CD-RW media! Of course, this is an irritating circumstance, but noting can be done about it.

The order of bytes in the sector is different from the order of bytes in the F1-frame. This means that when mapping the sector contents to a frame, even and odd bytes are swapped (Fig. 1.19). This mixing is intended to reduce the negative influence of disc defects that involve two adjacent bytes simultaneously.

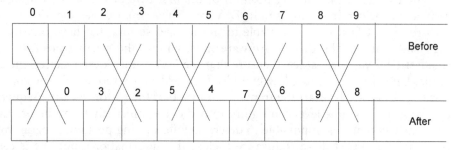

Fig. 1.19. Scheme of byte swapping in F1 frame

The software method of slicing a sector into frames is provided in the listing below. Here, the *sector* is the pointer to the initial sector, and *F1_frames* is the array of 98 frames, each containing 24 bytes:

Listing 1.8. An example demonstrating the technique for forming F1 frames (for the case, in which the frame and sector boundaries match)

```
/* Generate F1 frames */
for (a = 0; a < 98; a++)
{
    for (b = 0; b < 24; b++)
    {
    F1_frame[a][b]=((*sector&0xff00ff00UL)>>8)|((*sector&0x00ff00ffUL)<<8);
    }
}
```

F2-frame. Newly created F1-frames are supplied to the input of a special coder (*Cross-Interleaved Reed-Solomon Coder,* also known as *CIRC* coder), where their 24 bytes are complemented by 8 bytes of the Reed-Solomon checksum. As a result, F2-frames with a length of 32 bytes are produced at the coder output.

The contents of the bytes forming F1-frames remain unchanged at the bit level ("*The bit pattern of each of the 24 8-bit bytes of an F1-Frame remains unchanged*"). However, the bytes themselves are redistributed over 106 F2-frames. As a result, F1-frames are "spread" over the spiral track, which makes them less sensitive to radial scratches on the disc surface and any other local defects.

Mixing is achieved by means of so-called *delay lines*, and is carried out according to the following scheme (Fig. 1.20). The first delay section "swallows" the F1-frames supplied to its input. These frames are already split into 12 two-byte words, where the least significant and most significant bytes are designated by the letters A and B, respectively. The words are numbered sequentially from *W12n* to *W12n+11*. Thus, the first byte of the frame has the number "*W12n,A*", while the last one is numbered "*W12n+11,B*".

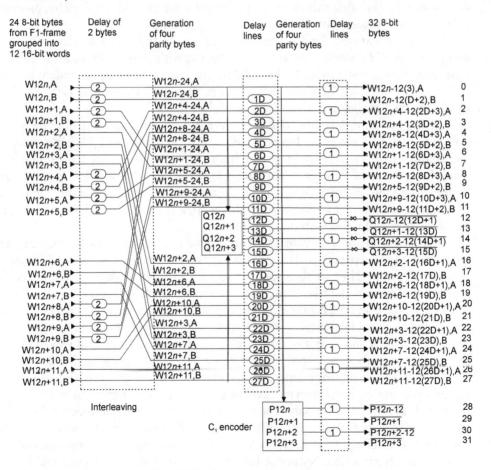

Fig. 1.20. Process of encoding bytes

The first delay line splits the frame contents into two groups of words, one of which ($W12n+2$, $W12n+3$, $W12n+6$, $W12n+7$, $W12n+10$, $W12n+11$) is supplied unhindered to the output, while the second ($W12n+0$, $W12n+1$, $W12n+4$, $W12n+5$, $W12n+8$, $W12n+9$) is forcibly delayed during the processing of the next two F1-frames. Words starting from the numbers $W12n+1$, ..., $W12n+10$ are carefully mixed according to a strictly defined scheme. In fact, a picture is worth 128 K words, because it is much easier to draw it graphically (Fig. 1.20) than describe it using normal language.

Mixed words are supplied to the input of the C_2-encoder, where they are complemented by four parity bytes computed according to the Reed-Solomon codes and sequentially numbered from $Q12n+0$ to $Q12n+3$.

The words complemented by parity Q-bytes are then supplied to the second delay line, where they are delayed for the length of the time interval required for processing F1-frames and ranging from $1D$ to $27D$ (where D is equal to 4).

The words that have finally been freed are sent to the next Reed-Solomon coder, designated as "C2", where they are supplemented with four parity bytes, sequentially numbered from $Pn+0$ to $Pn+3$. This kind of two-stage scheme of redundant encoding reduces the probability of irrecoverable errors considerably, because between C_1 and C_2 coders, the data being processed are carefully mixed!

Finally, the third delay line delays all even bytes in the data flow for the time required to process a single F1-frame. That's it! The newly created F2-frame then exits the output of the third delay line. This frame comprises 32 bytes sequentially numbered from 0 to 32: 24 bytes of payload, 4 Q-bytes of parity and 4 P-bytes of parity. At the same time, 24 bytes of useful data contained in the F2-frame include the data of a large set of different F1-frames! In other words, you can't consider the F2-frame to be the F1-frame supplied with the checksum.

When the data are read from a CD, an inverse process takes place (Fig. 1.21). First, the bytes being read pass the delay line that "grabs" even bytes for the interval required to process one frame. They are then supplied to the C_1 decoder, which checks the correctness of the checksum and tries, if necessary, to recover corrupted bytes. There is then another delay section (1D-27D Delay lines) and another decoder (C_2 decoder), which recover whatever couldn't be recovered by their predecessors. Finally, F1-frames that are ready for use leave the output of the last delay line. Further on, they are assembled into sectors. Sectors have already been covered, so we won't repeat ourselves here.

At such a level of redundancy, error-correction codes can recover up to 2 corrupted bytes per each 24/28-byte "slice" of the source data. If three or more bytes are corrupted, the decoder can only report an error, and is unable to recover the original contents of corrupted bytes. Still, it is possible to determine exactly which bytes were corrupted. Consequently, it might be possible to determine their approximate value by means of interpolation. Naturally, this technique of "recovery" is not suitable for recovering data CDs. However, it produces satisfactory results for Audio-CDs. Even on high-quality media, the number of irrecoverable errors is actually large enough. Therefore, CD drives must actively carry out their interpolation. Note that the vast majority of music lovers aren't even aware of its existence.

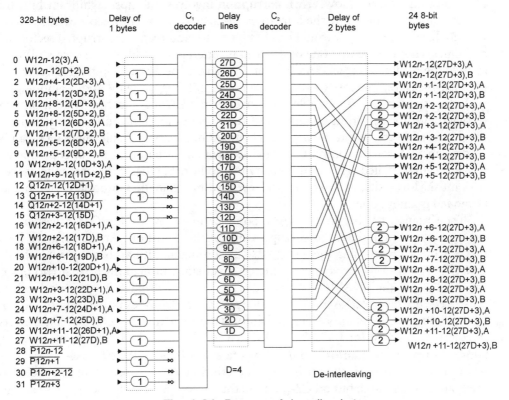

Fig. 1.21. Process of decoding bytes

First-generation CD-ROM drives intended for computers formally supported audio discs, and even managed to produce high-quality playback. However, any attempt to grab these discs and make a digital copy produced a result where the speakers issued continuous crackling sounds similar to those produced by old scratched vinyl gramophone records. While nostalgia isn't necessarily a bad thing, the days of vinyl records are long gone. The main reason for this situation is that CDs produce considerably better sound quality, which doesn't degrade with time, while records are inevitably decaying, even if you store them very carefully. Why, then, do our grabbed CDs become as crippled as records, also produce hissing and cracking sounds?.

This occurs because early CD-ROM drives read Audio CDs "as is," and didn't attempt to recover corrupted bytes when they occurred. Furthermore, they didn't even report the number of these bytes. As a result, application software didn't have any information and didn't know what to interpolate! If the corruption involves the least significant bits of a byte, this might remain undetectable to the human ear (even that of a true music lover). However, if corruption involves the most significant bits, this corruption can be heard by the human ear as a sharp click, noticeable even for those who are hard of hearing. It would be possible to try and read the corrupted sector several times (in the hope that one of the reading attempts would prove successful) or to analyze the read data to find and "smooth" all sharp "peaks" and "pits." However, this is a half-measure, as most of you will understand! High-quality audio grabbing on such drives is virtually impossible. Moreover, some CD manufacturers, keen on protecting their products from unauthorized copying, began to introduce a large number of irrecoverable errors into their products intentionally. As a result, these CDs can be read normally (even on computer CD drives), but any attempt to grab or copy them to CD-R inevitably failed. The sound quality was so horrible that it threatened to make a true music lover sick. The sound was even worse than that produced by an old-fashioned gramophone.

The situation has begun to correct. Some contemporary CD-ROM drives are capable of returning pointers to corrupted bits in the data flow. At the software level, this is achieved by passing the BEh (READ CD) command with a nonzero value for the *Error Flags* field to the drive. For reference, this field is located in the first two bits of the 9th byte of the ATAPI/SCSI packet. The result of using this command will be illustrated by the /etc/RAW.CD.READ/aspi32.C2.c demo example. Those of you who would like to get more detailed information on this topic are recommended to read the Standard for DVD/CD-ROM drives, which can be found at the following address: **http://www.stanford.edu/~csapuntz/specs/INF-8020.PDF** (page 143). Now, let us concentrate not so much on a description of the format of the fields of the READ CD command, but on C2-pointers themselves. Strictly speaking, these are not pointers at all, but, rather, normal bitmaps placed into the tail of the data returned by the drive. Each bit of the source data has its own corresponding bit of the C2-pointers. Analysis of the value of this bit allows us to determine whether or not this bit is corrupted without ambiguity. Taking into account the fact that the sector length is 2,352 bytes, it becomes easy to compute the total size of all C2-pointers bits, which is 2,352/8 = 294 bytes. The first byte of the sector corresponds to the first bit of the C2-pointers (Fig. 1.22).

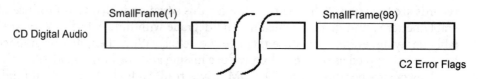

Fig. 1.22. Sequence of frames making up a block

To find out if a specific drive offers this possibility, just send the MODE SENSE 10 (5Ah) command to the drive with the Page Code equal to 2Ah (C/DVD Capabilities and Mechanical Status Page Format). Then the fourth bit of 13th byte of the returned data will specify that **C2 Pointers** option is supported. If this value is equal to 0, then this function is not supported (see the "/etc/RAW.CD.READ/aspi32.cfg.c" demo example). In particular, my PHILIPS CDRW 2400 doesn't provide this possibility.

But enough bad news. Let's return to our C1- and C2-decoders or, to be more precise, to the technique of computing the number of errors. There are at least six types of errors: *a*) single-character (recoverable) errors that correspond to the first stage of recovery (i.e., recoverable by the C_1 decoder); *b*) two-character (recoverable) errors corresponding to the first stage of recovery, and *c*) three-character (unfortunately, irrecoverable) errors that correspond to the same stage. A similar pattern is typical also for the second stage of recovery related to the C_2 decoder. It is a common practice to designate errors by the Latin character "E", followed by a two-digit number, the first digit of which specifies the number of errors (1, 2 or 3), while the second specifies the stage of correction (1 or 2). All possible combinations of these digits are outlined in Table 1.2.

Table 1.2. Conventional notation for all possible types of errors

E11	The number of single-character (recoverable) errors at the C1 stage
E21	The number of two-character (recoverable) errors at the C1 stage
E31	The number of three-character (irrecoverable) error at the C1 stage
E12	The number of single-character (recoverable) errors at the C2 stage
E22	The number of two-character (recoverable) errors at the C2 stage
E32	The number of three-character (irrecoverable) errors at the C2 stage

Three-character errors that cannot be recovered at the C1 stage (e.g., E31 errors) can be successfully recovered at the next recovery stage in most cases. However, a single E31 error can cause up to 30 E12 errors, because the data of 160 F1-frames are carefully mixed between C_1- and C_2 decoders!

Three-character errors irrecoverable at the C2 stage (e.g., E32 errors) serve as an evidence of a serious physical defect on the disc surface. Unfortunately, these errors are not as uncommon as they might seem at first glance, even on "virgin" discs. This is due to imperfect technological processes. Because of this, it is necessary to use redundant error correction codes on data CDs (for Audio CDs, interpolation is used in such cases, but for data CDs, interpolation is senseless). More detail on this topic was provided in *"Raw and Cooked Sectors."*

F3-frame. When an F2-frame produced as the output of the CIRC decoder is complemented by another byte of auxiliary data, called the *Control Byte,* an F3-frame is formed, which was already considered in *"Pits, Lands, Frames, and Sectors in Brief"*. The structure of the F3-frame is perfectly simple: first is the control byte, followed by 32 bytes inherited from the F2-frame. The control byte contains eight subcode bits, which, in turn, form channels that are 98 bytes long, which means that they span the entire sector comprising *98* F3-frames (for more detail, see *"Subcode Channels"*).

The structure formed by the 98 F3-frames is called a *section* and represents a self-sufficient entity not in any way bound to the sector boundaries. According to the ECMA-130 standard, *"These Sections are asynchronous with the Sectors, i.e., there is no prescribed relation between the number of the F1-Frame, in which the first byte of a Sector is placed, and the number of the F3-Frame, in which the first Control byte of the table is placed."* Another section of the same standard reads as: *"The address of a Sector is recorded in the Sector Header, also as an absolute time. It has no prescribed relation to the addresses of the Sections, because the mapping of a Sector on the Sections during recording is implementation-dependent due to the freedom left in clause 16. Therefore, the address of a Sector is filled in just before the Sector enters the CIRC encoder."*

The first bytes of the two F3-frames of each section (e.g., the first two control bytes of the section) are processed in a special manner. In contrast to other 3,232 bytes of the section, which are converted into 14-bit EFM-sequences that are directly written to the disc, these two bytes are replaced by fixed sync groups named *SYNC0* (00100000000001) and *SYNC1* (00000000010010), respectively (Fig. 1.23).

Byte	b_8	b_7	b_6	b_5	b_4	b_3	b_2	b_1
No.	p	q	r	s	t	u	v	w
0	SYNC 0							
1	SYNC 1							
2								
.								
.								
.								
96								
97								

Fig. 1.23. Section structure

Lead-in Area, Data Area, Lead-out Area, and TOC

The sequence of sectors of the same format is joined into the *track*, the minimum possible length of which is 300 sectors, while the maximum possible length can consume the entire disc. The first and last tracks of the disc are called the *Lead-in* and *Lead-out* areas and are used for special purposes, although most contemporary drives can do without them (with regard to recorders, they are obliged to do so).

Lead-In Area is an auxiliary disc area, which actually represents track number 9, always preceding the first PMA track. Each session of a multisession disc has its own Lead-in area. The size of the Lead-in area according to the standard is 9 MB (60 seconds, or 4,500 sectors). The Q subcode channel of the Lead-in session contains the TOC, where among other useful information, there are special pointers specifying either the Lead-out area address (closed disc), or the Lead-in area address of the next session (opened disc). The contents of the Lead-in area are unavailable for reading at the software level (drives from MSI provide this capability). Visually, the Lead-in area looks like a uniformly light shining ring.

Not every shining ring is the Lead-In! The actual Lead-In is always located at a distance of 23 mm from the disc edge, and is preceded by arbitrary trash.

CAUTION

Lead-Out Area. This is an auxiliary disc area designated by the track number AAh and terminating any closed session. The Lead-out area serves as a kind of indicator of disc and/or session termination. It helps the optical head to avoid being darted out of the disc limits. CD recorders must correctly process discs with open sessions. Normal CD-ROM drives and audio players, however, are not obliged to do so.

The lack of a Lead-out session (as well as specifying an incorrect address for it) might damage some drive models (for instance, PHILIPS).

CAUTION

The capacity of the Lead-out area of a single-session disc is, according to the standard, 13.5 MB (6,750 sectors, or 1.5 minutes). The capacities of the Lead-out areas for the second and subsequent sessions of multi-session discs are reduced to 4 MB (0.5 minutes, or 2,250 sectors). The contents of the Lead-out area are unavailable at the software level (the only exception are MSI drives). Visually, the Lead-out area looks like a shining ring.

TOC — Table Of Contents. This is an auxiliary area of the disc written in the Q subcode channel of the Lead-In area of the disc (it looks like a shining ring near the inner edge of the disc). Multisession discs have several independent TOCs, one TOC per each closed session. The TOC of an open session is stored in a special area in the PMA and, according to the standard, is available only to CD recorders. However, some models of CD-ROM drives can also read the TOC from the PMA.

The TOC contains information on the starting addresses of the disc Lead-in/Lead-out areas and the attributes of all its tracks (for instance, track type: audio or data. If the track type is data, then the data mode — Mode 1, Mode 2, etc., absolute starting address of the track and its corresponding session number). Besides this, the TOC also contains part of the ATIP and pointers to the location of its continuation.

The TOC is unavailable for reading directly or at the sector level,. However, to extract its contents in the raw form, it is possible to use the following SCSI/ATAPI command: *READ TOC/PMA/ATIP* (opcode: 43h) with `format field == 2h`.

The TOC should not be confused with the file system. In fact, the TOC and file system have nothing in common! File systems of CDs are stored directly in PMA and are easily available for reading at the sector level.

Program Area. This is the disc area located between the Lead-In and Lead-Out areas and containing information tracks with music or data. This is the main area of the disc, fully available at the sector level, including pauses between audio tracks. Most Data-CDs contain a single data track storing all of the necessary information recorded in a specific file system. However, file systems go beyond the limits of the topic under discussion. With regard to Audio-CDs, they have no file system at all. Rather, they use the TOC for this purpose, placing each song into a separate track.

If the Lead-out area is followed by a Lead-in area, the disc is described as *multisession*. Each *closed* session has its own Lead-in, Lead-out, and TOC, and the pointer contained in the Lead-out area contained in the TOC can include both the actual address of the Lead-out area of the current session and the address of the Lead-out area of the next session! The number of sessions is, in principle, unlimited. However, because of the pass-through numbering of tracks, the number of sessions cannot exceed 99. The session can be independent (the TOC specifies only tracks within a session) or connected (in this case, the TOC contains the addresses of tracks from previous sessions). However, not all drives recognize the existence of sessions. For example, a vast majority of audio players "see" only the first session and ignore all others. Because of this, it is possible to create discs that cannot be read on CD-ROM drives installed in computers, but can be read normally by standard CD players.

The session is considered to be closed if its data area is framed by Lead-in and Lead-out areas. Unclosed sessions can only be read by recording devices, which require access to the PMA. The pointer in the session's TOC pointing to the Lead-out area can contain either the actual address of the Lead-out area of the current session (closed disc), or the address of the Lead-in area of the next session. Recording is limited by the available disc space, the space in the PMA and the number of tracks (tracks are numbered using pass-through numbering, from 01 to 99). Sessions can also be connected at the level of the file system. The sessions mechanism allows for the "modification" of the CD-R by writing a new session.

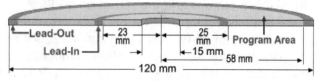

Fig. 1.24. CD structure

Chapter 2: Power of Reed-Solomon Codes

Entropy is blind, but patient. Sooner or later, by centering its fire on our position, square by square, it will strike the headquarters, or communication center. The first line of defense will then be destroyed. We will have to retreat to positions prepared beforehand. In other words, in such a situation a programmer has to rely on a backup copy of the volume.

E. V. Lishak
"32th Day of the year.
(Notes of para-system programmer)."

Practically everyone will already have heard of the existence of error-correction Reed-Solomon codes, widely used in data storage and transmission devices for the detection and *correction* of both single and multiple errors. Their application area is unusually large. Reed-Solomon encoders/decoders can be found in tape storage drives, RAM controllers, modems, hard disks, CD-ROM/DVD drives, etc. Thanks to these codes, some advanced archivers can survive the corruption of several sectors of the media-containing archive, or, sometimes, even the total destruction of an entire volume of a multi-volume archive. Besides this, Reed-Solomon codes enable the protection mechanism to restore bytes hacked by someone trying to crack the system or corrupted as a result of software or hardware failure.

In brief, although mastering the technique of error-correction encoding doesn't automatically give God-like powers, it at least raises you to that Olympus where great computer Gurus dwell among noiseless coolers and bug-free operating systems.

At the same time, only a small number of programmers can claim pride in original implementation of Reed-Solomon codes. After all, what is the point of bothering? There are lots of ready-to-use libraries, ranging from commercial software to free source codes distributed according to the GNU license agreement. There is a wide range of possibilities. Take any library of your choice[i]. Sure, there is pragmatic reason for using libraries. However, if you entrust control to the program *without understanding how it actually works*, are you a hacker? This book's intended audience, after all, mainly comprises hackers (naturally, in only the most positive sense of the term). On the other hand, when analyzing software distributed without source codes, you won't be able to identify the Reed-Solomon algorithm unless you carefully investigate it beforehand to gain a clear understanding of all of its intricacies. Suppose that you have encountered a protection mechanism that in some intricate way manipulates EDC/ECC fields of key sectors read from a CD. Further, assume that each of these sectors contains two mangled bits (plus errors that are generated in a natural way, provided that the CD is treated carelessly). At the same time, one of these is a *false* error and *shouldn't be corrected*. When copying the protected disc using a standard procedure, the microprocessor of the CD-ROM drive automatically correct all errors that the drive is capable of correcting. As a result, key marks will be erased. Consequently, the protected program will cease to operate. It is, of course, possible to copy the disc in the raw mode, e.g., without error correction. However, in this case, the copy will contain all of the errors of the original, both intentional and unintentional. As a result, even if the original is only slightly damaged, the correction capabilities of Reed-Solomon codes may be insufficient and the disc will become unreadable (What did you expect? Copying discs in raw mode results in error *accumulation*, and, therefore, is highly inefficient from any point of view). Mastering the basic principles of error-protected encoding will help us to grasp the logic of any protection mechanism. In particular, we will understand, which errors have to be corrected and which must be left "as is."

Unfortunately, most publications related to the Reed-Solomon codes are written in the language of higher mathematics. It is often beyond the average university graduate to understand these materials (how many hackers have math skills at the University level?)

---

[i] "*…due to implementation errors, this code adds new bugs instead of eliminating the existing ones. Therefore, this code is no longer available*" — this is the comment to the GNU source codes of the Reed-Solomon encoder/decoder. Having encountered such a comment, would you trust in Linux reliability in general and GNU library code in particular? Well, I never!

As a result, in the best case most of these abstract manuals end up buried at the back of hacker's bookshelves, where they gradually become covered with dust. In the worst case, they end up in the garbage can.

Software implementation of the Reed-Solomon error-correcting codes is actually very complicated and requires an above-average level of mathematical abilities. An explanation of the mathematical foundations of its implementation might seem boring and tiresome to system and hardware programmers, but, unfortunately, there is no other way around it. After all, no one promised that it was going to be easy to become a programmer. To become a really good programmer is significantly more difficult, so don't say you weren't warned beforehand! Just kidding :-). Don't worry, take it easy and don't be afraid of higher mathematics. You will encounter a few formulas in this chapter (what mathematician can live without formulas?), but, in most cases, I'll try to speak in the international programming language — C, which is familiar to all system programmers. So, fasten your seatbelts, and raise your heads from the keyboards, and off we go!

Basics of Error-Correcting Codes and Error-Correcting Encoding

Personal computers and bits and bytes have so inundated our everyday life that most people have ceased to think about information-encoding theory altogether, thinking of it as something self-evident. But things are not as simple as they might seem at the first glance.

In fact, encoding involves nothing more than the conversion of a *message* into a sequence of *code symbols,* also called *codewords.* Any *discrete message* contains a finite number of elements. In particular, any text is made up of letters, an image is made up of pixels, while a machine program is made up of commands, etc. Together, these building blocks form the *message source alphabet.* In the course of encoding, message elements are converted into corresponding numbers — *code symbols,* where each message element is assigned a unique sequence of code symbols, called a *code combination.* The set of code combinations that makes up the message is the *code.* The set of possible code symbols is called the *code alphabet,* while their total number (later on, designated by a lower-case m) is the *code base.*

Most likely, however, that you are aware of these facts already (even if you aren't, you can find a comprehensive explanation of encoding basics in any textbook on computer science). Are you, however, familiar with what is meant by the term *Hamming distance*? The Hamming distance is *the minimum number of differences between any two valid codewords* and it plays a fundamental role in the theory of error-correcting encoding. An official definition is as follows: "Hamming distance is a measure of the difference between two messages, each consisting of a finite string of characters, expressed by the number of characters that need to be changed to obtain one from the other." For instance, let us consider the following four-bit code:

Listing 2.1. An example of the simplest four-bit code with Hamming distance equal to one. Such a code is widely used in computing, despite its inability to detect errors

```
0 → 0000;   4 → 0100;   8 → 1000; 12 → 1100;
1 → 0001;   5 → 0101;   9 → 1001; 13 → 1101;
2 → 0010;   6 → 0110;  10 → 1010; 14 → 1110;
3 → 0011;   7 → 0111;  11 → 1011; 15 → 1111;
```

This is a normal binary code that might be encountered in some microcontrollers that hold 16 symbols in their 4 bits (meaning that, using this code, it is possible to encode 16 alphabetical characters). As can be easily checked, any two characters differ by at least one bit. Consequently, the Hamming distance for such a code is equal to 1 (e.g., d = 1).

Here is another four-bit code:

Listing 2.2. An example of a four-bit code with Hamming distance equal to 2. This code is already capable of detecting single errors

```
0 → 0000;   4 → 1001;
1 → 0011;   5 → 1010;
2 → 0101;   6 → 1100;
3 → 0110;   7 → 1111;
```

This time, any two arbitrarily taken symbols are different in at least two positions. Because of this, the information capacity of such a code has been reduced from 16 to 8 symbols. "But wait," some of you might cry out in surprise, "what gibberish? Where are combinations such as 0001 or 0010, for instance?" But this isn't gibberish. This code doesn't actually contain these combinations. To be more precise, they *are present*, but are declared *code violations*, also known as *noncode symbols* or *prohibited symbols*. Because of this circumstance, our code is capable of detecting any single error. For instance, let us take the 1010 symbol and invert there any arbitrary (but a single) bit.

Suppose that this is the second bit from the left. The corrupted symbol will then appear as follows: 1110. Since the 1110 combination is not a valid codeword, the decoder will report the occurence of an error. It can, alas, only detect an error, and is unable to fix it. In order to correct even a single erroneous bit, it is necessary to increase the Hamming distance to at least 3. Since four-bit code with d = 3 can comprise only two different symbols, it is not illustrative. Therefore, it is better to choose a wider code. Let's try a 10-bit code where d = 5.

Listing 2.3. An example of 10-bit code with Hamming distance equal to 5. This code can detect 4-bit errors and correct 2-bit errors

---

```
0000000000   0000011111  1111100000  1111111111
```

For example, let us take the 0000011111 symbol and invert any two bits. As a result, we will get something looking like 0100110111. Since this combination is not a valid codeword, the decoder detects that an error has occurred. Obviously, if the number of erroneous bits is smaller than the Hamming distance at least twice, the decoder is guaranteed to restore the initial symbol. In fact, if there are no less than 5 differences between any two valid symbols, then corruption of two bits of any such symbol will produce a new symbol of the alphabet (let us designate it as k). The Hamming distance between k and the original symbol is equal to the number of inverted bits (e. g., two in our case), while the distance to the nearest valid symbol is equal to d - k (3, in our case). In other words, while d - k > k, the decoder is guaranteed to restore the original symbol. In cases when d > k > d - k, successful restoration is not guaranteed. However, under favorable conditions it is possible in principle.

Returning to our symbol 0000011111, let us corrupt 4 bits: 0100110101 and try to restore the original symbol. Let us represent the recovery process graphically:

Listing 2.4. An attempt at correcting a 4-bit error

```
0000000000   0000011111  1111100000  1111111111

0100110101   0100110101  0100110101  0100110101

 -------     ----------   ----------   ----------

5 differences   4 differences  6 differences  5 differences
```

Roughly speaking, after detecting an error, the decoder sequentially compares the corrupted symbol with all of the valid symbols of the alphabet, trying to find the one that has the smallest number of differences with the corrupted one. To be more precise, it looks for the symbol that differs from the corrupted one in no more than (d - 1) bits. As can be seen easily, in this case we were lucky and the restored symbol actually matched the original one. However, if four corrupted bits were distributed as follows: 0111111111, the decoder would consider it to be 1111111111, and the restoration would be incorrect.

Thus, the correcting capability for a specific code is defined according to the following formula: to detect r errors, the Hamming distance must be greater than or equal to r, while for correcting r errors the Hamming distance must be greater than the duplicated number of errors r by at least one.

Listing 2.5. The correcting capabilities of a simple Hamming code

---

```
Error detection capability: d >= r
Error correction capability: d > 2r
Information capacity: 2^(n/d)
```

Theoretically, the number of detectable errors is unlimited, while, in practice, the information capacity of codewords dwindles rapidly with the growth of d. Suppose that we have 24 bytes of data and would like to correct up to two errors per each block. In this case, we will have to add 49 bytes more to this block, and, as a result, its information capacity would drop down to 30 percents! Is this a positive development? This deplorable result can be explained by the fact that bits of the codeword are isolated from one another, and changing one of them has no effect on the others. Is there any way out of this situation? There is!

Let all bits whose numbers represent powers of two, play the role of check bits, while the other bits will be normal bits carrying the information of the message. Each check bit must be responsible for the parity[i] of a specific group of bits controlled by it. Note that the same information bit can relate to different groups. One information bit will influence several check bits and, therefore, the information capacity of the codeword grows considerably (even "tremendously"). After that, it only remains to choose the optimal distribution of the spheres of influence.

According to the methods of error-protected encoding suggested by Hamming, in order to determine which check bits control the information bit in position k, it is necessary to factorize k by powers of two.

---

[i] E.g., if the sum of bits being checked is even, then the parity bit is equal to zero, and if it is odd, the parity bit is set to 1.

Table 2.1. Dividing bits into check bits and data bits

Position	Controlled by bits	
1 (A)	$2^0 = 1$	This is a check bit, it isn't controlled by any bit.
2 (B)	$2^1 = 2$	This is a check bit, it isn't controlled by any bit.
3	$2^0 + 2^1 = 1 + 2 = 3$	Controlled by check bits 1 and 2.
4 (C)	$2^2 = 4$	This is a check bit, it isn't controlled by any bit.
5	$2^0 + 2^2 = 1 + 4 = 5$	Controlled by check bits 1 and 4.
6	$2^1 + 2^2 = 2 + 4 = 6$	Controlled by check bits 2 and 4.
7	$2^0 + 2^1 + 2^2 = 1 + 2 + 4 = 7$	Controlled by check bits 1, 2 and 4.
8 (D)	$2^3 = 8$	This is a check bit, it isn't controlled by any bit.

Let's try to get a live "taste" of Hamming codes and manually calculate the check-sum of the `0101` four-bit symbol. After reserving places for check bits (highlighted in bold) our symbol will appear as follows: **AB**0**C**101. Now, it simply remains to calculate the values for bits A, B, and C:

❏ Bit A controlling bits 3, 5, and 7 is equal to *zero*, because their sum ($0 + 1 + 1$) is even.

❏ Bit B controlling bits 3, 6, and 7 is equal to *one*, because their sum ($0 + 0 + 1$) is odd.

❏ Bit C controlling bits 5, 6, and 7 s equal to *zero*, because their sum ($1 + 0 + 1$) is even.

Thus, the newly created codeword will appear as follows: **01**0**0**101, where the check bits are highlighted in bold.

Listing 2.6. The codeword with check bits

```
AB0C101
1234567
```

Now let us suppose that in the course of transmission, one of the bits of our code-word was inverted. As a result, the codeword began to appear as follows: `01001`◻`1`. Can we detect such an error? Let's try. Bit A must be equal to: ($0 + 1 + 1$) % $2 = 0$, which is true. Bit B must be equal to ($0 + 1 + 1$) % $2 = 0$. But in our codeword, it is equal to one. Let us memorize the number of "incorrect" bit and continue. Bit C must be equal to ($1 + 1 + 1$) % $2 = 1$; however, it is equal to zero. Aha! The check bits in positions 2 (bit B) and 4 (bit C) do not match reality. Their sum $(2 + 4 = 6)$ gives the position of the erroneous bit. Actually, in this case, the number of the mangled bit is equal to 6. Let's invert it to return our codeword into its original state.

What will happen if the corruption happens to a check bit rather than an information bit? The test will show that in this case, the corrupted bit can also be detected successfully. In this case, it can also be restored using the above-described technique (however, does this make any sense? After all, check bits are discarded in the course of decoding the codeword anyway).

At first glance, it might seem that Hamming codes are horribly inefficient, since for each 4 data bits we have 3 check bits. However, since the numbers of check bits are powers of two, they become more and more sparse with the growth of the codeword length. Thus, the check bit D, nearest to bit C, is located in position 8 (e.g., three steps away). The check bit E, however, is divided from bit D by $2^4 - 2^3 - 1 = 7$ steps, while check bit F is at a distance of $2^5 - 2^4 - 1 = 15$ steps.

Thus, the efficiency of Hamming codes rapidly increases with the growth of the length of the processed block. The program provided below clearly illustrates this:

Listing 2.7. Calculation of the effective information capacity of Hamming codes for codewords of different length

```
main()
{
        int a;
        int _pow = 1;
        int old_pow = 1;
        int N, old_N = 1;

        printf( "* * * Hamming code efficiency test * * * by Kris Kaspersky\n"\
            " BLOCK_SIZE    FUEL UP   EFFICIENCY\n"\
            "----------------------------------\n");
        for (a = 0; a < MAX_POW; a++)
        {
        N = _pow - old_pow - 1 + old_N;

        printf("%8d   %8d   %8.1f%%\n", _pow, N, (float) N/_pow*100);

        // NEXT
        old_pow = _pow; _pow = _pow * 2; old_N = N;

        } printf("----------------------------------\n");

}
```

Listing 2.8. Calculation of the effective information capacity of Hamming codes for codewords of different length

BLOCK_SIZE	FUEL UP	EFFICIENCY
1	0	0.0%
2	0	0.0%
4	1	25.0%
8	4	50.0%
16	11	68.8%
32	26	81.3%
64	57	89.1%
128	120	93.8%
256	247	96.5%
512	502	98.0%
1024	1013	98.9%
2048	2036	99.4%
4096	4083	99.7%
8192	8178	99.8%
16384	16369	99.9%
32768	32752	100.0%
65536	65519	100.0%
131072	131054	100.0%
262144	262125	100.0%
524288	524268	100.0%

From the listing provided above, it follows that in the course of processing blocks of a size of at least 1,024 bits, the overhead for processing check bits can be fully neglected.

Unfortunately, Hamming codes can correct only single errors, which means that they can tolerate the corruption of only one bit per entire block being processed. Naturally, error probability increases with the size of blocks being processed. Therefore, the choice of optimal codeword length is a non-trivial task, requiring at least the knowledge of error types and frequency, at which they occur in the communication links. For tape drives, CDs, hard disks, and other similar devices in particular, Hamming codes prove to be extremely inefficient. Why do we consider them? Well, for the simple reason that advanced encoding systems, including Reed-Solomon codes, are impossible to understand if you start attacking them from scratch. This is because they are actually based on complicated mathematical algorithms. However, after considering simpler methods such as Hamming codes, this, in fact, becomes possible.

Idea of Reed-Solomon Codes

Simply speaking, the basic idea of Reed-Solomon codes is multiplying the information word represented in the form of a polynomial D by the prime polynomial G^i, known to both parties. As a result, the codeword C will be obtained, also represented in the polynomial form.

Decoding is carried out in the inverse manner: If, after dividing the codeword C by the polynomial G, the decoder obtains a remainder, it can report an error. Accordingly, if the codeword can be divided without a remainder, this means that its transmission was completed successfully.

If the power of the polynomial G (also called the generator polynomial) exceeds the power of the codeword by at least two, then the decoder is capable not only of reporting, but also of correcting single errors. If the power of the generator polynomial exceeds that of the codeword by 4, double errors can also be corrected. Briefly speaking, the power of polynomial k is related to the maximum number of recoverable errors t as follows: k = 2*t. Consequently, the codeword must contain two auxiliary symbols per one recoverable error. Meanwhile, maximum number of recognizable errors is equal to t, i.e., one redundant symbol per each recognizable error.

In contrast to Hamming codes, Reed-Solomon codes can correct any reasonable number of errors with quite an acceptable level of redundancy. What helps to achieve this result? In Hamming codes, check bits controlled only data bits to the right of them and ignore all data bits located to the left. Let us return to Table 2.1. The addition of the 8th check bit D has in no way improved the noise immunity of encoding, since the check bit D has nothing to control. In Reed-Solomon codes, check bits expand their influence to all data bits. Therefore, increasing the number of check bits improves the quality of error detection/correction. Thanks to this, Reed-Solomon correcting codes have become so stunningly popular.

Now for the bad news. Normal arithmetic is not suitable for working with Reed-Solomon codes. Encoding assumes computations over polynomials, the coefficients of which must be added, subtracted, multiplied, and divided. These operations *must not* be accompanied by the rounding up of intermediate results (even division), in order to avoid the introduction of indeterminacy. Both intermediate and final results must not exceed the predefined limits of the bit width. But wait! This is impossible! Who believes that multiplication doesn't increase the bit width of the result?!

Still, if we call up a little brain power, we can grasp that it is not necessary to multiply the information word by the generator polynomial. It is possible to find a much more elegant solution.

1. Add r trailing zeroes to the source data word D. As a result, we will get a word that has the length of n = m + r and the polynomial X^r*D, where m is the length of the data word.

---

[i] I.e., the polynomial with integer coefficients that cannot be expressed as the product of two lower-degree polynomials with integer coefficients.

2. Divide the resulting polynomial x^r*D by the generator polynomial G and calculate the remainder from the division R, so that x^r*D = G*Q + R, where Q is the quotient which we ignore, since, at this stage, only the remainder is of interest.

3. Add the remainder R to the data word D, as a result we will get a code word C, the *data bits of which are stored separately from control bits.* In fact, *the remainder that was obtained as a result of division represents correcting Reed-Solomon codes.* The method of encoding, in which data and check symbols are stored separately, is known as *systematic coding.* Such coding is convenient from the point of view of hardware implementation.

4. Now, mentally scroll steps 1, 2, and 3, trying to detect, at which stage of calculation the bit width has been exceeded. You'll notice that there is no such stage! Everything is OK. It only remains to point out that the information word plus correcting codes can be written as T == x^r*D + R = GQ.

Decoding of the resulting keyword T is carried out in just the same manner as was described earlier. If, when dividing T (which, in fact, represents the product of G and Q) by the generator polynomial G, we get a remainder, this means that the word T is corrupted, and, accordingly, if there is no remainder, there was no error.

Now, the question arises as to how are we going to carry out division of polynomials within the framework of standard algebra? In integer arithmetic, division is not defined for all pairs of numbers (for instance, 2 cannot be divided by 3, and 9 cannot be divided by 4, — without the loss of value, of course). With regard to floating-point division, its precision is catastrophically insufficient for effective use with Reed-Solomon codes. Further, it is somewhat complicated for hardware implementation. If you are working with IBM PC based on a Pentium processor, it is equipped with high-performance math coprocessor. However, consider the situation from the point of view of manufacturers releasing hardware like tape drives, hard disks, CD drives. Are they going to equip these devices with Pentium 4 processors?! Of course not! It is much better to use special arithmetic — the *arithmetic of finite groups called Galois fields.* The advantage of this arithmetic is that operations of addition, multiplication, subtraction, and division are defined for all members of the field (except, naturally, for the case of division by zero). The number obtained as a result of any of these operations is guaranteed to be present in the group! This means that when dividing any integer number A, belonging to the set 0...255, by any integer number B belonging to the same set (naturally, B must not be equal to zero), we will get the number C, belonging to the same set. Consequently, there are no losses of value, and no uncertainty appears.

Thus, correcting Reed-Solomon codes are based on polynomial operations in the Galois fields and require the programmer to master several aspects of higher mathematics in the field of the theory of numbers. Like any other concepts of higher mathematics, Galois fields represent an abstraction that can't be presented in the form of illustration or "felt" in any other way. When dealing with such an abstraction, it is just necessary to accept it as a set of axioms, without trying to grasp its sense. It is sufficient to know that it works. That's all. Still, there are polynomials of vast powers, which will turn the normal system programmer a little green (unfortunately, programmers with higher math education are more of an exception than a rule).

Therefore, before rushing into the depths of a pathless mathematical forest of abstractions, let us construct the model of the Reed-Solomon coder/decoder operating according to the rules of normal integer algebra. Naturally, because the bit width must inevitably be extended in this case, it will be rather hard to find a reasonable area of application for such a coder/decoder. However, it works, it is illustrative, and it allows not only the understanding of the working principle of Reed-Solomon codes, but also allows you to feel them intuinively.

Let us base our considerations on the assumption that if $g = 2^n + 1$, then for any a belonging to the range of $0..2^n$, the product $a*g = c$ (where c is the codeword) will represent a jumble of bits from both source numbers.

Let us assume that $n = 2$, then $g = 3$. As can be easily seen, no matter by which number we multiply g — by 0, by 1, 2, or 3. Either way, the result will be exactly divisible by g only in case if no one of its bits is inverted (or, simply speaking, that there are no single errors).

The remainder from the division is a clear indication of the position in which the error has occurred (provided that it is a single error, because this algorithm is incapable of correcting group errors). To be more precise, if the error occurred in position x, then remainder of division will be equal to $k = 2^x$. To determine x by a given k value quickly, it is possible to use a trivial table algorithm. Nevertheless, for restoring the corrupted bit, it is not necessary to know its position. It is enough to simply carry out the following operation: $R = e \wedge k$, where e is the mangled codeword, $\wedge$ stands for the XOR operation, and R is the recovered codeword.

In general, the working implementation of the coder/decoder might appear as below. This implementation operates on the basis of normal arithmetic (e.g., with unjustified extension of the bit width), and corrects any single errors in a single 8-bit data word (naturally, it is not difficult to modify this program to operate with 16-bit information words). Note that the coder is implemented in a significantly simpler manner than decoder. In a real-world Reed-Solomon coder/decoder capable of correcting group errors, this gap is even more considerable.

**Listing 2.9. [/etc/EDC.ECC/rs.simplest.c] The simplest example
of implementation of the Reed-Solomon coder/decoder**

```c
/*-------------------------------------------------------------------------
 *
 *           SIMPLEST REED-SOLOMON CODER/DECODER
 *           =======================================
 *
 * Build 0x001 @ 02.07.2003
-------------------------------------------------------------------------*/
// ATTENTION! This coder/decoder is built on the basis
// of normal arithmetic, not on the Galois arithmetic.
// As a result, its functional capabilities are very limited.
// However, it is very easy and illustrative
#include <stdio.h>

#define SYM_WIDE    8       // width of the source data word (bits)

#define DATAIN  0x69        // input data (on byte)

#define ERR_POS 3           // number of corrupted bit

                            // prime polynomial
#define MAG (1<<(SYM_WIDE*1) + 1<<(SYM_WIDE*0))

// -----------------------------------------------------------------------------
// determining the error position x given the remainder k
// from the division of the codeword by the polynomial
// k = 2^x, where "^" — means raising to power
// The function accepts k and returns x
// -----------------------------------------------------------------------------
int pow_table[9] = {1, 2, 4, 8, 16, 32, 64, 128, 256};
lockup(int x) {int a; for(a=0; a<9; a++) if(pow_table[a]==x)return a; return -1;}

main()
{
     int i; int g; int c; int e; int k;

fprintf(stderr, "simplest Reed-Solomon encoder/decoder by Kris Kaspersky\n\n");
     i = DATAIN;         // input data (data word)
     g = MAG;            // prime polynomial
     printf("i = %08x    (DATAIN)\ng = %08x    (POLYNOM)\n", i, g);

     // REED-SOLOMON CODER (very simple, but working)
     // calculating the codeword intended for transmission
```

```
c = i * g;    printf("c = %08x    (CODEWORD)\n", c);
// End of CODER
   // transmission with errors
e = c ^ (1<<ERR_POS); printf("e = %08x    (RAW RECEIVED DATA+ERR)\n\n", e);
/*         ^^^^ inverting one bit to imitate the transmission error */


// REED-SOLOMON DECODER
// Check for transmission errors
// (the simplest Reed-Solomom decoder)
if (e % g)
{
   // errors detected, trying to correct
   printf("RS decoder says: (%x) error detected\n{\n", e % g);
   k = (e % g);  // k = 2^x, where x is the position of erroneous bit
   printf("\t0 to 1 err  position: %x\n", lockup(k));
   printf ("\trestored codeword is: %x\n}\n", (e ^= k));
}
printf("RECEIVED DATA IS: %x\n", e / g);
// END OF DECODER
}
```

Now, consider the results. Pay special attention to the fact that the corrupted bit was successfully restored. However, in order to achieve this, it was necessary to add three bits (instead of 2) to the source data word. Note that you take the maximum allowed 8-bit value 0xFF as the input word, then the code word will be equal to 0x1FE00. Since $2^{10} = 10000$, there will be no free positions, and the width must be increased up to 2^{11}, while the least significant bits of the code word remain unused. The "correct" coder must "connect" them in the manner of a ring.

Listing 2.10. The output of the simplest Reed-Solomon coder/decoder

```
i = 00000069      (DATAIN)
g = 00000200      (POLYNOM)
c = 0000d200      (CODEWORD)
e = 0000d208      (RAW RECEIVED DATA+ERR)

RS decoder says: (8) errors detected
{
   0 to 1 err  position: 3
   restored codeword is: d200
}
RECEIVED DATA IS: 69
```

General Concept

Reed-Solomon codes represent non-binary systematic block-based error correcting codes related to the class of cyclic codes with numeric field different from GF(2) and representing a subset of Bose-Chaudhuri-Hocquenghem codes. The correcting capabilities of Reed-Solomon codes directly depend on the number of check bytes. Adding r check bytes allows you to detect r arbitrarily corrupted bytes and guarantees the restoration of $r/2$ bytes out of them.

Recommended Reading

Despite the fact that this section is self-sufficient and explains all mathematical facts without referring to third-party sources, the desire to improve your knowledge is quite natural and can only be welcome. Therefore, it will be much better if you do not limit yourself to this book only and, instead, read a variety of specialized literature, each time noting the depth of the gap between your vague idea and a true understanding. The theory of error-correcting encoding is so vast that you could spend virtually your whole life studying it.

What are some starting points for this study?

❏ Blahut Richard *"Theory and Practice of Error Control Codes"*

This is a very good book — a "must have". According to obscure rumors, it has been published somewhere on the Net. I, however, have been unable to find it. The large number of references to it, however, is evidence of its quality.

❏ James Plank *"A tutorial on Reed-Solomon Coding for fault-tolerance in RAID-like systems"*

A very good reference on the use of Reed-Solomon codes for building fault-tolerant systems similar to RAID, oriented towards programmers lacking fundamental math education and explaining clearly the idea of error-correcting encoding. It also provides source codes in C. An electronic copy is available at: **http://www.cs.utk.edu/~plank/plank/papers/CS-96-332.pdf**. I strongly recommend that you read this manual, even if you are not going to create RAID systems.

❏ Joel Sylvester *"Reed-Solomon Codes"*

A very brief description of the Reed-Solomon codes' working principles, supplied with flowcharts instead of the source code. It isn't a comprehensive manual, but it still provides an understanding of the general pattern. Available at: **http://www.elektrobit.co.uk/pdf/reedsolomon.pdf**

❑ Tom Moore *"REED-SOLOMON PACKAGE"* (old tutorial)

An excellent compendium of several manuals on Reed-Solomon codes — probably the best that I've ever seen. Includes a brief description of the theory of Galois fields, the basic principles of constructing Reed-Solomon coders/decoders, and complete listings illustrated their implementation in C (unfortunately, very sparsely commented). This information was last posted in FIDO on 28.12.1994 in the comp.compression conference. It can be easily found using Google using the following keywords: "Reed-Solomon+main+ECC". Strongly recommended.

❑ Ross N. Williams *"A painless guide to CRC error detection algorithms"*

A detailed manual on CRC. Very useful because of the easily readable, understandable description of the polynomial arithmetic, without which operation with Reed-Solomon codes would simply be impossible. You can find it at **ftp://www.internode.net.au/clients/rocksoft/papers/crc_v3.txt**

❑ ftape (driver of the tape drive from the Linux distribution set)

No procedure of tape backup can do without error-correction codes! It's hard even to imagine. Therefore, this analysis of the source codes of the drivers for tape devices provides rich food for thought (provided, of course, that the driver being investigated actually uses the Reed-Solomon codes). The ftape Linux driver is the one you need. With regard to the code responsible for encoding/decoding Reed-Solomon codes, it is located in the ftape-ECC.c/ftape-ECC.h files. This is an example of good programming, so I recommend it.

❑ James S. Plank GFLIB *"C Procedures for Galois Field Arithmetic and Reed-Solomon Coding"*

A library for working with Reed-Solomon codes. Contains complete source codes of all required functions and is distributed according to GPL license. Can be found on any GNU site, including the following: **http://www.cs.utk.edu/~plank/plank/gflib/gflib.tar**.

Polynomial Arithmetic and Galois Fields

In the previous section of this chapter, we mentioned that error-protected Reed-Solomon codes are based on the following math components: *polynomial arithmetic* and the *arithmetic of Galois fields*. We can't proceed any further until we cover all of these aspects in detail, so let's be patient before assaulting the peaks of higher math. After that, we'll be engaged in pure coding without any sophisticated math.

Polynomial Arithmetic

The 6th section of *"Art of Programming"* by Donald Knuth is dedicated to the polynomial arithmetic. There, the following definition is given to this area of math: *"Formally speaking, polynomial over S is the following expression: $u(x) = u_n x^n + \dots + u^1 x + u_0$, where $u_n, \dots, u_1, u_0$ coefficients are elements of some algebraic system S, and variable x can be considered as a formal symbol without a determining value. Let us assume that algebraic system S represents a commutative ring with 1. This means that S allows addition, subtraction, and multiplication operations satisfying normal requirements: addition and subtraction are associative and commutative binary operations defined over S, multiplication is distributive in relation to addition. There are also elementary unit for addition 0 and elementary unit for multiplication 1, so that a + 0 == a and a * 1 == a for every a belonging to S. Subtraction is an inverse operation in relation to addition; however, no assumptions have been made for division as operation inverse to multiplication. The polynomial $0x^{n+m} + \dots + 0x^{n+1} + u_n x^n + \dots + u^1 x + u_0$ is considered as identical to $u_n x^n + \dots + u^1 x + u_0$, although formally these polynomials are different."*

Thus, instead of presenting data word D, codeword C, and the remainder from the division R as integer numbers (as we did earlier), we can relate them to the appropriate coefficients of a binary polynomial and carry out all further mathematical operations according to the rules of polynomial arithmetic. At first glance, the gain from this approach seems doubtful. However, let's not be hasty. Instead, let's present any number (the first one that comes to mind; for instance, let it be 69h) into a binary polynomial. Start the built-in Windows application named **Calculator,** or any other suitable application of your choice, and convert this number into binary form (with a bit of skill, it is possible to carry out this operation mentally: 69h → 1101001.

Well, the rightmost coefficient is equal to 1, then there are two zeroes, followed by 1... briefly speaking, we get the following: $1x^6 + 1x^5 + 0x^4 + 1x^3 + 0x^2 + 0x + 1$. In fact, the bit string 1101001 is one of the forms of writing the above-mentioned polynomial. Certainly, this form of data presentation might lack clarity from the beginner's point of view, but it is very convenient for machine processing. Stop. If 69h *already* represents a polynomial, then what is the difference between the addition of polynomials 69h and 27h and the addition of integer numbers 69h and 27h?! Undoubtedly, there is a difference. As Nietzsche has shown, there are no facts. All that exists are their interpretations. Interpretations of numbers and polynomials are different, and mathematical operations over them are carried out according to different rules.

Coefficients in polynomial arithmetic are strictly typified and the coefficient of x^k is of a different type than the coefficient of x^m (provided, of course, that $k \neq m$). Operations over numbers of different types are not allowed! All coefficients are processed independently and carry to the more significant bit or borrowing from the more significant bit are not taken into account. Let us demonstrate this with the example of adding 69h and 27h:

Listing 2.11. Addition carried out according to the rules of polynomial binary arithmetic (left) and according to the rules of normal binary arithmetic (right)

```
 1101001  (69h)       1101001  (69h)
+0100111  (27h)      +0100111  (27h)
 -------              -------
 1001110  (4Eh)      10010000  (90h)
```

Simple calculations show that modulo-2 addition of polynomials gives the same result as their subtraction and "magically" coincides with the XOR operation. The match with XOR is a purely accidental, though. However, the equivalence of addition and subtraction forces us to review the nature of things, to which most of us are accustomed. For instance, let us recall arithmetic problems such as "Mary has one apple. Pete takes it away from her. We gave another apple to Mary. How many apples does Mary have? How many apples would she have had if Pete hadn't robbed her?". From the modulo-2 arithmetic the answer would be: zero and one, respectively. Yes! If Pete didn't take the apple from Mary, 1 + 1 == 0 and the poor girl would not have any apples at all.

However, we are digressing. Let's forget the quarrels between the kids and return to the fictious member of our polynomial and its coefficients. Thanks to their typification and lack of mutual relations, we can process numbers of practically unlimited lengths by simply XOR'ing their bits. This is one of the main advantages of polynomial arithmetic that are unnoticeable at first glance, but thanks to which polynomial arithmetic became so widespread.

In our case, however, polynomial arithmetic alone is not sufficient. To implement a Reed-Solomon coder/decoder, we'll also need Galois fields. What are these, you ask?

Galois Fields

As long ago as the 1960s, when computers were iron-cast and 20 MB hard disks resembled washing machines, a beautiful legend was born about a green extra-terrestrial creature that came from stars and recorded the entire British Encyclopedia into a thin light-silvery rod, which the creature took with it as it left. These days, when the 100-GB hard disks are no bigger than a pack of cigarettes, this density of information recording is no longer a wonder. However, the point of this legend is that the extra-terrestrial creature has mastered the technology of writing an *infinite volume of information* on an *infinitely small media,* and the British Encyclopedia was chosen just as an example. The alien could copy the contents of all Internet servers by placing only a thin trace on its metal rod. You don't believe it? You have objections? Let us convert British Encyclopedia into digital form and obtain a very large number. Then let us place a decimal point before it, thus converting this number into a very long decimal fraction. Now it only remains to find two numbers, A and B, so that the result of dividing A by B is exactly equal to this decimal fraction with precision to the last digit. Writing these numbers to a metal rod can be carried out by placing a mark on the rod dividing the latter into two sections of lengths that are multiples of the values A and B, respectively. To read information from the rod, it will be enough to measure the lengths of the A and B sections and then divide A by B. The first ten digits following the decimal point will be more or less precise, after which… The practice here will outdo the perfect theory, burying the latter under a thick cover of information garbage that results from the impossibility of measuring exactly the geometric size of real-world objects.

In a digital world, the situation is even worse. Every programmer knows only too well that the division of integer and real numbers is subject to rather stringent limitations. First and foremost, division is a very resource-consuming operation, with regard to processor resources. If it's not enough that it is insufficient, the operation is mathematically inaccurate! This means that, if `c = a * b`, this doesn't necessarily mean that `a == c/b`! Thus, normal arithmetic is not suitable for practical implementation of Reed-Solomon codes. Therefore, one has to resort to a special branch of mathematics, namely, the mathematics of *finite Galois groups*.

Here, we interpret the *group* as a set of integer values, sequentially numbered from 0 to $2^n - 1$, for example: `{0, 1, 2, 3}` or `{00h 01h, 02h, 03h, 04h, 05h, 06h, 07h, 08h, 09h, 0Ah, 0Bh, 0Ch, 0Dh, 0Eh, 0Fh}`. Groups containing 2^n elements are called *Galois Fields* and denoted as follows: `GF(2^n)`.

Group members without fail are subject to associative, commutative, and distributive laws. However, they are processed in a way that might, at first glance, seem unnatural:

☐ The sum of any two group members is always present in this group.

☐ For any group member, designated as a, there always exists an *identity* member, which usually is denoted as e, and satisfies the following condition: `a + e = e + a = a`

☐ For each member a of a group there is an *inverse* member −a, so that `a + (-a) == 0`

Let us start with the first thesis. Does this seem like gibberish to you? Suppose that we have the following group: `{0, 1, 2, 3}`. Is it possible to obtain the number less than or equal to 3 when calculating the value $2 + 3$?! As it turns out, addition in Galois fields is carried out without accounting the carry, and the sum of two members of a Galois group is equal to: $c = (a + b) \% 2^n$, where the % operation stands for the calculation of the remainder from the division. As applied to our case: $(2 + 3) \% 4 == 1$. In mathematics, this operation is called *modulo-4 addition*, or *congruence addition*.

Naturally, the following question will likely interest you: Does modulo addition find a practical application or is it used only in abstract theoretical construction? Good question. You mechanically carry out this operation many times each day without even noticing or thinking that this is exactly that operation — addition without taking carry into account. For instance, suppose that you woke up at 6 p.m. and then worked on your computer for 9 hours without pauses. Then you accidentally look at your watch. Provided that the watch actually shows exact time, what will the position of the hour hand be? Obviously, the required value represents the modulo-12 sum of 6 and 9, which is equal to: $(6 + 9) \% 12 == 3$. Here is an illustrative example of using Galois arithmetic. And now, as an experiment, let us subtract 6 from 3... (if you find this difficult, just look at your watch).

Now, let us proceed with the most important fact: Since the result of dividing one group member by another group member (naturally, a non-zero one), must be present in this group, then, despite the fact that this is an integer division, this operation will be precise. In fact, the result will be precise rather than approximate! Consequently, if $c = a * b$, then $a == c/b$. In other words, multiplication and division are unambiguously and consistently defined for all group members, except for the case of division by zero. At the same time, multiplication doesn't result in the increase of the bit width!

Naturally, this is not a standard multiplication (and, of course, not in every Galois field $2*2=4$). However, Galois arithmetic must not necessarily correspond to "common sense." The most important thing about it is that it works, and works rather well. The existence of hard disks, CD-ROM/DVD drives is the best confirmation of this fact, since they all use this arithmetic for specific purposes of one sort or another.

As was already mentioned, modulo-2 Galois fields have become the most widespread in computing. This is because these fields are the most natural from machine processing point of view, since it is binary by the nature.

To implement Reed-Solomon coder/decoder, we will need four basic arithmetic operations: *addition, subtraction, multiplication*, and *division*. These operations will be covered in detail in the following few sections.

Addition and Subtraction in Galois fields

Modulo-2 addition in Galois fields is identical to subtraction, and is implemented by the XOR bitwise operation. This aspect was already discussed when studying polynomial arithmetic. Therefore, we will simply provide an example of software implementation of the addition/subtraction function:

Listing 2.12. The function implementing addition/subtraction in Galois fields

---

```
// This function returns the result of modulo-2 addition (subtraction)
// of two polynomials a and b
int gf_sum(int a, int b)
{
    return a ^ b;
}
```

Multiplication in Galois Fields

Having opened an elementary school math textbook, we will read there that multiplication represents the operation of addition repeated a number of times. If we have already learned how to carry out addition in Galois fields, should we feel confident that the multiplication function won't cause us any serious difficulties? Unfortunately, no. I always *knew* that two multiplied by two equals four. However, I never *believed* this to be an absolute truth. After encountering Galois fields for the first time, I understood how right I was[i]. As it turns out, there are other kinds of mathematics where two multiplied by two is not equal to four, and the multiplication operation is not defined using addition, but, rather, is based on quite a different concept.

In fact, if try to "wrap" the gf_sum function into the loop, we will get just the same addition, defined in a different way: a * b will be equal to a, if b is even, otherwise it will be equal to zero. Who needs this type of multiplication? Actually, the function implementing "real" Galois multiplication is so complicated and resource-consuming that to simplify its implementation, it is necessary to transform polynomials into index form, and then add indexes by modulo of GF, after which it is necessary to carry out an inverse transformation of the sum of indexes into polynomial form.

---

[i] In other words, when I press the button switch, I know that the light will be switched on. However, I am not sure (suppose that the electrician has cut the wires, or the light bulb has fused, etc.) The same thing is typical also for math. That set of trash that most of us are fed up from the secondary school, or even from colleges, is not a math. This is a set of *voodoo* rites that students must repeat to obtain the result, but which do not allow to grasp the underlying ideas — zen of math. I don't know whether or not this is for the better, but I feel it my duty to remind you that "math" taught in many educational institutions has no more relation to the real math than programming has to torturing the mouse when struggling with Microsoft Word or installing Windows.

What is the *index*? The index is the exponent of the power of two, which produces the required polynomial. For instance, the index of polynomial 8 is equal to 3 (2^3 = 8), while index of polynomial 2 is equal to 1 (2^1 = 2). It is quite easy to show that a * b = 2^i + 2^j = $2^{(i+j)}$. In particular, 2 * 8 = 2^3 + 2^1 = $2^{(3+1)}$ = 4^4 = 16. Now let us compose the following table and carry out some experiments with it:

Table 2.2. Polynomials (left column) and powers of two corresponding to them (right column)

i	alpha_of[i]
001	0
002	1
004	2
008	3
016	4

Up to this moment, we operated with the concepts of the customary arithmetic. Therefore, about two thirds of the table fields remained blank. In fact, equations such as 2^x = 3 have no integer solutions. Therefore, some indexes do not correspond to any polynomials! However, since the number of polynomials of any Galois field is equal to the number of possible indexes, we can map them to one another in specifically pre-defined way, without paying any attention to the fact that this action makes no sense from the customary mathematical point of view. The specific scheme of mapping can be chosen in any way. The only fact that matters here is that the mapping must be consistent., e.g., that it must satisfy all above-listed requirements of the groups (see *"Galois Fields"*).

Naturally, since the final result depends directly on the chosen mapping scheme, both parties (Reed-Solomon coder and decoder) must observe specific agreements. However, different Reed-Solomon coders/decoders can use different mapping schemes, incompatible to one another.

In particular, the Reed-Solomon decoder built into the CD-ROM drive carries out multiplication according to the table provided in Listing 2.13. Having encountered such a table in the disassembled listing of the program being investigated, you'll be able to quickly and reliably identify all functions that are using it.

Listing 2.13. Look-up table for GF(256). The leftmost column specifies polynomials/indexes (designated as `i`), the second column represents the table of powers of the trivial polynomial 2 (designated as `alpha`), the third column contains indexes corresponding to the current polynomial (designated as `index`)

i	alpha	index	i	alpha	index	i	alpha	index
000	001	-1	047	035	69	094	113	70
001	002	0	048	070	29	095	226	64
002	004	1	049	140	181	096	217	30
003	008	25	050	005	194	097	175	66
004	016	2	051	010	125	098	067	182
005	032	50	052	020	106	099	134	163
006	064	26	053	040	39	100	017	195
007	128	198	054	080	249	101	034	72
008	029	3	055	160	185	102	068	126
009	058	223	056	093	201	103	136	110
010	116	51	057	186	154	104	013	107
011	232	238	058	105	9	105	026	58
012	205	27	059	210	120	106	052	40
013	135	104	060	185	77	107	104	84
014	019	199	061	111	228	108	208	250
015	038	75	062	222	114	109	189	133
016	076	4	063	161	166	110	103	186
017	152	100	064	095	6	111	206	61
018	045	224	065	190	191	112	129	202
019	090	14	066	097	139	113	031	94
020	180	52	067	194	98	114	062	155
021	117	141	068	153	102	115	124	159
022	234	239	069	047	221	116	248	10
023	201	129	070	094	48	117	237	21
024	143	28	071	188	253	118	199	121
025	003	193	072	101	226	119	147	43
026	006	105	073	202	152	120	059	78
027	012	248	074	137	37	121	118	212
028	024	200	075	015	179	122	236	229
029	048	8	076	030	16	123	197	172
030	096	76	077	060	145	124	151	115
031	192	113	078	120	34	125	051	243
032	157	5	079	240	136	126	102	167
033	039	138	080	253	54	127	204	87
034	078	101	081	231	208	128	133	7
035	156	47	082	211	148	129	023	112
036	037	225	083	187	206	130	046	192
037	074	36	084	107	143	131	092	247
038	148	15	085	214	150	132	184	140
039	053	33	086	177	219	133	109	128
040	106	53	087	127	189	134	218	99
041	212	147	088	254	241	135	169	13
042	181	142	089	225	210	136	079	103
043	119	218	090	223	19	137	158	74
044	238	240	091	163	92	138	033	222
045	193	18	092	091	131	139	066	237
046	159	130	093	182	56	140	132	49

i	alpha	index	i	alpha	index	i	alpha	index
141	021	197	180	150	20	219	086	177
142	042	254	181	049	42	220	172	187
143	084	24	182	098	93	221	069	204
144	168	227	183	196	158	222	138	62
145	077	165	184	149	132	223	009	90
146	154	153	185	055	60	224	018	203
147	041	119	186	110	57	225	036	89
148	082	38	187	220	83	226	072	95
149	164	184	188	165	71	227	144	176
150	085	180	189	087	109	228	061	156
151	170	124	190	174	65	229	122	169
152	073	17	191	065	162	230	244	160
153	146	68	192	130	31	231	245	81
154	057	146	193	025	45	232	247	11
155	114	217	194	050	67	233	243	245
156	228	35	195	100	216	234	251	22
157	213	32	196	200	183	235	235	235
158	183	137	197	141	123	236	203	122
159	115	46	198	007	164	237	139	117
160	230	55	199	014	118	238	011	44
161	209	63	200	028	196	239	022	215
162	191	209	201	056	23	240	044	79
163	099	91	202	112	73	241	088	174
164	198	149	203	224	236	242	176	213
165	145	188	204	221	127	243	125	233
166	063	207	205	167	12	244	250	230
167	126	205	206	083	111	245	233	231
168	252	144	207	166	246	246	207	173
169	229	135	208	081	108	247	131	232
170	215	151	209	162	161	248	027	116
171	179	178	210	089	59	249	054	214
172	123	220	211	178	82	250	108	244
173	246	252	212	121	41	251	216	234
174	241	190	213	242	157	252	173	168
175	255	97	214	249	85	253	071	80
176	227	242	215	239	170	254	142	88
177	219	86	216	195	251	255	000	175
178	171	211	217	155	96			
179	075	171	218	043	134			

Using this table, you can easily carry out the transform from the polynomial form into the index form, and vice versa. How should you use this table? Let us assume that we need to multiply the polynomials 69 and 96. Let us find the number 69 in column i. The corresponding alpha value is 47. Let us memorize it (or write it down) and proceed with the number 96, for which the value of alpha is equal to 217. Let us carry out a modulo-256 addition of 47 and 217. As a result, we will get the following value: (217 + 47) % 256 = 8. Now, let us transform the result from the index form into the polynomial form. To do so, it is necessary to find the number 8 in column i and its corresponding polynomial — 3 — in column index. (If we carry out an inverse operation, by dividing 3 by 69, we will get 96, which proves the consistency of multiplication and division operations, as well as in the entire Galois arithmetic as a whole). This is rather fast, although sometimes it is unclear why the table is composed in this way rather than in some other. The worst thing is that the trustworthiness of the result cannot be felt intuitively, because all of these concepts represent a pure abstraction. This significantly complicates program debugging (it is rather difficult to debug anything where you don't fully understand the operating principle).

Still, it is not necessary to enter manually the multiplication table from the keyboard. It is possible to generate this table automatically, on the fly, at program execution time. A possible implementation of such a generator looks as follows:

Listing 2.14. The procedure of generating the lookup table of quick polynomial multiplication

```
#define m   8    // The exponent of the RS polynomial
// (equal to 8, according to the ECMA-130
// standard)
#define n   255 // n=2**m-1
        // (length of the codeword)
#define t   1    // number of errors to be corrected
#define k   253 // k = n-2*t
        // (length of the data word)

// prime generator polynomial
// According to ECMA-130: P(x) = x^8 + x^4 + x^3 + x^2 + 1
int p[m+1]={1, 0, 1, 1, 1, 0, 0, 0, 1 };

int alpha_to[n+1];      // table of exponents
                        // of the prime member
int index_of[n+1];      // index table
                        // for fast multiplication


//------------------------------------------------------------------
// Generating the look-up table for fast multiplication
// for GF(2^m) on the basis of prime generator polynomial
// from p[0] to p[m].
//
// Look-up table:
//      index->polynomial from alpha_to[]
//      contains j=alpha^i,
//      where alpha is the trivial member,
//      usually equal to 2
//      a ^ - operation of raising to the power
```

```
//        (not XOR!);
//
//        polynomial form -> index from
//        index_of[j=alpha^i] = i;
//
// © Simon Rockliff
//-------------------------------------------------------------------------

generate_gf()
{
   int i, mask;

   mask = 1; alpha_to[m] = 0;

   for (i = 0; i < m; i++)
   {
      alpha_to[i] = mask;
      index_of[alpha_to[i]] = i;
      if (p[i] != 0) alpha_to[m] ^= mask;
      mask <<= 1;
   } index_of[alpha_to[m]] = m; mask >>= 1;

   for (i = m+1; i < n; i++)
   {
      if (alpha_to[i-1] >= mask)
         alpha_to[i] = alpha_to[m] ^ ((alpha_to[i-1]^mask)<<1);
      else
         alpha_to[i] = alpha_to[i-1]<<1;

      index_of[alpha_to[i]] = i;
   } index_of[0] = -1;
}
```

The multiplication function itself looks rather trivial. In fact, it fits within five lines of code. In most software implementations of Reed-Solomon coder/decoder that I have seen, the division operation is not even implemented as a separate procedure but, rather, is carried out directly where it is called.

Listing 2.15. A function of fast multiplication in Galois Fields using a table

```
// The function returns the result of multiplication
// of two polynomials in Galois fields
int gf_mul(int a, int b)
```

```
{
    int sum;
    if (a == 0 || b == 0) return 0;      // Some optimization
                                         // won't hurt.
    sum = alpha_of[a] + alpha_of[b];     // Calculating the sum
                                         // of polynomial indexes
    if (sum >= GF-1) sum -= GF-1;        // Bringing the sum to
                                         // the GF module
    return index_of[sum];                // Transforming the
                                         // result to the
                                         // polynomial form
                                         // and return the result
}
```

Division in Galois Fields

Division in Galois fields is carried out practically the same way as multiplication, with the only exception that the indexes are not added but, rather, subtracted from one another. Actually, $a/b == 2^i/2^j == 2^{(i-j)}$. To transform this presentation from polynomial to index form and vice versa, the above-provided look-up table can be used.

Naturally, do not forget about the fact that, however perverse Galois fields might seem, even abstract arithmetic doesn't allow division by zero. Therefore, the division function must be supplied with the appropriate check.

Listing 2.16. The function of fast division of polynomials in Galois fields

```
// This function returns the result of division of two
// polynomials, a and b, in Galois fields.
// In case of attempt of division by zero, the function
// returns -1.
int gf_div(int a, int b)
{
    int diff;
    if (a == 0) return 0;                // Some optimization
                                         // won't hurt.
    if (b == 0) return -1;               // Division by zero
                                         // is not allowed!
    diff = alpha_of[a] - alpha_of[b];    // Calculating the
                                         // difference of indexes
    ff += GF-1;                          // Bringing the
                                         // difference to the
                                         // GF module
```

```
    return index_of[diff];              // Transforming the
                                        // result to the
                                        // polynomial form
                                        // and returning
                                        // the result

}
```

Simplest Practical Implementations

Ancient-model hard disks developed by IBM represent a good example of the implementation of the Reed-Solomon coder/decoder. The IBM 3370 model had very simple and illustrative Reed-Solomon coder/decoder of the (174,171) type in the Galois field GF(256). In other words, this coder/decoder operated with 8-bit cells (2^8=256), and there were 3 bytes of checksum field per 171 data bytes. As a result, this produced a codeword having the length of 174 bytes. As we will see later, all three checksum bytes were calculated absolutely independently from one another. Consequently, the Reed-Solomon coder/decoder operated only with *one byte*, which significantly simplified its architecture.

In contemporary hard disks, the Reed-Solomon coder/decoder has become significantly more complicated, and the number of check bytes has grown immensely. As a result, in implementations of this Reed-Solomon coder/decoder, one has to operate with numbers of unnatural lengths (about 1,408 bits or more). Consequently, the source code bristled with a thick layer of additional checks, loops, and functions that significantly complicate its understanding. Furthermore, most manufacturers of computer hardware have recently migrated to the hardware implementations of Reed-Solomon coders/decoders, which are implemented entirely by a single chip. In other words, despite all of our respect for technological progress, it is much better to study the basic operating principles of the Reed-Solomon coders/decoders on the examples of ancient models.

The listing provided below shows a fragment of the original code of the firmware for the IBM 3370 hard disk:

Listing 2.17. The key fragment of the Reed-Solomon coder/decoder from the original code of the IBM 3370 hard disk firmware

```
for (s0 = s1 = sm1 = i = 0; i < BLOCK_SIZE; ++i)
{
    s0  =                             s0 ^ input[i];
    s1  =             GF_mult_by_alpha[ s1 ^ input[i]];
    sm1 = GF_mult_by_alpha_inverse[sm1 ^ input[i]];
};
```

Listing 2.18. The key fragment of the Reed/Solomon coder/decoder from the IBM 3370 hard disk firmware

```
err_i = GF_log_base_alpha[ GF_divide[s1][s0] ];    // Calculating
                                                    // the error
                                                    // syndrome
input[err_i] ^= s0;                                 // Correcting the
                                                    // erroneous byte
```

Can we understand how it works? With regard to the s0 variable, everything is clear: This variable stores the checksum calculated according to the trivial algorithm. As you probably remember, addition in Galois fields is carried out by logical XOR operation. Therefore, s0 += input[i].

The goal of the s1 variable is more difficult to clarify. To understand the idea of its transformations, we must know the contents of the GF_mult_by_alpha table. Although, for the sake of brevity, this function is not provided here, it is easy to guess its goal because it has the speaking name: the contents of s1 are added to the next byte of the data flow being controlled, and then multiplied by so-called *primitive term*, designated as alpha, and equal to 2. In other words, s1 = 2 * (s1 + input[i]).

Now, let us assume that one of the bytes of the data flow becomes inverted (let us designate its position as err_i). Then the index of the inverted byte can be determined by the trivial division of s1 by s0. Why is this the case? In fact, s1 = 2 * (s1 + input[i]) is nothing other than the multiplication of the data word by the generated polynomial dynamically generated on the basis of its primitive member alpha. The checksum of the data word stored in the s0 variable actually represents the same data word, simply represented in more "compact" form. As already mentioned, if the error took place in position x, then the remainder generated by the division of the codeword by the generated polynomial will be equal to $k = 2^x$. Now, it only remains to calculate x by the given k, which in our case is carried out by means of looking up the GF_log_base_alpha table, which stores the pairs of mappings between k and 2^x. As long as the position of the erroneous byte is detected, it can be corrected by means of XORing it with the calculated checksum s0 (input[err_i] ^= s0). Naturally, this is true only for single errors. The above-described algorithm is unable of correcting errors comprising two or more corrupted bytes per data block. In fact, the third byte of the checksum — sm1 — is present for exactly this purpose. It protects the decoder from "incorrect" attempts at error correction, i.e., prevents error correction when the number of errors exceeds 1. If the expression s1/s0 == sm1 * s0 becomes false, then the disk controller can record the fact of multiple errors, but should report that these errors cannot be recovered.

As is well-known, the defects of a magnetic surface tend to group errors rather than cause single errors. To compensate for the weakness of the error-correction algorithm, IBM engineers resorted to byte *interleaving*. The IBM 3370 hard disk had the interleave of 3:1, which means that the first byte of the first block goes first, followed by the first byte of the second block, then by the first byte of the third block, and only after that — by the second byte of the first block. This trick increased the corrective capabilities of the hard disk from a single error to the sequence of three corrupted bytes... However, if bytes that were not directly adjacent to one another were subject to corruption, then the corrective capability once again dropped down to one corrupted byte per block. However, the probability of such an event was significantly lower.

Naturally, this kind of algorithm can be implemented not only in hard disks. By varying the block size and interleave factor, you'll be able to ensure more or less strong protection having higher or lower information redundancy. In fact, let us suppose that we have N sectors on the disk. Then, having divided them into blocks containing 174 sectors each and having dedicated 3 sectors per block for storing the checksum, we will be able to restore at least N/174 disk sectors. Based on an average disk capacity of 100 GB (which corresponds to 209,715,200 sectors), we will be able to restore up to 1,205,259 sectors — even in the case of their total physical destruction. At the same time, only 2 percent of disk space will be reserved for storing checksums. Most people would agree that the situations, when the destruction of a hard disk is so fast that correcting capabilities of the Reed-Solomon code prove to be insufficient for restoring information, are quite rare (provided, of course, that incipient disk corruption is noticed in due time, and provided that the interleave factor is chosen correctly — so that sectors belonging to the same plate of the hard disk were served by different correcting blocks. Otherwise, the corruption of the surface of one disk plate results in a group error that cannot be recovered by this algorithm).

What should we do if the entire hard disk is damaged? In this case, the most reasonable approach is to create an array of several disks storing useful information mixed with correcting codes. The main drawback of such an approach is its inefficiency with arrays comprising a small number of hard disks. The reasonable minimum is as follows: four data disks and one disk for check information. In this case, the loss of any of the data disks will be compensated by the check disk that remained functional. The damaged check disk can easily be replaced by a new one, and all check codes will be recalculated. However, if two disks fail simultaneously, this means a catastrophe. An array containing 15 disks, among which 12 are data disks, and 3 disks are reserved for check codes, provides a significantly higher level of fault tolerance. It tolerates simultaneous failure of any two disks, and under favorable circumstances, even simultaneous failure of three disks can be overcome.

Actually, there is nothing new in all this information. In fact, appropriate RAID controllers are available in practically any computer store. However... I can hardly imagine the cost of a RAID controller of level 15, and I am not sure that it will be possible to make it work (based on my own experience, RAID controllers even of basic levels are extremely error-prone, whimsical, and have extremely high requirements both to hardware and to the OS environment). Finally, practically all RAID controllers require either absolutely identical disks or, at least, ones that are very similar in their characteristics and/or interfaces). What if they are not available?

Software implementation of RAID, actively promoted by the author of this book, is free from all of the above-listed drawbacks. You can use disks of different geometry and even of different capacity. At the same time, nothing limits you to concentrating them in a single location. On the contrary, disks can be accessed even via the network. Furthermore, it is not necessary to reserve the entire disk for RAID storage. You can arbitrarily dedicate the desired part of the disk space for this purpose.

How can we use this in practice? The first idea that comes to mind is to use part of the hard disk space for storing redundant information that will allow the restoration of the disk contents in the event of a failure. If several computers are joined to form a network then, under conditions of relatively low overhead, we will be able to restore any of the hard disks in any computer connected to a network, even if its information is totally destroyed. This is thanks only to the redundant information distributed among all of the other computers. It would be hard to conceive of a more reliable system for information storage! This scheme was implemented by the author in the LANs of several enterprises. It has proven its high survivability, flexibility, and a wide range of functional capabilities. The need to constantly carry out backups of the hard disk contents was automatically eliminated. This is more than urgent under conditions of peer-to-peer networks, where there is no dedicated server! On the other hand, such networks exist, and they are not rare. (No, I do not promote the development of this type of network or claim that it is a good solution. I am simply noting the fact that they exist and are not going to be eliminated totally in the nearest future.)

The only drawback of software RAID implementation is its low performance. In particular, by installing software RAID on a server processing thousands of queries per second and modifying a large number of files intensively, you won't get a performance gain, but the concept of "performance" itself is rather relative. Having a sufficiently fast processor, it is possible to carry out information encoding/decoding on the fly without any losses in throughput! On the other hand, if read operations dominate over write operations, the installation of software RAID is a natural solution, since the integrity control of the information being read is carried out at the hardware level of the drive itself. Consequently, when using systematic encoding (i.e., data words separate from parity bytes), the Reed-Solomon decoder doesn't need to interfere with this process, and its help is needed only when part of the information is badly damaged. Realistically, this doesn't happen often. Thus, it is not worth paying a lot to firms specializing on hardware RAID implementations, especially since they don't provide home users and small businesses the attention that they deserve.

Reed-Solomon Codes in Practical Implementations

In previous sections, we have considered the basic mathematics that serve as the foundation for Reed-Solomon codes. We have also investigated the simplest coder/decoder, capable of correcting single errors and working with two parity symbols. These correcting capabilities are catastrophically insufficient for the overwhelming majority of problems. Therefore, it becomes necessary to implement a more powerful coder/decoder.

The coder/decoder considered in this section is highly configurable and can be tuned for operation with any number of parity symbols. This means that under conditions of reasonable redundancy, it is capable of correcting *any* imaginable number of errors. However, this flexibility and universality comes with a cost. Therefore, the design of such a decoder is about 100 times more difficult. The independent development of Reed-Solomon decoders requires a fundamental knowledge of higher mathematics in general, and the nature of correcting codes in particular. Therefore, do not be afraid or confused if the material provided in this section is not easily understandable. These topics are difficult and there is no simple way to explain them.

On the other hand, for practical usage in correcting codes, it is possible to simply compile the source codes of the Reed-Solomon coder/decoder provided here without obtaining further insight into it. The same approach is the case if you use any ready-to-use library from third-party developers. As an alternative example, the concluding part of this chapter will briefly describe the interface of the ElByECC.DLL library developed by the Elaborate Bytes company and distributed along with the popular Clone CD program. The best-known CD burner everywhere, Ahead Nero Burning ROM, has the similar library (NEWTRF.DLL).

Legend

Let us recall the main notation used in this chapter. The number of characters of the message being encoded (also called the data word) according to generally adopted agreement is designated by the letter k; the complete length of the codeword including the data being encoded and parity characters is equal to n. Consequently, the number of parity characters is equal to $n - k$. The maximum number of recoverable errors is designated by t. Since two parity symbols are required for correcting a single error, the total number of parity characters is equal to $2t$. The RS(n,k) expression describes a specific sort of Reed-Solomon correcting code, operating with n-symbol blocks, in which k symbols represent useful data, while all other symbols are used for parity symbols.

The polynomial obtained on the basis of the primitive term α is known as the generated polynomial.

Encoder

There are at least two types of Reed-Solomon codes: *non-systematic* and *systematic* encoders.

Non-systematic Reed-Solomon error-correcting codes are calculated by *multiplying* the data word by the generated polynomial. As a result, the codeword is generated that is absolutely different from the source information word and, therefore, not suitable for direct usage. For bringing the obtained data into their initial form, it is necessary to carry out the resource-consuming decoding operation, even if the data are not corrupted and do not require recovery!

When using systematic encoding, however, the source data word remains without changes, while the correcting codes (often called parity characters) are added to its end. Thanks to this, the decoding operation is needed only in the event of actual data destruction. Computation of non-systematic Reed-Solomon codes is carried out by the *division* of the data word by the generating polynomial. At the same time, all symbols of the data word are shifted by n-k bytes to the left, while the 2t bytes of the remainder are written to the released positions (see Fig. 2.1).

Since considering both types of encoders would require a lot of time, let us concentrate all of our attention on systematic coders, which are the most popular.

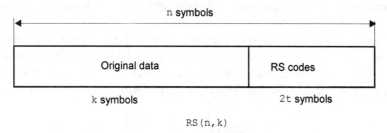

RS(n,k)

Fig. 2.1. Codeword structure

From the architectural point of view, the encoder represents the set of *shift registers*, joined by means of *integrators* and *multipliers*, operating according to the rules of Galois arithmetic. The shift register represents the sequence of memory cells, called *bits*, each of which contains one element of a Galois field GF(q). The symbol, contained in a specific position, is transmitted to the output line as it leaves this position. Simultaneously, the symbol from the input line is loaded into position. Replacement of symbols takes place discretely, at strictly defined time intervals, known as *clocks*.

In hardware implementation of the shift register, its elements can be connected both sequentially and in parallel. In the case of sequential connection, the sending of a single m-bit symbol will require m clocks, while in implementations using parallel connection, this operation requires only one clock.

The low efficiency of software implementations of Reed-Solomon codes is due to the fact that the developer cannot connect elements of the shift register in parallel. On the contrary, software developers are forced to work with the bit width "enforced" by specific hardware architecture. However, developing a 4-element, 8-bit shift register of the parallel type on processors of the IA32 family is a realistic task.

Circuits based on shift registers are usually called *filters*. The flow chart of a filter that carries out the division of a polynomial by a constant is shown in Fig. 2.2. Don't be confused by the fact that division is implemented by means of multiplication and addition. This technique is based on solving the system of two recurrent equalities:

$$Q^{(r)}(x) = Q^{(r-1)}(x) + R^{(r-1)}_{n-r} x^{k-r}$$

$$R^{(r)}(x) = R^{(r-1)}(x) - R^{(r-1)}_{n-r} x^{k-r} g(x)$$

Formula 2.1. Dividing a polynomial by a constant by means of multiplication and addition

Here: $Q(r)(x)$ and $R(r)(x)$ are the quotient and remainder at the r-th step or recursion, respectively. Since addition and modulo-2 computation are identical, for implementing the divider, we need only two devices — addition and multiplication devices. The subtraction device is not necessary.

After n shifts, the *quotient* will appear at the register output, while the register itself will contain the *remainder*, which represents the calculated parity symbols (they are the same as Reed-Solomon codes), while multiplication coefficients from g0 to g(2t-1) directly correspond to the multiplication coefficients of the generated polynomial.

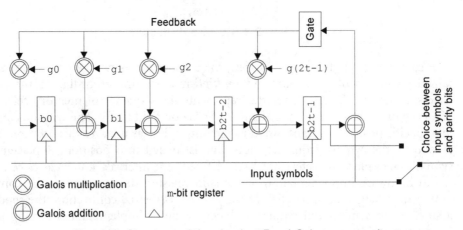

Fig. 2.2. Structure of the simplest Reed-Solomon encoder

The simplest software implementation of this type of filter is provided below. It represents a ready-to-use Reed-Solomon encoder, suitable for practical use. It could certainly be improved if desired. However, in this case, the listing would become less compact and less illustrative.

Listing 2.19. The source code for the simplest Reed-Solomon encoder

---

```
/*--------------------------------------------------------------------------
 *
 *                      Reed-Solomon encoder
 *
 *                      =====================
 *
 *
 *    The data being encoded are transmitted via the data[i] array, where i = 0...(k - 1),
 * and generated parity symbols are placed into the b[0]...b[2*t-1] array.
 * Source and resulting data must be represented in a polynomial
 * form (i.e., in standard form of machine data representation).
 *    Encoding is carried out using feedback shift register,
 * filled with appropriate elements of the g[] array with the generated
 * polynomial inside. The procedure of generating this polynomial was already
 * discussed in the previous section.
 *    The generated codeword is described by the following formula:
 * c(x) = data(x)*x^(n-k) + b(x), where ^ stands for the operator of raising
 *                      the number into the power of exponent.
 *
 *
 *                      Based on the source codes by
 *                      Simon'a Rockliff, from 26.06.1991
 *                      distributed according
 *                      to the GNU license
 *--------------------------------------------------------------------------*/
encode_rs()
{
    int i, j;
    int feedback;

    // Initializing the parity bit field by zeroes
    for (i = 0; i < n - k; i++) b[i] = 0;

    // Processing all symbols
    // of the source data from right to left
    for (i = k - 1; i >= 0; i--)
    {
            // preparing (data[i] + b[n − k −1]) for multiplication by g[i]
```

```
// i.e., adding the next "captured" symbol of the source
// data to the least significant symbol of the parity bits
// (corresponding to the b2t-1 register, see Fig. 2.2)
// and converting it into the index form,
// storing the result in the feedback register.
// As was already pointed out, the sum of the two indexes is
// the product of polynomials.
feedback = index_of[data[i] ^ b[n - k - 1]];

// Are there any more symbols for processing?
if (feedback != -1)
{
        // shifting the chain of bx registers
        for (j = n-k-1; j>0; j--)
                    // If the current coefficient g is a real one
                    // (i.e., non-zero) coefficient, then
                    // multiplying feedback by the appropriate g coefficient
                    // and adding it to the next element of the chain
            if (g[j]!=-1) b[j]=b[j-1]^alpha_to[(g[j]+feedback)%n];
else
                    // if the current coefficient g is equal to zero,
                    // then carrying out only shift without
                    // multiplication, by moving
                    // the character from one m-register
                    // to another m-register
            b[j] = b[j-1];

        // Looping the output symbol to the leftmost b0-register
        b[0] = alpha_to[(g[0]+feedback)%n];
}
else

{       // Division is complete,
        // carrying out the last shift of the register,
        // the quotient (which will be lost)
        // appears at the register output,
        // while the register itself
        // will contain the required remainder.
        for (j = n-k-1; j>0; j--) b[j] = b[j-1] ; b[0] = 0;
}
    }
}
```

Decoder

Decoding of Reed-Solomon codes is a complicated problem, the solution to which results in a bulky, complicated, and extremely complex code requiring the developer to have extensive knowledge of many areas of higher mathematics. A typical decoding scheme known as *auto-regressive spectral decoding method*, comprises the following steps:

1. Determining error syndrome (syndrome decoder).
2. Building error polynomial, carried out either using the highly efficient, but rather sophisticated Berlekamp-Massey algorithm, which is hard to implement, or using the simple, but very slow Euclidean algorithm.

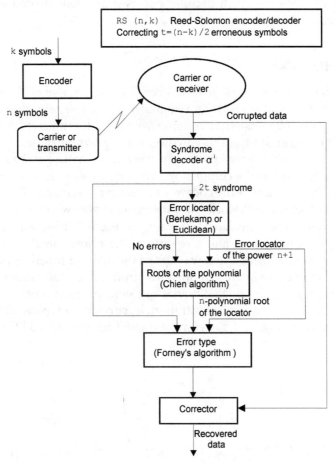

Fig. 2.3. Scheme of auto-regressive spectral decoder
for Reed-Solomon correcting codes

3. Finding the roots of this polynomial, which is usually carried out by means of trivial try-out (Chien search algorithm).

4. Determining the error type, which is carried out by building the bit mask calculated on the basis of Forney's algorithm or any other algorithm of matrix inversion.

5. Correcting erroneous symbols by means of superimposing the mask onto the data word and sequentially inverting all corrupted bits via XOR operation.

It is important to point out that this decoding scheme is neither the only one nor, probably, the best one. However, it is universal. In practice, there are about ten various decoding schemes, absolutely different from each other. As a rule, the choice of specific scheme depends on which decoder part is implemented programmatically, and for which part hardware implementation is chosen.

Syndrome Decoder

Roughly speaking, *syndrome is the remainder from the division of the codeword $c(x)$ by the generator polynomial $g(x)$*. If this remainder is equal to zero, the codeword is considered to be correctly transferred. A non-zero remainder indicates that there is at least one error. The remainder from the division is the polynomial, independent from the source message, which is determined exclusively by the nature of the error.

The received codeword v comprising components $v_i = c_i + e_i$, where $i = 0, ...,$ $n - 1$, represents the sum of the codeword c and error vector e. The goal of decoding is the separation of the codeword from the error vector, which is decried by the syndrome polynomial and calculated according to the following formula: $S_j = v(a^{j+j_0-1})$, where j ranges from 1 to $2t$, and a represents the prime member "alpha," which we have discussed earlier. Once again, we express the division function via multiplication, because division is a very inefficient operation from the performance point of view.

A flow chart of the device that carries out syndrome computation is presented in Fig. 2.4. As can be seen from this illustration, it represents a typical filter (compare it to the scheme shown in Fig. 2.2), therefore, it doesn't require any additional comment.

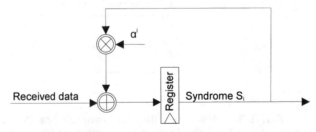

Fig. 2.4. Flow chart of the syndrome computation circuit

Computation of the error syndrome is carried out iteratively, so that the computation of the resulting polynomial (also called the *answer polynomial*) is completed directly at the moment when the last parity symbol passes through the filter. The total number of passes of the data being decoded through the filter is equal to $2t$ — one pass per symbol of the resulting polynomial.

The example of the simplest software implementation of the syndrome decoder is provided in Listing 2.2 and is much more illustrative than any verbal description.

Error Locator Polynomial

The obtained syndrome describes the error configuration, but it still doesn't specify, which symbols of the received message were corrupted. Actually, the power of the syndrome polynomial equal to $2t$ is significantly lower than the power of the message polynomial, which is equal to n, and there is no direct correspondence between their coefficients. The polynomial that has coefficients directly corresponding to the coefficients of corrupted symbols is called the *error locator polynomial* and, according to commonly adopted agreement, is designated by Λ (lambda).

If the number of corrupted symbols does not exceed t, the syndrome and error locator are related by unambiguous mapping, which can be expressed by the following formula: `GCD[x`^{n}`-1, E(x)] = `Λ`(x)`. Computation of the locator is reduced to the problem of finding the greatest common divisor. As a matter of fact, this problem was successfully solved by Euclid, and can be easily implemented both at the software and at the hardware level. However, the simplicity of implementation pays a price. In this case, the performance is sacrificed for simplicity, because the algorithm is very inefficient. In practice, the more efficient, but, at the same time, more sophisticated *Berlekamp-Massey* algorithm is used. A detailed description of this algorithm can be found in Volume 2 of the *"Art of Programming"* by Donald Knuth (see also *"Theory and Practice of Error Control Codes"* by Richard Blahut). The algorithm is reduced to the task of building a chain of shift registers with linear feedback, and, in its essence, is a kind of auto-regression filter, the multipliers in the vectors of which specify the polynomial Λ.

A decoder created according to such an algorithm requires no more than $3t$ multiplication operations in each iteration, and the total number of iterations doesn't exceed $2t$. Thus, the solution to this problem requires no more than $6t^2$ multiplication operations. In fact, the computation of the locator is reduced to solving the system of $2t$ equations with t unknown quantities — one equation per symbol of the syndrome. Unknown terms are positions of the corrupted symbols in the codeword v. As can be seen easily, if the number of errors exceeds t, the system of equations has no solution. In this case, it becomes impossible to recover the corrupted information.

The flow chart of the Berlekamp-Massey algorithm is shown in Fig. 2.5, and its complete software implementation can be found on the companion CD.

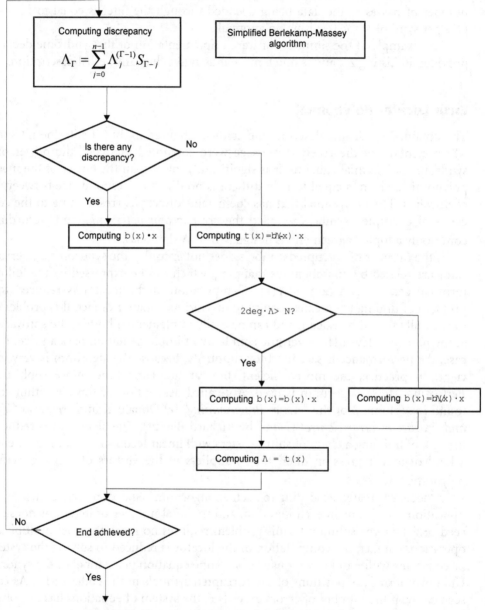

Fig. 2.5. Flow chart of the Berlekamp-Massey algorithm

Polynomial Roots

From what we know of the error locator polynomial, its roots determine the location of corrupted symbols in the received codeword. Now it only remains to find these roots. Most frequently, this is accomplished using the *Chien search* procedure, which by its nature is analogous to the inverse Fourier transform. In fact, it is reduced to exhaustive search and trying of all possible variants. All 2^m possible symbols, one by one, are substituted into the locator polynomial, and then the polynomial is computed. If the result is zero, then the required roots have been found.

Data Recovery

Thus, we know, which symbols of the codeword are corrupted. But, for the moment, we are not prepared to answer *how*. Using the syndrome polynomial and roots of the locator polynomial, it is possible to determine the character of corruption for each of the corrupted symbols. As a rule, the *Forney* algorithm is used for this purpose. This algorithm comprises two stages: first, by means of convoluting the syndrome polynomial by the locator polynomial Λ, we obtain some *intermediate polynomial*, conventionally designated as Ω. Then, based on the Ω-polynomial, the *zero error location* is computed, which, in turn, is divided by the derivative of the Λ-polynomial. As a result, the bit mask is obtained, in which each of the set bits corresponds to the corrupted bit. To restore the codeword to its initial state, all corrupted bits must be inverted, which is achieved by means of a logical XOR operation.

At this point, the procedure of decoding the received codeword can be considered accomplished. It only remains to discard n-k parity symbols, and the obtained data word is ready for use.

Source Code of the Decoder

The source code of a fully functional Reed-Solomon decoder, supplied with the necessary number of comments can be found on the companion CD. If you have difficulties when analyzing this listing, refer to the flow charts presented in Figs. 2.3, 2.4, and 2.5.

Interface to the ElByECC.DLL Library

Software implementation of the Reed-Solomon encoder/decoder provided in Listings 2.19 and on the companion CD is sufficiently illustrative. However, it is characterized by very low performance and requires optimization. As an alternative variant, it is possible to use ready libraries supplied by third-party developers, included in software products in any way related to processing Reed-Solomon error-correction codes. The list of such products includes utilities for CD copying/burning/restoration, drivers for tape drives (from streamer to ARVID), various telecommunication complexes, etc.

As a rule, all of these libraries are an integral part of the software product itself, and, therefore, are not documented in any way. Restoring the prototypes of the interface functions is a non-trivial task, requiring the investigator not only to have the disassembling skills, but also a knowledge of higher mathematics, otherwise the sense of all bit manipulations will remain unintelligible.

Is such disassembling legal? In fact, the disassembling of third-party software products is prohibited, but is still *legal*. In this case, it is appropriate to provide the analogy with unsealing your TV set, which results in voiding the warranty, but cannot be prosecuted by law. In just the same way, no one prohibits you to call the functions of someone else's library from your program. Distributing this library as part of your software product is illegal. However, what prevents you from asking the user to install this library on his own?

Provided below is a brief description of the most important functions of the ElByECC.DLL library included as part of the well-known copier of protected CDs — Clone CD. The shareware copy of this product can be downloaded from **http://www.elby.ch/**. The Clone CD product itself will be functional only for 21 days, after which it will require you to register the copy. However, there are no limitations on the usage of the ElByECC.DLL library.

Despite the fact that the ElByECC.DLL is oriented towards operation with sectors of CDs, it is also suitable for other purposes, for instance, for building fault-tolerant disk arrays, mentioned earlier in this chapter.

A brief description of the main functions of this library is provided below.

Linking the ElByECC.DLL Library to Your Programs

There are at least two methods of linking DLLs to your programs. When using dynamic linking, addresses of the required functions are determined by means of GetProcAddress calls. In this case, the ElByECC.DLL library itself must be loaded previously using LoadLibrary. For instance, this may look as follows (error handling is omitted for the sake of simplicity):

Listing 2.20. Dynamic loading of the ElByECC.DLL library

```
HANDLE h;
int (__cdecl *CheckECCAndEDC_Mode1) (char *userdata, char *header, char *sector);

h=LoadLibrary("ElbyECC.dll");
CheckECCAndEDC_Mode1 = GetProcAddress(h, "CheckECCAndEDC_Mode1");
```

Static linking assumes that a special lib-file is present, which can be automatically generated by the `implib` utility supplied as part of Borland C++ of any suitable version. This is a command-line utility called as follows: "`implib.exe -a ElByECC.lib ElByECC.lib`".

GenECCAndEDC_Mode1

The `GenECCAndEDC_Mode1` function generates error-correcting codes on the basis of a 2048-byte block of user data. This function has the following prototype:

Listing 2.21. The prototype of the GenECCAndEDC_Mode1 function

```
GenECCAndEDC_Mode1(char *userdata_src,  // Pointer to the 2048-byte array
                char *header_src, // Pointer to the header
                struct RAW_SECTOR_MODE1 *raw_sector_model_dst)
```

❏ `userdata_src` is the pointer to the 2,048-byte block of user data, for which it is necessary to compute the error-correction codes. The user data itself remains unchanged in the course of function execution. They are automatically copied to the buffer of the target sector, where they are supplemented by 104 + 172 parity bytes and 4 bytes of the checksum.

❏ `header_src` is the pointer to the 4-byte block containing the sector header. The first three bytes are taken for the absolute address written in the BCD form, while the fourth byte is responsible for the type of sector, to which it is necessary to assign the value 1, corresponding to the mode when correcting codes are enabled.

❏ `raw_sector_model_dst` is the pointer to the 2,352-byte block, in which the generated sector will be written, containing 2,048 bytes of user data and 104+172 bytes of error-correction codes along with 4 bytes of the checksum. Raw sector is presented by the following structure:

Listing 2.22. Structure of the raw sector

```
struct RAW_SECTOR_MODE1
{
    BYTE         SYNC[12];           // Sync group
    BYTE         ADDR[3];            // Absolute sector address
    BYTE         MODE;               // Sector type
    BYTE         USER_DATA[2048];    // User data
    BYTE         EDC[4];             // Checksum
    BYTE         ZERO[8];            // Zeroes (not used)
    BYTE         P[172];             // P parity bytes
    BYTE         Q[104];             // Q parity bytes
};
```

Provided that the function has been completed successfully, it returns a non-zero value, otherwise it returns zero.

CheckSector

The `CheckSector` function checks the integrity of the sector by the checksum, and restores it using Reed-Solomon redundant codes, if necessary.

Listing 2.23. The prototype of the CheckSector function

```
CheckSector(struct RAW_SECTOR *sector,  // Pointer to the sector buffer
int DO);                                 // Only checking/correcting
```

❏ `sector` — the pointer to the 2,352-byte data block containing the sector being tested. The sector is recovered on the fly, i.e., immediately when the error occurs. If the number of corrupted bytes exceeds the correcting capabilities of the Reed-Solomon codes, the source data remains unchanged.

❏ `DO` — the flag, the zero value of which specifies that modifying the sector is prohibited. In other words, this value corresponds to the TEST ONLY mode. A non-zero value allows data recovery, if they actually were corrupted.

❏ If the function terminates successfully, it returns a non-zero value. The function returns zero if the sector contains an error (in the TEST ONLY mode) or if the data recovery has failed (when calling the function in the data recovery mode). To prevent possible ambiguity, it is recommended that you call this function in two steps. First — in the test mode for checking data integrity, and second, in the data recovery mode (if data recovery is needed).

Final

Provided below is an example of practical usage of error-correcting code, suitable for solving practical real-world tasks.

Listing 2.24. An example of calling ElByECC.DLL functions from your program

---

```
/*------------------------------------------------------------------
 *
 *                    Demonstration of ElByECC.DLL
 *                    ========================
 *
 *
 *    This program demonstrates working with ElByECC.DLL library,
 * by generating redundant Reed-Solomon codes on the basis of
```

```
 * user data, and then deliberately corrupting and restoring them.
 * The number of bytes to be corrupted is passed in the first
 * command-line parameter (6 by default)
--------------------------------------------------------------------------------*/
#include <stdio.h>
#include "ElByECC.h"                              // Decompiled by MsIЦЬX

#define _DEF_DMG        6                         // Corrupt by default
#define N_BYTES_DAMAGE  ((argc>1)?atol(argv[1]):_DEF_DMG)  // How many bytes to corrupt?

main(int argc, char **argv)
{
    int a;
    char stub_head[HEADER_SIZE];                  // Sector header
    char user_data[USER_DATA_SIZE];               // User data area

    struct RAW_SECTOR_MODE1 raw_sector_for_damage;  // Sector for corruption
    struct RAW_SECTOR_MODE1 raw_sector_for_compre;  // sector checksum.


    // TITLE
    //-------------------------------------------------------------------------
    printf("= ElByECC.DLL usage demo example by KK\n");

    // Initializing user data
    //-------------------------------------------------------------------------
    printf("user data initialize..............");
    for (a = 0; a < USER_DATA_SIZE; a++) user_data[a] = a; // User_data  init
    memset(stub_head, 0, HEADER_SIZE); stub_head[3] = 1;   // src header init
    printf("+OK\n");

    // Generating Reed-Solomon codes on the basis of user data
    //-------------------------------------------------------------------------
    printf("RS-code generate..................");
    a = GenECCAndEDC_Mode1(user_data, stub_head, &raw_sector_for_damage);
    if (a == ElBy_SECTOR_ERROR) { printf("-ERROR!\x7\n"); return -1;}
    memcpy(&raw_sector_for_compre, &raw_sector_for_damage, RAW_SECTOR_SIZE);
    printf("+OK\n");

    // Intentionally corrupting user data
    //-------------------------------------------------------------------------
    printf("user-data %04d bytes damage........", N_BYTES_DAMAGE);
    for (a=0; a<N_BYTES_DAMAGE; a++) raw_sector_for_damage.USER_DATA[a]^=0xFF;
```

```
if(!memcmp(&raw_sector_for_damage, &raw_sector_for_compre, RAW_SECTOR_SIZE))
        printf("-ERR: NOT DAMAGE YET\n"); else printf("+OK\n");

// Checking the integrity of user data
//-------------------------------------------------------------------------
printf("user-data check...................");
a = CheckSector((struct RAW_SECTOR*)&raw_sector_for_damage, ElBy_TEST_ONLY);
if (a == ElBy_SECTOR_OK){
        printf("-ERR:data not damage\x7\n"); return -1;} printf(".data damge\n");

// Recovering user data
//-------------------------------------------------------------------------
printf("user-data recorder................");
a = CheckSector((struct RAW_SECTOR*)&raw_sector_for_damage, ElBy_REPAIR);
if (a == ElBy_SECTOR_ERROR) {
        printf("-ERR: NOT RECORVER YET\x7\n"); return -1; } printf("+OK\n");

// Checking if recovery was successful
//-------------------------------------------------------------------------
printf("user-data recorver check..........");
if(memcmp(&raw_sector_for_damage, &raw_sector_for_compre, RAW_SECTOR_SIZE))
        printf("-ERR: NOT RECORVER YET\x7\n"); else printf("+OK\n");

printf("+OK\n");
return 1;
}
```

Part II

Low-Level Control over Hardware

**Chapter 3: Practical Advice
on Urgent System Recovery 97**

**Chapter 4: Interfaces for Interaction
with the Hardware 137**

**Chapter 5: Methods
of Revealing Protection Mechanisms 211**

The sector level of interaction has been an attraction for developers of CD protection mechanisms, as well as for the developers of utilities designed for the copying of protected discs. The reading and writing of Raw sectors is even more promising, because it is the lowest possible level of interaction with the disc that can be supported by standard drives. In fact, most protection mechanisms operate this way. Some of them hide the key information in subcode channels, while others in some way corrupt ECC/EDC codes, or use non-standard formatting and similar methods.

Methods of operating with discs at the sector level are numerous, and descriptions of about dozen of these will be provided below. Most of the methods that will be discussed here are intended exclusively for Windows NT/W2K/XP and do not work on Windows 9x, which is likely to go the way of the wooly mammoth — interest in this operating system is fading swiftly, both for end users and for programmers. While Windows 9x will stay afloat for a while yet, in the long term it's not worth betting on, especially in view of the fact that Windows 9x does not support multiprocessor systems, and the triumphant arrival of Hyper-Threading is just around the corner.

Hyper-Threading technology is based on the implementation of Simultaneous Multi-Threading (SMT). In fact, this technology represents an intermediate stage between multithreading carried out in multiprocessor systems and parallelism at the level of instructions present in single-processor systems.

Since disc access at the sector level is initially oriented towards the developers of protection mechanisms, this section has a pronounced focus on the thwarting of hackers. It describes not only methods of low-level device management, but also discusses the internal function of protection mechanisms.

Some variations of protection against unauthorized copying cannot principally be cracked using standard home appliances. In particular, audio CD protection mechanisms based on an incorrect TOC (Table of Contents) render such a disc unreadable by computer CD-ROM drives. However, on audio players that do not delve into examining every TOC detail, such discs can be played satisfactorily. The only way of copying such a disc in a digital format is by patching the firmware of the CD-ROM drive to remove some of the "extra" checks, or by disassembling the drive to hot-swap the disc. More details on this topic will be provided in Chapter xxxx.

Therefore, it is indeed unwise to overestimate protection mechanisms designed to prevent the unauthorized copying of CDs.

Chapter 3: Practical Advice on Urgent System Recovery

1. Run-time errors have the highest priority. Only another error with a higher priority can terminate error execution.
2. Errors can ignore requests from the operating system.
3. Requests from errors to the operating system cannot be ignored.
4. When working with files, errors can use the file system of the basic OS and exploit its errors.
5. On a computer with parallel architecture, several errors can be executed simultaneously.

V.Tikchonov. *"Theory of Errors"*

Applications, Illegal Operations, and Everything Else

Low-level control over equipment requires extreme care and caution. Even the smallest error can result in the Blue Screen of Death (BSOD) or the abnormal termination of one or more applications. Driver developers and combat engineers have very much in common — neither of these professions is particularly forgiving of carelessness. ASPI and SPTI interfaces, despite their high-level wrappers, are equally aggressive. They can freeze the system or shut it down with or without pretext. It takes a long time to master the skill of writing stable and simple code. Until that level has been reached, the only guarantee of survival is the skill of recovering the system after critical errors and various kinds of malfunctions.

Different operating systems react to critical errors differently. For example, Windows NT reserves two regions of its address space for detecting stray pointers. One of them is located at the very "bottom" of the memory map and is intended for the "trapping" of zero pointers. Another is located between the heap and the memory area allocated for the operating system itself. It controls events that involve crossing the limits of the memory area allocated to user processes. Contrary to common opinion, it is in no way related to the WriteProcessMemory function (see MSDN article Q92764). Both regions take 64 K each, and any attempt of accessing them is interpreted by the system as a critical error. In Windows 9x, there is only one 4 K region for tracing stray pointers. Therefore, this system has significantly weaker controlling capabilities than Windows NT.

In Windows NT, the critical error screen (Fig. 3.1) contains the following information:

❑ The address of machine instruction that has caused the current exception
❑ A brief description of the exception category (or its code, if category is unknown)
❑ The exception parameters (address of invalid memory cell, type of operation, etc.)

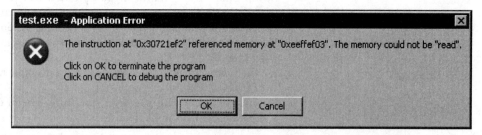

Fig. 3.1. Critical error message displayed by Windows 2000

Operating systems of the Windows 9x family are considerably more informative in this respect (see Fig. 3.2). Besides the exception category, they display the contents of CPU registers, stack condition and memory bytes located by the address CS:EIP (e.g., by the current execution address). However, the existence of the Doctor Watson tool, which will be described later in this chapter, diminishes this difference between the two families of operating systems. Therefore, in this case we can only point out that Windows 9x is more user-friendly and ergonomic, since it immediately provides the required minimum of error information, while in Windows NT error reports are created by a separate utility.

If no additional debugger has been installed in the system, then the critical error message window has only one button — **OK**. After the user clicks this button, the application that carried out the illegal operation will be terminated. If you wish, it is possible to add the **Cancel** button to this window. Clicking on this button will start the debugger or any other utility intended for analyzing the situation. It is important to understand that clicking the **Cancel** button doesn't cancel automatic termination of the incorrect application. However, having mastered some skills, you can close the "breach" manually and continue working in a normal way.

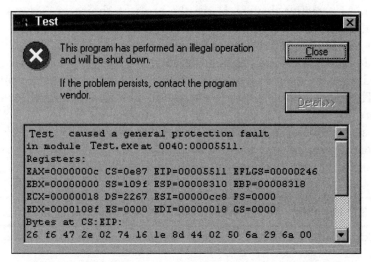

Fig. 3.2. Critical error message displayed by Windows 98

Start the Registry Editor application and go to the following registry key: HKLM\SOFTWARE\Microsoft\Windows NT\CurrentVersion\AeDebug. If there is no such key, just create it. The Debugger value specifies the path to the debugger with all of the required command-line options; Auto string parameter determines whether the debugger must start automatically (the value must be set to 1) or provide the user with a choice ("0"). Finally, the DWORD parameter UserDebuggerHotKey specifies the scancode for the hotkey for starting the debugger.

Doctor Watson

The Doctor Watson tool is the standard built-in debugger for critical errors that is included with all operating systems of the Windows family. Principally, it is a static tool for collecting all relevant information. Although Doctor Watson provides a detailed report on the causes of a failure, it lacks the active functions that would allow it to influence incorrectly operating programs. Thus, having only Doctor Watson at your disposal, you won't be able to make the application that has caused an error continue operating as if nothing has happened. To achieve this, you'll have to use interactive debuggers. The Microsoft Visual Studio Debugger, supplied as part of the Microsoft Visual Studio, is one of such tools. It will be considered later in this chapter.

That Doctor Watson is preferable for use on workstations, while interactive debuggers are the best for servers is a widely held opinion. Those who hold this view generally think that end users cannot understand all of the mysteries of the assembler, while interactive debuggers are the tools of choice on servers. This opinion is partially true. However, it isn't wise to ignore the point that not every cause of an error can be detected by static analysis tools. Furthermore, interactive tools simplify the procedure of analysis considerably. On the other hand, Doctor Watson is included with the operating system, while all other tools must be purchased separately. Therefore, it is up to you to choose the preferred debugger for handling critical errors.

To specify Doctor Watson as your default debugger, add the following entry to the system registry or issue the `Drwtsn32.exe -i` command (to carry out any of these operations, you must have administrative privileges):

Listing 3.1. Installing Doctor Watson as the default debugger

---

```
[HKEY_LOCAL_MACHINE\SOFTWARE\Microsoft\Windows NT\CurrentVersion\AeDebug]

"Auto"="1"

"Debugger"="drwtsn32 -p %ld -e %ld -g"

"UserDebuggerHotKey"=dword:00000000
```

Now the occurrence of any critical error will be followed by the generation of a report composed by Doctor Watson and containing a more or less detailed explanation on the error type and what has caused it.

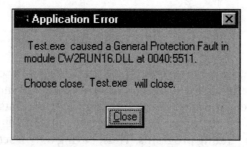

Fig. 3.3. Reaction of Doctor Watson to a critical error

An example of a report created by Doctor Watson is provided below. Comments are added by the author; the report's lines are in bold.

Listing 3.2. An example of report produced by Doctor Watson (with the author's comments in bold).

```
Exception in application:
    App:   (pid=612)
    ; pid of the process where the exception took place


    Time: 14.11.2003 @ 22:51:40.674
    ; Time when the exception took place


    Number: c0000005 (access rights violation )
    ; Code of the Exception category
    ; Code decoding can be found in WINNT.H
    ; included with SDK, supplied with any Windows compiler
    ; A detailed description of all exceptions can be found
        ; in supplementary documentation
        ; to all Intel and AMD processor, distributed freely
        ; by the respective manufacturers
    ; (Attention: To change the OS exception code to the CPU interrupt vector,
    ; you must reset the most significant word to zero.)
    ; In this case, this is 0x5 — an attempt to access
    ; an invalid memory address.



*----> System information <----*
    Computer name: KPNC
    User name: Kris Kaspersky
    Number of processors: 1
    Processor type: x86 Family 6 Model 8 Stepping 6
    Windows version: 2000: 5.0
    Current build: 2195
    Service pack: None
    Current type: Uniprocessor Free
    Registered organization:
    Registered user: Kris Kaspersky
    ; Brief info on the system



*----> Task list <----*
```

```
   0 Idle.exe
   8 System.exe
 232 smss.exe
...
1244 os2srv.exe
1164 os2ss.exe
1284 windbg.exe
1180 MSDEV.exe
1312 cmd.exe
 612 test.exe
1404 drwtsn32.exe
   0 _Total.exe
```

```
(00400000 — 00406000)
(77F80000 — 77FFA000)
(77E80000 — 77F37000)
; List of loaded DLLs
; According to documentation, the names of appropriate modules
; must be listed to the right of the addresses. They are
; masked so well, however, that they became practically invisible.
; Still, it is possible to extract their names from the log file.
; But this can't be done without the use of a few tricks (see character table below).
```

Memory copy for flow 0x188
```
; Provided below is a copy of the memory flow that has caused an exception.
```

```
eax=00000064 ebx=7ffdf000 ecx=00000000 edx=00000064 esi=00000000 edi=00000000
eip=00401014 esp=0012ff70 ebp=0012ffc0 iopl=0          nv up ei pl nz na pe nc
cs=001b  ss=0023  ds=0023  es=0023  fs=0038  gs=0000              efl=00000202
; Contents of registers and flags
```

Function: <nosymbols>
```
; Printout of the failure environment
```

```
    00400ffc 0000      add [eax],al      ds:00000064=??
    ; Writing the value into the cell that adds AL value to EAX
    ; The value of the cell address computed by Doctor Watson is equal to 64h,
    ; which, obviously, doesn't correspond to reality;
    ; Doctor Watson substitutes the value of the EAX register
    ; for the moment of failure into the expression
    ; and this value is different from the one
    ; that this register had at the moment of execution!
    ; Unfortunately, neither we nor Doctor Watson
```

```
; know the run-time value of the EAX register.
```

```
00400ffe 0000      add      [eax], al        ds:00000064=??
; Writing the AL value of the cell referenced by EAX
; What? again? what a pain?! Actually,
; it is the sequence 00 00 00 00 that is encoded this way.
; For all appearances, this sequence is a piece
; of some machine command incorrectly interpreted
; by the disassembling engine of Doctor Watson.
```

```
00401000 8b542408 mov      edx, [esp+0x8]    ss:00f8d547=????????
; Loading function argument into EDX
; It is impossible to tell for certain which argument we should load,
; since we do not know the address
; of the stack frame.
```

```
00401004 33c9      xor      ecx, ecx
; Resetting ECX to zero
```

```
00401006 85d2      test     edx, edx
00401008 7e18      jle      00409b22
; If EDX == 0, jumping to the 409B22h address
```

```
0040100a 8b442408 mov      eax, [esp+0x8]    ss:00f8d547=????????
; Loading the above-mentioned argument into EAX
```

```
0040100e 56        push     esi
; Saving ESI in the stack, thus moving the stack top pointer
; up by 4 bytes (into the area of lower addresses)
```

```
0040100f 8b742408 mov      esi, [esp+0x8]    ss:00f8d547=????????
; Loading the next argument into ESI
; Since ESP has just been changed, this isn't the argument
; with which we were dealing before.
```

```
00401013 57        push     edi
; Saving the EDI register in the stack
```

```
FAILURE -> 00401014 0fbe3c31    movsx  edi, byte ptr [ecx+esi] ds:00000000=??
       ; Well, we've got the instruction that has caused the access violation.
       ; it accesses the cell referenced by the sum of the ECX and ESI registers.
       ; What are their values? scroll the screen upwards slightly and find out that
       ; ECX and ESI are equal to 0, a fact about which
```

```
; Doctor Watson informs us: "ds:000000"
; Note that this information can be trusted, since substitution
; of the effective address was carried out at run time.
; Now, let us recall that ESI contains
; the copy of the argument passed to the function
; and that ECX was explicitly reset to zero. Consequently,
; in the [ECX+ESI] expression,
; the ESI register is the pointer, and ECX is the index.
; Since ESI is equal to zero, this means that our function
; passed the pointer to unallocated memory area.
; This usually happens
; either because of an algorithmic error in a program
; or because the virtual memory has been exhausted.
; Unfortunately, Doctor Watson doesn't disassemble
; the parent function, and we have to guess, which of the
; two possible variants is true.
; Although, it is possible to disassemble the memory dump
; of the process (provided, of course, that it has been saved),
; this isn't what we actually need…


00401018 03c7      add        eax, edi
; Add the contents of the EAX register
; to the EDI register and write the result to EAX.


0040101a 41        inc        ecx
; increase  ECX by one


0040101b 3bca      cmp        ecx, edx
0040101d 7cf5      jl         00407014
; Until ECX < EDX, jump to 407014
; (obviously, we are dealing with a loop controlled by the ECX counter).
; In the case of interactive debugging, we could forcibly exit the function
; that is returning the error flag, informing us so that the parent function
; (and the entire program along with it) can continue execution.
; In this case, only the last operation would be lost,
; while all the other data will remain correct.


0040101f 5f        pop        edi
00401020 5e        pop        esi
00401021 c3        ret
; exiting the function


*----> Backward tracing of the stack <----*
```

```
; Stack contents at the moment of failure
; prints addresses and parameters of previously executed functions.
; In the case of interactive debugging, we can simply pass control to one
; of the upper functions, which is equivalent to a return to the past.
; Only in reality is it impossible to fix smashed porcelain,
; in the computer universe, everything is possible!
FramePtr ReturnAd Param#1  Param#2  Param#3  Param#4  Function Name
; FramePtr: points to the value of the stack frame,
;          above (i.e., in smaller addresses) are the function arguments,
;          below are its local variables.
;
; ReturnAd: stores the return address to the parent function.
;          If this location contains garbage and back-tracing of the stack
;          starts to make a characteristic noise,
;          then it is highly likely
;          that we are dealing with the stack overflow error
;          or, possibly, that your computer is under attack.
;
; Param#: the first four parameters of the function —
;          this is the number of parameters
;          that Doctor Watson displays on the screen.
;          This is an overly stringent limitation,
;          since most functions have dozens of parameters
;          and the first four do not provide sufficient information.
;          However, a missing parameter can be retrieved easily
;          from the copy of the unprocessed stack manually.
;          To do so, it is enough to go by the address specified in the
;          FramePtr field
;
; Func Name: function name (if it is possible to detect it). In fact,
;          it displays only the names of functions imported from other DLLs,
;          since it is impossible to find a commercial program
;          compiled along with debug info.
;
0012FFC0 77E87903 00000000 00000000 7FFDF000 C0000005 !<nosymbols>
0012FFF0 00000000 00401040 00000000 000000C8 00000100 kernel32!SetUnhandledExceptionFilter
; Functions are listed in the order of their execution.
; The last one that was executed was the same
; kernel32!SetUnhandledExceptionFilter function that handles the current exception.

*----> Copy of unprocessed stack <----*
; The copy of the unprocessed stack contains it "as is."
; It is very helpful when detecting buffer overfull attacks — the entire shell-code
```

```
; passed by the intruder will be printed out by Doctor Watson,
; and you'll only have to detect it (for further details,
; see my book "Technique and philosophy of network attacks")
0012ff70  00 00 00 00 00 00 00 00 - 39 10 40 00 00 00 00 00   ........9.@.....
0012ff80  64 00 00 00 f4 10 40 00 - 01 00 00 00 d0 0e 30 00   d.....@.......0.
...
00130090  00 00 00 00 00 00 00 00 - 00 00 00 00 00 00 00 00   ...............
001300a0  00 00 00 00 00 00 00 00 - 00 00 00 00 00 00 00 00   ...............

*----> Symbol table <----*
; The symbol table contains the names of all loaded DLLs, along with the names
; of imported functions. Using these addresses as the starting point,
; we can easily restore the «list of loaded DLLs.»...

ntdll.dll
77F81106 00000000    ZwAccessCheckByType
...
                          77FCEFB0 00000000   fltused


kernel32.dll
77E81765 0000003d   IsDebuggerPresent
...
77EDBF7A 00000000   VerSetConditionMask
;
; Thus, let us return to the list of loaded DLLs.
; (00400000 - 00406000) - obviously,
; this is the memory area occupied by the program itself.
; (77F80000 - 77FFA000) - this is KERNEL32.DLL
; (77E80000 - 77F37000) - this is NTDDL.DLL
```

Microsoft Visual Studio Debugger

When you install the Microsoft Visual Studio programming environment, it registers its debugger as the default one for handling critical errors. Although this debugger is very easy to use, it has very limited functions, and doesn't even support such a simple operation as looking for a hex sequence in memory. Its only advantage in comparison to the most advanced (in every respect) option, Microsoft Kernel Debugger, is the ability to trace processes that have generated a critical exception.

In the hands of an experienced professional, Microsoft Visual Studio Debugger is capable of bringing wonders to reality, and one such wonder is making applications that have executed an illegal operation continue their work, even given that the operating system closes such applications abnormally without saving their data. Anyway, an interactive debugger (Microsoft Visual Studio Debugger is the one) provides much more detailed information on the failure and simplifies considerably the process of detecting its sources. Unfortunately, the limited space allowed in this chapter (even though it already contains a large amount of off topic information!) prevents the author from providing a detailed description of the entire methodic of debugging. Instead, I must limit myself to only a narrow range of the most interesting problems. For more details, see the section "*Inhabitants of the Shadowy Zone, or From Morgue to Reanimation*").

In order to set Microsoft Visual Studio Debugger as the default debugger for critical errors manually, add the following entries to the system registry:

Listing 3.3. Specifying Microsoft Visual Studio Debugger as your default debugger for critical errors

```
[HKEY_LOCAL_MACHINE\SOFTWARE\Microsoft\Windows NT\CurrentVersion\AeDebug]
"Auto"="1"
"Debugger"="\"C:\\Prg Files\\MS VS\\Common\\MSDev98\\Bin\\msdev.exe\" -p %ld -e %ld"
"UserDebuggerHotKey"=dword:00000000
```

Listing 3.4. A demo example that causes a critical exception

```
// The function returns the sum of n char characters.
// If it is passed the null-pointer, the function will "drop,"
// although itself isn't the source of error, rather,
// the arguments passed to it,
// by the parent function.
test(char *buf, int n)
{
    int a, sum;
    for (a = 0; a < n; a++) sum += buf[a]; // Here, the exception is thrown.
    return sum;
}

main()
{
    #define N    100
    char *buf = 0;                          // Initializing the pointer to the buffer

    /* buf = malloc(100); */                // "Forgetting" to allocate the memory,
```

```
// which is the error
    test(buf, N);                  // Passing the null-pointer to some function
}
```

Inhabitants of the Shadowy Zone, or From Morgue to Reanimation

Would you like to know how to make an application continue normal operation after a critical error message has appeared? In fact, this is an important, and sometimes urgent task. Suppose that an application containing unique data that have not been saved yet has crashed. In the best case, you'll have to enter this information once again, while in the worst case, you have lost the data for good. There are some utilities on the market aimed exactly at solving this problem (Norton Utilities is a typical example). Unfortunately, however, their abilities are far from comprehensive, and, on average, they turn out to be effective in only one in ten occasions. At the same time, manual "reanimation" of a faulty program is successful in 75 to 90 per cent of all cases.

Strictly speaking, it is impossible to recover fully the functionality of a crashed program or to roll back all of the actions that preceded the crash. In the best case, you'll be able to save the data before the program totally loses control and starts to behave unpredictably. Even this achievement would have to be counted as a success!

There are at least three different methods of reanimation: *a) forcibly exiting the function that has caused a critical exception; b) "unwinding" the stack and passing control back; c) passing control to the message handler function.* Let us consider each of these methods in the example of the testt.exe application, a copy of which can be found on the companion CD.

Jumping ahead a few steps, note that only faults that are caused by algorithmic errors can be reanimated. Errors caused by hardware faults are irrecoverable. If information stored in RAM was corrupted because of a physical defect in the memory, you probably won't be able to recover the crashed application. If, however, the failure did not affect vitally important data structures, there is some hope for successful recovery even in this case.

Forcibly Exiting the Function

Start the test program, enter some text in one or more of the windows, then select the **About TestCEdit** command from the **Help** menu. When the dialog opens, click the **Make error** button. Oops! The program displays a critical error message. If we click **OK**, all unsaved data will be lost, which isn't what we planned. However, if a previously installed debugger is present in the system, we can still make some attempts at saving the data. For the purposes of being specific, let's suppose that we have Microsoft Visual Studio Debugger.

Click **Cancel**, and the debugger will immediately disassemble the function that caused the exception (see the listing provided below).

Listing 3.5. Microsoft Visual Studio Debugger has disassembled the function that has thrown an exception

---

```
0040135C    push    esi
0040135D    mov     esi, dword ptr [esp+8]
00401361    push    edi
00401362    movsx   edi, byte ptr [ecx+esi]
00401366    add     eax, edi
00401368    inc     ecx
00401369    cmp     ecx, edx
0040136B    jl      00401362
0040136D    pop     edi
0040136E    pop     esi
0040136F    ret     8
```

Having analyzed the cause of the exception (the function has been passed the pointer to unallocated memory), we draw the conclusion that it is impossible to make the function continue execution, since we do not know the structure of the data passed to it. In such a case, we have to return forcibly to the parent function, without forgetting to set the error flag, which sends a signal to the program that the current operation has not been accomplished. Unfortunately, there are no commonly adopted error flags. Therefore, different functions use different agreements. To discover the situation in each specific case, we must disassemble the parent function and determine which error code it expects.

Place the cursor on the dump window and enter the name of the pointer to the stack top, ESP register, into the address line. Then press <Enter>. The stack contents will be immediately displayed:

Listing 3.6. Searching for the return address from the current function (in bold)

```
0012F488    0012FA64    0012FA64    004012FF
0012F494    00000000    00000064    00403458
0012F4A0    FFFFFFFF    0012F4C4    6C291CEA
0012F4AC    00000019    00000000    6C32FAF0
```

```
0012F4B8   0012F4C0   0012FA64   01100059
0012F4C4   006403C2   002F5788   00000000
0012F4D0   00640301   77E16383   004C1E20
```

The first two double words correspond to the POP EDI/POP ESI machine commands. Therefore, they are of little or no importance to us. As for the next double word, it contains the return address to the parent procedure (in the above-provided example, it is in bold). This is exactly what we need!

Press <Ctrl>+<D>, then click 0x4012FF, and debugger will display the following disassembled text:

Listing 3.7. Disassembled listing of the parent function

```
004012FA   call    00401350
004012FF   cmp     eax,0FFh
00401302   je      0040132D
00401304   push    eax
00401305   lea     eax, [esp+8]
00401309   push    405054h
0040130E   push    eax
0040130F   call    dword ptr ds:[4033B4h]
00401315   add     esp, 0Ch
00401318   lea     ecx, [esp+4]
0040131C   push    0
0040131E   push    0
00401320   push    ecx
00401321   mov     ecx, esi
00401323   call    00401BC4
00401328   pop     esi
00401329   add     esp, 64h
0040132C   ret
0040132C
0040132D   push    0
0040132D   ; This branch will get control if 401350h function returns FFh.
0040132F   push    0
00401331   push    405048h
00401336   mov     ecx, esi
00401338   call    00401BC4
0040133D   pop     esi
0040133E   add     esp, 64h
00401341   ret
```

Look at this: If the EAX register is equal to FFh, then the parent function passes the control to branch 40132Dh and terminates execution after several machine commands, passing control to a higher-level function. If, however, EAX != FFh, its value is passed to function 4033B4h. Consequently, we can assume that FFh is the error flag. Let us return to the function being tested by pressing <Ctrl>+<G> and clicking EIP. Then switch to the **Registers** pane and change the value of EAX to FFh.

Now, it is necessary to find a suitable point of return from the function. It is not possible to simply go to the RET machine command, because before returning from the function, it is necessary to balance the stack. Otherwise, the program will crash irreversibly, throwing us off to some unpredictable location.

In a general case, the number PUSH commands must correspond exactly to the number of POP commands. Also, take into account the fact that PUSH DWORD X is equivalent to SUB ESP, 4, and POP DWORD X — to ADD ESP, 4. After analyzing the disassembled listing of the function, it is possible to draw the conclusion that, to balance the good and the bad in this case, we must pop two double words from the stack top. They correspond to the following machine commands: 40135C:PUSH ESI and 401361:PUSH EDI. This can be achieved by passing the control to the 40136Dh address, where there are two benevolent POPs that bring the stack to a balanced state. Move the cursor to that position, right-click, and choose the **Set Next Statement** command from the context menu. As a variant, it is possible to switch to the registers window and change the EIP value from 401362h to 40136Dh.

Press <F5> to make the processor continue with program execution. Voila! The faulty program actually continues execution, and you can save your data. (A good-natured complaint about an error in the last operation can be ignored.)

Unwinding the Stack

It is not possible to forcibly exit from the function in every case. Some critical failures influence several nested functions simultaneously. In this case, in order to reanimate the "dead" program, we have to carry out a deep rollback, continuing program execution from the point, at which nothing threatened its operability. The exact depth of rollback must be selected experimentally. As a rule, it will be from three to five steps. Bear in mind that if nested functions modify global data (for instance, heap data), then any attempt at carrying out a rollback can result in a total crash of the program being debugged. Therefore, it is desirable to guess the rollback depth on the first attempt. If you are in doubt, just remember that an excess is better than a shortage. On the other hand, excessive rollback results in the loss of all unsaved data...

The rollback procedure comprises the following three steps: *a) building the tree of calls; b) determining the coordinates of the stack frame for each call; c) restoring the register context of the parent function.* A really good debugger will carry out all of these operations for you. The only thing that remains is to write appropriate values into EIP and ESP. Unfortunately, Microsoft Visual Studio Debugger cannot be qualified as a really effective debugger. It is good for tracing the stack, omitting FPO functions (*Frame Point Omission* — functions with optimized frame), but doesn't report coordinates of the stack frame; therefore, the most difficult part of your job must be carried out manually.

Still, even such a stack of calls is still better than nothing. By unwinding the stack manually, we will rely on the fact that frame coordinates are determined naturally by the return address. Let's suppose that that the contents of the **Call Stack** window appear as follows:

Listing 3.8. The contents of the Call Stacks window displayed by Microsoft Visual Studio Debugger

```
TESTCEDIT! 00401362()
MFC42! 6c2922ae()
MFC42! 6c298fc5()
MFC42! 6c292976()
MFC42! 6c291dcc()
MFC42! 6c291cea()
MFC42! 6c291c73()
MFC42! 6c291bfb()
MFC42! 6c291bba()
```

Let's try to find addresses 6C2922AEh and 6C298FC5h, corresponding to the two last steps of execution in the stack contents. Press <ALT>+<6> to switch to the dump window, then use the <Ctrl>+<G> hotkey combination to select the base address and select ESP. Scroll the dump window down, and you'll find both return addresses (in the listing provided below, they are framed):

Listing 3.9. Stack content after unwinding

```
0012F488  0012FA64  0012FA64  004012FF ← 0040136F:ret 8 the first return address
0012F494  00000000  00000064  00403458 ← 00401328:pop esi
0012F4A0  FFFFFFFF  0012F4C4  6C291CEA
0012F4AC  00000019  00000000  6C32FAF0
0012F4B8  0012F4C0  0012FA64  01100059
0012F4C4  00320774  002F5788  00000000
0012F4D0  00320701  77E16383  004C1E20
0012F4DC  00320774  002F5788  00000000
```

```
0012F4E8   000003E8   0012FA64   004F8CD8
0012F4F4   0012F4DC   002F5788   0012F560
0012F500   77E61D49   6C2923D8   00403458  ← 0040132C:ret;
0012F50C   00000111   0012F540   6C2922AE  ←6C29237E:pop ebx/pop ebp/ret 1Ch
0012F518   0012FA64   000003E8   00000000
0012F518   0012FA64   000003E8   00000000
0012F524   004012F0   00000000   0000000C
0012F530   00000000   00000000   0012FA64
0012F53C   000003E8   0012F564   6C298FC5
0012F548   000003E8   00000000   00000000
0012F554   00000000   000003E8   0012FA64
```

Memory cells below the return addresses represent the register values that are saved when entering the function and restored after exiting it. Memory cells located below return addresses are occupied by function arguments (if the function has any), or belong to the local variables of the parent function (if the nested function doesn't accept any arguments).

Returning to Listing 3.5, note that the two double words on the top of the stack correspond to the POP EDI and POP ESI machine commands, while the address that directly follows them — 4012FFh — is the one, to which the 40136Fh:RET 8 command passes control. To continue stack unwinding, we must disassemble the code by this address:

Listing 3.10. Disassembled listing of the "grandmother" function

```
004012FA   call    00401350
004012FF   cmp eax,0FFh
00401302   je  0040132D
00401304   push    eax
00401305   lea eax,[esp+8]
00401309   push    405054h
0040130E   push    eax
0040130F   call    dword ptr ds:[4033B4h]
00401315   add esp,0Ch
00401318   lea ecx,[esp+4]
0040131C   push    0
0040131F   push    0
00401320   push    ecx
00401321   mov ecx,esi
00401323   call    00401BC4
00401328   pop esi
00401329   add esp,64h
0040132C   ret                 ; SS:[ESP] = 6C2923D8
```

By scrolling the window downwards, we will notice the ADD ESP, 64 instruction that closes the current stack frame. Eight bytes more are popped by the 40136Fh:RET 8 instruction, and four bytes are taken by 401328:POP ESI. Thus, the position of return address in the stack is equal to current_ESP + 64h + 8 + 4 == 70h. Going down 70h bytes, you'll see:

Listing 3.11. Return address from the "grandmother" function

```
0012F500   77E61D49   6C2923D8   00403458 ← 00401328:POP ESI/ret;
```

The first double word is the value of the ESI register, which we will have to restore manually; the second is the return address from the function. Press <Ctrl>+<G>, enter 0x6C2923D8, and continue to unwind the stack:

Listing 3.12. Disassembled listing of the great-grandmother function

```
6C2923D8   jmp    6C29237B
...
6C29237B   mov    eax, ebx
6C29237D   pop    esi
6C29237E   pop    ebx
6C29237F   pop    ebp
6C292380   ret    1Ch
```

Now, we have finally got to restoring registers! Move to the right by one double word (it was just popped from the stack by the RET command), switch to the **Registers** window, and restore the ESI, EBX, and EBP registers by retrieving their saved values from the stack:

Listing 3.13. The contents of the registers saved in the stack along with the return address

```
0012F500   77E61D49   6C2923D8   00403458 ← 6C29237D:pop esi
0012F50C   00000111   0012F540   6C2922AE ←6C29237E:pop ebx/pop ebp/ret 1Ch
```

As an alternative, you can move the EIP register to the 6C29237Dh address, the ESP register — to the 12F508h address, and then press <F5> to continue program execution. This technique actually works. At the same time, the reanimated program doesn't report an execution error from the last operation (as was the case when restoring by means of forcibly exiting the function). Instead of this, the program doesn't execute that command. Very well!

Passing Control to the Message Handler Function

Neither of the above-described methods of reanimating faulty applications are free from limitations and drawbacks. If the stack is seriously damaged by buffer overflow attacks or by algorithmic errors, the contents of vitally important processor registers will be corrupted. In this case, we won't be able to roll back (because stack contents have been lost) or exit the current function (because EIP points to some unknown location, probably somewhere in outer space). For console applications, there is actually very little that can be done in such situations... GUI applications, however, are a different matter. The concept of event-driven architecture provides any windowing application with some server functions. Even if the current execution context is irreversibly lost, we can pass control to the message-handling loop, thus making the program continue processing user commands.

A classic message-handling loop appears as follows:

Listing 3.14. A classic message-handling loop

```
while (GetMessage(&msg, NULL, 0, 0))
{
TranslateMessage(&msg);
DispatchMessage(&msg);
}
```

All you need to do is pass control to the while loop, without even caring about the stack frame tuning, since optimized programs (which are overwhelming in the majority) address their local variables via ESP, rather than via EBP. Of course, when addressing to the msg variable, the function will ruin the stack contents that are located below its top. However, this is of little or no importance to us.

You should, however, realize that after you exit the application, it will definitely die (because instead of the address to return from the function, the RET machine command will find some unpredictable trash on top of the stack). However, this will be *after* you have saved all of your data, and, therefore, this crash doesn't present any threat. The only exception is in a group of freaky applications that "forget" to close all opened files and delegate this job to the ExitProcess function. However, even in this case, there is a way out: You can modify the return address in such a way as to make it point to the ExitProcess function!

Let us create the simplest Windows application and experiment with it. Start Visual Studio, choose **New → Project → Win32 Application** and then select **Typical Hello, World application**. Add a new item to the menu, and add the following: char *p; *p = 0; then compile this project with debug info.

Drop the application, then start the debugger. Move the cursor to the first line of the message-handling loop, right-click and select **Set Next Statement** from the context menu. Press <F5> to continue program execution and... it will actually continue to work!

Now, compile the project as a release (i.e., without debug info) and try to reanimate the application in naked machine code. Taking advantage of the fact that Windows is a truly multitasking environment, in which the crashing of one process doesn't interfere with the operation of others, start your favorite disassembler (IDA PRO, for instance) and analyze the import table of the program being debugged. Even freeware programs such as dumpbin are able to do this. However, the report produced by dumpbin is not as clear and illustrative as the results produced by fully functional disassemblers.

The main goal of our search will be the TranslateMessage/DispatchMessage functions and cross-references to the message-handling loop.

Listing 3.15. Searching TranslateMessage/DispatchMessage functions in the import table

---

```
.idata:004040E0 ; BOOL __stdcall TranslateMessage(const MSG *lpMsg)
.idata:004040E0  extrn TranslateMessage:dword; DATA XREF: _WinMain@16+71↑r
.idata:004040E0                                        ; _WinMain@16+8D↑r
.idata:004040E4 ; LONG __stdcall DispatchMessageA(const MSG *lpMsg)
.idata:004040E4  extrn DispatchMessageA:dword ; DATA XREF: _WinMain@16+94↑r
.idata:004040E8
```

The DispatchMessage function has the only related cross-reference that obviously leads to the message-handling loop we are after. The disassembled listing of this loop appears as follows:

Listing 3.16. The disassembled listing of the message-handling function

---

```
.text:00401050      mov    edi, ds:GetMessageA
.text:00401050 ; The first call to GetMessageA
               ; (this isn't the loop itself yet, it is only its threshold).
.text:00401050
.text:00401056      push   0         ; wMsgFilterMax
.text:00401058      push   0         ; wMsgFilterMin
.text:0040105A      lea    ecx, [esp+2Ch+Msg]
.text:0040105A ; ECX points to the memory area, through which GetMessageA
.text:0040105A ; will return the message. The current ESP value can be any value.
.text:0040105A ; The most important thing here is that it must
               ; point to the actually allocated memory area.
.text:0040105A ; (See memory map, if the ESP value turns out
```

```
.text:0040105A ; to be corrupted so that it points nowhere.)
.text:0040105A ;
.text:0040105E         push   0              ; hWnd
.text:00401060         push   ecx            ; lpMsg
.text:00401061         mov    esi, eax
.text:00401063         call   edi            ; GetMessageA
.text:00401063 ; Calling GetMessageA
.text:00401063
.text:00401065         test   eax, eax
.text:00401067         jz     short loc_4010AD
.text:00401067 ; Checking if there are unprocessed messages in the queue
.text:00401067

...

.text:00401077 loc_401077:                   ; CODE XREF: _WinMain@16+A9↓j
.text:00401077 ; Starting point of the message loop
.text:00401077
.text:00401077         mov    eax, [esp+2Ch+Msg.hwnd]
.text:0040107B         lea    edx, [esp+2Ch+Msg]
.text:0040107B ; EDX points to the memory area used for passing the messages.
.text:0040107B
.text:0040107F         push   edx            ; lpMsg
.text:00401080         push   esi            ; hAccTable
.text:00401081         push   eax            ; hWnd
.text:00401082         call   ebx            ; TranslateAcceleratorA
.text:00401082 ; Calling the TranslateAcceleratorA function
.text:00401082
.text:00401084         test   eax, eax
.text:00401086         jnz    short loc_40109A
.text:00401086 ; Checking if there are unprocessed messages in the queue
.text:00401086
.text:00401088         lea    ecx, [esp+2Ch+Msg]
.text:0040108C         push   ecx            ; lpMsg
.text:0040108D         call   ebp            ; TranslateMessage
.text:0040108D ; Calling the TranslateMessage function, if there is anything to translate
.text:0040108D
.text:0040108F         lea    edx, [esp+2Ch+Msg]
.text:00401093         push   edx            ; lpMsg
.text:00401094         call   ds:DispatchMessageA
.text:00401094 ; Dispatching the message
.text:0040109A
.text:0040109A loc_40109A:                   ; CODE XREF: _WinMain@16+86↑j
.text:0040109A         push   0              ; wMsgFilterMax
```

```
.text:0040109C      push    0                   ; wMsgFilterMin
.text:0040109E      lea     eax, [esp+34h+Msg]
.text:004010A2      push    0                   ; hWnd
.text:004010A4      push    eax                 ; lpMsg
.text:004010A5      call    edi                 ; GetMessageA
.text:004010A5 ; reading the next message from the message queue
.text:004010A5
.text:004010A7      test    eax, eax
.text:004010A9      jnz     short loc_401077
.text:004010A9 ; running the message handling loop
.text:004010A9
.text:004010AB      pop     ebp
.text:004010AC      pop     ebx
.text:004010AD
.text:004010AD loc_4010AD:                      ; CODE XREF: _WinMain@16+67↑j
.text:004010AD      mov     eax, [esp+24h+Msg.wParam]
                         .text:004010B1             pop     edi
                         .text:004010B2             pop     esi
.text:004010B3      add     esp, 1Ch
.text:004010B6      retn    10h
.text:004010B6 _WinMain@16 endp
```

We can see that the message-handling loop starts from the address 401050h. This is the address, to which it is necessary to pass control in order to continue the execution of the crashed program. Try it. The program works!

Naturally, the task of reanimating a real-world application is much more complicated, because the message-handling loop in this case will be distributed over a large number of functions. Note that it is very difficult to identify all of these functions in the course of "superficial" disassembling. Nevertheless, applications based on standard libraries (such as MFC or OVL) have a predictable architecture. Therefore, the reanimation of such applications isn't a hopeless task.

Let's consider the structure of the message-handling loop in MFC. MFC applications spend most of their time in the following function: CWinThread::Run(void). This function periodically polls the queue for the arrival of new messages and sends them to the appropriate handlers. If one of the handlers has caused a critical fault, program execution can be continued using the Run function. This is its main advantage!

The function has no explicit arguments, but accepts a hidden this argument, pointing to the CWinThread class instance or its derived class, without which the function will be unable to work. Fortunately, tables of virtual methods of the CWinThread class contain a sufficient amount of "birthmarks," allowing us to recreate the this pointer manually.

Let's load the Run function into the disassembler and mark all of the calls to the table of virtual methods addressed via the ECX register.

Listing 3.17. A fragment of the disassembled listing of the Run function

---

```
.text:6C29919D n2k_Trasnlate_main:                    ; CODE XREF: MFC42_5715+1F↑j
.text:6C29919D                                        ; MFC42_5715+67↓j ...
.text:6C29919D          mov     eax, [esi]
.text:6C29919F          mov     ecx, esi
.text:6C2991A1          call    dword ptr [eax+64h]   ; CWinThread::PumpMessage (void)
.text:6C2991A4          test    eax, eax
.text:6C2991A6          jz      short loc_6C2991DA
.text:6C2991A8          mov     eax, [esi]
.text:6C2991AA          lea     ebp, [esi+34h]
.text:6C2991AD          push    ebp
.text:6C2991AE          mov     ecx, esi
.text:6C2991B0          call    dword ptr [eax+6Ch]   ; CWinThread::IsIdleMessage (MSG*)
.text:6C2991B3          test    eax, eax
.text:6C2991B5          jz      short loc_6C2991BE
.text:6C2991B7          push    1
.text:6C2991B9          mov     [esp+14h], ebx
.text:6C2991BD          pop     edi
.text:6C2991BE
.text:6C2991BE loc_6C2991BE:                          ; CODE XREF: MFC42_5715+51↑j
.text:6C2991BE          push    ebx                   ; wRemoveMsg
.text:6C2991BF          push    ebx                   ; wMsgFilterMax
.text:6C2991C0          push    ebx                   ; wMsgFilterMin
.text:6C2991C1          push    ebx                   ; hWnd
.text:6C2991C2          push    ebp                   ; lpMsg
.text:6C2991C3          call    ds:PeekMessageA
.text:6C2991C9          test    eax, eax
.text:6C2991CB          jnz     short n2k_Trasnlate_main
.text:6C2991CD
```

Thus, the Run function expects to receive the pointer to the double word pointing to the table of virtual methods, elements 0x19 and 0x1B of which represent the PumpMessage and IsIdleMessage functions (or stubs to them), respectively. If DLL was not relocated, the addresses of imported functions can be found using the same disassembler. Otherwise, they should be reconstructed using the base address of the module, which is displayed by the debugger in response to the **Modules** command. Provided that these two functions were not blocked by the programmer, searching for the needed virtual table should be a trivial task.

For some unknown reason, the MFC42.DLL library doesn't export symbolic names for these functions, so we must get this information on our own. After processing the MFC42.LIB library using the `dumpbin` utility with the `/ARCH` command-line option, we will get the ordinals of both functions (for `PumpMessage`, this is 5307, and for `IsIdleMessage` — 4079). Now, it remains to find these values in the export list of MFC42.DLL (`dumpbin /EXPORTS mfc42.dll > mfc42.txt`), from which we will discover that the address of the `PumpMessage` function is 6C291194h, while the address of the `IsIdleMessage` is 6C292583h.

Now, it is necessary to find the pointers to the `PumpMessage`/`IsIdleMessage` functions in memory, or, to be more precise, in the data section, the base address of which is contained in the header of the PE-file. Bear in mind that in x86 processors, the least significant byte is located at the lower address, which means that all numbers are written in inverse order. Unfortunately, Microsoft Visual Studio Debugger doesn't support the memory-searching operation. Therefore, we must bypass this limitation by copying the content of the dump onto the clipboard, pasting it into a text file, and searching for addresses there by pressing <F7>. Finally, the required pointers are found at the addresses 403044h/40304Ch (naturally, in your system these addresses may be different). Note that the distance between the pointers is exactly equal to the distance between the pointers to [EAX + 64h] and [EAX + 6Ch], while the order, in which they appear in memory, is inverse to the order, in which virtual methods are declared. This is a good symptom, which indicates that we are likely on the right path.

Listing 3.18. The addresses of the IsIdleMessage/PumpMessage functions located in the data section

```
00403044    6C2911D4 6C292583 6C291194 ; IsIdleMessage/PumpMessage
00403050    6C2913D0 6C299144 6C297129
0040305C    6C297129 6C297129 6C291A47
```

The pointers referring to the 403048h/40304Ch addresses, obviously, are the candidates for membership in the virtual methods table of the `CWinThread` class, for which we are looking. By extending the search range to the entire address space of the process being debugged, we will find the following two stubs:

Listing 3.19. Stubs to the IsIdleMessage/PumpMessage functions located in the data segment

```
00401A20    jmp dword ptr ds:[403044h] ; IsIdleMessage
00401A26    jmp dword ptr ds:[403048h] ;
00401A2C    jmp dword ptr ds:[40304Ch] ; PumpMessage
```

We are getting closer! We have found the stubs to the virtual functions instead of the functions themselves. By unrolling this complicated puzzle, let us try to find the references to `401A26h`/`401A2Ch`, which pass control to the code provided above:

Listing 3.20. Virtual table of the CWinThread class

```
00403490 00401A9E 00401040 004015F0 ← 0x0,  0x1,  0x2  elements
0040349C 00401390 004015F0 00401A98 ← 0x3,  0x4,  0x5  elements
004034A8 00401A92 00401A8C 00401A86 ← 0x6,  0x7,  0x8  elements
004034B4 00401A80 00401A7A 00401A74 ← 0x9,  0xA,  0xB  elements
004034C0 00401010 00401A6E 00401A68 ← 0xC,  0xD,  0xE  elements
004034CC 00401A62 00401A5C 00401A56 ← 0xF,  0x10, 0x11 elements
004034D8 00401A50 00401A4A 00401A44 ← 0x12, 0x13, 0x14 elements
004034E4 00401A3E 004010B0 00401A38 ← 0x15, 0x16, 0x17 elements
004034F0 00401A32 00401A2C 00401A26 ← 0x18, 0x19, 0x1A elements (PumpMessage)
004034FC 00401A20 00401A1A 00401A14 ← 0x1B, 0x1C, 0x1D elements (IsIdleMessage)
```

Even a beginner will easily recognize the virtual functions table in this data structure. The pointers to stubs to `PumpMessage`/`IsIdleMessage` are divided by exactly one element, as required by the task conditions. Let us suppose that this virtual table is the one that we need. To check if this assumption is correct, count `0x19` elements upwards from `4034F4h`, and try to find the pointer that refers to its starting point. If you are lucky and it turns out to be of the `CWinThread` class, the program will be able to continue its operation correctly:

Listing 3.21. The instance of CWinThread, manually located in memory

```
004050B8   00403490 00000001 00000000
004050C4   00000000 00000000 00000001
```

Actually, something very similar to the truth can be found in the memory. Let us write the `4050B8h` value into the `ECX` register and locate the `Run` function in the memory (as already mentioned, its address — `6C299164h` — is known, provided that it hasn't been blocked). Then press <Ctrl>+<G>, enter `"0x6C299164"`, and choose the **Set Next Statement** command from the right-click menu. The program, having escaped with a slight fright, continues execution, while you have a good reason to be happy and go have a rest.

Hanged applications that react neither to keyboard entry nor to mouse clicks can be reanimated in a similar way.

How to Process Memory Dump

> ...In the software department, the entire floor was sown with the confetti from punch cards, and there were some guys crawling over the printout of a crash dump about 20 meters in length, trying to locate an error in the memory manager. The head of the department approached the president and informed him that there was some hope that the task could be achieved before dinner.
>
> J. Antonov. *"The Youth of Gates"*

Memory dump, also known as core, crash-dump, which is saved by the system in the event of a critical error, isn't the most useful tool for detecting the cause of the crash. However, there is often nothing else at the disposal of system administrator. What is the crash dump? This is the last moan of the operating system at the moment of irreversible fault, before it dies altogether. Digging it out is unlikely to please you. On the contrary, it is highly probable that you won't be able to detect the actual cause of the failure. Suppose, for instance, an incorrectly written driver has invaded the memory region belonging to another driver and ruined its data structures, sending all of the numbers there topsy-turvy. At the moment when the "victim" dies, the faulty driver may already be stopped and, in this case, it will be practically impossible using the memory dump alone to determine that it was the one that actually crashed the system.

Nevertheless, it doesn't make any sense to ignore the dump's existence. After all, it provided the only debugging method before the arrival of interactive debuggers. Contemporary programmers are spoiled by the availability of visual analysis tools. However, it doesn't provide them with much self-confidence in situations where pitiless entropy leaves them alone, face to face with their errors. But enough waxing lyrical. Let's take a closer look at this question.

First and foremost, it is necessary to edit the system configuration (**Control Panel** → **System**) and make sure that dump settings correspond to our requirements (**Advanced** → **Startup and Recovery**). Windows 2000 supports three types of memory dumps: small memory dump, kernel memory dump, and complete memory dump. To change the dump settings, you must have administrative privileges.

Small memory dump uses only 64 K (instead of 2 MB, as the context menu states) and includes: *a*) a copy of BSOD; *b*) a list of loaded drivers; *c*) the context of the crashed process with all of its threads; *d*) the first 16 K of the kernel stack of the crashed process. It's a disappointingly small amount of information, isn't it? Direct dump analysis provides us only with the address, at which the error has occurred and the name of the driver, to which that address belongs. Provided that system configuration didn't change after the moment of failure, we can start the debugger and disassemble the suspected driver. However, this is unlikely to produce a valuable result.

After all, the content of the data segment at the moment of failure is unknown to us. Furthermore, we cannot even say for sure that we see the same machine commands as those that caused the failure. Therefore, the small memory dump might be useful only for system administrators, for whom it is sufficient to know the name of the unstable driver. As practice has shown, this information is sufficient in the vast majority of cases. The administrator is expected to send complaints along with an error report and memory dump to driver developers, and replace the driver with a newer, more stable and reliable one. By default, small memory dump will be written to the directory called *%SystemRoot%*\Minidump, where it is assigned the name starting with the string "Mini", followed by the current date and number of the failure for the current day. For example: "*Mini110701-69.dmp*" — 69th system dump saved on November 7, 2001.

Kernel memory dump contains significantly more comprehensive information about the failure. It includes the entire memory allocated to the system kernel and its components — drivers, Hardware Abstraction Layer (HAL), and so on, as well as a copy of BSOD. The size of the kernel dump depends on the number of installed drivers and varies from system to system. Help system states that this value can vary from 50 to 800 MB. Eight hundred MB is too much to look realistic. A size of approximately 50 to 100 MB seems more likely. The technical documentation states that the approximate size of the kernel dump is about one third of the amount of RAM physically installed in the computer. This is the best compromise between disk space overhead, the speed of dump creation, and the information value of the latter. This option does actually provide you with the required minimum of information. Using this option, it is possible to locate practically all typical errors of the drivers and other kernel components, including those that are due to the hardware malfunction (however, the investigator must have some experience with studying memory crash dumps). By default, the kernel dump is written into the file named *%SystemRoot%*\ *Memory.dmp*. Depending on the current settings, the new dump will either overwrite the existing one or be added to its tail.

Full memory dump includes the entire content of the physical memory, both the memory occupied by kernel components and by application processes. Full memory dump turns out to be especially useful when debugging ASPI/SPTI applications, which, due to their specific features, are capable of dropping the kernel even from the application level. Despite its large size, the full memory dump is the favorite option of all system programmers (most administrators prefer the small memory dump). This isn't surprising, if we recall that hard disks long ago have passed the 100 GB threshold. From the programmer's point of view, it is much better to have an unneeded full memory dump than end up suffering because of its absence. By default, the full memory dump will be saved in the file named *%SystemRoot%*\ *Memory.dmp*. Depending on the current system settings, it will either overwrite the existing file or will be appended to its end.

Having chosen the preferred type of memory dump, let's simulate the system crash for the testing purposes. This will help us to get the required skills for recovering the system under fire. For this purpose, we'll need the following:

□ Windows Driver Development Kit (DDK), distributed by Microsoft for free and providing detailed technical documentation of the system kernel; several different C/C++ compilers, assembler, and some advanced tools for memory dump analysis.

□ The W2K_KILL.SYS or any other killer driver, such as BSOD.EXE by Mark Russinovitch, which allows you to get the dump at any given time instance, without needing to wait for a critical error to occur (the freeware version of BSOD.EXE can be downloaded from **http://www.sysinternals.com**).

□ *Symbol files*, required for kernel debuggers to function normally and making the disassembled code more readable and obvious. Symbol files are included in the "green" MSDN distribution set. In principle, you can get by without them. However, the environment variable _NT_SYMBOL_PATH must be defined anyway, otherwise the i386kd.exe debugger won't work.

□ One or more of the books describing the system kernel architecture. The best is *"Windows 2000 Internals"* by Mark Russinovitch and David Solomon. This book will be interesting both for system programmers and for administrators.

After installing DDK on your computer, close all applications and start the killer driver. The system will crash, display a BSOD informing of the causes of failure (see Fig. 3.4), and write the dump (the process might be accompanied by a rattling sound).

```
*** STOP: 0x0000001E (0xC0000005, 0xBE80B000, 0x00000000, 0x00000000)
KMODE_EXEPTION_NOT_HALTED

*** Address 0xBE80B000 base at 0xBE80A000, Date Stamp 389db915 - w2k_kill.sys

Beginning dump of physical memory
Dumping physical memory to disk: 69
```

Fig. 3.4. Blue Screen Of Death (BSOD), signaling the irrecoverable system failure and providing brief information about it

For most administrators, the appearance of BSOD means only one thing — the system was feeling so bad that it preferred death to the infamy of unstable operation. As for the enigmatic characters, they remain a total mystery, but not for true professionals!

Let's start from the top left position on the screen, and trace all BSOD elements, one by one.

□ *** STOP: actually means that the system has stopped. It doesn't carry any other useful information.

❑ 0x0000001E — this is the Bug Check code that classifies the failure. Decoding of the Bug Check codes is provided in DDK. In our case, the code is 0x1E — KMODE_EXEPTION_NOT_HALTED, which is specified by a line directly below. Brief explanations of the most typical Bug Check codes are provided in Table 3.1. Of course, it cannot serve as a replacement for the companion documentation. It will prove you, however, the need to download 70 MB of the DDK.

❑ Numbers in brackets are four Bug Check parameters, the physical meaning of which depends on a specific Bug Check code, which has no physical meaning outside its context. With regard to KMODE_EXEPTION_NOT_HALTED, the first Bug Check parameter contains the number of the exception that was thrown. According to Table 1, this is STATUS_ACCESS_VIOLATION — access to an invalid memory address. The fourth Bug Check parameter specifies the exact address. In this case, it is equal to zero, which means that a specific machine instruction attempted accessing by a null-pointer, corresponding to the initialized pointer that references unallocated memory region. Its address is contained in the second Bug Check parameter. The third Bug Check parameter is undefined in this case.

❑ *** Address 0xBE80B00 — this is the address, at which the failure took place. In this particular case, it is identical to the second Bug Check parameter. This, however, isn't always the case (Bug Check codes are not actually intended to store any addresses).

❑ base at 0xBE80A00 — contains the base loading address of the module that violated the system operating order, by which it is possible to restore the data about that module. (Attention: It isn't always possible to determine correctly the base address.) Using any suitable debugger (for instance, Soft-Ice from NuMega or i386kd from Microsoft), let's issue a command that produces the listing of all loaded drivers with their brief characteristics (in i386kd, this is achieved using the !drivers command). As a possible alternative, you can use the drivers.exe utility supplied as part of NTDDK. No matter which method you choose, the result will be approximately as follows:

```
• kd> !drivers!drivers
  Loaded System Driver Summary
  Base        Code Size       Data Size      Driver Name           Creation Time
  80400000  142dc0 (1291 kb)  4d680 (309 kb) ntoskrnl.exe  Wed Dec 08 02:41:11 1999
  80062000    cc20 (  51 kb)   32c0 ( 12 kb)      hal.dll  Wed Nov 03 04:14:22 1999
  f4010000    1760 (   5 kb)   1000 (  4 kb)  BOOTVID.DLL  Thu Nov 04 04:24:33 1999
  bffd8000    21ee0 ( 135 kb)   59a0 ( 22 kb)     ACPI.sys  Thu Nov 11 04:06:04 1999
  be193000   16f60 (  91 kb)   ccco ( 51 kb)   kmixer.sys  Wed Nov 10 09:52:30 1999
  bddb4000    355e0 ( 213 kb)  10ac0 ( 66 kb)   ATMFD.DLL  Fri Nov 12 06:48:40 1999
  be80a000     200 (   0 kb)    a00 (  2 kb)  w2k_kill.sys  Mon Aug 28 02:40:12 2000
  TOTAL:    835ca0 (8407 kb) 326180 (3224 kb) (    0 kb      0 kb)
```

❒ Note the highlighted string "w2k_kill.sys", located at the base address 0xBE80A00. This driver is exactly the one that we need! This step, though, isn't necessary, since the name of the faulty driver is displayed on the BSOD, anyway.

❒ Two lines at the bottom of the screen display the progress of the dump creation, entertaining the administrator by displaying a sequence of swiftly changing digits.

Below, you will find the physical meanings of the most common Bug Check hex codes with brief explanations. The popularity rating of the Bug Check codes was composed by counting the number of times they were referenced in Internet conferences (thanks to Google).

❒ 0x0A — symbolic name: IRQL_NOT_LESS_OR_EQUAL
Driver attempted to access the memory page at the DISPATCH_LEVEL or a higher level, which resulted in a crash, since Virtual Memory Manager (VMM) operates at lower level.

The possible source of failure can be BIOS, driver, or system service (this is especially typical for anti-virus scanners and FM tuner).

As a possible alternative, check the cable terminators SCSI drives and the Master/Slave settings on IDE drives. Try to disable the memory caching option in BIOS.

If this doesn't help, check the four Bug Check code parameters containing the reference to the accessed memory, IRQ level, access type (read/write) and the address of the driver's machine instruction.

❒ 0x1E — symbolic name: KMODE_EXCEPTION_NOT_HANDLED
The kernel component has thrown an exception, and then forgotten to handle it; the number of the exception is contained in the first Bug Check parameter. It usually takes one of the following values:

• 0x80000003 (STATUS_BREAKPOINT): A software breakpoint was encountered, which is a debugging rudiment that the driver neglected to remove.

• (0xC0000005) STATUS_ACCESS_VIOLATION: Access to invalid address (the fourth Bug Check parameter specifies the exact address) — error by the developer.

• (0xC000021A) STATUS_SYSTEM_PROCESS_TERMINATED: Failure of CSRSS and/or Winlogon processes. Both kernel components and user-mode applications can cause this error. As a rule, this happens if the machine is infected by a virus or when the integrity of system files has been violated.

• (0xC0000221) STATUS_IMAGE_CHECKSUM_MISMATCH: The integrity of one or more system files has been violated. The second Bug Check parameter contains the address of the machine command that has thrown an exception.

- 0x24 — symbolic name: NTFS_FILE_SYSTEM
  There is a problem with the NTFS.SYS driver. As a rule, this happens as a result of physical disc corruption or, more rarely, under conditions of an urgent shortage of physical memory.

- 0x2E — symbolic name: DATA_BUS_ERROR
  The driver accessed a non-existent physical address. If this isn't the driver's fault, this means that RAM or the processor cache memory (or video memory) is malfunctioning or was overclocked to unsupported frequency values.

- 0x35 — symbolic name: NO_MORE_IRP_STACK_LOCATIONS
  The higher-level driver called a lower-level driver via IoCallDriver interface, but there was no free space in the IRP stack and it was impossible to pass the entire IRP. This is a deadly situation that has no direct solutions; the only way out is trying to delete some of the least important drivers, in which case you may hope to get the system up and running again.

- 0x3F — symbolic name: NO_MORE_SYSTEM_PTES
  The excessive fragmentation of the PTE table, which results in the impossibility of allocating the memory block requested by the driver. As a rule, this situation is characteristic for audio/video drivers manipulating with vast memory blocks. Usually, such drivers fail to release allocated memory blocks in due time. To solve the problem, try to increase the PTE number (up to 50,000 at maximum) by editing the following registry entries: HKLM\SYSTEM\CurrentControlSet\Control\ SessionManager\Memory Management\SystemPages.

- 0x50 — symbolic name: PAGE_FAULT_IN_NONPAGED_AREA
  An attempt to access a non-existent memory page, which is usually caused either by hardware malfunction (as a rule, the faulty component is a RAM chip, or video/cache memory), or by an incorrectly designed service (this is typical for many anti-virus scanners), or by the corruption of the NTFS-formatted volume (run chkdsk with /f and /r command-line options). Also try to disable memory caching in BIOS.

- 0x58 — symbolic name: FTDISK_INTERNAL_ERROR
  Failure in the course of loading a RAID array. When trying to boot the system from the primary disk, the system has detected its corruption, after which it tried to access the mirror, but there was no partition table there.

- 0x76 — symbolic name: PROCESS_HAS_LOCKED_PAGES
  The driver failed to release locked pages after completion of the I/O operation; to detect the name of the faulty driver, open the HKLM\SYSTEM\CurrentControlSet\ Control\Session Manager\Memory Management branch of the system registry, find the TrackLockedPages DWORD parameter, and set its value to 1. Reboot the system, and it will then save the traced stack. If a faulty driver causes an error again, there will be a BSOD with a Bug Check code equal to 0xCB. This will help detect the driver that causes this error.

❑ 0x77 — symbolic name: KERNEL_STACK_INPAGE_ERROR

The memory page with the kernel data is not available for technical reasons. If the first Bug Check code is not equal to zero, it can take one of the following values:

- (0xC000009A) STATUS_INSUFFICIENT_RESOURCES — system resources are not sufficient.
- (0xC000009C) STATUS_DEVICE_DATA_ERROR — disk read/write error (or maybe bad sector).
- (0xC000009D) STATUS_DEVICE_NOT_CONNECTED — system cannot see the drive (controller malfunction, bad contact).
- (0xC000016A) STATUS_DISK_OPERATION_FAILED — disk I/O error (bad sector or malfunctioning controller).
- (0xC0000185) STATUS_IO_DEVICE_ERROR — incorrect termination of a SCSI drive or IRQ conflict of IDE drives.

A zero value got the first Bug Check code specifies an unknown hardware problem.

Such messages can appear if the system is infected by viruses, in the event of disk corruption, or in the case of RAM failure. Start Recovery Console and run the ChkDsk command with the /r command-line option.

❑ 0x7A — symbolic name: KERNEL_DATA_INPAGE_ERROR###

Kernel memory page is not available for technical reasons, the second Bug Check parameter contains the exchange status, and the fourth – the virtual page address that couldn't be loaded.

Possible reasons for the failure are bad sectors occupied by the pagefile.sys file, failures of the disk controller, or virus infection.

❑ 0x7B — symbolic name: INACCESSIBLE_BOOT_DEVICE

Boot device is unavailable because the partition table is corrupted or doesn't correspond to the content of the boot.ini file.

This message may appear after the replacement of the motherboard with an integrated IDE controller or the replacement of an SCSI controller, because each controller requires its "native" drivers. Thus, after installing a hard disk with the Windows NT operating system on a computer containing incompatible equipment, the OS won't start and needs to be reinstalled. Experienced administrators, however, can reinstall disk drivers, after booting into the Recovery Console.

It is also recommended to test the usability of equipment and scan the system for viruses.

❑ 0x7F — symbolic name: UNEXPECTED_KERNEL_MODE_TRAP

Processor exception unhandled by the operating system. As a rule, this situation is caused by hardware malfunction, incorrect CPU overclocking, its incompatibility with installed drivers, or algorithmic errors in drivers.

Check the usability of your equipment and remove all unnecessary drivers.
The first Bug Check parameter contains the exception number and can take the following values:

- 0x00 — attempt of dividing by zero
- 0x01 — system debugger exception
- 0x03 — breakpoint exception
- 0x04 — overflow
- 0x05 — generated by the BOUND instruction
- 0x06 — invalid opcode
- 0x07 — Double Fault

Descriptions of all other exceptions can be found in the technical documentation for Intel and AMD processors.

❏ 0xC2 — symbolic name: BAD_POOL_CALLER
The current thread has caused an incorrect pool-request, which is usually due to an algorithmic error by the driver developer. However, to all appearances, the system itself isn't bug-free, since to eliminate this error, Microsoft recommends the installation of SP2.

❏ 0xCB — symbolic name: DRIVER_LEFT_LOCKED_PAGES_IN_PROCESS
After completing the input/output procedure, the driver is unable to release locked pages (see PROCESS_HAS_LOCKED_PAGES).
The first Bug Check parameter contains the called address, while the second Bug Check parameter specifies the calling address. The last, fourth, parameter points to the UNICODE string with the driver name.

❏ 0xD1 — symbolic name: DRIVER_IRQL_NOT_LESS_OR_EQUAL
Same as IRQL_NOT_LESS_OR_EQUAL.

❏ 0xE2 — symbolic name: MANUALLY_INITIATED_CRASH
A manually generated system failure initiated by pressing the <Ctrl>+<Scroll Lock> hotkey combination, provided that the registry parameter CrashOnCtrlScroll located under HKLM\System\CurrentControlSet\Services\i8042prt\Parameters contains a nonzero value.

❏ 0x7A — symbolic name: KERNEL_DATA_INPAGE_ERROR
Kernel memory data page is not available for technical reasons. The second Bug Check parameter contains the exchange status. The fourth parameter specifies the virtual page address that couldn't be loaded.
Possible causes include bad sectors in pagefile.sys, disk controller failures, and virus infection.

Recovering the System after Critical Failure

> Unnatural, practically sexual inclination to the F8 button
> appeared in Rabbit with a good reason.
>
> *"14,400 bauds and 19,200 users"*

Operating systems of the Windows NT family can tolerate even critical faults — even if they occur in most unsuitable instances (for example, in the course of disk defragmentation). Fault-tolerant file system driver does everything on its own (although, it will be wise to run ChkDsk anyway).

If you have chosen the **Full memory dump** or **Kernel memory dump** options, then, after you boot successfully the next time, the hard disk will drag its read/write head for a long period of time, even if there are no attempts to access it. Don't worry! Windows simply relocates the dump from the virtual memory to its constant location. After starting Task Manager, you'll see a new process in the list — **SaveDump.exe**. This is the task that it carries out. The need for such a two-step scheme of saving the dump is explained by the fact that the operability of file system drivers isn't guaranteed at the moment of critical error, and the operating system can't risk using them. Instead, it limits itself to temporary storing the dump in virtual memory. By the way, if the available amount of virtual memory turns out to be insufficient (**Advanced** → **Performance** → **Virtual memory**), it will be impossible to save the dump.

If the system fails to boot, and this error is persistent, don't forget that you have the <F8> key at your disposal. Choose the **Last Known Good Configuration** menu option. Starting the system in safe mode with the required minimum of vitally important system services and drivers is a more radical step. System reinstallation is the last resort, and it isn't recommended to resort to this unless absolutely necessary. It is better to try to start the Recovery Console and relocate the dump to another machine, where you'll be able to investigate it.

Loading the Crash Dump

To load the crash dump into your Windows Debugger (windbg.exe), choose the **Crash Dump** option from the **File** menu, or press the <Ctrl>+<D> hotkey combination. If you are working with the i386kd.exe debugger, use the -z command-line option followed by the fully qualified path name to the dump file. The name of the dump file must be separated from the command by one or more blanks, and the _NT_SYMBOL_PATH environment variable must specify the full path to the symbol files. Otherwise, the debugger will terminate abnormally. As an alternative, you can use the -y command-line option. In this case, the console screen will appear approximately as follows: `i386kd -z C:\WINNT\memory.dmp -y C:\WINNT\Symbols`. Note that it is necessary to call the debugger from the **Checked Build Environment/Free Build Environment** console located in the Windows 2000 DDK folder. Otherwise, you'll fail.

Associating DMP files with the i386kd debugger is a good idea. After you do so, you'll be able to call the debugger by simply pressing the <Enter> key in FAR Manager. The choice of debugging tools, though, is a matter of personal preference. Some people prefer KAnalyze, while others are quite content with simple DumpChk. The range of analysis tools, from which you can choose, is broad (for instance, DDK contains four such tools). Thus, for the sake of distinctness, let us choose i386kd.exe, also known as Kernel Debugger.

As soon as the Kernel Debugger console appears on the screen (Kernel Debugger is the console application preferred by those who spent their youth sitting at terminals), the cursor will quickly disassemble the current machine instruction and drag us into the depths of machine code. Enter u from the keyboard, thus making the debugger to continue code disassembling.

According to symbolic identifiers PspUnhandledExceptionInSystemThread and KeBugCheckEx, we are somewhere deep in the kernel, or, to be more precise, somewhere in the surroundings of the code that displays the BSOD:

Listing 3.22. The results of disassembling the memory dump from the current address

```
8045249c 6a01      push    0x1
kd>u
_PspUnhandledExceptionInSystemThread@4:
80452484 8B442404 mov     eax, dword ptr [esp+4]
80452488 8B00     mov     eax, dword ptr [eax]
8045248A FF7018   push    dword ptr [eax+18h]
8045248D FF7014   push    dword ptr [eax+14h]
80452490 FF700C   push    dword ptr [eax+0Ch]
80452493 FF30     push    dword ptr [eax]
80452495 6A1E     push    1Eh
80452497 E8789AFDFF   call    _KeBugCheckEx@20
8045249C 6A01     push    1
8045249E 58       pop     eax
8045249F C20400   ret     4
```

There is nothing interesting in the stack (look for yourself. To view the stack contents, issue the kb command):

Listing 3.23. The stack contents don't provide any clues to the actual nature of the critical error

```
kd> kb
ChildEBP RetAddr  Args to Child
f403f71c 8045251c f403f744 8045cc77 f403f74c ntoskrnl!PspUnhandledExceptionInSystemThread+0x18
f403fddc 80465b62 80418ada 00000001 00000000 ntoskrnl!PspSystemThreadStartup+0x5e
00000000 00000000 00000000 00000000 00000000 ntoskrnl!KiThreadStartup+0x16
```

This turn of things is mystifying. You can disassemble the core as many times as you like, but it won't bring you any closer to the solution. This is logical, since the current address (8045249Ch) is far beyond the limits of the killer driver (0BE80A00h). So let's go another way. Do you recall the address that was displayed on the BSOD? If you don't, this isn't a problem! If the system settings don't prohibit it explicitly, copies of all BSODs are saved in the system log. Let's open it: **Control Panel → Administrative Tools → Event Viewer**):

Listing 3.24. A BSOD copy saved in the system log

```
The system was rebooted after a critical error:
0x0000001e (0xc0000005, 0xbe80b000, 0x00000000, 0x00000000).
Microsoft Windows 2000 [v15.2195]
Memory dump was saved: C:\WINNT\MEMORY.DMP.
```

Based on the category of the critical error (0x1E), we can easily determine the address of the killer instruction — 0xBE80B000 (in the above-provided listing, it is in bold). Now issue the u BE80B000 command to view its contents, and you'll see:

Listing 3.25. The results of disassembling of the memory dump by the address reported by BSOD

```
kd>u 0xBE80B000
be80b000 a100000000     mov eax,[00000000]
be80b005 c20800     ret 0x8
be80b008 90     nop
be80b009 90     nop
be80b00a 90     nop
be80b00b 90     nop
be80b00c 90     nop
be80b00d 90     nop
```

This looks much closer to the truth. The instruction pointed to by the cursor (in the text, it is in bold) calls on the cell that has a zero address, which causes the critical exception that crashes the system. Now, we know for certain, which branch of the program has caused this exception.

What should we do if we don't have a copy of the BSOD at our disposal? In fact, a copy of the BSOD is always available. You only need to know where to look for it. Try opening the dump file using any hex editor, and you'll find the following strings.

Listing 3.26. A copy of a BSOD in the program dump header

```
00000000:  50 41 47 45 44 55 4D 50 | 0F 00 00 00 93 08 00 00    PAGEDUMP☼.....У■.....
00000010:  00 00 03 00 00 80 8B 81 | C0 A4 46 80 80 A1 46 80    ..♥..АЛБ└┐FAA6FA.....
00000020:  4C 01 00 00 01 00 00 00 | 1E 00 00 00 05 00 00 C0    L☺..☺...▲...♣..└.....
00000030:  00 B0 80 BE 00 00 00 00 | 00 00 00 00 00 41 47 45    ▓A┘.........AGE.....
```

All main Bug Check parameters can be recognized immediately : 1E 00 00 00 is the failure category code — 0x1E (in x86 processors, the least significant byte is located at the lower address, which means that all numbers are written in the inverse order); 05 00 00 C0 is the STATUS_ACCESS_VIOLATION exception code; and 00 B0 80 BE specifies the address of the machine command that has thrown this exception. The combination 0F 00 00 00 93 08 can be recognized easily as the system Build number (just write it in decimal notation).

To view Bug Check parameters in more readable format, it is possible to use the following debugger command — dd KiBugCheckData:

Listing 3.27. Bug Check parameters displayed in more readable format

```
kd> dd KiBugCheckData
dd KiBugCheckData
8047e6c0   0000001e c0000005 be80b000 00000000
8047e6d0   00000000 00000000 00000001 00000000
8047e6e0   00000000 00000000 00000000 00000000
8047e6f0   00000000 00000000 00000000 00000000
8047e700   00000000 00000000 00000000 00000000
8047e710   00000000 00000000 00000000 00000000
8047e720   00000000 00000000 00000000 00000000
8047e730   00000000 e0ffffff edffffff 00020000
```

The list of other useful commands includes:

❏ !drivers — the command displaying the list of drivers that were loaded for the moment of failure
❏ !arbiter — the command displaying all arbitrators along with arbitration ranges
❏ !filecache — the command displaying the information about the file system cache and PT
❏ !vm — the command that produces the report on the virtual memory usage, etc.

Unfortunately, it is impossible to provide a complete listing of the commands here. If you need it, you'll find such a listing in the manual for your preferred debugger.

Naturally, it is much more difficult to detect the actual cause of the system crash in the real world. This is because any real driver consists of a large set of functions interacting with one another according to some intricate scheme. These functions form complicated hierarchies, sometimes crossed by tunnels of global variables, turning the driver into a labyrinth. Let us consider an example. The construction appearing as mov eax, [ebx], where ebx == 0, works quite normally, by obediently throwing an exception, and it is absolutely senseless trying to "talk" with it! It is necessary to locate the code that writes a zero value into EBX, which isn't an easy task. Of course, it is possible to scroll the screen upwards, hoping that the program code executes linearly at this section, but no one can guarantee that it is actually the case. The possibility to trace back is also missing. Roughly speaking, the address of the previous machine instruction is unknown, so it isn't recommended to rely on screen scrolling.

Having loaded the driver being tested into any intellectual disassembler that automatically restores cross-references (such as IDA PRO), we will get a more or less complete idea about the topology of the program's controlling branches. Naturally, disassembling, because of its static nature, doesn't guarantee that control hasn't been passed somewhere else. It does, however, narrow the search range. Generally speaking, there are lots of good books about disassembling (for instance, I have written one myself — "Hacker Disassembliny Uncovered" by Kris Kaspersky); therefore, I won't concentrate on this topic here. I'll simply wish you good luck.

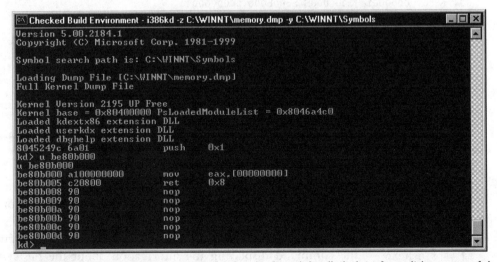

Fig. 3.5. The i386kd debugger at work; despite its minimalistic interface, it is a powerful and convenient instrument, allowing you to carry out prodigious tasks by pressing a couple of shortcut keys or keyboard combinations (one of which calls up your own script)

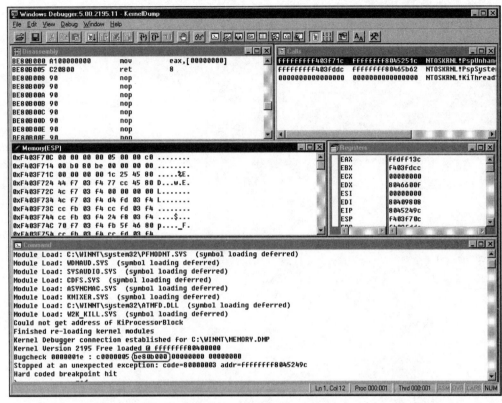

Fig. 3.6. Windbg with loaded memory dump. Note that the debugger automatically highlights the Bug Check codes without waiting for us to instruct it to do so, and when attempting to disassemble the instruction that has caused the critical exception, the screen displays the string specifying the name of the killer driver: "Module Load: W2K_KILL.SYS" — a nice touch

Chapter 4: Interfaces for Interaction with the Hardware

The methods of interacting with hardware are numerous. Depending on the particular features of the problem to be solved and on those of the equipment itself, one of a number of control interfaces may be the most important. At the highest level of the interface hierarchy, there is the family of operating system API functions that carry out the basic input/output operations (for instance, opening a file, or reading data from a file). For most applications, this proves to be more than enough. Unfortunately, however, this set of functions doesn't allow you to write even the simplest CD-copying program. In order to achieve this, it is necessary to go by at least one level deeper in the hierarchy, calling on the driver of specific device directly.

Standard disc drivers supplied as part of the Windows 9*x* and Windows NT operating systems support a limited set of basic commands (such as read a sector, view a TOC, etc.), which do not allow for the full implementation of all of the capabilities of contemporary CD-ROM/R/RW drives. However, their set of functions is sufficient for the writing of the simplest protection mechanisms.

The overwhelming majority of protection mechanisms of this type can be copied well enough by standard copying. This, by the way, is not surprising, since both the copier and the "protection" feed from the same "trough", that is, from the same set of instructions. On second thought, perhaps it's better to say that they use the same set of control commands working with the device at the logical level.

To create protection that can't be cracked, you must dive to the very bottom of the well, and "talk" to the device in its native language. Although optical drive controllers support a high-level set of commands (in fact, at a considerably higher-level than floppy drives do), and despite the fact that drive interface is based on specific equipment and CD-ROM/R/RW discs were not initially designed with an eye on protection, it is still possible to create discs that are practically impossible to copy at this level.

Despite popular opinion, it isn't necessary to write a custom driver to achieve low-level control over drives. All of the required drivers have already been written. The developer has only to choose one of the competing interfaces, which ensures low-level interaction with SCSI/ATAPI devices from the user-mode application level. This list is quite long, and it includes ASPI, SPTI, and even MSCDEX (which has been practically forgotten, but is still supported by Windows 98/ME operating systems). Each of these interfaces has its own advantages and drawbacks. That's why commercial products must support them all.

Since the programming of optical drives goes far beyond the limits of the topic of CD protection (which still is the main topic of this book), we will cover hardware interfaces only briefly and in a simplified form.

The information that will be provided below is sufficient for studying all of the above-listed interfaces from scratch, and for doing this on your own. Even if you have never encountered the topic of programming SCSI/ATAPI devices before, it is unlikely that you will experience any difficulties while reading this chapter.

Access via the CD-ROM Driver

In operating systems of the Windows family, management of device drivers is carried out by means of calls to the DeviceIoControl function responsible for sending special FSCTL/IOCTL commands. The FS prefix denotes that this command belongs to the file system management group, and is of no interest to us in the context of this book. The commands with the IO prefix relate to the input/output device, or, to be more precise — to its driver.

The DeviceIoControl function simply passes on these commands "as is," without going deeper into its "physical sense." Therefore, it doesn't make any sense to look for a list of available IOCTL commands in the description of DeviceIoControl. The description doesn't contain anything like this! It merely provides the list of standard IOCTL commands, while all remaining information related to this topic is provided by Windows DDK.

There you will discover, in particular, that the IOCTL_CDROM_READ_TOC command is used for reading disc TOC, while for listing session block addresses of multi-session discs, there is the IOCTL_CDROM_GET_LAST_SESSION command. It is also necessary to pay attention to the `IOCTL_CDROM_READ_Q_CHANNEL` command, which ensures the retrieval of the information from the Q-channel of subcode (this is important for retrieving key marks).

Reading CD-ROM sectors in the Raw mode is carried out by the `IOCTL_CDROM_RAW_READ` command, the capabilities of which, unfortunately, are limited to CDDA discs only. Reading data from CDDATA discs, sector by sector, is not supported on Raw or on user levels. According to the adopted security policy, no application has the right to bypass the security subsystem. If this were not the case, intruders would easily be able to access confidential data by simply reading the disc at the sector level. Built-in drivers supplied as part of the Windows operating system fully comply with this requirement, although third-party developers may violate this restriction if they so chose. Windows NT DDK includes the source code of a demo CD-ROM driver (NTDDK\ src\storage\class\cdrom\). After introducing some small modifications, this driver will agree to read discs of all types without asking any silly questions. To do this, simply open the cdrom.c file, find the string `"if (rawReadInfo->TrackMode == CDDA) {"`, and go to the branch whose `OperationCode` is equal to `SCSIOP_READ`. Then, modify the code in such a way as to ensure that this branch gets control in all other cases.

The `IRP_MJ_READ` function, which is present in DDK and which, in the theory, ensures that it is possible to read individual logical blocks, is an internal function of the driver. Access to this function from the application level is closed and it doesn't make any sense to use it in combination with `DeviceIoControl`.

Table 4.1. Description of IOCTL commands of the standard CD-ROM driver (more detailed information is provided in Windows NT DDK)

IOCTL command	Description
`IOCTL_CDROM_CHECK_VERIFY,` `IOCTL_STORAGE_CHECK_VERIFY (0x24800h)`	Detects the fact of disc replacement (opening/closing the tray)
`IOCTL_CDROM_CLOSE_DOOR*,` `IOCTL_STORAGE_LOAD_MEDIA (0x2D480Ch)`	Closes the drive tray
`IOCTL_CDROM_FIND_NEW_DEVICES,` `IOCTL_STORAGE_FIND_NEW_DEVICES` `(0x24818h)`	Lists new drives connected after OS startup or since the last call to this command
`IOCTL_CDROM_GET_CONTROL`	Reports the current position of audio playback
`IOCTL_CDROM_GET_DRIVE_GEOMETRY` `(0x2404Ch)`	Determines the disc type and its geometry (number of sectors on disc, sector size, etc.)

continues

Table 4.1 Continued

IOCTL command	Description
IOCTL_CDROM_GET_LAST_SESSION (0x24038h)	Lists starting addresses of sessions and writes them to the TOC buffer read by IOCTL_CDROM_READ_TOC
IOCTL_CDROM_GET_VOLUME (0x24014h)	Returns the current volume from CD-ROM
IOCTL_CDROM_PAUSE_AUDIO (0x2400Ch)	Temporarily pauses audio playback
IOCTL_CDROM_PLAY_AUDIO_MSF (0x24018h)	Initiates audio playback process from specified position up to the specified position
IOCTL_CDROM_RAW_READ (0x2403Eh)	Reads raw sectors from audio discs
IOCTL_CDROM_READ_Q_CHANNEL (0x2402Ch)	Reads data from the Q subcode channel
IOCTL_CDROM_READ_TOC (0x24000h)	Reads the disc TOC
IOCTL_CDROM_RESUME_AUDIO (0x24010h)	Resumes audio playback
IOCTL_CDROM_SEEK_AUDIO_MSF (0x24004h)	Positions optical head
IOCTL_CDROM_SET_VOLUME (0x24028h)	Sets volume from the CD-ROM
IOCTL_CDROM_STOP_AUDIO (0x24008h)	Stops audio playback

* — obsolete and currently removed from the DDK

The DeviceIoControl function is always preceded by a call to the CreateFile function, which returns the handle of the appropriate device specified in the following format: \\.\X:, where X is the letter of the drive, with which you are going to work. Note that the dwCreationDisposition flag must be set to OPEN_EXISTING, or your attempt to access the drive will fail. A typical example of a call to this function is provided in Listing 4.1.

NOTE

Windows NT registers the CD drive under the following name: \\.\CdRomx, where x is the number of the drive (starting from zero) that references the same drive as the drive letter, and provides the same set of functions.

Listing 4.1. An Example illustrating the opening of the device

```
HANDLE hCD;                          // drive descriptor
hCD=CreateFile("\\\\.\\X:", GENERIC_READ, FILE_SHARE_READ, 0, OPEN_EXISTING, 0,0);
if (hCD == INVALID_HANDLE_VALUE)                    // error
```

The prototype of the `DeviceIoControl` function itself appears as shown in Listing 4.2.

Listing 4.2. The prototype of the *DeviceIoControl* function

```
BOOL DeviceIoControl(
    HANDLE hDevice,              // Device descriptor
    DWORD dwIoControlCode,       // IOCTL code of the command to be executed
    LPVOID lpInBuffer,          // Pointer to the input buffer
                                // (Irp->AssociatedIrp.SystemBuffer)
    DWORD nInBufferSize,        // Size of the input buffer, in bytes
    LPVOID lpOutBuffer,         // Pointer to the output buffer
                                // (Irp->AssociatedIrp.SystemBuffer)
    DWORD nOutBufferSize,       // Size of the output buffer, in bytes
    LPDWORD lpBytesReturned,    // Pointer to the counter of returned bytes
    LPOVERLAPPED lpOverlapped   // Pointer to the structure for asynchronous operations
);
```

Here:

❑ `hDevice` — the descriptor that was just returned by `CreateFile`.

❑ `dwIoControlCode` — the IOCTL code for our operation.

❑ `lpInBuffer` — the pointer to the buffer that contains the data prepared for passing to the device (as a rule, these are command arguments). In the course of function execution, the buffer contents are copied into `Irp->AssociatedIrp.SystemBuffer`. This is mentioned here in order to prevent you from feeding the entire IRP structure to `DeviceIoControl` when you see this form of abracadabra in DDK.

❑ `nInBufferSize` — the size of the input buffer in bytes. In the course of function execution, it is copied into the `Parameters.DeviceIoControl.InputBufferLength` structure.

❑ `lpOutBuffer` — the pointer to the output buffer, where the contents of `Irp->AssociatedIrp.SystemBuffer` are returned.

❑ `nOutBuffersSize` — pointer to the double word, where the number of bytes returned by the driver via output buffer will be written.

If the operation has been accomplished successfully, the function will return a non-zero value. Otherwise, it will return zero. For more detailed information on the error, call `GetLastError`.

Passing of IOCTL commands to the device doesn't require that you have administrative privileges (except for cases where the device is opened with the GENERIC_WRITE flag). This significantly improves the "ergonomic" properties of protection mechanisms based on this function. (*Let us consider protection mechanisms for a moment, or, to be more precise, their ability to resist the attempts at cracking them. Since, obviously, the* `DeviceIoControl` *function isn't employed in common programs very often, it "unmasks the headquarters" of the protection mechanism. Consequently, it becomes quite easy to "get a bearing" on it. It is enough to set a breakpoint to the* `DeviceIoControl` *function and wait until the* `IOCTL` *command passed to it takes one of the above-listed values. Setting a breakpoint to* `CreateFile` *is not wise, because it will produce a large number of garbage debugger popups (*`CreateFile`* is called any time when a file is opened/created). However, it makes sense to search for the* "\\.\" *string in the program body. If you succeed, the only thing left to do is to click on the cross-reference and then press <Enter>. That's it! Here is the protection code for you.*

In order to ensure a better understanding of this method of interaction between an application and the device driver, consider a key fragment of the function that carries out this type of interaction (error handling has been omitted for the sake of simplicity).

Listing 4.3. [/IOCTL.CDDA.raw.read.c] A function demonstrating techniques for reading raw sectors via a CDFS driver (intended for CDDA discs *only*)

```
//--[ReadCDDA]-----------------------------------------------------------
//
//              Reads RAW sectors from CDDA discs
//              ==========================================
//
// ARG:
//   drive       - name of the device from which to read
//               (for example, "\\\\.\\X:")
//   start_sector  - number of the first sector to read
//   n_sec       - number of sectors to read
//
// RET:
//   == 0        - error
//   != 0        - pointer to the buffer containing read sectors
//
// NOTE:
//   This function supports discs only of the types supported by
//   the CDFS driver, which is the one that it uses.
//   The built-in Windows NT driver supports only CDDA discs
//-------------------------------------------------------------------------
char* ReadCDDA(char *drive, int start_sector, int n_sec)
{
// Supported track types
typedef enum _TRACK_MODE_TYPE {
    YellowMode2,          // native MODE 2 (not CD-data)
    XAForm2,            // XA MODE 2 Form 2 (Video-CD)
```

```
    CDDA                  // Audio-CD
} TRACK_MODE_TYPE, *PTRACK_MODE_TYPE;

// the arugment of the IOCTL_RAW_READ command
typedef struct __RAW_READ_INFO {
    LARGE_INTEGER     DiskOffset;     // logical block offset in bytes
    ULONG             SectorCount;    // number of sectors to read
    TRACK_MODE_TYPE   TrackMode;      // mode of the track to read
} RAW_READ_INFO, *PRAW_READ_INFO;

#define CDROM_RAW_SECTOR_SIZE       2352
#define CDROM_SECTOR_SIZE           2048

int a;
HANDLE hCD;
DWORD  x_size;
char   *szDrive;
BOOL   fResult = 0;
unsigned char *buf;
RAW_READ_INFO rawRead;

// PREPARING THE RAW_READ_INFO STRUCTURE, passed to the CD-ROM driver
rawRead.TrackMode = CDDA;              // disc type - Audio CD
rawRead.SectorCount = n_sec;          // number of sectors to read
rawRead.DiskOffset.QuadPart = start_sector * CDROM_SECTOR_SIZE;
//                                     ^^^^^^^^^^^^^^^^^^
// The starting sector is specified by the number of its first byte,
// rather than by its logical number. Theoretically,
// pass-through numbering of bytes from the first
// to the last bytes of the disc ensures full abstraction
// from the hardware (sector size is returned by the
// IOCTRL_CDROM_GET_DRIVE_GEOMETRY command).
// In practice, however, driver architects
// have made a blunder, as a result of which the driver,
// instead of the pass-through byte numbers, accepts
// start_address * CDROM_SECTOR_SIZE,
// where CDROM_SECTOR_SIZE is the logical block size,
// which, in this case, is equal to the standard sector size
// of the CDDATA disc (2048 bytes), while the sector size
```

```
// of CDDA discs is 2352 bytes. Therefore, DiskOffset
// is equal to start_secor * CDROM_SECTOR_SIZE,
// while buffer size must be equal to
// start_secor * CDROM_RAW_SECTOR_SIZE

// ALLOCATING MEMORY
buf = malloc(CDROM_RAW_SECTOR_SIZE * n_sec);

// GETTING THE DEVICE DESCRIPTOR
hCD = CreateFile(drive,GENERIC_READ,FILE_SHARE_READ,0,OPEN_EXISTING,0,0);
if (hCD != INVALID_HANDLE_VALUE)

// PASSING THE IOCTL_CDROM_RAW_READ COMMAND TO THE DRIVER
fResult = DeviceIoControl(  hCD, 0x2403E /* IOCTL_CDROM_RAW_READ */,
              &rawRead, sizeof(RAW_READ_INFO),
              buf, CDROM_RAW_SECTOR_SIZE*n_sec,
              &x_size, (LPOVERLAPPED) NULL);

// OUTPUT OF THE RESULT (if there is any)
if (fResult)
    for (a = 0; a <= x_size; ++a) printf("%02X%s", buf[a], (a%24)?" ":"\n");
else
    printf("-ERROR"); printf("\n");

// EXITING
CloseHandle(hCD); return (fResult)?buf:0;
}
```

Studying TOC contents may be useful when analyzing some protected discs.

Listing 4.4. [/IOCTL.read.TOC.c] A sample program interacting with the CDFS driver via IOCTL and reading the TOC contents (with decryption)

```
/*-----------------------------------------------------------------------
 *
 *                     READING AND DECODING TOC
 *                     ========================
 *
 * build 0x001 @ 26.05.2003
 -----------------------------------------------------------------------*/
main(int argc, char **argv)
```

```
{
        int       a;
        HANDLE        hCD;
        unsigned char    *buf;
        WORD      TOC_SIZE;
        BYTE      n_track;
        DWORD         x_size,b;

        #define DEF_X    "\\\\.\\G:"              // default drive
        #define argCD     ((argc>1)?argv[1]:DEF_X)

        // CHECKING ARGUMENTS
        if (argc < 2) {fprintf(stderr, "USAGE: IOCTL.read.TOC \\\\.\\X:\n"); return 0;}

        // TITLE
        fprintf(stderr, "simple TOC reader via IOCTL\n");

        // ALLOCATING MEMORY
        buf = (char *) malloc(buf_len);

        // OPENING THE DEVICE
        hCD=CreateFile(argv[1], GENERIC_READ, FILE_SHARE_READ, 0, OPEN_EXISTING, 0, 0);

        // EXIT IN CASE OF ERROR
        if (hCD == INVALID_HANDLE_VALUE)
            {fprintf(stderr, "-ERR: %x\n", GetLastError()); return 0;}

        // PASSING THE CDROM_READ_TOC COMMAND TO THE DRIVER
        if (DeviceIoControl( hCD, 0x24000 /* IOCTL_READ_TOC */,
                        0, 0, buf, buf_len, &x_size, 0) != 0)
        {
            // GETTING TOC LENGTH (it is written in reverse order)
            TOC_SIZE = buf[0]*0x100L + buf[1];
            printf("TOC Data Length........%d\n", TOC_SIZE);

            // DECODING OTHER INFORMATION
            printf("First Session Number...%d\n", buf[2]);
            printf("Last Session Number....%d\n\n", (n_track=buf[3]));
            for (a = 1; a <= n_track; a++)
            {
                    printf("track %d\n{\n",a);
                    printf("\treserved............%x\n", buf[a * 8 - 4]);
                    printf("\tADR|control.........%d\n", buf[a * 8 - 3]);
```

```
            printf("\ttrack number.........%d\n", buf[a * 8 - 2]);
            printf("\treserved............%d\n", buf[a * 8 - 1]);
            printf("\treserved............%d\n", buf[a * 8 + 0]);
            printf("\tmin................%d\n", buf[a * 8 + 1]);
            printf("\tsec................%d\n", buf[a * 8 + 2]);
            printf("\tframe..............%d\n", buf[a * 8 + 3]);
            printf("}\n\n");
    }


    // PRINTING TOC CONTENTS IN RAW FORMAT
    printf("\n\t\t\t* * RAW * * *\n");
    for(a = 0; a < x_size; a++)
            printf("%02X%s", (unsigned char)buf[a], ((a+1)%22)?" ":"\n");
    printf("\n\t\t\t* *  *  * * *\n");
    }

}
```

Listing 4.4 is another demo example. It illustrates the technique of reading the *TOC (Table of Content)* — in audio CDs, it represents an analog of the partition table.

Access in the Cooked Mode (Block Reading Mode)

The Windows NT operating system is distinguished positively from other systems in that it supports the device block reading mode — the so-called *cooked-mode*, in which all disc contents are interpreted as one large file. Within this "file", it is possible to carry out navigation by calling on the SetFilePointer function, and to read/write individual sectors by calling on ReadFile/WriteFile functions, respectively. The current pointer position is specified in bytes (not in sectors!); however, the pointer value must be a multiple of the logical sector length (512 bytes for floppy and hard disks, and 2,048 bytes for CD-ROM). Otherwise, an error will occur. The number of bytes read (or written) at one time must also fit within an integer number of sectors. An attempt to read a part of a sector will fail.

Despite all the elegance and ease of implementation, this method of controlling the drive is also not free from serious drawbacks. First, it doesn't support file systems other than ISO 9660/Joliet and High Sierra File System. Put simply, this means that block reading mode is suitable only for processing data discs, and is useless for reading sectors from audio discs. Second, reading raw sectors is impossible in cooked mode, and you will have to do only with those parts of these sectors that contain user data. This situation significantly weakens the protection mechanism and allows it to easily be deceived. For instance, let us assume that protection based on physical defects of the medium surface attempts to read its key sector to check its readability. Since the content of correction codes is unavailable to the protection mechanism, it cannot distinguish actual physical defects from their rough imitation (e.g., from delibe- rate distortion of ECC/EDC codes by copying in order to emulate unrecoverable read errors).

To check whether or not the protection uses this method of disc access, try the following easy method: Set the breakpoint to the `CreateFile` function, thus making the debugger to react in those — and only those — cases where the first four charac- ters of the filename to be opened are "\\.\" (which means that the function tries to open a device instead of a file). These strings might look similar to the following: `bpx CreateFileA if (*esp->4=='\\\\.\\')`. After that, all that remains is to make sure that the last back-slash is followed by the drive letter of the required drive (on my computer, this is the "\\.\G:" drive). Having waited for the exit from the `CreateFile` function by "`P RET`" and having viewed the device descriptor returned to it (this descriptor will be loaded into the `EAX` register), you will be able to trap all calls to `SetFilePointer/ReadFile`, the analysis of which will disclose the operating algorithm of the protection mechanism.

The demo example provided below represents a ready-to-use utility for grabbing discs with data at the sector level and writing all grabbed information into a file.

Listing 4.5. [/cooked.sector.read.c] An example illustrating the technique for reading sectors in cooked mode

---

```
/*-------------------------------------------------------------------------
 *
 *                      READS SECTORS FROM A CD IN BLOCK MODE
 *
 *                      ================================================
 *
 *
 *        This program works only under Windows NT, without requiring
 * administrative privileges
 *
 * Build 0x001 @ 19.05.03
-------------------------------------------------------------------------*/
#include <windows.h>
#include <winioctl.h>
#include <stdio.h>


// DEFAULT PARAMETERS
#define DEF_FN          "sector"
#define DEF_TO          0x666
```

```
#define DEF_FROM         0x000
#define CDROM_SECTOR_SIZE   2048     // for MODE1/MODE2FORM1 only!

// COMMAND-LINE ARGUMENTS
#define argCD         (argv[1])
#define argFN         ((argc > 2)?argv[2]       :DEF_FN)
#define argFROM   ((argc > 3)?atol(argv[3]):DEF_FROM)
#define argTO      ((argc>4)?(atol(argv[4])>argFROM)?atol(argv[4]):argFROM:DEF_TO)

main(int argc, char **argv)
{
        int     a;
        FILE    *f;
        HANDLE      hCD;
        Char    *buf;
        DWORD       x_read;
        Char    buf_n[1024];

        // CHECKING ARGUMENTS
        if (argc<2)
        {
            printf("USAGE: cooked.sector.read PhysCD [filename] [from] [to]\n");
            printf("\tPhysCD   - physical name of CD (\"\\\\.\\G:\")\n");
            printf("\tfilename - file name to store follow sector\n");
            printf("\tfrom     - start sector\n");
            printf("\tto       - end sector\n");
            return 0;
        }

        // TITLE
        fprintf(stderr,"cooked sector reader for NT\n");

        // ALLOCATING MEMORY
        buf = malloc(CDROM_SECTOR_SIZE);
        if (!buf){printf("-ERR:low memory\n"); return -1;}

        // OPENING THE DEVICE
        hCD = CreateFile(argCD, GENERIC_READ, FILE_SHARE_READ, 0, OPEN_EXISTING, 0, 0);
        if (hCD == INVALID_HANDLE_VALUE) {
            printf("-ERR: error CreateFile(%s,....)\n", argCD); return -1;
```

```
    }


    // INFO
    printf("read sector from %04d to %04d in %s file\n", argFROM, argTO, argFN);


    // POSITIONING THE POINTER TO THE FIRST SECTOR TO BE READ
    SetFilePointer (hCD, CDROM_SECTOR_SIZE * argFROM, NULL, FILE_BEGIN);


    // READING SECTORS ONE BY ONE
    for (a = argFROM; a <= argTO; a++)
    {
        // READING THE NEXT SECTOR
        if (ReadFile(hCD, buf, CDROM_SECTOR_SIZE, &x_read, NULL) && x_read)
        {
            // WRITING THE SECTOR JUST READ INTO THE FILE
            sprintf(buf_n, "%s[%04d].dat", argFN, a);
            if (f=fopen(buf_n, "wb")){fwrite(buf, 1, x_read, f); fclose(f);}
            printf("sector [%04d.%04d] read\r", a, argTO);
        }
        else
        {
            printf("sector %04d read error\n", a);
        }
    }
}
```

Access via SPTI

One of the most interesting architectural features of the Windows NT operating system is its ability to interact with IDE devices via the SCSI interface! Unfortunately, this technology is poorly documented. For instance, sources such as Platform SDK, MSDN, and DDK contain only odds and ends. Thus, only a true professional or very clever and inquisitive beginner can make sense of this information.

As one could conclude from reading most discussions in teleconferences, most programmers haven't properly mastered the techniques of device management via the SCSI interface. Therefore, it is useful to cover this problem in more detail.

To solve this problem, we'll need the following items:

❑ *Description of the SCSI interface* (see the "*SCSI Architecture Model — 3*" document, which describes the main concepts of SCSI architecture, and the "*SCSI Primary*

Commands — 3" document that determines the basic set of commands for all SCSI devices; draft versions of both documents are available for downloading from: **http://www.t10.org/ftp/t10/drafts/sam3/sam3r08.pdf** and **http://www.t10.org/ftp/t10/drafts/spc3/spc3r14.pdf**, respectively. As a quick-start manual, a good recommendation is to study the "*The Linux SCSI programming HOWTO*" document, which can be downloaded from **http://www.ibiblio.org/pub/Linux/docs/HOWTO/other-formats/pdf/SCSI-Programming-HOWTO.pdf**).

❏ *Description of SCSI commands specific for CD-ROM drives* (see the "*Multimedia Commands — 4*" document describing the principles of programming CD-ROM/R/RW drives. The electronic version of this document can be found here: **http://www.t10.org/ftp/t10/drafts/mmc4/mmc4r02b.pdf**).

❏ *Description of ATAPI interface for CD-ROM/DVD drives* (for instance, see the "*ATA Packet Interface for CD-ROMs*" and "*Specification for ATAPI DVD Devices*" documents. Note that DVD specifications provide better and more comprehensive descriptions of the CD-ROM architecture than "native" documentation written specially for CD-ROM. Versions of these documents (not the newest, but still quite suitable revisions) can be found here: **www.stanford.edu/~csapuntz/specs/INF-8020.PDF** and **ftp.seagate.com/sff/INF-8090.PDF**. Descriptions of SCSI and ATAPI commands duplicate each other in many respects. However, some particularly difficult aspects are sometimes described better in one document than the other. Therefore, professional programmers should have both of them on hand.

❏ *Description of data storage formats, used with CDs* (see the "*Data interchange on read-only 120 mm optical data disks*" ECMA-130 standard, known as the "Yellow Book"), which can be found here: **http://www.ecma-international.org/publications/files/ecma-st/Ecma-130.pdf**. This is a basic standard for CD-ROM drives.

❏ Besides this, any literature that in any way considers the aspects of CD-ROM programming is useful. So, what is SCSI? It is the standardized, platform-independent interface that ensures coordinated interaction of different devices and high-level applications. In fact, the acronym *SCSI* stands for *Small Computer System Interface*. Thanks to SCSI for low-level device management, it is not necessary to write custom drivers (writing a driver with the only purpose to overcome API limitations is absolutely senseless), and this task can be solved at the application level by means of sending special *CDB blocks* to the device. These CDB blocks might contain either standard or device-specific control commands, along with all of the parameters that they require. In fact, CDB stands for *Command Descriptor Block*. An example of such a block is provided below.

Table 4.2. An example of a CDB which, being transmitted to a SCSI device, makes it read sector 0x69

Offset, bytes	Contents	
0x0	0x28	Code of the "read sector" command
0x1	0x00	Reserved
0x2	0x00	Sector number — 0x69
0x3	0x00	
0x4	0x00	
0x5	0x69	
0x6	0x00	Number of sectors
0x7	0x01	
0x8	0x00	Reserved
0x9	0x00	Reserved
0xA	0x00	Reserved

The first byte of the block stands for the *operation command* (in our case: 0x28 — read one or more sectors), and all other bytes of the block are *parameters of this command*. Pay special attention to the fact that the least significant byte of the word resides at higher address, i.e., the exact opposite to what you are accustomed to on the IBM PC! Therefore, if you transmit the 0x69 0x00 0x00 0x00 sequence as the number of the first sector, the sector with the number 0x6900000 will be read instead of sector 0x00000069, as would be expected.

A brief description of standard SCSI commands can be found in the "*The Linux SCSI programming HOWTO*" document mentioned earlier. However, this is unlikely to be sufficient for our purposes. Therefore, the commands specific to CD-ROM drives will be covered separately. Nevertheless, you must first understand how CDB blocks are encapsulated in *SRB* envelopes (SRB stands for *SCSI Request Block)*. Without these envelopes, the operating system will simply be unable to understand what you are going to do (as a matter of fact, any computer program only does the things that it is instructed to do. Sometimes, this is exactly the thing that the user wanted it to do, but not always).

The structure of the SRB block is described in detail in NT DDK. Therefore, you won't cover it here in detail but, rather, will only briefly consider its main fields.

Listing 4.6. Brief description of the SCSI_REQUEST_BLOCK structure

```
typedef struct _SCSI_REQUEST_BLOCK {
        USHORT Length;              // The length of the SCSI_REQUEST_BLOCK structure

        UCHAR Function;             // Function (usually, SRB_FUNCTION_EXECUTE_SCSI == 0,
                                    // e.g., send the command for execution to the device)
        UCHAR SrbStatus;            // Here, the device displays the command execution
                                    // progress. The most frequently encountered values are:
                                    // SRB_STATUS_SUCCESS == 0x1 - the command
                                    // completed successfully.
                                    // SRB_STATUS_PENDING == 0x0 - the command
                                    // is being executed.
                                    // SRB_STATUS_ERROR == 0x4 - an error was encountered.
                                    // Other values are also possible,
                                    // for a complete list see DDK.

        UCHAR ScsiStatus;           // Here the device returns the command completion status.
                                    // If the command didn't return SUCCESS,
                                    // then there was an ERROR.

        UCHAR PathId                // SCSI port to which the device controller is attached.
                                    // For virtual SCSI devices, this is always set to 0.

        UCHAR TargetId;             // Controller of the device on the bus.
                                    // For IDE devices usually set to the following values:
                                    // 0 - primary, 1 - secondary

        UCHAR Lun;                  // Logical device ID within the controller
                                    // For IDE devices usually set to the following values:
                                    // 0 - master, 1 - slave

        CHAR QueueTag;              // Not used, as a rule, and must be equal to zero
        CHAR QueueAction;           // Not used, as a rule, and must be equal to zero

        CHAR CdbLength;             // Length of the CDB block.
                                    // For ATAPI devices always set to 12 (0Ch)
        CHAR SenseInfoBufferLength; // the length of the SENSE buffer (see later )

        LONG SrbFlags;              // Flags that usually take two values:
                                    // SRB_FLAGS_DATA_IN == 0x40 - data move from
                                    // device to computer (read)
```

```
                    // SRB_FLAGS_DATA_OUT == 0x80 - data move from
                    //                        computer to device (write)

        ULONG DataTransferLength;    // Length of data block to be read or written

        LONG TimeOutValue;    // Time-out value in seconds

        PVOID DataBuffer;        // The pointer to the buffer containing
                        // data to be read/written

        PVOID SenseInfoBuffer;    // The pointer to the SENSE buffer (see later)

        struct _SCSI_REQUEST_BLOCK *NextSrb; // The pointer to the next SRB.
                                // Not executed, as a rule

        PVOID OriginalRequest; // The pointer to IRP. Practically not used

        PVOID SrbExtension; // Not used, as a rule, and must be equal to zero

        UCHAR Cdb[16];        // The CDB block per sec
} SCSI_REQUEST_BLOCK, *PSCSI_REQUEST_BLOCK;
```

After filling the fields of the SCSI_REQUEST_BLOCK structure appropriately, you can pass the SRB to the chosen device by calling on the DeviceIoControl function. All you have to do is specify an appropriate IOCTL code. That's it! Having swallowed the bait, the operating system will pass the CDB block to the appropriate device, and that device will (or won't) carry out the command contained in the CDB block. Pay special attention: The *CDB block is not processed by the device driver. Instead, it is the device itself that processes the CDB.* Because of this, you have virtually unlimited capabilities for device management. Note that you get all of these capabilities from the application level.

However, everything has its dark side. The device management procedure is rather capricious. A single error in filling in one of the fields can result in that the device will refuse to carry out the commands passed to it. Instead of command execution, it will either return an error code, or nothing at all. Besides this, even the slightest negligence can ruin all of the data on all of the hard drives. Therefore, it is necessary to be especially careful when choosing the TargetID and lun values! (*To determine automatically the CD-ROM address, it is possible to use the SCSI_INQUIRY command — see the DDK demo example, which you can find in the* \NTDDK\src\win_me\block\wnaspi32 *file*). However, let's forget about the dangers (after all, the life would be boring without them). Now you are going to discuss the most interesting aspect of our problem, namely, searching the IOCTL code passed on in the specific SRB.

As it turns out, it isn't easy to carry out this procedure directly. In fact, using only legal tools, it is simply impossible! For a number of reasons, the Windows developers decided only to provide full access to the fields of the SCSI_REQUEST_BLOCK structure to driver developers. As for application developers, they are limited to using structures such as SCSI_PASS_THROUGH and SCSI_PASS_THROUGH_DIRECT. Actually, these structures have a goal similar to SRB, but are somewhat limited in their functionality. Fortunately, there are no limitations on the contents of CDB blocks and, therefore, there is still the possibility of low-level control over the hardware. Further details on this topic can be found in the section "*9.2 SCSI Port I/O Control Codes*" in the Windows NT DDK documentation and in the source code of the demo example that can be found in the \NTDDK\src\storage\class\spti directory. Also, pay special attention to the spti.htm file in the same directory. This file provides a detailed description of how to control the device via the SCSI interface.

In line with the name of the directory containing this demo example, this method of interaction with the device is known as *SPTI* (standing for *SCSI Pass Through IOCTLs*). Let us briefly list the main, specific features and limitations of SPTI.

First, you must have administrative privileges for passing CDBs to devices. This isn't always convenient (although it is a positive situation from the security point of view).

Second, using of multi-target commands is not permitted (it means that you cannot issue the command for copying data from device A to device B that bypasses the processor — although, contemporary drives support such commands and it would be wonderful if it were possible to copy CDs without loading the processor).

Third, there is no support for the reversible (i.e., bidirectional) movement of data. At any given moment, data can be moved either from device to the computer or from computer to the device, but simultaneous bidirectional data movement is impossible).

Fourth, if a class driver has been installed for the target device, CDBs must be directed to the class driver, rather than to the SCSI device itself. This means that to control the CD-ROM drive, you must interact with it via the \\.\X: device, where X is the letter representing the CD-ROM drive. An attempt to access the \\.\Scsi0: device will return error code. As experience has shown, this is the main stumbling block for all inexperienced programmers who rush ahead without reading the documentation first.

NOTE

It is possible to address to the device as \\.\CdRom0 or \\.\CdRom1, without the terminating colon, where 0 or 1 stands for the ordinal number of the CD-ROM drive in the system. In contrast to a common fallacy, stating that the \\.\CdRom0 device is located at the lower level as compared to \\.\X:. From the operating system's point of view, these are synonyms. To make sure that this is true, it is enough to view the contents of the object table (objdir \DosDevice), which shows that \\.\X: is just a symbolic link to \\.\CdRomN.

Fifth, there are strict limitations on the maximum size of the data being sent (MaximumTransferLength). These limitations are imposed by specific features of the hardware device and the miniport driver serving it. The limitations relate to the maximum size allowed for the data block and to the number of physical pages that it takes up. In order to determine specific characteristics, it is necessary to send the IOCTL_SCSI_GET_CAPABILITIES command to the device. This command will return the IO_SCSI_CAPABILITIES structure (its definition can be found in the NTDDSCSI.h file). Along with other information, this structure contains the MaximumTransferLength and MaximumPhysicalPages_in_bytes values. The maximum size of the data to be sent is calculated using the following formula: largest transfer = min(MaximumTransferLength, MaximumPhysicalPages_in_bytes). Another way is to limit the data blocks to 64 Kbytes, which, guaranteed, will be supported by all devices. The buffer must be aligned by the value equal to AlignmentMask, which is returned in the IO_SCSI_CAPABILITIES structure. The alignment level ensured by the malloc function is sufficient for this, and no problems will arise when using it. The situation is different where memory allocation is carried out by the "char buf[BUF_SIZE]" construction — in this case, there is no guarantee that your program will operate properly.

Sixth, the SCSI_PASS_THROUGH_DIRECT structure itself contains a significantly smaller number of fields and, at the same time, the values contained in fields such as PathId, TargetId, and Lun are simply *ignored*! The physical address of the device on the bus is determined directly by the operating system by means of the symbolic name of the descriptor for the device, to which the SCSI_PASS_THROUGH_DIRECT request is sent.

Listing 4.7. The format of the SCSI_PASS_THROUGH_DIRECT structure (the SCSI_PASS_THROUGH structure is similar to it in many respects. However, it doesn't ensure data transmission through DMA)

```
typedef struct _SCSI_PASS_THROUGH_DIRECT {
        USHORT Length;                 // Structure size SCSI_PASS_THROUGH_DIRECT
        UCHAR ScsiStatus;              // Status of the command execution
                                       // by SCSI device
        UCHAR PathId;                  // Ignored
        UCHAR TargetId;                // Ignored
        UCHAR Lun;                     // Ignored
        UCHAR CdbLength;               // Length of the CDB packet sent to the
                                       // device (in bytes)
        UCHAR SenseInfoLength;         // Length of the SENSE buffer
                                       // to return error
        UCHAR *DataIn;                 // Direction of the data transmission
        ULONG DataTransferLength;      // Size of the data exchange buffer
                                       // (in bytes)
```

```
        ULONG TimeOutValue;          // Time-out value
        PVOID DataBuffer;            // Pointer to the data exchange buffer
        ULONG SenseInfoOffset;       // Pointer to the SENSE buffer
                                     // with error information
        UCHAR Cdb[16];               // Buffer containing CDB packet
                                     // (16 bytes maximum)
}SCSI_PASS_THROUGH_DIRECT, *PSCSI_PASS_THROUGH_DIRECT;
```

Fortunately, the "censorship" mainly relates to fields that are rarely used in practice anyway. Therefore, nothing has been lost. Just fill the remaining fields, and the structure will be ready!

Naturally, before passing it to the device, it is necessary to first get the descriptor for the required device. This can be done as follows:

Listing 4.8. Opening the drive in order to get its descriptor, which will be used for device control

```
HANDLE hCD = CreateFile ("\\\\.\\X:", GENERIC_WRITE | GENERIC_READ,
            FILE_SHARE_READ | FILE_SHARE_WRITE, 0, OPEN_EXISTING, 0, 0);
```

Making sure that hCD is not equal to INVALID_HANDLE_VALUE, pass the received descriptor along with the IOCTL_SCSI_PASS_THROUGHT_DIRECT structure to DeviceIoControl function. The function can be called as follows:

Listing 4.9. Passing the IOCTL_SCSI_PASS_THROUGH structure

```
DeviceIoControl(hCD, 0x4D014h /* IOCTL_SCSI_PASS_THROUGH_DIRECT */, &srb,
        sizeof(SCSI_PASS_THROUGH_DIRECT), sense_buf, SENSE_SIZE, &returned, 0);
```

Here, srb is the filled instance of the IOCTRL_SCSI_PASS_THROUGHT_DIRECT structure, and returned is the variable, to which the number of bytes returned by the device will be written. The sense_buf is the buffer, in which the filled instance of the IOCTL_SCSI_PASS_THROUGHT_DIRECT structure will be returned, along with the *sense info* — error code of the operation being executed. If the operation is completed without errors, sense info is not returned, and sense_buf contains only IOCTL_SCSI_PASS_THROUGH. The position of the sense info location within the buffer is determined by the contents of the SenseInfoOffset field. The value of this field must be chosen in such a way as to avoid overlapping with the IOCTRL_SCSI_PASS_THROUGHT structure. Simply speaking, the minimum possible offset of the Sense Info is equal to: srb.SenseInfoOffset = sizeof(SCSI_PASS_THROUGH_DIRECT).

Note that `SenseInfoOffset` is not a pointer to the sense info but, rather, it is the index of the first byte of sense info in the returned buffer!

To detect an error, it is necessary to analyze the number of bytes returned by the `DeviceIoControl` function in the returned variable. If it exceeds the size of the `IOCTL_SCSI_PASS_THROUGH` structure, then the buffer contains sense info. If this is the case, the sense info presence indicates that there is an error! The sense info format is shown in Fig. 4.1.

Byte \ Bit	7	6	5	4	3	2	1	0
0	Valid	Error code (70h or 71h)						
1	Segment number (reserved)							
2	Reserved		ILI	Reserved	Sense key			
3 6	Information							
7	Additional sense length ($n - 7$)							
8 11	Command-specific information							
12	Additional sense code							
13	Additional sense code qualifier (optional)							
14	Field replaceable unit code (optional)							
15	SKSV (optional)	Sense key specific (optional)						
17								
18 n	Additional sense bytes							

Fig. 4.1. SENSE INFO format. Sense info is returned by the device in case of error

The first byte specifies the error type and usually takes the value of 70h (*current error*) or 71h (*deferred error*). Error codes from 72h to 7Eh are reserved, and errors with the code 7Eh indicate vendor-specific sense-info format. Error codes from 00h to 6Fh are not defined in the ATAPI CD-ROM specification. Therefore, their use is undesirable (this warning is intended mainly to hardware developers, and not programmers).

Error description is encoded by the following three numbers: Sense Key, Additional Sense Code (ASC for short) and Additional Sense Code Qualifier (ASCQ). On top of this hierarchy is the Sense Key, containing the generic error categories, followed by the ASC, which describes the error in more detail. At the lowest hierarchical level, there is the ASCQ, which qualifies the additional sense code itself. If the error is exhaustively described only by the Sense Key and ASC, the ASCQ is missing (or, to be more precise, is undefined).

Description of the main error codes is provided in two tables below. It should be pointed out that the Sense Key value is not critical for error analysis, since each ASC will belong to the one Sense Key value. In contrast to this, the same ASCQ can belong to different ASCs and, therefore, it makes no sense without the precisely specified ASC value.

Table 4.3. Main Sense Key values (error categories) and their descriptions

Sense Key	Description
00h	NO SENSE. No additional sense info. The operation was completed successfully.
01h	RECOVERED ERROR. The operation has completed successfully. However, some problems were encountered in the course of its execution. These problems were eliminated by the drive itself. Additional information is provided by ASC and ASCQ.
02h	NOT READY. The device is not ready.
03h	MEDIUM ERROR. An irrecoverable error was encountered in the course of operation execution. Most probably, this error was caused by medium defects or incorrect data. This sense key may also be returned in cases when the drive is unable to distinguish the medium defect from hardware failure.
04h	HARDWARE ERROR. Irrecoverable hardware error (for instance, controller failure).
05h	ILLEGAL REQUEST. Illegal parameters passed to the drive in the CDB packet (for instance, the starting address is larger than the ending address).
06h	UNIT ATTENTION. The medium has been replaced or the device controller has been reset.
07h	DATA PROTECT. An attempt at reading protected data.
8h—0Ah	Reserved.
0Bh	ABORTED COMMAND. Command execution was for some reason aborted.
0Eh	MISCOMPARE. Source data do not correspond to the data read from the medium.
0Fh	Reserved.

Table 4.4. Main ASC and ASCQ codes

ASC	ASCQ	DROM	Description
00	00	DROM	No additional sense information
00	11	R	Play operation in progress
00	12	R	Play operation paused
00	13	R	Play operation successfully completed
00	14	R	Play operation stopped due to error
00	15	R	No current audio status to return
01	00	R	Mechanical positioning or changer error
02	00	DROM	No seek complete
04	00	DROM	Logical drive not ready — cause not reportable
04	01	DROM	Logical drive not ready — in progress of becoming ready
04	02	DROM	Logical drive not ready — initializing command required
04	03	DROM	Logical drive not ready — manual intervention required
05	01	DROM	Media load — eject failed
06	00	DROM	No reference position found
09	00	DRO	Track following error
09	01	RO	Tracking servo failure
09	02	RO	Focus servo failure
09	03	RO	Spindle servo failure
11	00	DRO	Unrecovered read error
11	06	RO	CIRC unrecovered error
15	00	DROM	Random positioning error
15	01	DROM	Mechanical positioning or changer error
15	02	DRO	Positioning error detected by read of medium
17	00	DRO	Recovered data with no error correction applied
17	01	DRO	Recovered data with retries

continues

Table 4.4 Continued

ASC	ASCQ	DROM	Description
17	02	DRO	Recovered data with positive head offset
17	03	DRO	Recovered data with negative head offset
17	04	RO	Recovered data with retries and/or CIRC applied
17	05	DRO	Recovered data using previous sector ID
18	00	DRO	Recovered data with error correction applied
18	01	DRO	Recovered data with error correction & retries applied
18	02	DRO	Recovered data — the data were auto-reallocated
18	03	R	Recovered data with CIRC
18	04	R	Recovered data with L-EC
1A	00	DROM	Parameter list length error
20	00	DROM	Invalid command operation code
21	00	DROM	Logical block address out of range
24	00	DROM	Invalid field in command packet
26	00	DROM	Invalid field in parameter list
26	01	DROM	Parameter not supported
26	02	DROM	Parameter value invalid
28	00	ROM	Not ready to ready transition, medium may have changed
29	00	ROM	Power on, reset, or bus device reset occurred
2A	00	ROM	Parameters changed
2A	01	ROM	Mode parameters changed
30	00	ROM	Incompatible medium installed
30	01	RO	Cannot read medium — unknown format
30	02	RO	Cannot read medium — incompatible format
39	00	ROM	Saving parameters not supported

continues

Table 4.4 Continued

ASC	ASCQ	DROM	Description
3A	00	ROM	Medium not present
3F	00	ROM	ATAPI CD-ROM drive operating conditions have changed
3F	01	ROM	Microcode has been changed
40	NN	ROM	Diagnostic failure on component *NN* (80h–FFh)
44	00	ROM	Internal ATAPI CD-ROM drive failure
4E	00	ROM	Overlapped commands attempted
53	00	ROM	Media load or eject failed
53	02	ROM	Medium removal prevented
57	00	R	Unable to recover table of contents
5A	00	DROM	Operator request or state change input (unspecified)
5A	01	DROM	Operator medium removal request
63	00	R	End of user area encountered on this track
64	00	R	Illegal mode for this track
B9	00	R	Play operation aborted
BF	00	R	Loss of streaming

As you can see, it's easy! The only thing you have yet to clarify is *ATAPI*. Since you aren't going to interact with ATAPI directly (thanks to Windows architects, you don't have this capability), let us consider its main aspects and features only briefly. As a matter of fact, ATAPI specification was adopted in 1996 for devices logically different from hard disks, including optical, magneto-optical, and tape drives. This is a packet extension of the interface, which allows for the reception of blocks of control information whose structure was borrowed from SCSI, via ATA bus. This fact allows us to understand why Windows is so dashing when "turning" ATAPI devices into SCSI ones. If you neglect the hardware differences between interfaces, which are not "visible" at the application level, ATAPI will be very similar to SCSI. Control over ATAPI devices is carried out using the same CDBs that you have considered earlier.

Naturally, in order to control the device, it is necessary to know its controlling commands. To get this information, you'll need the "*ATAPI Packet Commands for CD-ROM devices*" reference manual. Open this manual to the description of the READ CD command (BEh code), and you'll find the following table.

Byte \ Bit	7	6	5	4	3	2	1	0
0	Operation code (BEh)							
1	Reserved			Expected sector type			Reserved	
2	MSB							
3	Starting Logical Block Address (LBA)							
4								
5								LSB
6	MSB							
7	Transfer length in blocks							
8								LSB
	Flag bits							
9	Synch field	Header(s) code		User data	EDC& ECC	Error flag(s)		Reserved
10	Reserved				Sub-channel data selection bits			
11	Reserved							
18	Additional sense bytes							
n								

Fig. 4.2. Description of the READ CD command

Let's try to clarify this table. The first byte, representing the code of the command being executed, doesn't raise any questions. However, it is followed by the *Expected Sector Type* field specifying the type of required sector. If you jump ahead a few pages, you'll find the codes corresponding to all of the existing sector types: CDDA, Mode 1, Mode 2, Mode 2 Form 1, and Mode 2 Form 2. If sector type is not known beforehand, pass the 0x0 value in this field, meaning that any type of sector is acceptable.

The next four bytes contain the *address of the first sector to be read*, specified in the LBA (*Logical Block Address*) format. This abbreviation hides elegant method of pass-through sector numbering. If you have ever programmed ancient hard disks, you'll recall the bulky computations that had to be carried out in order to determine to which head, cylinder, and sector each byte belongs. Now it is possible to do this without all that fuss. The first sector has the number 0, followed by 1, 2, 3... and so on, until the last sector of the disk is reached. The only important thing that you should bear in mind is that the byte order in this double word is inverse, which means that the most significant byte of the most significant word comes first.

Bytes with numbers from six to eight are occupied by the parameter specifying the *number of sectors to be read*. Note that for sector address, four bytes are allocated, while for the number of sectors to be read — there are only three. However, you are not going to read the entire disc in one operation! Byte order in this case is also inverse, so be careful to avoid errors. Otherwise, you'll request a reading of half of the entire disc when attempting to read only a single sector.

The ninth byte is especially interesting, because it stores *flags that determine which parts of the sector must be read*. Besides user data, you can request sync bytes, the header, *EDC/ECC codes, and even read error flags* (for cracking some protection mechanisms, this information is indispensable, although, unfortunately, not every drive supports this feature).

The tenths bit is responsible for retrieving subchannel data. However, since the same data are already present in the header, it is possible, in principle, to do without this information.

Finally, the last (eleventh, counting from zero) byte, isn't used because it is reserved. Therefore, in order to ensure compatibility with newer drive models, it must be set to zero.

Naturally, depending on the type and volume of the requested data, the length of the returned sector can vary to a great degree.

Table 4.5. Interrelation between the type of requested data and the length of the returned sector

Data to be transferred	Flag Bits	CD-DA	Mode 1	Mode 2 non XA	Mode 2 Form 1	Mode 2 Form 2
User Data	10h	2352	2048	2336	2048	2338
User Data + EDC/ECC	18h	(10h)	2336	(10h)	2336	(10h)
Header Only	20h	(10h)	4	4	4	4
Header Only + EDC/ECC	28h	(10h)	Illegal	Illegal	Illegal	Illegal
Header & User Data	30h	(10h)	2052	2340	Illegal	Illegal
Header & User Data + EDC/ECC	38h	(10h)	2344	(30h)	Illegal	Illegal
Sub Header Only	40h	(10h)	8	8	8	8

continues

Table 4.5 Continued

Data to be transferred	Flag Bits	CD-DA	Mode 1	Mode 2 non XA	Mode 2 Form 1	Mode 2 Form 2
Sub Header Only + EDC/ECC	48h	(10h)	Illegal	Illegal	Illegal	Illegal
Sub Header & User Data	50h	(10h)	(10h)	(10h)	2056	2336
Sub Header & User Data + EDC/ECC	58h	(10h)	(10h)	(10h)	2344	(50h)
All Header Only	60h	(10h)	12	12	12	12
All Header Only + EDC/ECC	68h	(10h)	Illegal	Illegal	Illegal	Illegal
All Header & User Data	70h	(10h)	(30h)	(30h)	2060	2340
All Header & User Data + EDC/ECC	78h	(10h)	(30h)	(30h)	2340	2340
Sync & User Data	90h	(10h)	Illegal	Illegal	Illegal	Illegal
Sync & User Data + EDC/ECC	98h	(10h)	Illegal	Illegal	Illegal	Illegal
Sync & Header Only	A0h	(10h)	16	16	16	16
Sync & Header Only + EDC/ECC	A8h	(10h)	Illegal	Illegal	Illegal	Illegal
Sync & Header & User Data	B0h	(10h)	2064	2352	Illegal	Illegal
Sync & Header & User Data + EDC/ECC	B8h	(10h)	2344	(30h)	Illegal	Illegal

Table 4.5 Continued

Data to be transferred	Flag Bits	CD-DA	Mode 1	Mode 2 non XA	Mode 2 Form 1	Mode 2 Form 2
Sync & Sub Header Only	C0h	(10h)	Illegal	Illegal	Illegal	Illegal
Sync & Sub Header Only + EDC/ECC	C8h	(10h)	Illegal	Illegal	Illegal	Illegal
Sync & Sub Header & User Data	D0h	(10h)	(10h)	(10h)	Illegal	Illegal
Sync & Sub Header & User Data + EDC/ECC	D8h	(10h)	(10h)	(10h)	Illegal	Illegal
Sync & All Headers Only	E0h	(10h)	24	24	24	24
Sync & All Headers Only + EDC/ECC	E8h	(10h)	Illegal	Illegal	Illegal	Illegal
Sync & All Headers & User Data	F0h	(10h)	2064	2352	2072	2352
Sync & All Headers & User Data + EDC/ECC	F8h	(10h)	2352	(F0h)	2352	(F0h)
Repeat All Above and Add Error Flags	02h	294	294	294	294	294
Repeat All Above and Add Block & Error Flags	04h	296	296	296	296	296

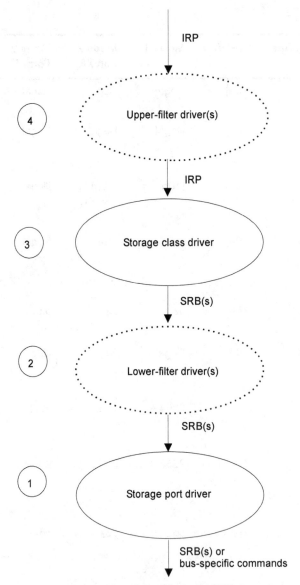

Fig. 4.3. Windows NT internals

At the application level, IDE devices are interpreted as SCSI devices. Naturally, the drive doesn't undergo any changes at the physical level. Therefore, IDE CD-ROM drive remains an IDE drive, with all of its advantages and drawbacks. However, IRP requests to these drivers, while passing via the Storage Class Driver, are translated into SRBs (SCSI request blocks). SRB requests then go to the Storage port driver (e.g., directly to the device driver), where they are once again translated into physical commands specific to that device (see Fig. 4.3). Detailed information on this absorption process are provided in NT DDK (see section "*1.1 Storage Driver Architecture*"). Here, it is enough to emphasize the fact that, beside the commands from the `IRP_MJ_EEE` family, you can also pass SRB requests, which provide significantly more freedom and flexibility, to the device. However, it is impossible to organize this interaction directly from the application level because IRP commands are *private* ones, while the `DeviceIoControl` API function passes only public commands that can be explicitly processed by the driver in `IRP_MJ_DEVICE_CONTROL` manager.

Now, to get some practical experience, let us create a program reading raw sectors from CDs. The key fragment of such a program (along with the required comments) is provided below:

Listing 4.10. [/SPTI.raw.sector.read.c] The function that reads raw sectors via SPTI

```
#define RAW_READ_CMD      0xBE // ATAPI RAW READ
#define WHATS_READ        0xF8 // Sync & All Headers & User Data + EDC/ECC
#define PACKET_LEN        2352 // length of one sector
//#define WHATS_READ      0x10 // User Data
//#define PACKET_LEN      2048 // length of one sector


//-[SPTI_RAW_SECTOR_READ]-------------------------------------------------
//   The function reads one or more sectors from the CDROM in RAW format,
//   according to the flags passed to it.
//
//   ARG:
//        CD        - The drive to be opened
//                    (something like "\\\\.\\X:" or "\\\\.\\CdRom0")
//   buf            - The buffer, to which the data must be read
//   buf_len        - Buffer size in bytes
//   StartSec       - Number of the starting sector, counting from zero
//   N_SECTOR       - Number of sectors to read
//   flags          - What information must be read
//                    (see SCSI/ATAPI specification )
//
//   RET:
//        != 0      - The function was executed successfully
//        == 0      - The function returned error
//
```

```
//    NOTE:
//        - Works only under NT/W2K/XP and requires
//          administrative privileges
//
//        - 64 K of data per operation at maximum
//--------------------------------------------------------------------------------
SPTI_RAW_SECTOR_READ(char *CD,char *buf,int buf_len,int StartSec,int N_SEC,char flags)
{
        HANDLE                hCD;
        SCSI_PASS_THROUGH_DIRECT srb;
        DWORD                 returned, length, status;

        // OPENING THE DEVICE
        hCD = CreateFile (   driver, GENERIC_WRITE|GENERIC_READ,
                             FILE_SHARE_READ|FILE_SHARE_WRITE, 0, OPEN_EXISTING, 0, 0);
        if (hCD == INVALID_HANDLE_VALUE) { printf("-ERR: open CD\n"); return 0;}

        // FORMING SRB
        memset(&srb,0,sizeof(SCSI_PASS_THROUGH_DIRECT)); // Initialization

        srb.Length = sizeof(SCSI_PASS_THROUGH_DIRECT);
        srb.PathId = 0;                                  // SCSI controller ID
        srb.TargetId = 6;                                // Ignored
        srb.Lun = 9;                                     // Ignored
   srb.CdbLength = 12;                                   // Length of the CDB
                                                         // packet

        srb.SenseInfoLength = 0;                         // SenseInfo not needed
        srb.DataIn = SCSI_IOCTL_DATA_IN;                 // We are going to read.
        srb.DataTransferLength = PACKET_LEN*N_SECTOR;    // Length of data
                                                         // to read
        srb.TimeOutValue = 200;                          // TimeOut value
        srb.DataBufferOffset = buf;                      // Pointer to the
                                                         // buffer
        srb.SenseInfoOffset = 0;                         // SenseInfo is
                                                         // not needed


        // CDB packet containing ATAPI commands
        srb.Cdb[0] = RAW_READ_CMD;                       // Read RAW sector.
        srb.Cdb[1] = 0x0;                                // Any type of the disk
                                                         // format is acceptable.


        // The number of the first sector to be read. Most significant byte
```

```
// of the most significant word goes first, least significant byte
// of the least significant word goes last
srb.Cdb[2] = HIBYTE(HIWORD(StartSector));
srb.Cdb[3] = LOBYTE(HIWORD(StartSector));
srb.Cdb[4] = HIBYTE(LOWORD(StartSector));
srb.Cdb[5] = LOBYTE(LOWORD(StartSector));

// Number of sectors to be read
srb.Cdb[6] = LOBYTE(HIWORD(N_SECTOR));
srb.Cdb[7] = HIBYTE(LOWORD(N_SECTOR));
srb.Cdb[8] = LOBYTE(LOWORD(N_SECTOR));

srb.Cdb[9] = flags;        // What should be read
srb.Cdb[10] = 0;           // Subchannel Data Bits
srb.Cdb[11] = 0;           // Reserved

// SENDING SRB TO ATAPI device
status = DeviceIoControl(hCD, IOCTL_SCSI_PASS_THROUGH_DIRECT,
            &srb, sizeof(SCSI_PASS_THROUGH_DIRECT), &srb, 0, &returned, 0);

return 1;
}
```

It only remains to note that protection mechanisms that interact with the disc via SPTI can be cracked easily by setting a breakpoint to the `CreateFile/ DeviceIoControl` functions. To prevent "extra" popups of the debugger, the breakpoint filter must react only to those calls to the `CreateFile` function, whose leftmost argument is set to `\\.\X:` or to `\\.\CdRomN`. The second left argument of the `DeviceIoControl` must automatically represent either `IOCTL_SCSI_PASS_ THROUGHT`, or `IOCTL_SCSI_PASS_THROUGHT_DIRECT`, the hex codes of which are equal to `0x4D004` and `0x4D014`, respectively.

Access via ASPI

> A debugged program is one, for which
> the failure conditions haven't been found yet.
>
> *Programmer folklore*

There are two main drawbacks of the above-described SPTI interface: It requires administrative or root privileges for controlling the device and, even worse, it is supported only by operating systems of the Windows NT family. Windows 9x/ME operating systems lack support for this interface. The only legitimate method of accessing the CD-ROM under Windows 9*x* is using 16-bit thunk for directly accessing the MSCDEX MS-DOS driver, which provides a considerably wider set of functional capabilities than in the Windows driver. Naturally, parallel support of two families of operating systems requires significant efforts from programmers, which results in a considerable increase of the cost of software products.

To simplify the development of cross-platform applications, *Adaptec* has developed a special system-independent interface allowing for the control of various SCSI devices from the application level. This interface became known as *ASPI*, which stands for *Advanced SCSI Programming Interface* (although, unofficially, it is often called Adaptec SCSI Programming Interface).

System independence in ASPI is ensured by the two-layer model of its organization: Architecturally, it comprises the *low-level driver and application-level wrapper library*. ASPI driver was developed taking into account specific features of the OS. It is responsible for directly controlling the SCSI bus (regardless of whether this bus is physical or virtual). Since the interface between the operating system and drivers changes from system to system, a special ASPI library is used for hiding these differences. This library provides the common unified interface for all operating systems.

Let us consider how ASPI interface is implanted into the OS in the example of Windows ME (see Fig. 4.4). At the highest level of the hierarchy are the WNASPI32.DLL and WINASPI.DLL libraries, intended for 32- and 16-bit applications, respectively. These DLLs export the following three basic ASPI functions: `GetASPI32DLLVersion`, `GetASPI32SupportInfo` and `SendASPI32Command` (the latter being the most important), and three helper functions: `GetASPI32Buffer`, `FreeASPI32Buffer`, `TranslateASPI32Address` (the latter is present only in the 32-bit version of the library).

By calling the `DeviceIoControl` function, they communicate with the ASPI driver, which resides lower in the hierarchy. Depending on the OS, this driver is called either APIX.VXD (Windows 9x), or ASPI.SYS (Windows NT). In the course of its initialization, this driver creates the `MbMmDp32` device. Don't ask me what this name means, since the answer is buried deep inside the Adaptec company.

NOTE

16-bit applications communicate with the driver via the `1868h` function of the `2Fh` interrupt. The details of this process can be discovered by disassembling the winaspi.dll library. By the way, this DLL is tiny — its size is just 5 K.

In principle, nothing prevents us from communicating directly with ASPI driver, bypassing the WNASPI32.dll. In fact, most developers of protection mechanisms choose this method. To do so, it is enough to disassemble WNASPI32.dll and discover the correspondence between ASPI commands and IOCTL codes (for obvious reasons, ASPI protocol isn't documented). Actually, nothing could be easier than setting the breakpoint to SendASPI32Command, after which the hacker can easily locate the protection code. With regard to DeviceIoControl calls, they are more difficult to handle, because they are too numerous. Moreover, beginner crackers of protection mechanisms (the most common group of hackers) have only a vague idea of the input/output architecture, to say nothing about the ASPI protocol. For qualified and experienced hackers, though, this protection doesn't present a serious obstacle (more details are provided in *"Revealing protection mechanisms"*).

The ASPI driver itself "connects" to SCSI and IDE/ATAPI ports, thanks to which it allows for the control of all these devices (including CD-ROM drives).

NOTE

Client modules (in Fig. 4.4, they are designated by the numbers 1, 2, and 3) send their requests to the Installable File System driver (designated by the number 6). Client modules also have ASPI libraries for 32- and 16-bit applications at their disposal (they are designated by the numbers 4 and 6). They, to a degree, stand apart from the rest of the system because they are optional components developed by a third-party company — Adaptec. The file system driver redirects a request it has received to one of the following specialized drivers, among which is the CD-ROM driver, CDFS.VxD, designated by the number 8. Its tasks include supporting CD file systems such as ISO 9660, High Sierra, etc. One level below, there is the Volume Tracker (14), which traces events such as disc replacement, and, even lower, there is the driver that supports this particular CD-ROM model itself. This is the so-called CD type-specific driver, implemented by CDVSD.VxD module. Among other tasks, it is responsible for assigning the CD drive letter. In fact, this is the sector level of interaction with the CD, and there are no file systems here. Although this driver is specific to the CD-ROM drive model, it is absolutely independent of its physical interface, because it relies on the CD-ROM device SCSI'zer (21), which converts IOP requests arriving from higher-level drivers into SRB packets directed to lower-level drivers (more details on this topic are provided in the section "Access via the SCSI Port"). The SCSI CD-ROM helper (23) resides even lower, ensuring interaction between the SCSI'zer and the SCSI port. The SCSI port itself, created by the SCSI ports manager (26), represents a unified, system-independent tool for organizing the interaction between medium-level drivers and physical (or virtual) devices. The ASPI driver (18) relates to one of these SCSI ports. The ASPI driver is implemented in the APIX.VxD file and goes up to its "wrappers" — WNASPI32.DLL and WNASPI.DLL (numbers 11 and 12, respectively). Below the SCSI manager reside the mini-port drivers, which translate SCSI requests into the "language" of the specific interface bus. In particular, the driver ensuring support for IDE devices is implemented by the ESDI_506.PDR file (number 29). Naturally, if necessary, you can communicate with IDE devices via IDE/ATAPI ports (25), which are implemented by the same driver — ESDI_506.PDR (the ASPI driver, due to performance considerations, does exactly this). The left part of the flowchart, representing the hierarchy of drivers of all other disk drives, will not be covered here, since it isn't related to our discussion in any way.

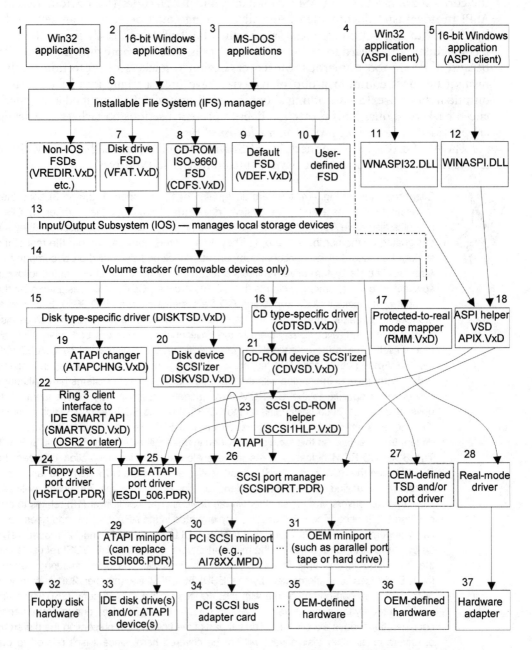

Fig. 4.4. Architecture of the Windows 98/ME Input/Output system

For ASPI programming, at least two things are required: the ASPI *driver* and ASPI *SDK*. The driver is freely downloadable from the Adaptec Web server (the drivers for the following operating systems are available: MS-DOS, Novell, Windows 9*x*, Windows NT/W2K/XP). As for SDK, at some point it ceased to be a freeware, and is distributed on a commercial basis, although its price is relatively small (somewhere around $10). However, all of the materials required for your work, including documentation, header files, and libraries can be borrowed from Windows Me DDK (which is included as part of Windows 2000 DDK). Thus, if you have a copy of W2K DDK, there's no need to worry. If this is not the case, get MSDN library, which is distributed along with Microsoft Visual Studio 6.0. Here, you'll find documentation and header files, while the missing libraries for the appropriate DLLs can be produced on your own (lib.exe with the /DEF command-line key). Anyway, it is possible to do without these libraries by loading all required functions via LoadLibrary/GetProcAddress.

Since the ASPI interface comes with good documentation (the programmer's manual comprises about 35 pages), mastering it shouldn't cause any serious problems (at least after you have become acquainted with SPTI). Besides, Windows Me DDK includes a completed demo example, which can be found in the \src\win_me\block\ wnaspi32\ folder. Despite the fact that it is intended for Windows Me, it is also suitable for other operating systems, including Windows 98, Windows 2000, Windows XP, etc.

However, this example is extremely awkward, with a large number of errors. In relation to clarity and readability, I have to say that it would be hard to find a less illustrative example demonstrating ASPI operation! It is definitely much better to investigate the source codes of the CD slow program, which can be easily found on the Internet. The only problem is that this program is in Assembly language. Therefore, it is necessary to have previous experience in this language.

Let us briefly list the main drawbacks of the aspi32ln.c demo example. First, this is not a console application. Therefore, most of its code has no relation to ASPI, since it implements the program's GUI. Second, this example uses the unified function for receiving notifications from two commands: SCSI_INQUIRY and SCSI_READ10. In 50% of the cases, the latter is replaced by its constant 0x28, which also doesn't improve code readability. Third, CD-ROM drives are only partially supported by this program. The poorly designed architecture of this application did not allow the developers to achieve their goals. Consequently, the branch responsible for reading from CD-ROM in the ASPI32Post function is specially commented out. If you remove this blocking, there will be read errors, since the program is oriented only towards the drives where sector size equals 0x200 bytes. CD-ROM drives, designed to work with discs having sector size four times greater than this value, do not fall within this category. If you want to avoid redesigning the entire program, the only option is to increase the size of the requested block to 0x800 bytes (in this case, four sectors will be read from hard disks at a time, which is more than acceptable). Finally, the increment (e.g., the computation of the address of the next block to be read) is designed so terribly that it is not usable at all.

There's no point in concentrating on criticisms of demo examples (even an imperfect demo program is still better than nothing), so let's proceed with studying the ASPI interface, or, to be more precise, its most important command — SendASPI32Command, which ensures the passing of SRB blocks to the device. Hopefully, you'll be able to master all of the other problems on your own, without encountering any difficulties.

The SRB_ExecSCSICmd structure, which contains the data on the SRB request, is almost a twin of SCSI_PASS_THROUGH_DIRECT, as there are more similarities than differences between them. Look at the following:

Listing 4.11. The SRB_ExecSCSICmd structure

```
typedef struct
{
BYTE SRB_Cmd;                      // ASPI command code = SC_EXEC_SCSI_CMD
BYTE SRB_Status                    // ASPI command status byte
BYTE SRB_HaId;                     // ASPI host adapter number
BYTE SRB_Flags;                    // ASPI request flags
DWORD SRB_Hdr_Rsvd;                // Reserved, MUST = 0
BYTE SRB_Target;                   // Target's SCSI ID
BYTE SRB_Lun;                      // Target's LUN number
WORD SRB_Rsvd1;                    // Reserved for Alignment
DWORD SRB_BufLen;                  // Data Allocation Length
LPBYTE SRB_BufPointer;             // Data Buffer Pointer
BYTE SRB_SenseLen;                 // Sense Allocation Length
BYTE SRB_CDBLen;                   // CDB Length
BYTE SRB_HaStat;                   // Host Adapter Status
BYTE SRB_TargStat;                 // Target Status
LPVOID SRB_PostProc;               // Post routine
BYTE SRB_Rsvd2[20];                // Reserved, MUST = 0
BYTE CDBByte[16];                  // SCSI CDB
BYTE SenseArea[SENSE_LEN+2];       // Request Sense buffer
}
SRB_ExecSCSICmd, *PSRB_ExecSCSICmd;
```

Note that in order to control the device, you needn't know its descriptor! It is enough to specify its physical address on the bus (i. e., correctly fill the SRB_HaId and SRB_Target fields). How can you find them? Quite easily. Just send the INQUIRY (code 12h) command to all physical addresses. The device, physically or virtually associated with that port, will return identification information (among other useful data, it will contain the device name). Non-existent devices won't return anything and the operating system will report an error.

The simplest program for device polling might appear as follows:

Listing 4.12. Sequential polling of ports in order to detect devices connected to them

```
#define MAX_ID          8
#define MAX_INFO_LEN    48
SEND_SCSI_INQUITY()
{
        #define MAX_LUN 8    // max. possible number of logical devices
        BYTEAdapterCount;
        DWORD   ASPI32Status;
        unsigned char buf[0xFF];
        unsigned char str[0xFF];
        unsigned char CDB[ATAPI_CDB_SIZE];
        long a, real_len, adapterid, targetid;

        // Getting the number of adapters on the bus
        ASPI32Status = GetASPI32SupportInfo();
        AdapterCount = (LOBYTE(LOWORD(ASPI32Status)));

        // Preparing the CDB block
        memset(CDB, 0, ATAPI_CDB_SIZE);
        CDB[0] = 0x12;          // INQUIRY
        CDB[4] = 0xFF;          // Response size

        // Spamming the ports in order to find the required device
        for (adapterid = 0; adapterid < MAX_LUN; adapterid++)
        { // Attention! The use of ^^^^^^^^^^^^^^ AdapterCount is not
          // permitted here, as recommended in some manuals, because device
          // adapter numbers do not necessarily follow one another directly.
          // If there is a "gap" in numbering,
          // one or more devices will remain undetected

                for (targetid = 0; targetid < MAX_ID; targetid++)
                {
                        a = SEND_ASPI_CMD(adapterid, targetid, CDB,
                                    ATAPI_CDB_SIZE, 0, buf, 0xFF, ASPI_DATA_IN);
                        if (a == SS_COMP)
                        {
                                real_len = (buf[4]>MAX_INFO_LEN)? buf[4]:MAX_INFO_LEN;
                                memcpy(str, &buf[8], real_len); str[real_len] = 0;
```

```
                    printf("%d.%d <-- %s\n", adapterid, targetid, str);
            }
        }
    }
}
```

The result of program execution on the author's computer looks as shown below. (Pay special attention to the fact that the addresses of the devices connected to a virtual SCSI bus created by the ASPI driver might differ from their actual physical addresses. For example, in this case, the PHILIPS drive sitting on the physical IDE port with the number 0, happened to occur on virtual port 1, since the port number 0 was occupied by the Virtual Clone CD driver. Note that if the latter is removed from the system, the mapping between virtual and physical addresses, in principle, should be fully restored. However, this isn't guaranteed.) The leftmost digit represents the adapter ID. The following digit stands for the target ID.

Listing 4.13. Devices connected to the author's computer

```
0.0 <-- ELBY      DVD-ROM          1.0
1.0 <-- IBM-DTLA-307015            TX2O
1.1 <-- PHILIPS CDRW2412A          P1.55VO1214DM10574
2.0 <-- ST380011A                  3.06
2.1 <-- TEAC      CD-W552E         1.09
3.0 <-- AXV       CD/DVD-ROM       2.2a
3.1 <-- AXV       CD/DVD-ROM       2.2a
3.2 <-- AXV       CD/DVD-ROM       2.2a
```

Another important advantage of the ASPI interface in comparison to SPTI is support for the *asynchronous mode* of request processing. Having sent a request to read a certain number of sectors, you can continue the execution of your program without waiting for the sector-reading process to be completed. Of course, to achieve a similar result using SPTI interface it is enough to create another thread. However, this solution is not as elegant as the previous one.

Listing 4.14. [\etc\RAW.CD.READ\aspi32.raw.c]. Demo example of a program that reads raw sectors from the CD

```
#include "scsidefs.h"
#include "wnaspi32.h"

void ASPI32Post (LPVOID);
```

```
#define F_NAME      "raw.sector.dat"

/* ASPI SRB packet length */
#define ASPI_SRB_LEN    0x100

#define RAW_READ_CM 0xBE

#define WHATS_READ  0xF8        // Sync & All Headers & User Data + EDC/ECC
#define PACKET_LEN  2352

//#define WHATS_READ    0x10    // User Data
//#define PACKET_LEN    2048


#define MY_CMD      RAW_READ_CMD

HANDLE hEvent;

//-[DWORD READ_RAW_SECTOR_FROM_CD]---------------------------------------------
//      This function reads one or more sectors from the CD-ROM
//      in RAW mode, according to the flags passed to it.
//
//  ARG:
//      adapter_id  - Bus number (0 - primary, 1 - secondary)
//      read_id     - Number of the device on the bus
//                      (0 - master, 1 - slave)
//      buf         - Buffer, into which the data must be read
//      buf_len     - Buffer size in bytes
//      StartSector - Starting number of the sector from which to read
//                      (numbering starts from 0)
//      N_SECTOR    - Number of sectors to be read
//      flags       - Information to be read (see the ATAPI specification)
//
//  RET:
//                  - Doesn't return anything
//
//  NOTE:
//      The function returns control before accomplishing the request.
//      Therefore, at the moment of exiting, the data buffer is still
//      empty. It gets filled only when calling
//      the ASPI32Post function (you can modify it as needed).
```

```
//      For signaling the operation completion, it is recommended to use
//      events.
//
//      The function operates under Windows 9x/ME/NT/W2K/XP
//      and _doesn't_ require administrative privileges.
//      However, ASPI driver must be installed.
//----------------------------------------------------------------------------
READ_RAW_SECTOR_FROM_CD(int adapter_id,int read_id,char *buf,int buf_len,
                        int StartSector,int N_SECTOR,int flags)
{
        PSRB_ExecSCSICmd SRB;
        DWORD       ASPI32Status;

        // Allocating memory for SRB request
        SRB = malloc(ASPI_SRB_LEN); memset(SRB, 0, ASPI_SRB_LEN);

        // PREPARING SRB block
        SRB->SRB_Cmd = SC_EXEC_SCSI_CMD;            // Execute SCSI
                                                    // command
        SRB->SRB_HaId = adapter_id;                 // Adapter ID
        SRB->SRB_Flags = SRB_DIR_IN|SRB_POSTING;    // Asynchronous
                                                    // data read
        SRB->SRB_Target = read_id;                  // Device ID
        SRB->SRB_BufPointer = buf;                  // Buffer for
                                                    // loading data
        SRB->SRB_BufLen = buf_len;                  // Buffer length
        SRB->SRB_SenseLen = SENSE_LEN;              // SENSE buffer
                                                    // length
        SRB->SRB_CDBLen = 12;                       // Size of ATAPI
                                                    // packet

        SRB->CDBByte [0] = MY_CMD;                  // ATAPI command
        SRB->CDBByte [1] = 0x0;                     // CD format - any

                                                    // Number of the first sector
        SRB->CDBByte [2] = HIBYTE(HIWORD(StartSector));
        SRB->CDBByte [3] = LOBYTE(HIWORD(StartSector));
        SRB->CDBByte [4] = HIBYTE(LOWORD(StartSector));
        SRB->CDBByte [5] = LOBYTE(LOWORD(StartSector));

                                                    // Number of sectors to be read
        SRB->CDBByte [6]  = LOBYTE(HIWORD(N_SECTOR));
```

```
SRB->CDBByte [7] = HIBYTE(LOWORD(N_SECTOR));
SRB->CDBByte [8] = LOBYTE(LOWORD(N_SECTOR));

SRB->CDBByte [9] = flags      // What info must be read?
SRB->CDBByte [10] = 0;        // Subchannel data are not needed
SRB->CDBByte [11] = 0;        // Reserved

// Address of the procedure that will receive notifications
SRB->SRB_PostProc = (void *) ASPI32Post;

// Sending an SRB request to the device
SendASPI32Command(SRB);

// Returning from the function _before_ accomplishing
// execution of the request
return 0;
}


//-----------------------------------------------------------------------------
//   This callback function is called up by ASPI and gains control
//   after the accomplishment of request execution or in case of error.
//   As a parameter, it receives the pointer to the instance of
//   the PSRB_ExecSCSICmd structure, containing all required information
//   (status, pointer to the buffer, etc.)
//-----------------------------------------------------------------------------
void ASPI32Post (void *Srb)
{
    FILE *f;

    // Has our request completed successfully?
    if ((((PSRB_ExecSCSICmd) Srb)->SRB_Status) == SS_COMP)
    {
    // THIS CODE CAN BE MODIFIED AS YOU NEED
    //----------------------------------------------------------
    // Writes the sector contents into the file.
    // ATTENTION:
    // PSRB_ExecSCSICmd) Srb)->SRB_BufLen contains the buffer size
    // rather than the actual length of read data. If the number of bytes
    // returned by the device is smaller than the buffer size,
    // then its tail will contain the garbage!
    // Here we use the SRB_BufLen field
    // only because when calling the SendASPI32Command function
```

```
      // we carefully trace the buffer size to ensure
      // its correspondence to the volume of returned information.
      if (f=fopen(F_NAME, "w"))
      {
      // Writes the sector into the file
            fwrite(((PSRB_ExecSCSICmd) Srb)->SRB_BufPointer, 1,
                        ((PSRB_ExecSCSICmd) Srb)->SRB_BufLen, f);
            fclose(f);
      }
      // Beeping and "unfreezing" the flow, thus notifying that
      // read procedure has been completed
      MessageBeep(0); SetEvent(hEvent);
      //---------------------------------------------------------
      }
}

main(int argc, char **argv)
{
      void *p; int buf_len, TIME_OUT = 4000;

      if (argc<5)
      {
            fprintf(stderr, "USAGE:\n\tRAW.CD.READ.EXE adapter_id"\",
            read_id, StartSector, n_sec\n"); return 0;
      }

      // Calculating the buffer length and allocating memory for it
      // ATTENTION: proceeding in such a way, you can use blocks
      // only up to 64 K.
      // If you need larger buffers, use the GetASPI32Buffer function.
      buf_len = PACKET_LEN*atol(argv[4]); p = malloc(buf_len);

      // Creating an event
      if ((hEvent = CreateEvent(NULL,FALSE,FALSE,NULL)) == NULL) return -1;

      // Reading one or more sectors from the CD
      READ_RAW_SECTOR_FROM_CD(atol(argv[1]), atol(argv[2]), p, buf_len,
                  atol(argv[3]), atol(argv[4]), WHATS_READ);

      // Waiting until the operating is completed
      WaitForSingleObject(hEvent, TIME_OUT);

      return 0;
}
```

Having compiled and run this example, you can make sure that it runs successfully both under Windows 9x and under Windows NT without having administrative privileges! On one hand, this is all very well, but, on the other hand... the presence of the ASPI driver creates a large hole in security system, which will help malicious software do whatever it is instructed in relation to controlling your hardware. Would you like to infect MBR/boot sectors? Here you are. Or perhaps you'd like to wipe the entire hard drive clean? Nothing could be easier. Therefore, if you care about the security of your information, it's advisable to delete the ASPI32 driver from your computer (to do so, you only need to remove the ASPI.SYS file from the WINNT\System32\Drivers directory). Naturally, all of the above-mentioned information relates only to operating systems from the NT family, since, in Windows 9x, direct access to equipment can be gained even without all of this mess.

Access via the SCSI Port

As was already mentioned above (see the *"Access via SPTI"* section), you can, independent of the physical interface of the disk drive (be it SCSI or IDE), communicate directly with it via the unified SCSI interface. In other words, the driver for a specific device (CD-ROM drives, in particular) is absolutely abstracted from specific features of the bus interface implementation of that specific device. This means that even if drives working via infrared ports appear tomorrow, the CDROM.SYS driver won't know anything about it, and will control such devices via an SCSI port.

Even if there are no SCSI controllers installed on your computer, a couple of usable SCSI can be found anyway. Of course, these ports are virtual rather than physical. However, from the software point of view, they look as if they are physical. Try to use the CreateFile function to open the \\.\SCSI0: device and it will be opened successfully, thus confirming the existence of virtual SCSI ports (do not forget that the string must be terminated by a column). By sending specific IOCTL commands to SCSI ports, you can control any physical or virtual device connected to that port. In fact, there is another abstraction level between the virtual SCSI port and the physical interface bus, the level occupied by *SCSI miniport*, which, actually, abstracts the SCSI port driver from specific physical equipment (see *"Access via SCSI miniport"* for more details).

Naturally, before sending IOCTL commands to the SCSI port, it would be nice to know what equipment is connected to that port. There are numerous methods for solving this problem. These methods range from the IOCTL_SCSI_GET_INQUIRY_DATA command sent to the device (see the source code of the Windows NT DDK demo example located in the NTDDK\src\storage\class\spti directory), after which the device, along with other information, will report its name (something like PHILIPS CDRW2412A), to the *object table* viewed, which you will carry out here. Windows NT DDK contains the objdir.exe utility, which, as its name suggests, allows the contents of the device object tree object to be displayed in the form of a directory. Devices available to open using the `CreateFile` function are stored in a directory with the name `\DosDevices\`. Looking at the name, you might think that it contains the names of devices available from under MS-DOS that Windows NT must emulate to ensure backward compatibility. In reality, however, this directory is used actively by the Win32 subsystem of the Windows NT operating system. Any time the `CreateFile` function accesses a specific logical device (for example, when it tries to open the C:\MYDIR\myfile.txt file), the Win32 subsystem looks in the `\DosDevices\` directory to find out to which internal device this logical device is connected. Internal devices are visible only under Native-NT, while they are senseless for all of its subsystems other than Win32. In particular, disk C: under Native-NT has the name of `\Device\HarddiskVolume1`, while the fully qualified path to the myfile.txt file looks as follows: `\Device\HarddiskVolume1\MYDIR\myfile.txt`. However, try to feed this string to the CreateFile functions, since it probably won't understand what do you want from it.

Thus, the `\DosDevices\` directory serves as a kind of connecting link between the Win32 subsystem and the Windows NT kernel. Now, return to our problem and consider, to which native device the "SCSI" logical device is connected. Start objdir with the `\DosDevices` command-line option and redirect its output to the file (`objdir \DosDevices | MORE` as alternative). Along with lots of other information, you will find the following strings (if you don't have DDK, use the Soft-Ice debugger, where it is necessary to give the `objdir \??` command to achieve a similar result. Note the two question marks in the command line, since the `\DosDevices` directory isn't actually a directory but, rather, a symbolic link to the `\??` directory, or its shortcut).

Listing 4.15. The relationship between logical SCSI devices and native-NT devices

---

```
Scsi0:      SymbolicLink - \Device\Ide\IdePort0
Scsi1:      SymbolicLink - \Device\Ide\IdePort1
Scsi2:      SymbolicLink - \Device\Scsi\axsaki1
```

As it turns out, SCSI0: and SCSI1 devices represent nothing other than symbolic links to IDE ports with numbers 0 and 1, respectively. The `IdePort0` and `IdePort1` devices, though, are not IDE ports in a physical sense. These are virtual SCSI ports created by the ATAPI.SYS driver in the course of its initialization. The same driver creates the symbolic links `\DosDevices\SCSI0:` and `\DosDevices\SCSI1:`, as well as the shortcuts `\Device\ScsiPort0` and `\Device\ScsiPort1`, unavailable for the Win32 subsystem and intended for internal use at the driver level. Naturally, ATAPI.SYS is not limited to the creation of all of the devices listed above, but also serves them by providing higher-layer drivers with a unified interface for interacting with the installed equipment.

As concerns the SCSI2: device, it is not connected to any physical bus, and the virtual CD-ROM drive is connected to its corresponding SCSI port. This virtual drive is created by the Alcohol 120% program, or, to be more precise, by its driver — AXSAKI.SYS! Higher-level drivers (in particular, CDROM.SYS), won't suspect anything. Instead, they will work with the virtual disk as if it were a physical one. This is not surprising, since the SCSI port concept ensures the independence of higher-level drivers from specific hardware, with which they "operate." This is why NT allows such an easy implementation of various physical device emulators!

By the way, after disassembling the Alcohol 120% program, you might reveal some dirty and obscene words used as variable names or labels.

SCSI devices can be managed from the application level via the STPI interface. However, instead of the drive letter, it is necessary to specify the name of the SCSI port, to which this drive is connected. The main advantage of such a method of controlling devices lies in that you don't necessarily need administrative privileges to communicate with the drive. Normal user privileges are more than sufficient. Besides, direct operation with the SCSI port is somewhat faster than accessing the device via a long chain of higher-level drivers and the numerous filters wrapping them.

However, all attempts at passing an SRB block via the SCSI port inevitable end with an error. For example, the following code refuses to work. Why?

Listing 4.16. An example of incorrect operation with a virtual SCSI port

```
// Getting the SCSI port descriptor
hCD = CreateFile ("\\\\.\\SCSI1", GENERIC_WRITE|GENERIC_READ,
FILE_SHARE_READ|FILE_SHARE_WRITE, 0, OPEN_EXISTING, 0, 0);


// Forming the SRB block



// Sending the SRB block directly to the SCSI port
status = DeviceIoControl(hCD, IOCTL_SCSI_PASS_THROUGH_DIRECT, &srb,
                 sizeof(SCSI_PASS_THROUGH), &srb, 0, &returned, FALSE);
```

Newsletters are swarming with questions relating to this problem. Some users report that this code operates correctly, while the majority complains that it doesn't. The answer can be found in the DDK (if you read it carefully, of course). Here it is: *9.2 SCSI Port I/O Control Codes:* "If a class driver for the target type of device exists, the request must be sent to that class driver. Thus, an application can send this request directly

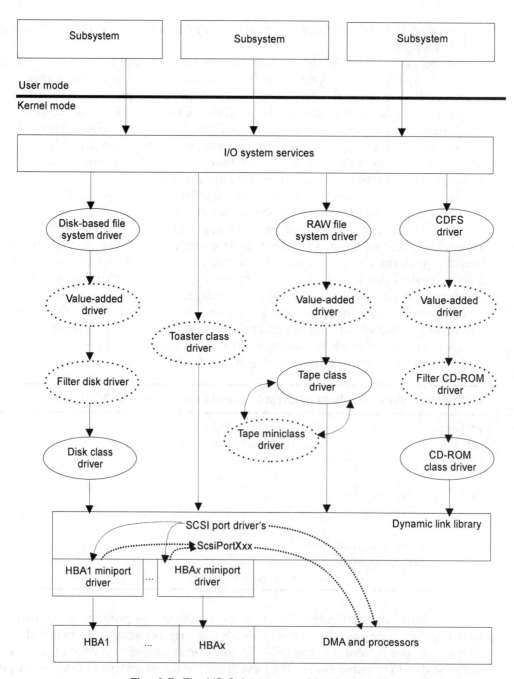

Fig. 4.5. The I/O Subsystem architecture in NT

to the system port driver for a target logical unit only if there is no class driver for the type of device connected to that LU." In less technical language, direct control over the SCSI port from the application level is possible only *for those devices that have no class driver installed.* For instance, suppose that you have connected some non-standard hardware to your computer. In this case, it is possible to control this hardware directly via the SCSI port, since this hardware has no class driver! However, CD-ROM drives, which you are discussing here, are a different matter. They always have a class driver installed and, therefore, the operating system does everything possible to prevent direct communication with such hardware via the SCSI port, since this is the only reliable way of avoiding conflicts.

Does this mean that direct access to CD-ROM drives via the SCSI port is impossible? Well, only partially. Attempts to access the SCSI port directly are actually blocked by the operating system. However, the same operating system provides you with the ability to control the device via an SCSI miniport. What is a miniport? This is exactly what you will consider now.

Accessing the Drive via SCSI Miniport

The SCSI miniport driver allows the system to abstract from the details of the physical interfaces for specific equipment. In the interest of brevity, let us simply call it the *minidriver,* although this is actually only partially true. After all, along with the minidrivers for SCSI ports, there are also drivers for video and network miniports. However, since neither of these relates to the context of our discussion in any way, there won't be any misunderstanding.

Hierarchically, the miniport driver resides between the physical (virtual) devices connected to specific interface buses of the computer (IDE/PCI/SCSI) and the SCSI port driver. The miniport driver is a system-independent driver, which, at the same time, depends on specific features of the *HBA* (*Host Bus Adapter*), i.e., the physical/virtual equipment that it serves. The miniport driver exports a range of functions of the ScsiPortXXX family, which are intended for use by higher-level drivers. Usually, it is implemented as a Dynamic Link Library (DLL), which, quite naturally, executes in ring 0 of the kernel level.

It is this driver that translates SCSI requests into commands for the device connected to it, creates virtual SCSI ports with names such as \Device\ScsiPortx, and ensures support for storage media having interfaces different from SCSI. For example, drivers such as ATAPI.SYS, serving CD-ROM drives with the ATAPI interface, and DISK.SYS, serving hard disks, are implemented in the form of miniport drivers.

Control of the miniport is carried out using special IOCTL code passed to the DeviceIoControl function and defined as IOCTL_SCSI_MINIPORT in the NTDDSCSI.H file. If you don't have a copy of NT DDK, here is its direct value: 0x4D008. Naturally, before calling on the `DeviceIoControl` function, you must first open an appropriate SCSI port using the `CreateFile` function. The code that carries out this task might appear as shown in the listing below. Pay special attention to the fact that the port name must appear as `SCSIx:`, rather than `ScsiPortx`; the name must be terminated with a colon. Otherwise, the attempt will fail.

Listing 4.17. Opening the SCSI port for controlling the miniport driver

```
h = CreateFile("\\\\.\\SCSI1:", GENERIC_READ | GENERIC_WRITE, FILE_SHARE_READ |
FILE_SHARE_WRITE, NULL,OPEN_EXISTING, 0, NULL);
```

Here, you open the first (numbered from zero) SCSI port that, as you already know, corresponds to the first IDE channel, or, to put it in other words, to the secondary IDE controller (on the author's computer, the CD-ROM drive is connected to that particular controller). To detect the drive location on an unknown computer, you can use the `IOCTL_SCSI_GET_INQUIRY_DATA IOCTL` code, which makes the miniport driver list all the equipment at its disposal, after which it only remains to correctly determine its type (for more details, see NTDDK\SRC\STORAGE\CLASS\SPTI).

However, miniport control is carried out in a different way from that used to control the SCSI port! At this level, there are no standard commands, and you have to take into account the specific features of the implementation of specific hardware. Instead of SRB requests, the minidriver accepts the `SRB_IO_CONTROL` structure defined as follows:

Listing 4.18. The purpose of the SRB_IO_CONTROL structure fields

```
typedef struct _SRB_IO_CONTROL
{
ULONG HeaderLength;     // sizeof(SRB_IO_CONTROL)
UCHAR Signature[8];     // Minidriver signature
ULONG Timeout;          // Max. waiting time for the request
                        // to be completed (in seconds)
ULONG ControlCode;      // Command code
ULONG ReturnCode;       // Here we will get the return code.
ULONG Length;           // The length of entire transmitted buffer
} SRB_IO_CONTROL, *PSRB_IO_CONTROL;
```

Well, you understand the meaning of the `HeaderLength` field, but what is the *signature*? The point is that the controlling codes of miniport drivers aren't standardized. On the contrary, they are defined by the drivers' developers. Therefore, the control codes of one driver are unlikely to fit those of another. In order to avoid conflicts, each miniport driver contains a unique signature, which it compares carefully to the one passed on by an application in the signature field of the SRB_IO_CONTROL structure. If these signatures do not match, the driver responds with the following message: SRB_STATUS_INVALID_REQUEST. Unfortunately, the interfaces of the standard minidrivers — ATAPI.SYS and DISK.SYS — are not documented. As a result, it's a difficulty for those who are unable to disassemble. With regard to the disassembler, it immediately shows that the signatures of both drivers appear as *SCSIDISK*. The signature of the Alcohol 120% minidriver appears as *Alcoholx* (the latter doesn't present any special interest to us because it doesn't correspond to standards).

It is somewhat more difficult to understand program codes. Although the specialists constantly reading MSDN and therefore, having a sound knowledge in it, might recall that "…this specification describes the API for an application to issue SMART commands to an IDE drive under Microsoft Windows 95 and Windows NT. Under Windows 95, the API is implemented in a Vendor Specific Driver (VSD), Smartvsd.vxd. SMART functionality is implemented as a 'pass-through' mechanism, whereby the application sets up the IDE registers in a structure and passes them to the driver through the DeviceIoControl API."

Well, one of the drivers facilitates the manipulation of the registers of the IDE controller as needed, which means that it provides low-level access to the disk — very well. The interface with the SMART driver is well documented (see *"MSDN →Specifications a Platforms → SMART IOCTL API Specification"*). But the silence in relation to Windows NT appears to be somewhat irritating. Clearly, there are no VxDs in Windows NT. However, it is clearly stated in this document that SMART API is implemented there. If you use a few gray cells and a little bit of intuition work, you might be able to guess that SMART support in NT is through standard means! The only question that remains is as follows: How and by what means? Neither SDK nor DDK contain any information on this topic. However, careful study of the header files included with NT DDK can help. Look at what you can find in the scsi.h file.

Listing 4.19. The SMART control commands in Windows NT, which can be passed to the miniport driver via the ControlCode field of the SRB_IO_CONTROL structure

---

```
//
// SMART support in atapi
//
#define IOCTL_SCSI_MINIPORT_SMART_VERSION          ((FILE_DEVICE_SCSI<<16) + 0x0500)
#define IOCTL_SCSI_MINIPORT_IDENTIFY               ((FILE_DEVICE_SCSI<<16) + 0x0501)
#define IOCTL_SCSI_MINIPORT_READ_SMART_ATTRIBS     ((FILE_DEVICE_SCSI<<16) + 0x0502)
#define IOCTL_SCSI_MINIPORT_READ_SMART_THRESHOLDS  ((FILE_DEVICE_SCSI<<16) + 0x0503)
#define IOCTL_SCSI_MINIPORT_ENABLE_SMART           ((FILE_DEVICE_SCSI<<16) + 0x0504)
```

```
#define IOCTL_SCSI_MINIPORT_DISABLE_SMART             ((FILE_DEVICE_SCSI<<16) + 0x0505)
#define IOCTL_SCSI_MINIPORT_RETURN_STATUS             ((FILE_DEVICE_SCSI<<16) + 0x0506)
#define IOCTL_SCSI_MINIPORT_ENABLE_DISABLE_AUTOSAVE((FILE_DEVICE_SCSI<<16) + 0x0507)
#define IOCTL_SCSI_MINIPORT_SAVE_ATTRIBUTE_VALUES   ((FILE_DEVICE_SCSI<<16) + 0x0508)
#define IOCTL_SCSI_MINIPORT_EXECUTE_OFFLINE_DIAGS    ((FILE_DEVICE_SCSI<<16) + 0x0509)
#define IOCTL_SCSI_MINIPORT_ENABLE_DISABLE_AUTO_OFFLINE (FILE_DEVICE_SCSI<<16) + 0x050a
```

You might suspect that, in Windows, NT SMART isn't implemented in the miniport driver, and disassembling of ATAPI.SYS actually confirms this. So "why include IOCTL commands in the header file without documenting them?" would be a fair question for Microsoft's technical writers. And, according to the license agreement, disassembling any OS components is prohibited. Instead of complaining, let's read the "*SMART IOCTL API Specification*" once again. In this document, you discover that in order to control the miniport driver under Windows NT, it is necessary to pass the code of one of the above-listed commands to the ControlCode field of the SRB_IO_CONTROL structure. For example, IOCTL_SCSI_MINIPORT_IDENTIFY.

Immediately following the end of the SRB_IO_CONTROL structure, there must be SENDCMDINPARAMS, defined as shown in Listing 4.20.

Listing 4.20. The SENDCMDINPARAMS structure providing direct access to IDE registers

```
typedef struct _SENDCMDINPARAMS
{
DWORD     cBufferSize;          // Buffer size in bytes or zero
IDEREGS   irDriveRegs;          // The structure containing
                               // the values of IDE registers
BYTE      bDriveNumber;         // Physical disk number,
                               // starting from zero
BYTE      bReserved[3];         // Reserved
DWORD     dwReserved[4];        // Reserved
BYTE      bBuffer[1];           // The starting point of the input buffer
} SENDCMDINPARAMS, *PSENDCMDINPARAMS, *LPSENDCMDINPARAMS;
```

This means that the input buffer of the DeviceIoControl function must look as follows:

SRB_IO_CONTROL	SENDCMDINPARAMS	DBuffer (if available)

Fig. 4.6. Structure of the input buffer of the DeviceIoControl function for controlling the miniport driver under Windows 9x/NT

The first structural element, cBufferSize, containing the bBufferSize, is obvious and, therefore, of little interest. As for the IDREGS structure, it represents a virtual goldmine of information. Just look for yourself:

Listing 4.21. The IDEREGS structure providing low-level access to IDE registers

```
typedef struct _IDEREGS
{
BYTE bFeaturesReg;          // IDE Features register
BYTE bSectorCountReg;       // IDE SectorCount register
BYTE bSectorNumberReg;      // IDE SectorNumber register
BYTE bCylLowReg;            // IDE CylLowReg register
BYTE bCylHighReg;           // IDE CylHighReg register
BYTE bDriveHeadReg;         // IDE DriveHead register
BYTE bCommandReg;           // Command register
BYTE bReserved;             // Reserved
} IDEREGS, *PIDEREGS, *LPIDEREGS;
```

Anyone who has ever read the ATA/ATAPI specification and programmed devices with the IDE interface should immediately recognize the well-known registers — Command, Drive/Head, Cylinder High, Cylinder Low, Sector Number, Sector Count, and Features. That they are listed in reverse order in the IDEREGS structure is only a minor implementation detail. The main fact is that using this structure, it is possible to do whatever you like with the drive, implementing all of the tricks of which it is capable. It is hard to believe that the security subsystem contains such a security loophole. This is aggravated further by the fact that administrative privileges are not required for controlling the miniport. Jumping with joy, let's fill in the remaining fields of the SENDCMDINPARAMS structure, namely: bDriveNumber — the physical number of the drive, numbering from zero, and the buffer for passing the data.

IMPORTANT

This is a buffer itself, rather than a pointer to a buffer.
However, for the moment, you are not going to write any data to the disc, are we? Well, then let's leave this field blank.

Alas! An attempt to "feed" the drive with a command other than those from the SMART family, will fail. After all, the miniport driver isn't as stupid as you supposed. It checks the contents of the IDEREGS structure before passing it to the IDE drive. The only exception has been made for the drive identification command — 0xEC, about which Microsoft has openly informed us: "There are three IDE commands supported in this driver, ID (0xEC), ATAPI ID (0xA1), and SMART (0xB0). The 'subcommands' of the SMART commands (featuring register values) are limited to the currently defined values (0xD0 through 0xD6, 0xD8 through 0xEF). SMART subcommand 0xD7, write threshold value, is not allowed. Any other command or SMART subcommand will result in an error being returned from the driver. Any SMART command that is not currently implemented on the target drive will result in an ABORT error from the IDE interface".

At first glance, it seems that you have failed altogether. However, this is not so the case! After all, this check can be disabled. Let us disassemble the ATAPI.SYS driver and see what can be done. The following fragment is responsible for checking IDE commands passed to the drive in order to determine whether they belong to the allowed list.

Listing 4.22. A fragment of the disassembled listing of the ATAPI.SYS driver

```
.text:00013714 aScsidisk       db 'SCSIDISK',0   ; DATA XREF: SCSI_MINIPORT + CC↓o
; here is our signature              ^^^^^^^^
;
.text:000137DF
.text:000137DF loc_137DF:                        ; CODE XREF: SCSI_MINIPORT + B5↑j
.text:000137DF mov    [edi], ebx
.text:000137E1 mov    eax, [ebx+18h]
.text:000137E4 push   8                          ; The length of the string
                                                 ; to be compared
.text:000137E6 add    eax, 4
.text:000137E9 push   offset aScsidisk           ; Pattern signature
.text:000137EE push   eax                        ; The signature passed
                                                 ; by an application
.text:000137EF call   ds:RtlCompareMemory        ; Do signatures match?
.text:000137F5 cmp    eax, 8
.text:000137F8 jnz    oc_13898                    ; No match, exiting
.text:000137F8
.text:000137FE mov    esi,[ebx+18h]
.text:00013801 mov    eax,[esi+10h]              ; Getting Control code
.text:00013804 cmp    eax, 1B0500h               ; IOCTL_SCSI_MINIPORT_SMART_VERSION
.text:00013809 jz     loc_1389F                   ;  Processing ...SMART_VERSION
.text:0001380F mov    ecx, 1B0501h               ; IOCTL_SCSI_MINIPORT_IDENTIFY
.text:00013814 cmp    eax, ecx                   ;
.text:00013816 jz     short loc_1382D            ;    Processing ...IDENTIFY
.text:00013818 jbe    short loc_13898            ; IF ControlCode < IDENTIFY THEN go to exit
.text:0001381A cmp    eax, 1B050Ah               ; IOCTL_SCSI_MINIPORT_ENABLE_DISABLE..
.text:0001381F ja     short loc_13898            ; IF ControlCode > ENABLE_DISAB.. go to exit
.text:00013821 push   ebx                        ;
```

```
.text:00013822    push    edi               ;
.text:00013823    call    sub_12412         ; processing other SMART commands
.text:00013828    jmp     loc_1393E
.text:0001382D    ; -------------------------------------------------------------


.text:00012412    sub_12412 proc near       ; CODE XREF: SCSI_MINIPORT+106↓p
...
.text:00012433    cmp     [ebp+var_1E], 0B0h ; SMART-command
.text:00012437    jnz     loc_12633         ; If this isn't SMART, go to exit
.text:00012437                              ; Checks start from here

.text:0001243D    movzx   eax, [ebp+var_1C]
.text:00012441    mov     eax, [ebx+eax*4+0B0h] ; Loading Drive/Head register into EAX
.text:00012448    test    al, 1             ; Comparing the least significant bit
                                            ; of AL to one
.text:0001244A    jz      loc_1262F         ; If the least significant bit
                                            ;is equal to zero, then exit
.text:00012450    test    al, 2             ; Comparing the next bit of AL to one
.text:00012452    jnz     loc_1262F         ; If it isn't equal to zero, exit
.text:00012458    mov     al, [ebp+var_24]  ; Loading the Feature register to AL
.text:0001245B    cmp     al, 0D0h          ; Is this SMART READ DATA?
.text:0001245D    mov     [ebx+0CCh], al
.text:00012463    jz      loc_12523         ; If yes, start processing
.text:00012469    cmp     al, 0D1h          ; Is it obsolete?
.text:0001246B    jz      loc_12523         ; If yes, start its processesing
.text:00012471    cmp     al, 0D8h          ; Is this SMART ENABLE OPERATIONS?
.text:00012473    jz      short loc_12491   ; If yes, start its processing
.text:00012475    cmp     al, 0D9h          ; Is this SMART DISABLE OPERATIONS?
.text:00012477    jz      short loc_12491   ; If yes, start its processing
.text:00012479    cmp     al, 0DA           ; Is this SMART RETURN STATUS?
.text:0001247B    jz      short loc_12491   ; If yes, start its processing
.text:0001247D    cmp     al, 0D2h          ; Is this SMART ENBL/DSBL ATTRIBUTE AUTOSAVE?
.text:0001247D    cmp     al, 0D2h          ; It this really the case?!
.text:0001247F    jz      short loc_12491   ; If yes, start its processing
.text:00012481    cmp     al, 0D4h          ; Is this SMART EXECUTE OFF-LINE IMMEDIATE?
.text:00012403    jz      short loc_12401   ; If yes, start its processing
.text:00012485    cmp     al, 0D3h          ; Is this SMART SAVE ATTRIBUTE VALUES?
.text:00012487    jz      short loc_12491   ; If yes, start its processing
.text:00012489    cmp     al, 0DBh          ; Is this SMART ENABLE OPERATIONS?
.text:0001248B    jnz     loc_12633         ; If no, then exit
.text:00012491
.text:00012491    loc_12491:                ; CODE XREF: sub_12412+61↑j
.text:00012491          ; Command processing starts from here
```

```
.text:00012491                                           ;
.text:00012491      push    1
.text:00012493      pop     eax
.text:00012494      cmp     ds:0FFDF02C0h, eax
.text:0001249A      jnz     short loc_124A5
.text:0001249C      cmp     dword ptr [ebx+4], 640h
.text:000124A3      jz      short loc_124A7
.text:000124A5

.text:000124A5      loc_124A5:                            ; CODE XREF: sub_12412+88↑j
.text:000124A5      xor     eax, eax
.text:000124A7

.text:000124A7      loc_124A7:                            ; CODE XREF: sub_12412+91↑j
.text:000124A7                                            ; Writing to the port starts from here!
.text:000124A7                                            ;
.text:000124A7      mov     esi, ds:WRITE_PORT_UCHAR
.text:000124AD      test    al, al
.text:000124AF      jz      short loc_124C0
.text:000124B1      mov     al, [ebp+var_1C]
.text:000124B4      shr     al, 1
.text:000124B6      and     al, 1
.text:000124B8      push    eax
.text:000124B9      push    432h
.text:000124BE      call    esi                      ; WRITE_PORT_UCHAR
```

Thus, in order to allow the driver to send any commands to the IDE drive, you must change the conditional jump located by the address 0x12437 (in the listing, it is highlighted and surrounded by a rectangle) for the unconditional jump passing the control to the write command by the address 0x12491. After modifying the driver, don't forget to correct its checksum, which can be carried out, for example, using the EDITBIN.EXE utility supplied with Microsoft Visual Studio. Otherwise, Windows NT will refuse to load the hacked driver.

Naturally, I recommend that you carry out such an operation only with your own driver, because others are unlikely to be pleased by the newly-created security hole. Moreover, distribution of the modified version of ATAPI.SYS violates the licensing agreement and Microsoft's copyright. Draw your own conclusions. Nevertheless, your application can patch ATAPI.SYS on your own computer and on the computers of your users (naturally, you must inform them of the things that you are going to do, ask their permission or, at least, mention this aspect in companion documentation).

This method of interacting with the drive mustn't be neglected altogether, since it significantly complicates the cracking of protection mechanisms based on it. After all, not every hacker is well acquainted with specific features related to controlling the miniport. Therefore, with good probability, the vast majority will make fools of themselves.

The example program provided below demonstrates the passing of ATA commands to the IDE drive via the miniport driver.

Listing 4.23. [/etc/SCSI.mini-port.c] A sample program demonstrating the technique of interacting with the SCSI miniport

---

```
int ATAPI_MINIPORT_DEMO(void)
{
        int a;
        HANDLE  h;
        Char*buf;
        Int LU = 0;
        DWORD    returned;
        Int controller;
        CharScsiPort [16];
        Charbuffer [sizeof (SRB_IO_CONTROL) + SENDIDLENGTH];

        SRB_IO_CONTROL  *p = (SRB_IO_CONTROL  *) buffer;
        SENDCMDINPARAMS *pin = (SENDCMDINPARAMS *) (buffer + sizeof (SRB_IO_CONTROL));

        // Testing both IDE controllers in a loop
        for (controller = 0; controller < 2; controller++)
        {
                // Forming ScsiPort for each controller
                sprintf (ScsiPort, "\\\\.\\Scsi%d:", controller);

                // Opening the required ScsiPort
                h = CreateFile (ScsiPort,GENERIC_READ | GENERIC_WRITE,
                             FILE_SHARE_READ | FILE_SHARE_WRITE, NULL, OPEN_EXISTING, 0, 0);

                if (h == INVALID_HANDLE_VALUE) { // EXIT IF ERROR
                        printf("-ERR:Unable to open ScsiPort%d\n", controller);
                        return -1;
                }

                // Testing both devices on each of the IDE controllers
                for (LU = 0; LU < 2; LU++)
                {
                        // Initializing the input buffer
                        memset (buffer, 0, sizeof (buffer));

                        // PREPARING THE SRB_IO_CONTROL STRUCTURE,
```

```
                          // intended for the miniport driver
                          p -> Timeout = 10000;                        // Wait
                          p -> Length = SENDIDLENGTH;                  // Max. length
                          p -> HeaderLength = sizeof (SRB_IO_CONTROL); // Header size
                          p -> ControlCode = IOCTL_SCSI_MINIPORT_IDENTIFY;
                          // ^^^ code of the command sent to the driver

                          // Signature for ATAPI.SYS - "SCSIDISK"
                          strncpy ((char *) p -> Signature, "SCSIDISK", 8);

                          // PREPARING THE SENDCMDINPARAMS STRUCTURE,
                          // containing ATA commands passed to the IDE drive
                          pin -> bDriveNumber = LU;
                          pin -> irDriveRegs.bCommandReg = IDE_ATA_IDENTIFY;

                          // SENDING THE REQUEST TO THE MINIPORT DRIVER
                          if (DeviceIoControl (h, IOCTL_SCSI_MINIPORT, buffer,
                          sizeof (SRB_IO_CONTROL) + sizeof (SENDCMDINPARAMS) - 1,
                                  buffer, sizeof (SRB_IO_CONTROL) + SENDIDLENGTH,
                                  &returned, 0))
                                  if (buffer[98]!=0)
                                          {// In response, get the string with
                                          // the identifier of
                                          // the IDE- drive, which we display on
                                          // the screen.
                                          for (a = 98; a < 136; a+=2 )
                                          printf("%c%c", buffer[a+1], buffer[a]);
                                          printf("\n");
                                          }
                  }
          CloseHandle (h); // Close the descriptor of the given SCSI miniport.
  }
      return 0;
}
```

Communication via Input/Output Ports

The Windows NT operating system carefully guards Input/Output ports from application's attempts at accessing them. This measure was implemented due to the requirements of the chosen security policy. The freedom of applications is intentionally limited in such a way as to prevent any attempts at damaging the system or unauthorized access to confidential data. The right to access the hardware directly is provided only to drivers and DLLs executing in the kernel mode (see *"Access via SCSI Miniport"*).

To paraphrase Benjamin Franklin, a nation that has exchanged essential liberties for a little temporary safety deserves neither of these things. Oh yes — as if it were impossible to hang the system via SPTI/ASPI! This is even more true when you recall that administrative privileges aren't required for this. In fact, security policy and discretionary access are useless, because ASPI provides access to the disk at the sector level without checking if this operation is legitimate. For example, nothing could be simpler than infecting the boot sector with a boot virus. At the same time, the lack of access to Input/Output ports significantly complicates the task of managing the equipment, not to mention the development of reliable and strong protection mechanisms.

Operating systems of the Windows 9x family behave more democratically, but this level of indulgence is applicable only to MS-DOS programs, while Win32 applications are deprived of direct access to the ports.

Nevertheless, it is still possible to control the hardware from the application level. There are at least two ways of solving this problem: *a) The development of the pass-through driver implementing more or less transparent interface for communicating with ports using the IOCTL mechanism* and *b) Modifying the I/O Permission Map (IOPM)* in such a way as to have port access migrate to the list of non-privileged operations that can be carried out from the application level. Both methods will be covered in detail. Let us start with the interface driver.

Windows NT DDK includes the rather interesting PORTIO demo driver, which creates a virtual device and implements a special IOCTL interface. Using this interface, applications are able to manipulate the ports of this device in any way they like. The source code of this demo driver with the required minimum of comments can be found in the following directory: \NTDDK\src\general\portio. Clearly, a virtual device is not exactly what you need, since the range of its Input/Output ports can't overlap with the ports belonging to other devices, as the system would detect an error and warn the user of the hardware conflict in Device Manager. Although such a conflict doesn't influence system usability, users won't really benefit from viewing conflicting devices labeled with the "exclamation mark" icon.

In fact, nothing prevents the kernel-mode driver from accessing any port. To read the entire range of ports, it is enough to delete the following lines from the source code of the genport.c program.

Listing 4.24. Checking whether addresses of accessed ports belong to the range of virtual device ports created by the driver

---

```
if (nPort >= pLDI->PortCount ||
        (nPort + DataBufferSize) > pLDI->PortCount ||
            (((ULONG_PTR)pLDI->PortBase + nPort) & (DataBufferSize - 1)) != 0)
{
        return STATUS_ACCESS_VIOLATION;    // Illegal port number
}
```

It is necessary to pay attention to the fact that the driver expects to receive a relative port address rather than an absolute one. A relative port address is counted from the base port address specified when adding a virtual device to the system. For instance, consider the following listing:

Listing 4.25. Calculating the actual port address via the base address

---

```
case IOCTL_GPD_READ_PORT_UCHAR:
*(PUCHAR)pIOBuffer=READ_PORT_UCHAR((PUCHAR)((ULONG_PTR)pLDI->PortBase + nPort));
break;
```

Obviously, the text highlighted in bold must be deleted. In this case, the driver will be able to operate with absolute ports rather than with the relative ones. Consequently, this will allow us to access any port in the system! If you port the modified driver to Windows 9x, our applications will run in both operating systems and will depend only on the hardware. On the other hand, anyone who wants to control these ports must understand clearly for what purpose and what difficulties this might generate.

Naturally, since the possibility of uncontrolled access to all existing Input/Output ports significantly weakens the operating system, which is vulnerable even without it, it would be wise to introduce some additional checks and limitations in the driver. For example, it would be useful to deny direct access to anything that does not represent a CD-ROM drive. Otherwise, in the event that your program becomes popular and widely used, crowds of vandals will rush to write malicious code, such as Trojans. Note that the destructive power of these tools would be practically unlimited, and it would be very difficult to bring the situation under control. On the other hand, during ASPI's existence, no attempts at using it for destructive purposes have been reported, although the possibility still exists.

Another drawback in the suggested method of controlling devices is its catastrophically low performance. The calls to the DeviceIoControl split into thousands of machine commands (!), because of which the request-processing time becomes too long, while measurements of the physical characteristics of the spiral track (if you actually need to measure these characteristics) becomes imprecise. Furthermore, the DeviceIoControl function is too bulky and ungraceful. The most unpleasant thing is that it is very easy to set a Break Point to this function. Therefore, the fate of such protection is a foregone conclusion. In the days of MS-DOS, when controlling equipment was carried out using the IN and OUT machine commands, it was much more difficult to locate the protection code in the program body. However, controlling devices using these commands was considerably easier, and such communications were characterized by significantly higher performance.

It is assumed that under Windows NT direct access to the ports is possible only at the kernel level, while applications must access the ports via the high-level interface provided by a driver. Although this interface can be completely transparent (nothing is easier for the driver than to intercept the exception thrown in the course of an attempt at reading or writing to the port from the application level, and do it on its own), it is still not quite what you need...

Actually, the IN/OUT commands can also be executed at the application level. However, to achieve this, you'll need to use undocumented features of the operating system, as well as documented but little known features of the protected mode implementation in Intel 80386+ processors. Let us start our discussion with processors. Open the *"Instruction Set Reference"* and view how the OUT machine command is implemented. Among other useful information, we'll find its pseudo-code, which appears approximately as follows:

Listing 4.26. Pseudo-code of the OUT instruction

```
if ((PE == 1) && ((CPL > IOPL) || (VM == 1)))
{
        /* Protected mode with CPL > IOPL or virtual-8086 mode */
        if (Any I/O Permission Bit for I/O port being accessed == 1)
            #GP(0);          /* I/O operation is not allowed */
        else
            DEST ← SRC;   /* Writes to the selected I/O port */
}
        else
{
        /* Real Mode or Protected Mode with CPL <= IOPL */
        DEST ← SRC;     /* Writes to the selected I/O port */
}
```

Attention! Having detected that the privileges of the current level are insufficient for the execution of this machine instruction, the processor is in hurry to throw out the General Protection Fault exception. On the contrary, it gives this instruction another chance by carrying out the check of the state of the *I/O permission bitmap*. If the memory bit corresponding to the current port is not set to 1, the output to this port is carried out in spite of any prohibitions from CPL!

Thus, in order to have access to ports from the application level, it is sufficient to correct the I/O permission bitmap, after which the Windows NT security subsystem will stop interfering with our work, since the control of access to the ports is carried out at the hardware level, rather than at the software level. Consequently, if the processor stops throwing out exceptions, the operating system will never know what's happening!

The main problem is that the vast majority of the authors of the books on assembler never mention the I/O permission bitmap. Programmers that know about its existence are few. These are mainly individuals who prefer original documentation to poor translations and retellings.

From the *"Architecture Software Developer's Manual Volume 1: Basic Architecture"*, you know that the I/O permission bitmap is located in the *TSS* (*Task State Segment*). To be more precise, its actual offset from the TSS starting point is defined by the 32-bit field located in the bytes 0x66 and 0x67 of the Task State Segment. The zero bit of this map is responsible for the zero port, the first bit controls the first port, and so on, up to the most significant bit — bit 0x2000, which controls port 65535. The bitmap is terminated by the so-called terminator byte, which has the value of 0xFF. That's all. The ports with their bits set to zero are available from the application level without any limitations. Naturally, the I/O permission bitmap is available only to drivers, and not to applications. Therefore, it is impossible to proceed any further without writing a custom driver. However, this driver will operate only at the stage of its initialization, and all subsequent I/O operations will be carried out directly, even if you unload the driver from the memory.

Now for the bad news. In Windows NT, the offset of the I/O permission bitmap by default is located beyond the limits of the Task State Segment. Therefore, modifying the I/O bitmap is not an easy task, since it is simply missing (there is no such thing). The processor reacts to this situation adequately. However, it denies access to the Input/Output ports from the application level.

The Input/Output map actually does exist in the TSS, but it is intentionally disabled by the system in order to prevent applications from behaving in a way that is not allowed. The only exception is made for high-performance graphic libraries that access Input/Output ports from the application mode. As can be easily guessed, such a trick provides Microsoft with a significant advantage over its competitors, since they are forced to control the ports either from the kernel level or via the interface provided by the video driver. Naturally, both methods are outclassed by direct access to the ports.

However, attempts to correct the pointer to the Input/Output map don't produce the desired result, since Windows NT stores the copy of this value in the process context. Therefore, the pointer to the previous copy of the I/O map is restored automatically after context switching. On one hand, this is good, because every process can have its own I/O map. On the other, Microsoft's documentation doesn't contain any tips on using this map.

It is possible, however, to use the trick of increasing the TSS size in such a way as to make the I/O map address, which earlier pointed to somewhere beyond the TSS limits, reside in the valid and available memory area. Since there are only 0xF55 bytes in the tail of the last page occupied by TSS, the maximum size of the map that you can create in this gap spans only 31,392 I/O ports. To be honest, other ports are unlikely to be necessary. Therefore, this limitation doesn't cause any serious inconvenience.

Nevertheless, there are more elegant methods for solving this problem. The efforts of Dale Roberts have resulted in the discovery of three completely undocumented functions: `Ke386SetIoAccessMap()`, `Ke386QueryIoAccessMap()`, and `Ke386IoSetAccessProcess()`. As follows from their names, these functions ensure a legal method of controlling the I/O map. When I say that these functions are absolutely undocumented, I mean that even header files from the DDK do not contain the prototypes for these functions. As a matter of fact, DDK header files list a wide range of undocumented functions. Still, the NTOSKRNL library exports them, and these functions are easily available from the driver level.

More detailed information on this topic can be read in the article written by their discoverer — Dale Roberts. Here, you will cover them only briefly. So, the `Ke386SetIoAccessMap` function takes two arguments: a `DWORD`, which, being set to one, makes the function copy the I/O map to the pointer, which is passed to it with the second argument. The `Ke386QueryIoAccessMap` function accepts the same arguments, but carries out an inverse operation. Namely, it retrieves the current I/O map from the TSS and copies it to the specified buffer. Finally, the `Ke386IoSetAccessProcess` function accepts the pointer passed to it with its second argument and pointing to the structure of the process received by means of calling on the `GetCurrentProcess()` documented function. The first argument plays the same role as the first argument of the previous two functions. A zero value moves the pointer to the I/O map outside the limits of the TSS, thus denying access to the ports from the application level, while a value of 1 activates the I/O map passed earlier.

The example provided in Listing 4.27 demonstrates the use of these functions.

Listing 4.27. [/etc/GIVEIO.c] A demo example of the drive opening direct access to the I/O ports from the application level

---

```
/*----------------------------------------------------------------------
 *
 *      This driver allows the execution of the
 *   IN/OUT machine command from the application level
 *
 *   =================================================
 *
 *   ATTENTION: I, Chris Kaspersky, have not been involved in the creation of and assume
 * no responsibility for this program!
 *   -----------------------------------------------------------------
 *
 *   GIVEIO.SYS: by Dale Roberts
 *   COMPILING: Use the DDK BUILD tools
 *   GOAL: Providing access to direct I/O from the user mode
 ----------------------------------------------------------------------*/

#include <ntddk.h>
```

```
/* The name of our device driver */
#define DEVICE_NAME_STRING L"giveio"


// The IOPM structure is simply an array of bytes having the size of 0x2000
// and containing 8K * 8 bits == 64K bits IOPM, which cover the entire 64 K
// address space of x86 processors.
// Each bit set to 0 provides access to the appropriate port
// to the user-mode process; each bit set to 1 denies access via the respective
// port.
#define IOPM_SIZE 0x2000
typedef UCHAR IOPM[IOPM_SIZE];


// The array of zeroes that is copied to the actual IOPM in the TSS by means
// of calling the dsKe386SetIoAccessMap() function
// Required memory is allocated in the course of driver loading
IOPM *IOPM_local = 0;


// These are two undocumented functions that we use in order,
// to provide I/O access to the calling process
// * Ke386IoSetAccessMap()      - copies the passed I/O map to the TSS
// * Ke386IoSetAccessProcess() - changes the pointer to the IOPM offset,
//                               after which the I/O map just copied
//                               begins to be used
void Ke386SetIoAccessMap(int, IOPM *);
void Ke386QueryIoAccessMap(int, IOPM *);
void Ke386IoSetAccessProcess(PEPROCESS, int);


// RELEASE ALL EARLIER ALLOCATED OBJECTS
VOID GiveioUnload(IN PDRIVER_OBJECT DriverObject)
{
UNICODE_STRING uniDOSString;
WCHAR DOSNameBuffer[] = L"\\DosDevices\\" DEVICE_NAME_STRING;

if(IOPM_local) MmFreeNonCachedMemory(IOPM_local, sizeof(IOPM));
RtlInitUnicodeString(&uniDOSString, DOSNameBuffer);
IoDeleteSymbolicLink (&uniDOSString);
IoDeleteDevice(DriverObject->DeviceObject);
}


//---------------------------------------------------------------------------
//   Setting IOPM of the calling process in such a way as to
//   provide it with full access to I/O ports. The IOPM_local[] array
```

```
//   contains zeroes, consequently, IOPM will be reset to zero.
//   If OnFlag == 1, the process is provided access to I/O;
//   If this flag is set to 0, access is denied.
//-----------------------------------------------------------------------------
VOID SetIOPermissionMap(int OnFlag)
{
Ke386IoSetAccessProcess(PsGetCurrentProcess(), OnFlag);
Ke386SetIoAccessMap(1, IOPM_local);
}


void GiveIO(void)
{
SetIOPermissionMap(1);
}


//-----------------------------------------------------------------------------
//   The handler for processing user-mode call to CreateProcess().
//   This function is introduced into the function call table using
//   DriverEntry(). When user-mode application calls CreateFile(),
//   this function gets control in the context of the calling application,
//   but with CPL (current privilege level of the processor) set to 0.
//   This allows for the carrying out of operations possible only in kernel mode.
//   GiveIO is called for providing the calling process with access to I/O.
//   All that the user-mode application needing access to I/O must do,
//   is open this device using CreateFile().
//   No other actions are needed.
//-----------------------------------------------------------------------------
NTSTATUS GiveioCreateDispatch(IN PDEVICE_OBJECT DeviceObject,IN PIRP Irp)
{
GiveIO(); // give the calling process I/O access

Irp->IoStatus.Information = 0;
Irp->IoStatus.Status = STATUS_SUCCESS;

IoCompleteRequest(Irp, IO_NO_INCREMENT); return STATUS_SUCCESS;
}


//-----------------------------------------------------------------------------
//   The driver entry procedure. This procedure is called only once after
//   loading the driver into the memory. It allocates the resources required
//   for driver operation. In our case, it allocates the memory for the IOPM array
//   and creates the device that can be opened by the user-mode application.
//   This function also creates a symbolic link to the device driver.
```

```
//   This allows the user-mode application to access our driver
//   using the \\.\giveio notation.
//-------------------------------------------------------------------------
NTSTATUS DriverEntry(IN PDRIVER_OBJECT DriverObject, IN PUNICODE_STRING RegistryPath)
{
NTSTATUS       status;
PDEVICE_OBJECT    deviceObject;
UNICODE_STRING    uniNameString, uniDOSString;

WCHAR NameBuffer[] = L"\\Device\\" DEVICE_NAME_STRING;
WCHAR DOSNameBuffer[] = L"\\DosDevices\\" DEVICE_NAME_STRING;

// Allocating the buffer for local IOPM and setting it to zero
IOPM_local = MmAllocateNonCachedMemory(sizeof(IOPM));
if(IOPM_local == 0) return STATUS_INSUFFICIENT_RESOURCES;
RtlZeroMemory(IOPM_local, sizeof(IOPM));

// Initializing the device driver and device object
RtlInitUnicodeString(&uniNameString, NameBuffer);
RtlInitUnicodeString(&uniDOSString, DOSNameBuffer);
status = IoCreateDevice(DriverObject, 0, &uniNameString, FILE_DEVICE_UNKNOWN,
0, FALSE, &deviceObject);
if(!NT_SUCCESS(status)) return status;

status = IoCreateSymbolicLink (&uniDOSString, &uniNameString);
if (!NT_SUCCESS(status)) return status;

// Initializing driver entry points in the driver object
// All that we need are Create and Unload operations
DriverObject->MajorFunction[IRP_MJ_CREATE] = GiveioCreateDispatch;
DriverObject->DriverUnload = GiveioUnload;

                        return STATUS_SUCCESS;
}
```

Listing 4.28. [/etc/GIVEIO.demo.c] An example of input/output to the port from the application level

```
/*-------------------------------------------------------------------------
 *
 *       Demonstration of the in/out call at the application level
 *    (ATTENTION: The GIVEIO.SYS driver must be previously loaded.)
 *    ===========================================================
```

```
*
*    ATTENTION: I, Chris Kaspersky, have not been involved in the creation of and assume
*    no responsibility for this program!
* --------------------------------------------------------------------------------
*
* GIVEIO.TST: by Dale Roberts
* GOAL: Testing the GIVEIO driver by carrying out some I/O operation
*    (for example, accessing the internal PC speaker)
--------------------------------------------------------------------------------*/
#include <stdio.h>
#include <windows.h>
#include <math.h>
#include <conio.h>

typedef struct {
short int pitch;
short int duration;
} NOTE;

// NOTES TABLE
NOTE notes[] = {{14, 500}, {16, 500}, {12, 500}, {0, 500}, {7, 1000}};

// SETTING THE SPEAKER FREQUENCY IN HZ
// THE SPEAKER IS CONTROLLED BY THE INTEL 8253/8254 TIMER WITH 0X40-0X43 I/O PORTS
void setfreq(int hz)
{
hz = 1193180 / hz;    // Speaker base frequency 1.19MHz
_outp(0x43, 0xb6);    // Choosing timer 2, write operation, mode 3
_outp(0x42, hz);      // Setting frequency divider
_outp(0x42, hz >> 8);    // Most significant bit of the divider
}


//--------------------------------------------------------------------------------
//   Note that duration is specified in fractions of the 400 Hz frequency, the number 12
//   specifies the scale. The speaker is controlled via port 0x61. Setting two
//   least significant bits allows channel 2 of the 8253/8254 timer
//   and activates the speaker.
//--------------------------------------------------------------------------------
void playnote(NOTE note)
{
_outp(0x61, _inp(0x61) | 0x03);       // Activating the speaker
setfreq((int)(400 * pow(2, note.pitch / 12.0))); Sleep(note.duration);
_outp(0x61, _inp(0x61) & ~0x03);      // Deactivating the speaker
```

```
}

//----------------------------------------------------------------------------
//   Opening and closing the GIVEIO device, which gives us direct access to I/O;
//   then trying to play music
//----------------------------------------------------------------------------
int main()
{
int      i;
HANDLE        h;

h = CreateFile("\\\\.\\giveio", GENERIC_READ, 0, NULL, OPEN_EXISTING,
FILE_ATTRIBUTE_NORMAL, NULL);
if(h == INVALID_HANDLE_VALUE)
{
printf("Couldn't access giveio device\n"); return -1;
}
CloseHandle(h);

for(i = 0; i < sizeof(notes)/sizeof(int); ++i) playnote(notes[i]);

                              return 0;

}
```

Now let us discuss how this method of accessing I/O ports can be used for the benefit of protection mechanisms. Suppose that our protection is based on the presence of a physical defect of the CD surface. In this case, all you need to do is to make reading this sector remain as unnoticeable as possible: if this sector is actually is unreadable, then you are dealing with an original disc. Otherwise, this disc is an illegal copy. Direct control over I/O ports will not be picked up with close to 100 percent probability. This is true even if you are dealing with experienced hackers. They are simply unlikely to guess such a ruse. The only thing that you should care about is preventing them from detecting the protection code by cross-references left by the error message that is displayed on the screen in the event that the disc in question is considered to be illegal.

Nevertheless, qualified hackers won't swallow this kind of bait. With a malicious grin, they will just set a breakpoint to the Input/Output operations to the ports 0x1F7/0x177 (for Primary and Secondary drives, respectively). To avoid drowning in the mess of API calls to the drive, they will use conditional breakpoints, instructing the debugger to show up only in case when the address of machine command that carries out I/O operation is below 0x70000000 (i.e. that it belongs to the application rather than to the kernel).

However, is there anything that prevents us from executing the I/O command using the address belonging to the kernel from the application level? To do so, it is enough to scan the upper half of the address space for the presence of the following commands: OUT DX, AL (0xEE opcode) and IN AL, DX (0xEC opcode). The question can be asked: How are you going to return the control? The answer to this question is straightforward — this can be carried out by means of handling structural exceptions. If the machine command that follows IN/OUT throws out an exception (by the way, such commands are a numerous), then by catching this exception and handling it, you can continue program execution as if nothing happened.

The advantage of this technique is that the breakpoint set by the hacker to the Input/Output ports won't work (to be more precise, it will actually work, but it will be immediately "swallowed" by the filter). The drawback of this approach is the complication of the protection mechanism.

Access via the MSCDEX Driver

The famous MSCDEX, created in the days of MS-DOS glory, provided the required functional capabilities to programmers, despite its multiple drawbacks. It ensured with a sufficient level of comprehensiveness all of the capabilities of the drives that existed at that time. For example, the reading of individual sectors was carried out by the 1508h function of the INT 2Fh interrupt. If it was necessary to go to the raw level, it was always possible to ask MSCDEX to pass the ATAPI packet directly. This task was accomplished by the 1510h function of the same interrupt (see the Interrupt List by Ralf Brown, if you need more detailed information).

Curiously enough, the functional capabilities of the newer OS, Windows 9x, are incomparably weaker. For instance, under this more powerful OS, it is rather problematic to go down to the sector level without encountering a large number of problems. To all appearances, the system architects have decided that the sector level is something unneeded and, furthermore, system-dependent. Therefore, according to their point of view, "proper" applications must be developed as fully portable, and must use only standard Win32 API calls — all other calls are illegal.

Meanwhile, to support backward compatibility with programs written for MS-DOS and Windows 3.1, the Windows 95 operating system supports MSCDEX interface. As a result of performance considerations, this interface isn't implemented in "native" MSCDEX, which could be missing on the disk. Rather, these functions are implemented in a CD-ROM driver that executes in 32-bit protected mode. This means that all of the required functionality is present in the system. Consequently, there remains a hope to get hands over it in some way or another. Naturally, this problem can be easily solved at the kernel level, but writing a custom driver just to provide an interface to the existing one is very inefficient.

Fortunately, there is a documented and ready-to-use interface between Win32 applications and the MSCDEX driver in Windows 9*x*. Unfortunately, it is awkwardly implemented. In general, because the MSCDEX interface is callable only in V86-mode, Win32 applications must thunk to a 16-bit DLL, and the 16-bit DLL must use the DOS Protected Mode Interface (DPMI) Simulate Real Mode Interrupt function to call its functions.

NOTE

DPMI (DOS Protected Mode Interface) is the interface designed specially to enable developers of protected-mode MS-DOS applications to use the functions of 16-bit operating system such as MS-DOS itself.

Particularly, you are interested in the 1508h function — *DPMI Simulate Real Mode Interrupt,* which allows for the calling of real-mode interrupts from the protected mode. By calling the emulator of the MSCDEX driver via its native INT 2Fh interrupt, you can do whatever you like with the drive, since the MSCDEX interface, as was have mentioned before, is very powerful.

Thus, you can predict the following programming route: Win32 application — 16-bit DLL — DMPI Simulate RM Interrupt — MSCDEX — CDFS. Isn't it too bulky? Or isn't it better to use ASPI (because it is present in Windows 95) or undertake the development of a custom driver? Nevertheless, even if you are not planning to control the drive via MSCDEX, it is useful to know about the existence of such a method to communicate with hardware, especially if you plan to crack someone else's programs. In this case, setting breakpoints to API functions won't produce anything, because reading sectors is carried out via INT 31h (DMPI) and INT 2Fh interrupts. Unfortunately, setting breakpoints directly to these interrupts results in a large number of garbage debugger popups. Using filters is unlikely to be efficient because the number of possible variations is too large. It would be much better to search for interrupt calls in the disassembled program listing!

Additional information on this topic can be found in the Q137813 article included in the MSDN documentation supplied along with Microsoft Visual Studio. The title of this article is "*How Win32 Applications Can Read CD-ROM Sectors in Windows 95*". A complete listing of DMPI- and MSCDEX-functions can be found in the Interrupt-List composed by Ralf Brown. Thus, you shouldn't encounter any difficulties when using this technique. (Although, it is rather difficult nowadays to find a compiler capable of generating 16-bit code and linker for Windows 3.1! By the way, Microsoft Visual Studio 6.0 is not suitable for this purpose any more, since beginning with one of its earlier versions, it lacks the capability for creating projects for MS-DOS/Windows 3.1.)

Provided below is a key fragment quoted from MSDN. This example illustrates the technique for calling real-mode interrupts from 16-bit DLL executed in the Windows environment.

Listing 4.29. A key fragment of a program illustrating the technique for communicating with the MSCDEX driver from 16-bit DLL executed in Windows

```
BOOL FAR PASCAL MSCDEX_ReadSector(BYTE bDrive, DWORD StartSector, LPBYTE RMlpBuffer)
{
RMCS callStruct;
BOOL fResult;

// Prepare DPMI Simulate Real Mode Interrupt call structure with
// the register values used to make the MSCDEX Absolute read call.
// Then, call MSCDEX using DPMI and check for errors in both the DPMI call
// and the MSCDEX call.
BuildRMCS (&callStruct);
callStruct.eax = 0x1508;                 // MSCDEX "ABSOLUTE READ" function
callStruct.ebx = LOWORD(RMlpBuffer);     // Buffer offset for reading a sector
callStruct.es = HIWORD(RMlpBuffer);      // Buffer segment for reading a sector
callStruct.ecx = bDrive;                 // Drive letter 0=A, 1=B, 2=C, etc.
callStruct.edx = 1;                      // Read one sector
callStruct.esi = HIWORD(StartSector);    // Number of the sector to be read
                                         // (most significant word)
callStruct.edi = LOWORD(StartSector);    // Number of the sector to be read
                                         // (least significant word)

// Calling the real-mode interrupt
if (fResult = SimulateRM_Int (0x2F, &callStruct))
fResult = !(callStruct.wFlags & CARRY_FLAG);

return fResult;
}

BOOL FAR PASCAL SimulateRM_Int(BYTE bIntNum, LPRMCS lpCallStruct)
{
BOOL fRetVal = FALSE; // Assume failure

__asm
{
push  di                 ; Saving the DI register
mov   ax, 0300h          ; DPMI Simulate Real Mode Interrupt
mov   bl, bIntNum        ; Number of the real-mode interrupt for the call
mov   bh, 01h            ; Bit 0 = 1; all other bits must be set to zero
xor   cx, cx             ; Do not copy anything from the PM stack to RM stack.
les   di, lpCallStruct   ; Pointer to the structure with registers values
int   31h                ; Gateway to DMPI
```

```
jc      END1                    ; If error, jump to END1.
mov     fRetVal, TRUE           ; Everything's OK.
END1:
pop di                          ; Restoring the DI register
}


// Return
return (fRetVal);
}
```

Communicating via the Custom Driver

Although Windows also allows for the controlling of devices from the application level, most developers prefer to carry out such control using a custom driver capable of interacting with the drive both directly and via its driver. The latter method is preferable, since it allows for abstracting from specific equipment and ensures a unified interface for all drives. Most drivers of this type "connect" to ATAPI and/or SCSI ports and interact with the disk in a way similar to the ASPI driver that you have considered before.

Communication with applications is usually carried out by means of special IOCTL codes passed to the driver by the DeviceIoControl function. These IOCTL codes are labelled "special", since the development of the protocol for organizing interaction between the driver and device is entirely on the conscience (and in the fantasies) of the developer of that specific driver. There is no such thing as standardization here! Furthermore, the DeviceIoControl function is not the only possible variant. Executing in ring 0 formally provides the right to access all resources of the operating system. If desired, even the most unimaginable perversions are possible. For example, it is possible to communicate with the application via the common memory area. In this case, breakpoints set on DeviceIoControl won't produce any result. However, the overwhelming majority of drivers operate via IOCTL and are not distinguished by original ideas. In some way, this position is justified. Actually, the more non-standard features are implemented in the driver, the higher is the probability of conflicts, and the lower its compatibility with other programs (including operating systems). Moreover, a sophisticated driver is much more difficult to debug and bring to perfection than a simple one. On the other hand, however, an unsophisticated driver is very easy to crack, and, therefore, the efforts spent on its development are not justified. In this case, it is much more reasonable to use ASPI, which ensures fully functional low-level interface, which is also system-independent. When using this approach, you won't have to create implementations of your driver intended for all existing operating systems and end up involved in feverish activity related to rewriting the code with the release of each new Windows version.

Summary Table of Characteristics of Various Interfaces

The summary table provided below shows the main characteristics of all of the methods of access described above. As can be seen from this table, the best results are produced by the method of access via ASPI, which ensures an easy, convenient, and system-independent interface for controlling storage media. The next most-positive result is produced by STPI. The main drawback of this method lies in that it is supported only by operating systems of the Windows NT family and doesn't work on Windows 9x. The development of a custom driver looks like a good idea. Implementing such a driver for both Windows NT and Windows 9x (by the way, WDM drivers at the source code level ensure compatibility) will ensure support for your application under both operating systems.

Table 4.6. The comparison of different methods of access (undesired characteristics are highlighted)

	CDFS	cocked	MSCDEX	ASPI	SPTI	SCSI port	mini port	own driver	IOPM
Windows 9x	–	–	+	+	–	–	–	+	N/a
Windows NT	+	+	–	+	+	+	+	+	+
Requires administrative privileges	no	no	–	no	yes	no	no	id[*]	[**]
Supports CDDA	yes	no	yes	yes	yes	yes	yes	yes	yes
Supports CD data	yes	yes	yes	yes	yes	yes	yes	yes	yes
Raw read from CDDA	yes	no	yes	yes	yes	yes	yes	yes	yes
Raw read from CD data	no	no	yes	yes	yes	yes	yes	yes	yes
Potentially dangerous	no	no	no	yes	no	no	no	yes	yes
Well documented	yes	yes	yes	yes	no	no	no	yes	no
Ease of use	yes	yes	no	yes	yes	yes	no	no	no

[*] Here and further on, "id" means "implementation-dependent".

[**] Driver installation requires administrative privileges on the local computer; however, its subsequent use doesn't.

Chapter 5: Methods of Revealing Protection Mechanisms

Can God create such a stone that he would be unable to lift, it is a question that can't be answered by science. Programmers, however, can easily find such a thing that they can't debug.

Programmers' folklore

Protection requiring low-level access to the CD will inevitably give itself away by the presence of functions such as `DeviceIoControl` and/or `SendASPI32Command` in the import table. If protection mechanism loads these functions dynamically, this can be revealed by setting breakpoints to the `LoadLibrary/GetProcAddress` functions (however, experienced programmers can search for the required functions in the memory, — this task is not as complicated as it seems).

Furthermore, the program body might contain strings such as: "\\.\", "SCSI", "CdRom", "wnaspi32.dll", etc. By setting a breakpoint on the first byte of the string, we will be able immediately to locate the protection code as soon as it is called for the first time. To avoid this, developers often encrypt all text strings. However, most of them usually limit themselves to primitive static encryption (which usually is carried out by ASPack or other similar programs). Therefore, if we wait until decryption is completed and call the debugger after starting the program, instead of doing so before it, all text strings will be displayed in plain text! Dynamic encryption is much more reliable. In this case, text strings are decrypted directly before passing them to the appropriate API function, after which they are encrypted again. However, if desired, it is also possible to overcome dynamic encryption! To achieve this, it is enough to set a conditional breakpoint on the CreateFile function to which these text strings are passed, popping up only in the event that the first four bytes of the filename are equal to "\\.\". An example of such a call would look as follows:

```
bpx CreateFileA if (*esp->4=='\\\\.\\')
```

after which it remains only to enjoy the results.

Naturally, the "results" as we understand them include, first, the name of the file to be opened, or, to be more precise, the driver name (this is a result in itself), and, second, the descriptor returned by the CreateFile function. To proceed further, it is possible to choose one of the following two approaches: Either set the breakpoint at the memory cell, in which this descriptor is saved, or set a conditional breakpoint to the DeviceIoControl, catching only those calls to it that are necessary for us. An example of a debugger session is provided in Listing 5.1.

Listing 5.1. An example illustrating the determination of the protection mechanism using Soft-Ice

```
:bpx CreateFileA if (*esp->4=='\\\\.\\')    (setting a breakpoint)
:x                                          (exiting the debugger)
...
(Debugger pauses for a moment, and then pops up at the moment of call to CreateFileA.)
:P RET                                      (exit CreateFileA)
:? eax                                      (get the descriptor value)
00000030  0000000048   "0"                  (response from debugger)
:DeviceIoControlA if (*esp->4==0x30)        (setting the breakpoint to DeviceIoCntrol)
(after a pause, the debugger pops up at the moment of call to DeviceIoControl)
:P RET                                      (exit DeviceIoControl)
: U                                         (That's all. The protection is detected!)
001B:00401112    lea    ecx, [ebp-38]
001B:00401115    push   ecx        ;
001B:00401116    push   0004D004    ; Here it is, IOCTL_SCSI_PASS_THROUGH_DIRECT!
001B:0040111B    mov    edx, [ebp-0C]
001B:0040111E    push   edx
001B:0040111F    call   [KERNEL32!DeviceIoControl]
```

As can be seen, the search for DeviceIoControl didn't take long. It only remains now to analyze the IOCTL code passed to it (in our example, this is IOCTL_SCSI_PASS_THROUGH_DIRECT) and its parameters passed via the stack one double word higher.

Some developers place the critical part of the protection code in the driver, hoping that hackers won't find it there. Vain and naive hope! Drivers are very easy to analyze because of their small size. Consequently, there is no place in a driver to hide the protection code. However, if you "dissipate" the protection code by several megabytes of the application code, the analysis will take a horribly long time. Thus, if hackers have no special interest in cracking that protection, they are better off purchasing a legal copy rather than spending several weeks jumping from disassembler to debugger and vice versa.

What tricks are used by developers to complicate driver analysis? One method is to encrypt the text string with the symbolic name of the device created by the driver at the time of loading. As a result, the hacker knows for sure that the protection code opens the device "\\.\MyGoodDriver", but can't determine quickly to which driver this name corresponds. In the case that there is no encryption, the problem is solved easily by a trivial context search. For example, let's assume that we need to know which driver creates the device with the name MbMmDp32. Open the WINNT\System32\Drivers folder with Far Manager, press <ALT-F7>, and enter the name of the string to be searched for: "MbMmDp32". Do not forget to select the **Use all installed character tables** checkbox (otherwise, nothing will be found, since the string must be specified in Unicode). After some disk activity, Far Manager will produce the only correct answer: ASPI32.SYS. This is the driver that we need! Now imaging that string containing the name is encrypted... If the driver is loaded dynamically, the situation is not too bad. Simply set the breakpoint to the IoCreateDevice and wait until the debugger pops up. Then, issue the P RET command and search the map of loaded modules (displayed by the mod command) to find what can be discovered in this memory region. Drivers that load during the OS boot are significantly more difficult to overcome. Quite often, you will have to search for the required driver by means of trial and error. The date of file creation can often help in this search — the driver installed by the protected application must bear the same data of creation as all of its other files. However, the protection mechanism can freely manipulate the creation data at its discretion, so this technique is not reliable. A positive result can be produced by comparing the contents of the WINNT\System32\Drivers directory before and after installation of the protected application. Clearly, the protection can only be hidden among one of the newly installed drivers.

CD Burning: Pros, Cons, and Something about

To protect CDs from copying, it is not necessary to undertake the development of a custom CD-burning program. Instead of this, you can work with "raw" disc images supported by Alcohol or Clone CD. Despite the fact that all of these programs impose certain limitations on the images they create, the development of high-quality protection mechanisms is still possible. In other words, these programs easily burn the things that they are unable to copy on their own!

When creating a custom copying program for protected discs, it is possible to do this without the burning functionality — it is enough to prepare the disc image (i.e., correctly read the protected disc). Mass-production of the hacked image doesn't present any problem. Thus, it is better to focus directly on the analysis of protected discs rather than to reinvent the wheel, so to speak, developing once again things that were invented long ago. Alcohol and Clone CD have excellent burning capabilities. However, the reading engine of these programs is obviously weak, so that even minor distortions of the control structures of the CD are able to confuse them.

If, despite all of this, you are still convinced that you need a custom program like Nero CD-ROM Burner, there is an answer! Make a call to Maxwell's daemon[i], where it is easier to fall into its clutches than to escape (just kidding). The biggest problem, however, lies in technique of CD burning, and even a brief overview of it would require a separate book. Having only the standards and specifications for SCSI commands will be insufficient, since they don't clarify many details of the process for generating various data structures required by the drive for correctly burning the source image onto a CD. In my opinion, the best manual on CD burning is the *"Functional Requirements for CD-R (Informative)"* supplement to the *"SCSI-3 Multimedia Commands"* document, a version of which can be downloaded from: **http://www.t10.org/ ftp/t10/drafts/mmc/mmc-r10a.pdf** (note that in later revisions of this document, this supplement was removed).

It would also be useful to analyze the source code of the **CDRTOOLS** utility, which can be found on the site: **http://prdownloads.sourceforge.net/cdromtool/ cdromtool_2002-11-26.zip?download.** Of course, a little more than seven megabytes of source code is rather appalling than appealing prospect. However, I do not know simpler programs.

A more laborious (but, at the same time, more tempting) method is disassembling executable files of the Alcohol, Clone CD, CDRWin, and other programs, including the monstrous Nero. It is not actually necessary to carry out complete disassembling. It is sufficient to intercept SCSI commands passed to the drive and analyze the sequence of their calls, without forgetting about the values of arguments, which, in fact, contain all of the key data structures.

Depending on the method chosen by the developer of an application intended for communicating with the device, espionage is carried out either by intercepting the `DeviceIoControl` function with the arguments `IOCTL_SCSI_PASS_THROUGH/`

---

[i] An imaginary creature who is able to sort hot molecules from cold molecules without expending energy, thus bringing about a general decrease in entropy and violating the second law of thermodynamics. After James Clerk Maxwell.

IOCTL_SCSI_PASS_THROUGH_DIRECT (4D004h/4D014h), or the SendASPI32Command function for SPTI and ASPI interfaces, respectively. Applications interacting with the drive via a custom driver can also be intercepted. However, there are no universal solutions here and each specific case must be considered individually.

Let's look at the Alcohol copier for detecting the algorithms of clearing and burning CD-RW discs (CD-R is burned in a similar way, but doesn't require clearing, for obvious reasons). Start Alcohol, go to Alcohol copier and then to the **Settings** tab, click on the **General** link, and choose the **WinASPI Layer Interface (safe mode)** option in the **Disk management interface** drop-down list (if it was not chosen before). After changing the interface, the program must be restarted. Exit the program and start it again to make sure that it is usable.

Now, start soft-ice (or any other debugger supporting breakpoints on API functions) and, having previously loaded ASPI export (NuMega Symbol Loader → File → Load Exports → wnaspi32.dll), open the Alcohol.exe process, unpacking it if necessary (as a rule, it is packed with UPX).

Now, try to set the breakpoint on SendASPI32Command, giving the following command to the debugger: bpx SendASPI32Command. However, nothing useful will come of this. Soft-Ice will complain that it can't find such a function, despite the fact that its name is spelled correctly. This is not surprising, if we suppose that wnaspi32.dll is loaded dynamically in the course of program execution, and the address of ASPI functions are unknown at the stage of loading Alcohol.exe.

It is possible to set the breakpoint on LoadLibraryA, tracking the process of loading of all DLLs. However, since Alcohol loads an enormous number of various DLLs, the debugging session will take a long time, during which we have to watch the screen and endure the monotonous activity of pressing <CTRL-D> repeatedly. A more advanced monitoring approach is setting a conditional breakpoint that will automatically discard all obviously false calls. The command corresponding to it might look, for example, as follows: bpx LoadLibraryA if *(esp->4) == "SANW", where SANW are the first two characters of the wnaspi32.dll name written in inverse order, with the account of the case chosen by the program developer (if you do not know this beforehand, it is possible to use the case-insensitive comparison function).

The bpx GetProcAddress command will then allow all of the ASPI functions to be intercepted, including SendASPI32Command. The name of the loaded function can be viewed by means of issuing the d esp → 4 command. Having waited until the SendASPI32Command appears, click P RET and, having set the breakpoint to bpx eax, press <Ctrl>+<D> to exit Soft-Ice (all the other breakpoints can be deleted if desired).

When the debugger pops up, issue the "d esp → 4" command, and the contents of the SRB_ExecSCSICmd structure will appear in the memory dump window. Now the byte number 30h will be the first byte of the CDB (Attention: This is the first byte of the packet, rather than the pointer to the packet itself); bytes 03h and 10h are the data direction flags and pointer to the clipboard, respectively.

Provided below are examples of spy protocols intercepted in the course of clearing and burning CD-RW.

Listing 5.2. The contents of intercepted CDB blocks sent by Alcohol to the device in the course of fast clearing of the disc

---

```
1E 00 00 00 01 00     PREVENT REMOVAL (ON) -----------+
51 00 00 00 00 00     READ DISK INFORMATION-------+   |
1E 00 00 00 00 00     PREVENT REMOVAL (OFF) ------|---+
BB 00 FF FF FF FF     SET SPEED ----------+       |   |
5A 00 2A 00 00 00     MODE SENSE -----+   |       |   |
BB 00 FF FF 02 C2     ----------------|---+       |   |
5A 00 2A 00 00 00     ----------------+           |   |
1E 00 00 00 00 00     ---------------------------|---+
51 00 00 00 00 00     ---------------------------+
A1 11 00 00 00 00     BLANK
```

Pay special attention to the fact that, for clearing the disc, Alcohol uses the BLANK SCSI command, a detailed description of which can be found in the *"Multimedia Commands — 4"* and *"Information Specification for ATAPI DVD Devices"* documents.

Let's continue our activity in the field of espionage by tracing the process of CD burning. The sequence of SCSI commands sent to the device will appear as follows:

Listing 5.3. The contents of intercepted CDB blocks sent by Alcohol to the device in the course of CD burning

---

```
Choosing "burn" from the menu
BB 00 FF FF FF FF     SET SPEED
5A 00 2A 00 00 00     MODE SENSE
AC 00 00 00 00 52     GET PERFORMANCE

"Write" dialog appears
1E 00 00 00 00 01     PREVENT REMOVAL (LOCK)
51 00 00 00 00 00     READ DISK INFORMATION
1E 00 00 00 00 00     PREVENT REMOVAL (UNLOCK)

CD burning in progress
43 02 04 00 00 00     READ ATIP
51 00 00 00 00 00     READ DISK INFORMATION
...
52 00 00 00 00 00     READ TRACK/ZONE INFORMATION
```

```
5A 00 05 00 00 00      MODE SENSE
55 10 00 00 00 00      MODE SELECT
51 00 00 00 00 00      READ DISK INFORMATION
2A 00 FF FF D2 AC      WRITE(10) -+
2A 00 00 00 D2 BC      ------------+-- write Lead-In
2A 00 00 00 D2 CC      -----------+
...
2A 00 00 00 65 B3      WRITE(10) -+
2A 00 00 00 65 CD      ------------+-- write track
2A 00 00 00 65 E7      -----------+
```

To conclude, let us mention the list of SCSI commands directly related to CD burning and recommended for future careful investigation: BLANK, CLOSE TRACK/SESSION, FORMAT UNIT, READ BUFFER CAPACITY, READ DISC INFORMATION, READ MASTER CUE, READ TRACK INFORMATION, REPAIR TRACK, RESERVE TRACK, SEND CUE SHEET, SEND OPC INFORMATION, SYNCHRONIZE CACHE, WRITE (10). All of the above-listed commands relate to the MMC-1 standard and, therefore, are easy to understand. The text of the standard can be downloaded from the site: **http://www.t10.org/ftp/t10/drafts/mmc/mmc-r10a.pdf.**

Locking and Unlocking the EJECT Button

If the application interacting with the CD carries out an operation that must not be interrupted under any circumstances, it is possible to use the IOCTL command for blocking the tray IOCTL_CDROM_MEDIA_REMOVAL (0x24804). In this case, any attempt to eject the disc from my PHILIPS CDRW triggers malicious blinking of the red LED, showing that the disc is "IN", but locked. The disc cannot be ejected until the tray is unlocked by the pin or by means of rebooting the system.

This circumstance alone creates a rich set of possibilities for numerous intruders or for simply incorrectly operating programs that can fall slain by a crucial fault before unlocking the media. Is it possible to overcome the situation? It's easy. Just unlock the tray on your own!

The point is that the system does not require the unlocking procedure to be carried out in the context of the process that has carried out the blocking. It simply counts the locks and, if the counter is equal to zero, then the tray is free. Consequently, if the block counter is equal to six, we must give the unlocking command six times before the CD can be ejected.

The utility (the source code of which is provided in Listing 5.4) allows us to manipulate the block counter according to our needs. The "+" command line argument increases the counter by one, while "-" carries out an inverse operation. When the counter value reaches 0, any attempts of decreasing it will bring no result.

How can we use this? Suppose, for example, that the untimely ejection of the disc has occurred before the burning operation has been accomplished, which is certainly useful for experimentation. Another application is as follows: When leaving your computer for several minutes, you can lock the disc to make sure that no one takes it away. If someone still manages to do this (by rebooting the computer), lock the trays of their CD-ROM drives and make them reboot!

Listing 5.4. The [/etc/CD.lock.c] Utility for locking/unlocking the CD-ROM tray

```
/*--------------------------------------------------------------------------
 *
 *                      LOCKS AND UNLOCKS THE CD-ROM TRAY
 *                      =====================================
 *
 * build 0x001 @ 04.06.2003
 ----------------------------------------------------------------------------*/
#include <windows.h>
#include <winioctl.h>
#include <stdio.h>

#define IOCTL_CDROM_MEDIA_REMOVAL 0x24804
main(int argc, char **argv)
{
        BOOL                    act;
        DWORD                   xxxx;
        HANDLE                  hCD;
        PREVENT_MEDIA_REMOVAL   pmrLockCDROM;

        // CHECKING ARGUMENTS
        if (argc<3){printf("USAGE: CD.lock.exe \\\\.\\X: {+,-}\n"); return -1;}

        if (argv[2][0]=='+') act=TRUE;              // INCREMENT THE LOCK COUNTER
            else if (argv[2][0]=='-') act=FALSE;    // DECREMENT THE LOCK COUNTER
                else {printf(stderr, "-ERR: in arg %c\n", argv[2][0]); return -1;}

        // GET THE DEVICE DESCRIPTOR
        hCD=CreateFile(argv[1],GENERIC_READ,FILE_SHARE_READ,0,OPEN_EXISTING,0,0);
        if (hCD == INVALID_HANDLE_VALUE) {printf("-ERR: get CD-ROM\n"); return -1;}

        // LOCK OR UNLOCK THE CD-ROM TRAY
        pmrLockCDROM.PreventMediaRemoval = act;
        DeviceIoControl (hCD, IOCTL_CDROM_MEDIA_REMOVAL,
                &pmrLockCDROM, sizeof(pmrLockCDROM), NULL, 0, &xxxx, NULL);
}
```

Hacking Secrets. Brake Fluid for CDs

The arrival of high-speed CD-ROM drives has resulted in a large number of problems. The popular opinion is that the cons far outnumber the pros. The list of drawbacks includes terrible noise, vibration, and broken discs. Who needs it? Besides, many algorithms for binding to CD feel somewhat uncertain at high speeds. Hence, protected discs do not start on the first attempt, if they ever start at all. What can we do about this? Naturally, we just slow them down! Fortunately, most drives support the SET CD SPEED (opcode 0BBh) command. At first glance, there is no problem at all — just specify the required parameters. However, things are not as simple as they seem.

The first nuisance (minor, but still annoying) is that the speed is specified in KB per second, rather than in "x" (note that the measurement unit is KB rather than bytes). At the same time, single speed corresponds to a throughput of 176 KB per second. What about double speed? If you deduce that it will be 352 (2 × 176), you are mistaken. The speed is actually 353! Triple speed does equal what we would expect: 176 × 3 = 528. However, 4x speed once again deviates from what would seem logical, being 706 rather than 704 (4 × 176). An incorrectly specified speed will result in the setting of the speed one grade lower than expected, and the correspondence between the grades and stages will be ambiguous. Suppose that the drive supports the following range of speeds: 16x, 24x, 32x, and 40x. If the specified speed (in kilobytes per second) is lower than the nominal 32x speed, the drive will operate at the next lower supported speed, 16x in our case. Hence, to translate the "x" into kilobytes per second, they must be multiplied by 177 rather than by 176!

The second nuisance (much more significant and considerably more frustrating) is that the standard specification does not contain a command producing the complete list of supported speeds. This information must be obtained by means of trial and error. Before starting the trial, a properly operating program must make sure that there is no disc in the drive. If there is, it must forcibly eject it. As a matter of fact, running a low-quality disc at high speeds might result in the disc exploding, rendering the drive unusable. The user must be absolutely sure that the disc inserted into the drive will rotate at exactly the speed that is requested, and that the program won't increase the rotation speed without justification.

The third nuisance (of a horrifying nature this time) is that some drives (TEAC 522E, for instance) successfully swallow the SET CD SPEED command and confirm the changing of the rotation speed by returning its new value in MODE SENSE. However, the actual rotation speed remains as before until the disc is accessed once again. Therefore, it is wise to issue a command for reading a sector from the disc directly after the SET CD SPEED command (if the disc is present). Measuring the drive speed without a disc in the tray is pointless, suitable only for building the sequence of supported speeds, because all of the previous speed settings become invalid after inserting a new disc into the drive. Thus, the optimal rotation speed for each disc (from the drive's point of view) must be determined for each individual disc. The drive also has the right to change the rotation speed by decreasing it if the read operation is not going well, or increasing it if everything is OK.

Investigation of Real Programs

To summarize all of this material and acquire practical skills, let's look at several popular programs working with CDs at a low level to find out how this interaction is carried out.

Having called on the indispensable Soft-Ice and set the breakpoint to `bpx CreateFileA if (*esp->4=='\\\\.\\')`, let us sequentially start the following three programs: *Alcohol 120%*, *Easy CD Creator*, and *Clone CD*, each time noting the name of the opened device.

Alcohol 120%

Alcohol 120%, depending on the settings, can access the disc in three different ways: via its own custom driver (by default), via *ASPI/SPTI interface*, and via *ASPI Layer*. Let's start with the custom driver. Setting the breakpoint on `CreateFileA` shows that Alcohol opens the \\.\SCSI2: device (the number, naturally, depends on the hardware configuration), and a further check confirms that the `DeviceIoControl` function receives the same descriptor that was returned when opening the SCSI device! Consequently, Alcohol considers as "custom driver" the miniport driver that it has installed in the system in the course of program installation.

Now, let's change the Alcohol 120% settings to make it work via the SPTI/ASPI interface. After restarting the program (and Alcohol requires that you restart after changing the access method), we once again will see the procedure of opening the \\.\SCSI2 device, and then the disk \\.\G: will be opened (the drive letter, naturally, depends on the hardware configuration). Essentially, in the course of interaction with the device via SPTI interface, things are proceeding in exactly this way. To be more precise, they *must proceed in such a way*. Alcohol 120% opens the \\.\G: disk *multiple times*, which is an indication of its "freaky architecture". This complicates our task significantly, since we must trace all descriptors simultaneously. If we miss just one of them, the reconstructed working algorithm will be incorrect (isn't it interesting to find out how Alcohol 120% copies protected discs?).

Finally, by switching Alcohol 120% to the last mode of interaction with the disc, we will get the following result: \\.\\SCSI2, \\.\MbMmDp32, \\.\G:. The device with the name "MbMmDp32" is the ASPI driver that we have already encountered. However, in this case it is not absolutely clear why Alcohol 120% opens disk \\.\G:, since the ASPI interface doesn't require it.

Easy CD Creator

Easy CD Creator accesses the drive directly by its "native" name (on my computer, this is "CDR4_2K"), then opens the "MbDlDp32" device, which CDR4_2K registers itself.

Consequently, Easy CD Creator works with the disc via the custom driver. To clarify how it works, we will have to, first, disassemble the CDR4_2K driver and analyze, which IOCTL codes correspond to which driver actions, and, second, trace all DeviceIoControl calls (simply set a conditional breakpoint, which pops up when passing its "own" descriptor returned by the CreateFileA("\\\\.\\CRDR_2K",...) and CreateFileA("\\\\.\\MbDlDp32",...) functions).

After formatting the sequence of IOCTL calls in the form of an improvised program, we will be able to reconstruct the protocol of interaction with the disc and find the protection (if there is any).

Clone CD

The breakpoint set to the CreateFileA function indicates that Clone CD communicates with the disc via the custom driver "\\.\ELBYCDIO", and, for reasons that are unclear, it is opened in the loop, so that the driver descriptor is returned multiple times.

Part III

Protection against Unauthorized Copying and Data Recovery

Chapter 6: Anti-Copying Mechanisms 225

Chapter 7: Protection Mechanisms for Preventing Playback in PC CD-ROM 345

Chapter 8: Protection against File-by-File Disc Copying 353

Chapter 9: Protection Mechanisms Based on Binding to Storage Media 375

Chapter 10: Data Recovery from CDs 393

Chapter 6: Anti-Copying Mechanisms

This chapter covers the organization of various mechanisms for protection against the unauthorized copying of CDs and provides explanations of the principles, by which they operate, as well as examples of how these mechanisms are implemented in different software. It also demonstrates how these protection mechanisms can be neutralized.

Classification of protection mechanisms: Methods of protection against unauthorized copying can be classified in relation to a number of criteria, the most important among which are the following:

❐ *The strength of the protection mechanism* (can the protected CD be copied by a standard copier; by a specialized copier capable of emulating protected media; or can it simply not be copied at all).

❐ *Principle by which the protection operates* (non-standard disc formatting; binding to physical characteristics of a specific media).

❐ *Compatibility with hardware and software* (the protection mechanism is fully compliant with the standard and is compatible with all standard equipment; the protection mechanism doesn't formally violate the standard but, however, relies on undocumented features of hardware implementation that aren't guaranteed to be supported; or the protection mechanism clearly violates the standard and relies on a specific equipment line).

❏ *Implementation level* (software level — the creation of the master disc is carried out using standard equipment; hardware level — the creation of the master disc requires special equipment).

❏ *Interface of communication with the CD drive* (standard C and/or Pascal library; OS API; low-level hardware access.

❏ *Object of protection* (protection of the entire disc; protection against file-by-file copying; protection against digital grabbing of audio content.

The strength of the protection mechanism against cracking: There is no absolute protection against copying for optical media. Such a mechanism is, in principle, impossible to design, because, if the disc can be read, this means that it can also be copied. Naturally, if hardware protection is effectively built into the drive chipset, the procedure for cracking it can be extremely difficult, if not impossible, using standard equipment. However, what prevents a hacker from modifying the firmware for the drive at his or her disposal, or from introducing certain constructive modifications, thus blocking the protection mechanism? It is enough to recall the sensational story of MOD chips to make all of the illusions of copyright holders disappear like smoke.

Struggling against professional crackers is absolutely pointless. No one has ever won this battle. The faster the process of improving protection mechanisms evolves, the more promising are the prospects for cracking them. Even the most perfect protection mechanisms can be cracked. Realistically, this is merely a question of time, motivation, and financial resources (bear in mind that, in this case, the financial potential is almost infinite).

Therefore, it is necessary to protect against qualified users instead of protecting against hackers. Standard copiers (Ahead Nero, Roxio Easy CD Creator), at minimum, must not be able to copy the disc. Maximum protection assumes that it is impossible to copy the protected CD using specialized copiers designed for protected discs (Alcohol 120%, Clone CD). Nevertheless, protection against copying can be very different. Physical defects on the surface cannot, in principle, be copied using standard equipment. However, they can easily be *simulated* by corrupting the sector checksum. Naturally, this can be detected easily by a more "intelligent" protection mechanism. For this purpose, however, the protection must delve to lower levels, in comparison with API, in order to get direct access to the hardware. Note that this is not positive from the point of view of compatibility and security.

Emulation of the original media is even more difficult to overcome. Some advanced copiers (such as Alcohol 120%) create a virtual drive that behaves exactly in the same manner as the protected disc. Software of this type carefully reproduces practically all of the physical characteristics of the disc's surface. Hence, the difficulties involved in copying the original disc depend not so much on the complications associated with imitating the specific features of the disc, but, rather, by their hidden location.

In other words, it is necessary to find a set of specific distinguishing features, the presence of which would be extremely difficult to detect. Good candidates for this role are the subcode channels of unreadable sectors. Because of the specific features of CD-drive design, the precision of positioning for subchannel data is low, and, consequently, the result of the READ SUBCHANNEL SCSI/ATAPI command is not only unpredictable, but also impossible to reproduce! Each time this command is executed it returns the sub-channel data for sector $N \pm \delta + k$, where N is the address of the requested sector, δ is the random drive error, and k the systematic drive error. Thus, grabbing the subchannel data of all sectors will take too long. If the subchannel data are intentionally mixed and/or corrupted, the problem posed by their copying will become practically unsolvable. Copying such a disc is practically impossible, whether using existing copiers or any of the advanced models that will certainly appear in the future.

The strength of the protection mechanism against a bit-hack is, generally, not critical. Even the most advanced and sophisticated protection mechanism will be cracked, provided that the hacker has enough motivation! Therefore, the only attainable goal that that is considered here is the *complication* of the process for copying original CDs using standard or hacker tools. What methods allow us to complicate this copying?

When MS-DOS and 3,5"/5,25" floppy drives were still dominant, the most popular protection methods were *non-standard disc formatting* and *creation of extremely difficult to reproduce surface defects*. These protection mechanisms could be implemented at both the *hardware* and *software* levels. In this context, the "hardware level" is understood as non-standard equipment used for recording a protected disc (for example, a device for creating laser marks by means of vaporizing the magnetic layer at a strictly defined location, or even a commonplace variable capacitor, connected in parallel to quartz in order to change its frequency and, consequently, its track length. Software methods of protection were limited to the use of standard equipment. This considerably reduced the expense involved in duplicating original discs (when it was only necessary to reproduce a small number of items, this was very important). Curiously enough, the strength of hardware protection was no higher than that ensured by the protection at the software level. All kinds of protection mechanisms could be cracked using software methods, and, most often, this could be achieved in a completely automatic mode.

Generally speaking, all of the existing methods of CD protection can be divided into the following two types: *non-standard disc formatting* and *binding to the physical characteristics of the media surface*. Protection mechanisms of the first type can be implemented by means of aberration from the standard. On the other hand, the vast majority of "loyal" programs attempt to comply with standards. As a result, the protected disc cannot be copied using standard methods, and this is exactly the result that copyright holders were looking for. The idea of non-standard formatting is not new. It was widely used even in the times of "Amiga," "Spectrum," and other ancient computers.

This type of protection couldn't withstand an attack carried out by a reasonably intelligent individual. However, the problems that it caused to legal users became legend long ago. Any deviation — even the slightest — from the standard would void any guarantee that the disc would be readable at all! Because of the wide variety of the equipment available on the market, it is impossible to test protected discs on all existing drive models. Consequently, there is the risk that owners of untested models will encounter serious problems. The more significant are the deviations from the standard, the higher this risk will be.

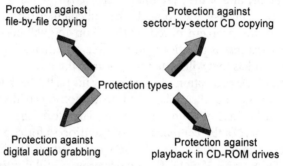

Fig. 6.1. Classification of protection mechanisms

Disc protection against playback in computer CD-ROM drives, also called protection against digital playback, is the most infamous of all protection mechanisms. The main goal of this type of protection is the prevention of unauthorized copying the disc and grabbing its contents into MP3 format, without preventing normal playback. Obviously, the requirements of the protection here are mutually exclusive, because the playback of an audio disc is, in itself, an example of grabbing. Whether the grabbed data are supplied to the DAC input or to the input of an MP3-compressor is not important, because the drive doesn't inform the disc which circuitry it will use to read it (why should a crocodile chat with its breakfast).

In practice, however, the situation is somewhat different. Low-end audio players and computer CD-ROM drives differ significantly in their design and interpret the same information written on a CD differently. With regard to computer CD-ROM drives, they most frequently play audio discs through a special audio channel, which differs significantly from the digital data channel. Thus, the creation of a protection mechanism is reduced to the intentional introduction of errors into the disc structure that will manifest themselves only in the digital grabbing mode, while remaining unnoticeable in all other situations.

As has already been mentioned, any modification of the disc structure going beyond the limitations implied by the standard renders this disc "non-standard." The behavior of non-standard discs on arbitrary-selected equipment is unpredictable! At the same time, the processing of non-standard audio discs is significantly different from the processing of non-standard data discs. A protection mechanism built into an executable file is, in fact, a program. Consequently, it knows everything about the format corruption of the protected disc and knows how to process it. Just one thing is required of the CD-ROM drive — to read the data and do what, and only what, it is instructed to do. The situation is completely different when an audio disc is processed by CD-ROM firmware. In this case, an *external* program (CD-ROM firmware) that corresponds to the standard is used for processing of the corrupted data. As a result, CD-ROM drive firmware can interpret *any* deviations from the standard as a situation where there is a "non-audio disk" or there is "no disk present." The large variety of digital equipment considerably complicates the problem of testing protection mechanisms for compatibility.

Actually, the protection of audio CDs against copying turns into protection against playback. Often, these discs can not even be played on standard audio players, let alone CD-ROM drives. On CD-ROM drives, they can only be played if they can be played at all, through an audio channel, which gradually dies away. Windows 2000 and Windows XP, for example, use digital playback of audio discs actively. On Macs, according to rumors I've heard, this is the main playback mode. Since the discussion of the advantages of digital playback in comparison to analog playback is a topic for another book, we won't concentrate on this topic here. It is enough to note that every user has the right to choose his or her preferred playback method. Consequently, cracking this kind of "protection" is justifiable — if not a noble deed!

The PHILIPS Corporation, which is one of the inventors of CD technology, strongly opposes any deviations from the standard and insists on that protected discs including anti-copying technology should not use the "Compact Disc" logo. Legislation in many countries supports this stance. Any disc protected by a non-standard format must be marked with an unequivocal warning that, although the piece of plastic you are purchasing bears a resemblance to a CD, in reality, *it is not a proper CD.*

Nostalgic reminiscence

Long ago, when Spectrum computers were quite popular, one publisher of an e-zine (after so many years, the name of the company escapes me) invented a protection system in the following form. The controller chip for the drive is supplied with a specific clock frequency, which forms the basis for its operation. Because, In this case, the MFM recording method is used, the track length depends on the frequency. Normally (if my memory serves me well), the track length was in the range of 6,200 bytes (unformatted). Well, this company, or, more likely, one bunch of guys :), created a shorter track on the disc, of about 5,000 bytes. Thanks to the PLL in controller, it could be read quite normally. However, the length of 5,000 bytes was preserved. This protection was *impossible* to overcome on a standard computer (obviously). However, hackers immediately came up with the idea to connect a variable capacitor in parallel to the quartz. By tuning this variable capacitor, it was possible to obtain a track of the desired length. For the moment, it was difficult to say for sure who was the first to invent this method, because it was invented and reinvented many times. However, Bob Johns, who was writing a copier for discs protected in this manner exactly by that time, was the first to provide information on this method to the wide user community.

Built-in CD Protection

CD protection against unauthorized copying was initially built into CDs. Even in times immemorial, when there were no PCs and no data CDs, and the problem of piracy didn't really exist, the Red Book already described a special bit called the *digital copy prohibited/permitted*, which prohibited digital reading from the medium if the copyright holder so desired (view the CONTROL field of the Q subcode channel — if the first bit, starting from zero, is reset to zero, then digital reading is permitted, and vice versa). However, neither of the CD-copying programs of which the author is aware takes this bit into account. For instance, Ahead Nero Burning ROM displays a warning message, but nothing more. Neither of the CD-ROM drives blocks digital reading, even in the case that it is "prohibited." This is the result, partially, of the fact that digital playback has considerable advantages over analog playback (lower parasitic noise, software correction of sound, etc.). For these reasons, analog audio is rapidly being squeezed out of the market. Devices that do not support digital playback have little chance of finding a niche in the market. Consequently, device manufacturers have little choice but to ignore this standard as a result of consumer demand.

Protection Mechanisms Based on Non-Standard Disc Formats

Incorrect TOC and its Consequences

TOC invalidation is a cruel, ugly, but strangely widespread technique in protection mechanisms. End-user copiers (Easy CD Creator, Stomp Record Now!, Ahead Nero) actually go a little nuts when encountering discs of this type. Copiers of protected disks (Clone CD, Alcohol 120%) are much more loyal to an incorrect TOC. However, in order to obtain a usable copy, they require a specific combination of reading and burning devices. Even given this, successful copying of these discs is not guaranteed.

The burning device must support the *RAW DAO* (*Disc At Once*) mode, i.e., the mode by which the entire disk is written at a single pass. The *RAW SAO* (*Session At Once*) mode isn't suitable for this purpose, since it orders the drive to write the session contents before writing the TOC. Consequently, the drive has to analyze the TOC on its own in order to determine the session length and its starting address. An attempt to write an incorrect TOC in SAO mode generally results in unpredictable drive behavior. Consequently, it is pointless to hope for the generation of a usable copy of a protected disc! As a rule, the first session with an incorrect TOC encountered by the drive proves to be the last. This is because there is *no room* to write all of the other sessions (TOC invalidation is usually aimed at increasing the session size to several gigabytes).

The CD-reading device, besides reading in a Raw mode (which is supported by practically all drives), must be able to recognize an incorrect TOC. When it encounters such a case, it must automatically switch to a "reserved" addressing resource, namely, to the Q subcode channel. Otherwise, the session containing the incorrect TOC will be unavailable for reading even at the sector level.

Thus, *not all equipment is appropriate for copying discs with incorrect TOCs.* About one third of all available copier models are unsuitable for this purpose. In order to find out if the model that you have chosen supports the RAW DAO mode, refer to the online Help system of Clone CD, which provides a long list of various drives (unfortunately, the ones that I have chosen are not listed here), along with their characteristics. Another approach is to issue the 46h (GET CONFIGURATION) SCSI/ATAPI command and check the drive's response. Of my two copiers, only NEC supports the RAW DAO mode. The situation is even more complicated with regard to determining the ability of reading incorrect sessions, since this ability represents exclusively internal drive logic. As a rule, even if the drive is capable of working with an incorrect TOC, the drive itself does not indicate this, and drive manufacturers usually do not advertise this feature. This information has to be found experimentally. For instance, take a disk with an intentionally invalidated TOC (later in this chapter, I'll explain how to create one), insert it into the drive, and try to read sectors from an incorrect session. Different drives might react very differently. For instance, PHILIPS, depending on the "mood" of its circuitry, might either report a read error or return a stream of unintelligible gibberish, where even a SYNC in the raw header isn't recognizable.

The main drawback of protection mechanisms based on TOC invalidation is that some drives refuse to recognize these disks, and, therefore, make playback impossible. A legal user, who has suffered inconveniences due to the incompatibility of his or her hardware with the protection mechanism, will, in the best case, complain and return the disk to the manufacturer. Naturally, this can be only done if he or she is able to eject this trash from the drive. This question is problematic, since the embedded microprocessors of some drives simply "hang" when they attempt to analyze an incorrect TOC. In these cases, the drive, literally speaking, retreats into its shell. It becomes fully abstracted from all of the "irritants" of the outside world, including the user's attempts to eject the disk. Of course, the hole for ejecting disks in emergency cases[i] hasn't been removed entirely, but, according to some rumors, it isn't present on all drives (although myself have never encountered a drive lacking this feature). On the other hand, this hole in many cases is concealed behind the decorative panel. Cases where the user isn't aware of the existence of this feature or how to use it, are even more frequent. Macintosh systems lack these holes (or Mac users never suspected that they might exist). Anyway, the number of law suits that they have filed is virtually uncountable. The most interesting fact here is that the courts have ruled in favor of an overwhelming majority of these suits. As a result, the developers have had to pay for the "repair" of equipment, moral injury, and, finally, the legal costs for the cases. *(By the way, removing protection from disks written with crude violations of the standard, and in particular, those with an incorrect TOC, is not considered to be cracking. Consequently, it can't be prosecuted by Law. Therefore, if you encounter discs of this type, crack them without any qualms).*

Incorrect Starting Address for the Track

To create a protected disk with a incorrect TOC, we will need: Any burner capable of creating multi-session disks (Roxio Easy CD Creator, for example); a copier of protected disks that stores the TOC contents in a text file that can be edited (we will work with Clone CD); and, finally, a burning drive that supports the RAW DAO writing mode. Although I don't like this style of presenting materials, for the sake of simplicity, all actions will be described in the form of step-by-step instructions.

Step One: Creating an Original Disk. Take a virgin CD-R disk from the pack, or, better still, an "old stager" CD-RW. Insert it into the drive and write a couple of sessions in standard mode. It would be even better (or, to be more precise, more obvious) if the second session includes all of the files from the first session — the one, the TOC of which we are going to disfigure. The most interesting question is whether or not the drive will be able to read its contents.

Step two: Obtaining the image of the original disk. Start Clone CD and instruct it to create an image of the original disk (at this stage, the chosen profile for settings is not critical. Because the disk isn't protected yet, we can use both the **Data CD** and **Protected PC Game** options with the same level of success. Note that it isn't necessary to click the **Create "Cue-Sheet"** checkbox, because this option is available only for single-session CDs).

---

[i] Carefully look at the front panel of your CD-ROM. Do you see a tiny hole about 1 mm in diameter below the tray? Use any long, thin, and sufficiently firm object, for instance, such as metallic clip to slightly open the tray by entering the "picklock" into the hole up to the stop and press slightly. Here you are! Now, it is possible to open the tray manually. Attention: First of all, do not forget to power down the computer before doing this operation. Second, hold the "picklock" strictly horizontally, otherwise you can miss and damage some sensitive unit.

Step three: Invalidating the starting address of the first track in the CD image. If everything has been done correctly and both the software and the hardware operate normally, the following three files will be created on your hard disk: IMAGE.CCD — containing the contents of the Q subcode channel of the Lead-in area or, simply speaking, the TOC; IMAGE.IMG — the raw disk image containing all sectors starting from 00:00:02 and including the total number of available sectors; and IMAGE.SUB — the contents of the subcode fields of the Program Memory Area. In principle, the latter file might not be present (it is created only if the **Read subchannels from data tracks** checkbox is set). This circumstance is not critical, however, because, at this point, we are mainly interested in the TOC itself and not the subcode channels! Open the IMAGE.CCD file using any plain-text editor and try to translate the language of the disk geometry into normal, human-friendly language. The contents of a valid TOC in RAW format are shown in Listing 6.1.

Listing 6.1. The contents of a valid TOC in RAW format

```
[CloneCD]                     ; Information on the Clone CD product
Version=3                     ; Clone CD version. Of little importance

[Disc]                        ; Disk information
TocEntries=12                 ; Number of TOC entries
Sessions=2                    ; Number of sessions = 2
DataTracksScrambled=0         ; DVD field (see inf-8090), for CDs this info is pointless
CDTextLength=0                ; No CD-Text in subcode fields of the Lead-in area

[Session 1]                   ; Session 1 information
PreGapMode=1                  ; Track type — Mode 1 (data track, 2048 bytes of data)
PreGapSubC=0                  ; No subchannel data

[Session 2]                   ; Session 2 information
PreGapMode=1                  ; Track type — Mode 1 (data track, 2048 bytes of data)
PreGapSubC=0                  ; No subchannel data

[Entry 0]                     ; Information of the TOC entry №0
Session=1                     ; Entry of session 1
Point=0xa0                    ; 1st track of session 1 number in PMin/disk type in PSec
ADR=0x01                      ; q-Mode == 1
Control=0x04                  ; Digital copy prohibited ;-)
TrackNo=0                     ; The track we are currently reading —
                              ; this is the Lead-in track (i.e., the TOC)
AMin=0                        ; \
ASec=0                        ; + Absolute address of the current track
```

```
AFrame=0                    ; /
ALBA=-150                   ; LBA-address of the current track
Zero=0                      ; This field must be set to zero, which is the case
PMin=1                      ; Number of the first track of session 1
PSec=0                      ; Disk type CD-DA or CD-ROM in Mode 1
PFrame=0                    ; No useful information
PLBA=4350                   ; Track number presented by CloneCD as the LBA-address,
                            ; i.e., trash

[Entry 1]                   ; Information of TOC entry №1
Session=1                   ; Entry of session 1
Point=0xa1                  ; Number of the last track of session 1 in PMin
ADR=0x01                    ; q-Mode == 1
Control=0x04                ; Digital copy prohibited ;-)
TrackNo=0                   ; Track that we are currently reading — Lead-in track
                            ; (i.e., the TOC)
AMin=0                      ; \
ASec=0                      ; + Absolute address of the current track
AFrame=0                    ; /
ALBA=-150                   ; LBA-address of the current track
Zero=0                      ; This field must be set to zero, which is the case
PMin=1                      ; Number of the last track of session 1
                            ;(only one track in the session)
PSec=0                      ; No useful information
PFrame=0                    ; No useful information
PLBA=4350                   ; Track number presented by CloneCD as LBA-address,
                            ; i.e., trash

[Entry 2]                   ; Information of the TOC entry №2
Session=1                   ; Entry of session 1
Point=0xa2                  ; Position of Lead-out area in PMin:PSec:PFrame
ADR=0x01                    ; q-Mode == 1
Control=0x04                ; Digital copy prohibited ;-) TrackNo=0
                            ; Track that we are currently reading —
                            ; Lead-in track (i.e., TOC)
AMin=0                      ; \
ASec=0                      ; + — Absolute address of the current track
AFrame=0                    ; /
ALBA=-150                   ; LBA-address of the current track
Zero=0                      ; This field must be set to zero, which is the case
PMin=0                      ; \
PSec=29                     ; + — Absolute address of the Lead-out area of session 1
PFrame=33                   ; /
```

```
PLBA=2058            ; LBA-address of Lead-out area of session 1

[Entry 3]            ; Information of the TOC entry №3
Session=1            ; Entry of session 1
Point=0x01           ; Information of track 1 of session 1
ADR=0x01             ; q-Mode == 1
Control=0x04         ; Digital copy prohibited ;-)
TrackNo=0            ; Track that we are currently reading — Lead-in track
                     ; (i.e., TOC)
AMin=0               ; \
ASec=0               ; + — Absolute address of the current track
AFrame=0             ; /
ALBA=-150            ; LBA-address of the current track
Zero=0               ; This field must be set to zero, which is the case
PMin=0               ; \
PSec=2               ; + — Absolute address of the starting point
                     ; of track 1 of session 1
PFrame=0             ; /
PLBA=0               ; LBA-address of the starting point of track 1 of session 1

[Entry 4]            ; Information of the TOC entry №4
Session=1            ; Entry of session 1
Point=0xb0           ; Position of the next writable area in AMin:ASec:AFrame
ADR=0x05             ; q-Mode == 1
Control=0x04         ; Digital copy prohibited ;-)
TrackNo=0            ; Track that we are currently reading — Lead-in track (i.e., TOC)
AMin=2               ; \
ASec=59              ; + — Absolute address of the next writable area
AFrame=33            ; /
ALBA=13308           ; LBA-address of the next writable area
Zero=3               ; Number of pointers in Mode 5
PMin=22              ; \
PSec=14              ; + — Absolute address of the maximum writable area
PFrame=34            ; /
PLBA=99934           ; LBA-address of the maximum writable area

[Entry 5]            ; Information of TOC entry №5
Session=1            ; Entry of session 1
Point=0xc0           ; Starting address of the Lead-in area of Hybrid disk
                     ; (if there is any)
ADR=0x05             ; Mode 5 (Orange book)
Control=0x04         ; Digital copy prohibited ;-)
TrackNo=0            ; Track that we are currently reading —
                     ; this is the Lead-in track (i.e., TOC)
```

```
AMin=162                  ; Recommended laser power for burning
ASec=128                  ; Application code
AFrame=140                ; Reserved
ALBA=288590               ; LBA-"address" of three preceding fields
Zero=0                    ; Reserved
PMin=97                   ; \
PSec=27                   ; + — Absolute Lead-in address of the disk hybrid area
PFrame=21                 ; / (Address is beyond the limits of the disk,
                          ; i.e., there is no Hybrid disk)
PLBA=-11604               ; LBA-address of Lead-in area of Hybrid
                          ; (computed with overflow)


[Entry 6]                 ; Information of the TOC entry №6
Session=1                 ; Entry of session 1
Point=0xc1                ; Copy of ATIP information
ADR=0x05                  ; -+
Control=0x04              ; -+
TrackNo=0                 ; -+
AMin=4                    ; -+
ASec=120                  ; -+
AFrame=96                 ; -+
ALBA=26946                ; -+ — ATIP information
Zero=0                    ; -+
PMin=0                    ; -+
PSec=0                    ; -+
PFrame=0                  ; -+
PLBA=-150                 ; -+


[Entry 7]                 ; Information of TOC entry №7
Session=2                 ; Entry of session 2 (here we have finally got to session 2!)
Point=0xa0                ; Number of first track of session 2 in PMin/disk type in PSec
ADR=0x01                  ; q-Mode == 1
Control=0x04              ; Digital copy prohibited ;-)
TrackNo=0                 ; Track that we are currently reading — Lead-in track
                          ; (i.e., TOC)
AMin=0                    ; \
ASec=0                    ; + — Absolute address of the current track
AFrame=0                  ; /
ALBA=-150                 ; LBA-address of the current track
Zero=0                    ; This field must be set to zero, which is the case
PMin=2                    ; Number of the first track of session 2
                          ; (track numbering is pass-through!)
PSec=0                    ; Disk type CD-DA and CD-ROM disk in Mode 1
```

```
PFrame=0                      ; No useful information
PLBA=8850                     ; Track number presented by CloneCD as LBA-address, i.e., trash

[Entry 8]                     ; Information of TOC entry №8
Session=2                     ; Entry of session 2
Point=0xa1                    ; Number of the last track of session 2 in PMin
ADR=0x01                      ; q-Mode == 1
Control=0x04                  ; Digital copy prohibited ;-)
TrackNo=0                     ; Track that we are currently reading — Lead-in track (i.e., TOC)
AMin=0                        ; \
ASec=0                        ; + — Absolute address of the current track
AFrame=0                      ; /
ALBA=-150                     ; LBA-address of the current track
Zero=0                        ; This field must be set to zero, which is the case
PMin=2                        ; Number of the last track of session 2
                              ; (the session has only one track)
PSec=0                        ; No useful information
PFrame=0                      ; No useful information
PLBA=8850                     ; Track number presented by CloneCD as LBA-address,
                              ; i.e., trash

[Entry 9]                     ; Information of TOC entry №9
Session=2                     ; Entry of session 2
Point=0xa2                    ; Position of the Lead-out area in PMin:PSec:PFrame
ADR=0x01                      ; q-Mode == 1
Control=0x04                  ; Digital copy prohibited ;-)
TrackNo=0                     ; Track that we are currently reading — Lead-in track (i.e., TOC)
AMin=0                        ; \
ASec=0                        ; + — Absolute address of the current track
AFrame=0                      ; /
ALBA=-150                     ; LBA-address of the current track
Zero=0                        ; This field must be equal to zero, which is true
PMin=3                        ; \
PSec=24                       ; + — Absolute address of the Lead-out area of session 2
PFrame=23                     ; /
PLBA=15173                    ; LBA-address of the Lead-out area of session 2

[Entry 10]                    ; Information of TOC entry №10
Session=2                     ; Entry of session 2
Point=0x02                    ; Information of track 2 of session 2
ADR=0x01                      ; q-Mode == 1
Control=0x04                  ; Digital copy prohibited ;-)
TrackNo=0                     ; Track that we are currently reading — Lead-in track (i.e., TOC)
```

```
AMin=0                  ; \
ASec=0                  ; + — Absolute address of the current track
AFrame=0                ; /
ALBA=-150               ; LBA-address of the current track
Zero=0                  ; This field must be equal to zero, which is the case
PMin=3                  ; \
PSec=1                  ; + — Absolute address of the starting point
                        ; of track 2 of session 2
PFrame=33               ; /
PLBA=13458              ; LBA-address of the starting point of track 2 of session 2

[Entry 11]              ; Information of TOC entry №11
Session=2               ; Entry of session 2
Point=0xb0              ; Address of the next writable area in AMin:ASec:AFrame
ADR=0x05                ; Mode 5
Control=0x04            ; Digital copy prohibited ;-)
TrackNo=0               ; Track that we are currently reading — Lead-in track
                        ; (i.e., TOC)
AMin=4                  ; \
ASec=54                 ; + — Absolute address of the next writable area
AFrame=23               ; /
ALBA=21923              ; LBA-address of the next writable area
Zero=1                  ; Number of Mode 5 pointers
PMin=22                 ; \
PSec=14                 ; + — Absolute address of the last possible Lead-out area
PFrame=34               ; / (in fact, the disk contains 23 minutes.
                        ; Just look at the rounding error 22:14:34)
PLBA=99934              ; LBA-address of the last possible Lead-out area

[TRACK 1]               ; Information of track 1
MODE=1                  ; Mode 1
INDEX 1=0               ; Post-gap?

[TRACK 2]               ; Information of track 2
MODE=1                  ; Mode 1
INDEX 1=0               ; Post-gap?
```

Generally speaking, the disk contains two sessions, with one track in each. The absolute address of the starting point of the first track is 00:00:02, while the absolute address of the Lead-out area of the first session is 00:29:33 (the address of the track's last sector is shorter by two seconds). The absolute address of the starting point of the second track is 03:01:33, while the absolute Lead-out address of the second session is 03:24:33. The maximum achievable disk capacity is 22:14:34 (although it is labeled as a 23-minute disk).

Now let's corrupt the TOC by increasing the starting address of the first track so that it exceeds the limits of the first session. For the moment, it doesn't matter where it points. It will point somewhere. To find the entry that corresponds to it quickly, use the context search. Press <F7> and enter point=0x1:

Listing 6.2. Attributes of track 1

```
[Entry 3]          ; Information of TOC entry №3
Session=1          ; Entry of session 1
Point=0x01         ; Information of track 1 of session 1
ADR=0x01           ; q-Mode == 1
Control=0x04       ; Digital copy prohibited ;-)
TrackNo=0          ; Track that we are currently reading — Lead-in track
                   ; (i.e., TOC)
AMin=0             ; \
ASec=0             ; + — Absolute address of the current track
AFrame=0           ; /
ALBA=-150          ; LBA-address of the current track
Zero=0             ; This field must be equal to zero, which is the case
PMin=0             ; \
PSec=2             ; + — Absolute address of the starting point
                   ; of track 1 of session 1
PFrame=0           ; /
PLBA=0             ; LBA-address of the starting point of track 1 of session 1
```

As we can see, here we have both the *absolute* track address, measured in minutes:seconds:frames, and the LBA address of the track. The LBA address is nothing more than the logical number of the sector, starting from zero. In practice, the LBA-address field is lacking in the TOC. Here (in the Clone.ccd file) it was added by Clone CD on its own initiative. Actually, the TOC doesn't contain an entry for the LBA-address. Presumably, Clone CD computes the LBA-address for the sake of convenience (and, in fact, it is much more comfortable to work with LBA-addressing). However, when you introduce any modifications into CCD-files, you have to track the correspondence between both types of addresses on your own. In order to translate the absolute addresses into LBA format, it is possible to use the following formula:

Logical Sector Address = (((Minute * 60) + Seconds) * 75 +Frame) − 150.

The listing below shows the attributes of track 1 before and after the introduction of intentional errors.

Listing 6.3. The attributes of track 1 before distortion (left), and after distortion (right)

```
[Entry 3]                              [Entry 3]
     Session=1                              Session=1
     Point=0x01                             Point=0x01
     ADR=0x01                               ADR=0x01
     Control=0x04                           Control=0x04
     TrackNo=0                              TrackNo=0
     AMin=0                                 AMin=0
     ASec=0                                 ASec=0
     AFrame=0                               AFrame=0
     ALBA=-150                              ALBA=-150
     Zero=0                                 Zero=0
     PMin=0                         □       PMin=10
     PSec=2                         □       PSec=2
     PFrame=0                       □       PFrame=0
     PLBA=0                         □       PLBA=-1
```

The crafty author used a clever trick instead of calculating the LBA-address. In fact, I placed my bet on the fact that my version of Clone CD would always use absolute addresses and ignore the LBA. You may use any address of the first track. However, it was done in such a way as to ensure that an invalid address is guaranteed to go beyond the limits of the first session, whose Lead-out area is located at the address 00:29:33 (see TOC entry 2).

Step Four: Mounting the invalidated image to the virtual drive. Now let's mount the invalidated disk image on the Alcohol 120% virtual drive. What good will come of this? Naturally, we cannot be sure that the virtual drive will behave as an actual drive. But, on the other hand, real drives also behave unpredictably when dealing with corrupted disks! Therefore, the use of Alcohol 120% as a working model makes sense, especially since it allows you to save both time and writing media. After all, mounting a virtual drive instead of burning a real CD can be done almost instantly (provided, of course, that it is done at all). Up to version 1.4.3 — the newest version at the moment of writing — Alcohol 120% essentially couldn't deal with corrupted disk images. The program refused to mount them, informing the user that the file image was not available: Unable to mount image. File not accessible. Presumably, Alcohol 120% understands the incorrect TOC too literally, trying to find something that is guaranteed to be missing from the image file (in fact, there is no track starting at address 10:02:00 and terminating with the address 00:29:33).

What a pity! The ability to mount disk images with incorrect TOCs would enable us to overcome the protection not only on those drives supporting the RAW DAO mode, but on every burning drive. In this case, we could save the image of the protected disk to the media in the form of a normal file, and then mount it dynamically using Alcohol 120% as necessary. Thus, Alcohol 120% is considerably less "hardboiled" than it seems.

Step five: Writing an invalidated image to the disk. As an experiment, let's try to burn the invalidated image in the RAW SAO mode, in which, as was shown earlier, the proper writing of sessions with incorrect TOCs is impossible. To guarantee the elimination of possible side effects, it is best to use a drive that doesn't provide hardware support for RAW DAO mode (what if the copier decides to demonstrate a wonder of artificial intelligence and automatically switches to a more suitable writing mode, ignoring our manual settings).

The image burning wizard in Alcohol 120% provides the information shown in Listing 6.4 for the image to be written. Pay specific attention to the size and address of the first track of the first session (they are in bold).

Listing 6.4. The summary information on the image to be written, displayed by Alcohol

---

```
Type:      CloneCD image file
Path:      L:\
Name:      Image.ccd
           Image.img
           Image.sub
Size:      8.81 MB
Sessions:  2
Tracks:    2

Session 01:
   Track 01: Mode 1, Length: -42942(8191.92 GB), Address: 045000
Session 02:
   Track 02: Mode 1, Length: 001715(3.3 MB), Address: 013458
```

Beautiful! If we believe Alcohol 120%, then the length of the first track is 8 TB. This monstrous amount of data will never fit on a DVD, let alone a CD. In fact, track length is not stored anywhere in the TOC. On the contrary, it is computed as the difference between the starting addresses of two adjacent tracks (if the session contains only one track, then the address of the Lead-out area adjacent to the track is used).

The invalidation of the starting address of the first track has resulted in a negative difference between the starting addresses of this track and the Lead-out area. Actually, $00:29:33 - 10:02:00 = 2058 - 45000 == -42942$. If we remember that, according to the standard, LBA-addresses are 32-bit non-negative numbers, it becomes clear how Alcohol has obtained such an unnatural value (negative numbers always have the most significant bit set, hence a very small negative number corresponds to a very large positive one). Simple calculations show that the value of 8 TB, identified by Alcohol, is achieved only when using 43-bit variables. As it turns out, Alcohol 120% is designed with a reserve for the future. As a matter of fact, discs larger than 30 GB are anticipated. For addressing such disks, 32-bits will be insufficient. Besides, it is necessary to account for the reserve required for "trapping" negative lengths that appear as a result of TOC invalidation, since Alcohol is a protected copier!

Finally, the most important moment arrives, namely, the burning of the invalidated image on CD-R/CD-RW.

CAUTION

If you are using a CD-RW disc, you must be aware that you could ruin it! If the only CD-RW drive that you have at your disposal refuses to recognize such a disk, it will be impossible to erase it.

After "swallowing" the invalidated image, Alcohol 120%, without any complaint, burns the write indicator (if, of course, your drive has one) and proceeds with the burning process. A minute or two passes, but the progress bar will remain at the zero mark. By the end of the 6th minute, when the write head reaches the disk edge, the burning process terminates abnormally, and Alcohol 120%, after producing a sad "bang," reports a hardware error.

Viewing the resulting disc on ASUS and NEC drives allows you to see only the first session. No traces of the second session can be found. It seems that it has passed like a witch in the night. The situation is even worse with the PHILIPS drive, since it refuses to recognize what you insert as a CD. After short time, during which it produces raspy sounds from its mechanical internals, accompanied by strained wails of the motor as it tries different speeds, the "DISC IN" indicator blinks sadly and goes out. The "sadness" means that, if you have invalidated the disk, you'll have to kiss it goodbye. If it was a cheap CD-R, this doesn't matter. However, a usable CD-RW is a greater loss. Fortunately, on NEC drives, CD-RW can be cleared successfully. Encouraged by this circumstance, let us continue with our disk harassment.

Clone CD copier, in this respect, behaves differently. First, it evaluates the length of the corrupted track as 4,294,868,664 bytes (see the listing provided below). This indicates that this copier uses 32-bit variables, and, consequently, is unable to distinguish positive values from negative values. Pay special attention to the size of the first track of the first session (in bold).

Listing 6.5. The summary information on the image to be written displayed by Clone CD

```
INFORMATION ON THE IMAGE FILE:

Number of sessions: 2
Disk space required: 34850 KB
Sectors: 15173
Time: 03:22:23 (minutes:seconds:framesк)

INFORMATION ON SESSION 1:

Session size: 4726 KB
Number of tracks: 1
Pregap: Mode 1 data, size: 103359 KB
Track 1: Mode 1 data, size: 4294868664 KB

INFORMATION ON SESSION 2:

Session size: 3939 KB
Number of tracks: 1
Track 2: Mode 1 data, size: 3939 KB
```

Second, having detected that the burning of an incorrect TOC is impossible on this drive, Clone CD fixes the TOC so that it takes a correct form. As a result, the burning process goes on without any errors and we obtain a disc that *looks* like a usable and functional CD. The starting address of the first track starts where the Lead-in area of the first session ends (or, to be more precise, the Pre-gap area of the first track starts at the point where the Post-gap Lead-in area of the first session ends. This fact, however, is of minor importance to us). Such a disk will normally be read by any CD-ROM drive. There is, however, a trap! If a protection mechanism reads the TOC contents, it will easily detect that it is dealing with a copy and not with the original disc. Why, then, do we need this type of copying, if only the copier could display at least some warning? Well, professionals will quickly recognize the trap. Beginners or simply, normal users, however, will have problems. In other words, it's a tough job.

However, *in RAW DAO mode the burning of the invalidated image carries on just fine, and Clone CD doesn't introduce a wheeze into the TOC, thanks to which we get a truly protected CD*, which will now try to crack.

Step six: Testing the usability of a protected disk. Viewing a protected disk on a NEC drive displays all of the files. This includes those that belong to the first track, namely, those whose staring address was badly corrupted. By double-clicking on those files, you can make sure not only that they are present in the directory, but also that they can be opened successfully by associated applications. To all appearances, these files look OK. But some uneasy doubts start to torture our souls: Did the CD-RW drive actually burn the starting address of the first track as we required?

To answer this question, we have to analyze the disk geometry, i.e., to simply read the TOC. Let's start Roxio Easy CD Creator, which we have already grown to love, and find the **CD Information** command in the **CD** menu. Click on it, and you'll immediately see a dialog displaying the disk layout.

CAUTION

Not every product is capable of understanding an incorrect TOC! Easy CD Creator can do this, while Stomp Record Now!, for instance, isn't capable of doing so. If there is no suitable program at your disposal, you can use the `raw.TOC.exe` utility supplied along with this book.

As we might have expected, the starting address of the first track is far beyond its "native" session, and its length, expressed as a positive number, significantly exceeds the available disk capacity (Fig. 6.2). Thus, all of our concerns are absolutely groundless!

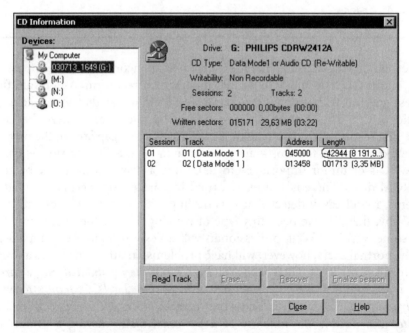

Fig. 6.2. Negative length of the first track drives the standard copier crazy

But how do we access the contents of the first track? Well, who said you that a CD is addressed on the basis of tracks in the first place? The base addressing unit for data CDs is the *sector*. The absolute address of each sector is unambiguously defined by its Q-subcode channel (on account of the fact that the boundaries of sections and sectors might differ, the maximum possible difference allowed by the standard is 1 second, i.e., 75 sectors. Therefore, this method is used only for the rough positioning of an optical head). Precise positioning is carried out directly by the sector header, which contains its absolute address in a native form. Track numbers do not take part in the process of sector processing, or, to be more precise, *may or may not take part in this process.* This depends on the drive model and its firmware. Their participation and the details of this process represent a deep secret on the part of the drive's developers. They do not advertise these! However, some way or other, some drives become confused when encountering an incorrect TOC.

The results of testing that I have conducted are as follows: NEC and TEAC show the contents of both sessions and process their contents correctly. ASUS shows only the first, incorrect session, and doesn't see the second session, making it unavailable even at the sector level. However, files of the first session are processed properly enough. PHILIPS sees both sessions, but it correctly processes only the files of the last session (i.e., the one that isn't invalidated). The incorrect session is available at the sector level, but access to it is not stable. Sometimes, without any visible reason, PHILIPS goes crazy and returns only senseless gibberish.

Thus, the following conclusion can be drawn: *Protection mechanisms based on an incorrect TOC cannot bind to any session. Therefore, both sessions must duplicate the contents of the other in hope that the drive at the user's disposal will read at least one of them.* What is the sense in this kind of protection then? Still, there is some sense in this. Although the protection cannot be bound to sessions, it can be bound to the raw contents of the TOC. Later in this chapter, we will discuss how to carry out this kind of binding in practice. For the moment, let's try to copy the protected disk using our favorites — Clone CD and Alcohol 120%, not forgetting, of course, about standard copiers.

Automatic Copying and a Discussion of its Results

My favorite and most beloved program, *Stomp Record Now!*, when attempting to copy a disk with an incorrect starting address for the first track, displays the `Invalid disk` error message and refuses to start the operation. This isn't a surprise. After all, what else could be expected from a copier intended for end users?

It is much more interesting to test the behavior of *Ahead Nero* — the most popular professional copier. A test shows that, independently of the state of the **Ignore Illegal TOC Type** checkbox on the **Read options** tab, and independently of other options that the user may set, it is impossible to copy the protected disk. Nero doesn't make any attempt at reading the disk and displays the `Invalid track mode` error message! The CD Speed utility supplied as part of Nero also works improperly. It carries out scanning of the area where the illegal address is located rather than the first track. The second track is not displayed at all.

Now let's proceed with copiers of protected disks. *Clone CD* is one tool of this type, and its developers insist that it is capable of overcoming any protection that exists today.

Regardless of the drive, into which we insert the protected disk, Clone CD always produces the same result, which has no relation to reality. According to its humble opinion, the disk contains only one session, 4.6 MB long, but the size of its single track is as big as 3.9 TB! Clone CD copier sees the protected disk as shown in Listing 6.6.

Listing 6.6. Note that Clone CD has recognized only the first session, and, further, done it incorrectly

```
INFORMATION ON THE CD IN THE DRIVE:


Number of sessions: 1

Disk space taken: 4726 KB

Sectors: 2058

Time: 00:27:33 (min:sec:frame)


INFORMATION ON SESSION 1:


Session size: 4726 KB

Number of tracks: 1

Pregap: Mode 1 data, size: 103359 KB

Track 1: Data, size: 4294868664 KB
```

Long before the completion of the copying process, we begin to doubt if the disk will be copied correctly. More realistically, this doubt turns into the firm certainty that the disk will be copied incorrectly. And, in fact, our doubts turn to be true! Let's create the image of the copied disk and compare the resulting TOC to the original.

Listing 6.7. The image of the protected disk obtained using the Clone CD program (Incorrect fields are highlighted in bold)

```
[CloneCD]                    ; Copier information
Version=3                    ; Clone CD version

[Disc]                       ; Information about the disk
TocEntries=7                 ; Number of TOC entries == 7
                             ; (in the original TOC there were 12)
Sessions=1                   ; Number of sessions == 1
                             ; (in the original TOC there were 2)
DataTracksScrambled=0        ; DVD field
CDTextLength=0               ; No CD-Text in subcode fields of the Lead-in area

[Session 1]                  ; Session 1 information
PreGapMode=1                 ; Track type == Mode 1
PreGapSubC=0                 ; No subchannel data

[Entry 0]                    ; Information of the TOC entry №0
Session=1                    ; Entry of session 1
Point=0xa0                   ; Number of the first track of session 1
                             ; in PMin/disk type in PSec
ADR=0x01                     ; q-Mode == 1
Control=0x04                 ; Digital copy prohibited ;-)
TrackNo=0                    ; Track that we are currently reading — Lead-in track
(e.g., TOC)
AMin=0                       ; \
ASec=0                       ; + — Absolute address of the current track
AFrame=0                     ; /
ALBA=-150                    ; LBA-address of the current track
Zero=0                       ; This field must be set to zero, which is the case
PMin=1                       ; Number of the first track of session 1
PSec=0                       ; Disk type CD-DA and CD-ROM disk in Mode 1
PFrame=0                     ; No useful information
PLBA=4350                    ; Track number represented by CloneCD
                             ; as LBA-address, i.c., trash

[Entry 1]                    ; Information of TOC entry №1
Session=1                    ; Entry of session 1
Point=0xa1                   ; Number of the last track of session 1 in PMin
ADR=0x01                     ; q-Mode == 1
Control=0x04                 ; Digital copy prohibited ;-)
TrackNo=0                    ; Track that we are currently reading —
```

```
                                 ; Lead-in track (i.e., TOC)
AMin=0                           ; \
ASec=0                           ; + — Absolute address of the current track
AFrame=0                         ; /
ALBA=-150                        ; LBA-address of the current track
Zero=0                           ; This field must be equal to zero, which is the case
PMin=1                           ; Number of the last track of session 1
                                 ; (session has only one track)
PSec=0                           ; No useful information
PFrame=0                         ; No useful information
PLBA=4350                        ; Track number represented by CloneCD as
                                 ; LBA-address, i.e., trash


[Entry 2]                        ; Information of TOC entry №2
Session=1                        ; Entry of session 1
Point=0xa2                       ; Position of the Lead-out area in PMin:PSec:PFrame
ADR=0x01                         ; q-Mode == 1
Control=0x04                     ; Digital copy prohibited ;-)
TrackNo=0                        ; Track that we are currently reading —
                                 ; Lead-in track (i.e., TOC)
AMin=0                           ; \
ASec=0                           ; + — Absolute address of the current track
AFrame=0                         ; /
ALBA=-150                        ; LBA-address of the current track
Zero=0                           ; This field must be set to zero, which is true
PMin=0                           ; \
PSec=29                          ; + — Absolute address of the Lead-out
                                 ; area of session 1
PFrame=33                        ; /
PLBA=2058                        ; LBA-address of the Lead-out area of session 1


[Entry 3]                        ; Information of TOC entry №3
Session=1                        ; Entry of session 1
Point=0x01                       ; Information of track 1 of session 1
ADR=0x01                         ; q-Mode == 1
Control=0x04                     ; Digital copy prohibited ;-)
TrackNo=0                        ; Track that we are currently reading —
                                 ; Lead-in track (i.e., TOC)
AMin=0                           ; \
ASec=0                           ; + — Absolute address of the current track
AFrame=0                         ; /
ALBA=-150                        ; LBA-address of the current track
Zero=0                           ; This field must be set to zero, which is the case
```

```
PMin=10                     ; \
PSec=2                      ; + — Absolute address of the starting point of
                            ; track 1 of session 1
PFrame=0                    ; /
PLBA=45000                  ; LBA-address of the starting point of
                            ; track 1 of session 1

[Entry 4]                   ; Information of the TOC entry №4
Session=1                   ; Entry of session 1
Point=0xb0                  ; Position of the next
                            ; writable area in AMin:ASec:AFrame
ADR=0x05                    ; q-Mode == 1
Control=0x04                ; Data disk protected against copying ;-)
TrackNo=0                   ; Track that we are currently reading —
                            ; Lead-in track (i.e., TOC)
AMin=2                      ; \
ASec=59                     ; + — Absolute address of the next writable area
AFrame=33                   ; /
ALBA=13308                  ; LBA-address of the next writable area
Zero=3                      ; Number of pointers in Mode 5
PMin=22                     ; \
PSec=14                     ; + — Absolute address of the maximum writable area
PFrame=34                   ; /
PLBA=99934                  ; LBA-address of the maximum writable area

[Entry 5]                   ; Information of the TOC entry №5
Session=1                   ; Entry of session 1
Point=0xc0                  ; Starting address of Lead-in area of Hybrid disk
                            ; (if any)
ADR=0x05                    ; Mode 5 (Orange book)
Control=0x04                ; Data disk protected against copying ;-)
TrackNo=0                   ; Track that we are currently reading —
                            ; Lead-in track (i.e., TOC)
AMin=162                    ; Recommended power of laser for
ASec=200                    ; Application code (original contained 128 here)
AFrame=224                  ; Original contained 140 here
ALBA=294074                 ; LBA-"address" of the previous three fields
Zero=0                      ; Reserved
PMin=97                     ; \
PSec=27                     ; + — Absolute address of Lead-in area of Hybrid disk
PFrame=21                   ; /   (address is outside the disk limits,
                            ; i.e., no Hybrid disk)
PLBA=-11604                 ; LBA address of Lead-in area of Hybrid
```

```
                              ; (computed with overflow)

[Entry 6]                     ; Information of the TOC entry №6
Session=1                     ; Entry of session 1
Point=0xc1                    ; Copy of ATIP information
ADR=0x05                      ; -+
Control=0x04                  ; -+
TrackNo=0                     ; -+
AMin=4                        ; -+
ASec=192                      ; -+
AFrame=150                    ; -+- ATIP (changed!)
ALBA=32400                    ; -+
Zero=0                        ; -+
PMin=0                        ; -+
PSec=0                        ; -+
PFrame=0                      ; -+
PLBA=-150

[TRACK 1]
MODE=0
INDEX 1=45000
```

The reduction of the number of sessions to one is rather embarrassing. Where the second, correct (!) session, has gone is unclear. And, although the incorrect data from the first track have been preserved, the Application Code and ATIP fields have changed unexpectedly (despite the fact that these data were written to the same CD-RW disc, although its burning was carried out on different drives). The most surprising thing is that Clone CD has displayed some garbage instead of the actual address of the Lead-out area. According to it, the absolute Lead-out address is equal to 00:29:33, while the Lead-out of the original disk was located at position 03:24:23, and the starting address of the first track of the copied disk was 10:02:00. Yes! The Lead-out address proved to be located before the starting point of the first track! There you are. The copier could not handle the "native" disk protection, and has applied its own instead.

The consequences are as follows: The copied disk is not usable on all drives (ASUS, NEC, and TEAC will read it, although they'll see only the first session, but PHILIPS will refuse to recognize the disc altogether). What is more, there is nothing easier for the protection than to read the current TOC and compare it to the original. Because the TOC of the copied disk was badly damaged, it becomes only too easy to distinguish the original from its illegal copy.

To put it frankly, it has all fizzled out. Well, let's try to appeal to *Alcohol 120%* — surely it must handle this situation! In fact, Alcohol 120% views both sessions — correct and incorrect (Fig. 6.3).

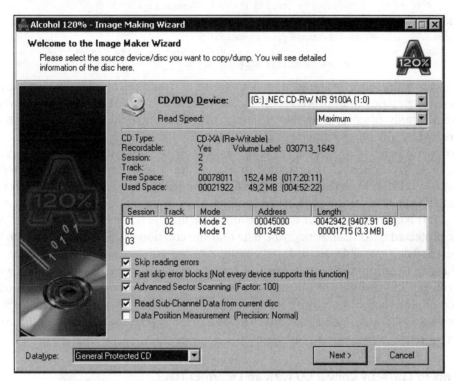

Fig. 6.3. Alcohol 120% views both sessions of the protected disk.
However, the disk copy obtained using it will also be unusable

However, for some unknown reason, it saves only the second (by comparison, remember that Clone CD saved the first). Well, what's the problem? As it appears, there is no need to compare the TOC contents — after all, the TOC of the copy is unlikely to contain the contents expected by the protection. Nevertheless, in contrast to pessimistic expectations, the TOC contents copied by Alcohol 120% correspond almost completely to the original. The only error made by Alcohol 120% is that it has determined the Pregap type of both tracks as Mode 2 instead of Mode 1. Still, because session 1 is missing from the image, the disk copy obtained using it proves to be unusable.

During the image burning process, Alcohol 120% says: Image size DOESN'T match the Lead-out, written in TOC! (which is the direct consequence of the erroneous creation of the image by Alcohol 120% itself, due to the invalid start address of the first track). The address of the Lead-out area in the TOC is 03:22:23. The image size is 12:54:65.

```
08:46:48 (G:) TEAC CD-W552E (1:1): An error occurred during the write process!
08:46:48 Error: [05/26/00] — Invalid Field In Parameter List
08:46:48 (G:) TEAC CD-W552E (1:1): An error occurred during the write process!
08:46:48 Loading of the image file canceled!
08:46:51 There were errors during the write process! View the report file
         and contact the technical support service.
```

But wait! It was claimed that both Clone CD and Alcohol 120% are capable of copying practically all protected discs that exist at the moment. Having believed this, we suddenly discover that they are unable to overcome the protection mechanisms created by any programmer (even a beginner)! Furthermore, they are unable to overcome it separately or working in combination! At the same time, the equipment used in these experiments is guaranteed to ensure the correct copying of corrupted disks (after all, I did these tests on my own)! Consequently, the developers of both copiers won't be able to use the physical limitations of the equipment being used as an excuse.

It is hard to believe that such a primitive technique simply "blinds" the best copiers of protected disks. Can it really be true that the creation of disks that can virtually not be copied is possible on ordinary home equipment? Yes, it's true! Of course, you shouldn't confuse the impossibility of copying the disk by automatic copiers with the principal impossibility of obtaining its absolutely identical copy. In manual mode, the copying of such disks is possible (provided, of course, that your CD-RW drive supports RAW DAO mode and the CD-ROM drive can read sectors from both sessions). In the next session, we will discuss how to achieve this.

How to Correctly Copy a CD with an Incorrect TOC?

Using the "Pinch of File" (or any other block file copier), HIEW, two images of the protected disk (one with the first session from Clone CD, and the other with the second session from Alcohol 120%), and having exercised our brain a bit, it is possible to re-create an identical copy of the original disk by means of combining them. However, this isn't the proper way and, for a true hacker, isn't a particularly elegant approach.

To avoid writing a custom program for CD burning, let us limit ourselves to using Clone CD. Provided that the disk image supplied to Clone CD is correct, this program will carry out burning successfully.

Thus, we have a more or less correct IMAGE.CCD file, containing the TOC (it can be taken from Alcohol 120%). However, the image file IMAGE.IMG is missing. Well, let's try to obtain it. We will base it on the fact that LBA addresses for all disks are numbered sequentially, including the Lead-in/Lead-out area and other auxiliary stuff. Naturally, it is impossible to read the control disk areas directly at the sector level, but this is exactly the method that we are going to use! Reading the disk sequentially, from first sector to the last, we will discover that sectors having LBA addresses from 0 to 2,055 can be read without any problems. After that, there follows a "shadowy zone" of unreadable sectors, spanning up to sector 13,307. Here, the sectors are either totally unreadable or are returned in a severely mutated form, easily recognizable by the lack of a correct sync sequence in their headers. Finally, starting from address 13,308, reading can be continued without problems.

It appears to be the case that we are dealing with a two-session disk, and the "shadowy zone" between the sessions is nothing other than the Lead-out/Lead-in areas. Adding two seconds for Post-gap (assuming that it was written according to the standard), we will find that the LBA address of the last significant sector of the first session is 2,057 or, converted into absolute units, — 0 minutes, 29 seconds, and 32 frames. Accordingly, the address of the first sector of the second session is equal to: `13308 + 150 (pre-gap) == 13458`, or 3 minutes, 1 second, 33 frames. Of course, if the disk being investigated contains many errors, its analysis becomes more complicated, since physical defects at the sector level may look exactly like Lead-in/Lead-out areas, provided, of course, that the defective areas have the appropriate length. This, fortunately, is unlikely.

Having discarded sectors located in the pre- and Post-gap zones (e.g., 150 sectors from the end of the first readable area and the same number from the start of the next), we must unite them into a common file using any file copier (for instance, this may be the built-in MS-DOS copy command: `copy file_1 /b + file_2 image.img`). After that, it only remains to read the raw TOC using the READ TOC SCSI/ATAPI command (opcode: `43h`, format: `2h`) and write it into the IMAGE.CCD file according to Clone CD syntax. As an alternative, you can use the CCD file created by Alcohol 120%, having previously corrected the Pre-gap mode (as already mentioned, Alcohol 120% has determined it incorrectly, having confused Mode 1 with Mode 2). According to the standard, the sector mode is specified by 15th byte of its header (starting from zero). If this byte is set to 1 (which is true in our case), then the mode of this sector will also be 1, not 2.

Provided that everything has been done correctly, after writing the manually formed disk image we'll have a disk practically identical to the original. Is it that simple? Yes, it's as simple as that! And the procedure for writing an automatic copier for automating our efforts takes no more than a few hours! If reading raw sectors from the disks represents a problem for you, just use the source codes of the ASPI32.raw/SPTI.raw utilities, which carry out exactly this operation.

Thus, corrupting the TOC isn't a reliable mechanism for copy protection. It will prevent normal users with Clone CD/Alcohol 120% at their disposal from copying the disc. Note that, in most cases, this is all that is actually required from the protection mechanism.

An Example of Implementing Protection at the Software Level

Now let us demonstrate how to implement this type of protection programmatically. The simplest thing to do is to send a command to read a raw TOC to the drive (opcode: 43h, format: 2h) and compare the result returned by this command with the predefined pattern. It is up to the protection (it's its private affair), which fields that command will check. It is at least sufficient to check the number of sessions and the starting address of the corrupted track. At the maximum protection level, it is possible to check the entire TOC. Naturally, it is recommended to avoid a byte-by-byte comparison of the TOC being checked with the original, since this approach implies laying a stake on the specific features of the drive's firmware. The standard remains silent about the order, in which the TOC contents must be returned. Therefore, its binary representation might vary from drive to drive (although, in practice this does not happen). A competently designed protection system must analyze only those fields where it is explicitly bound to their contents.

The demo example provided below illustrates the technique for correct binding to the TOC. Naturally, explicit binding can be detected easily by a qualified hacker and deleted from the program as something unnecessary. Therefore, don't blindly use this example in your programs. It would be much better to use the values of the TOC fields as working constants that are vitally important for the correct operation of your program. In this case, the resemblance of real faces to the photos in the "passports," so to speak, won't be so evident. Naturally, explicit checks for disk authenticity must be present in the program. However, the main goal here isn't the protection of the program against cracking! On the contrary, it is informing the user that the disk being checked isn't a legal copy.

Listing 6.8. [crackme.9822C095h.c] A demo example of the simplest protection binding to the incorrect TOC and preventing unauthorized copying

---

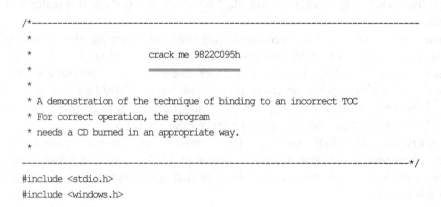

```
/*---------------------------------------------------------------------
 *
 *                     crack me 9822C095h
 *                     ================
 *
 *
 * A demonstration of the technique of binding to an incorrect TOC
 * For correct operation, the program
 * needs a CD burned in an appropriate way.
 *
 *
 ---------------------------------------------------------------*/
#include <stdio.h>
#include <windows.h>
```

```
#include "CD.h"
#include "SPTI.h"
#include "ASPI32.h"

// Parameters of protected disk that we are going to check
//---------------------------------------------------------
#define _N_SESSION      2               // Number of sessions
#define _TRACK          1               // Number of the track being checked
#define _TRACK_LBA      0x6B124         // Starting LBA address of the _TRACK track

// Program parameters
//--------------------
#define MAX_TRY         3               // Max. Number of attempts at reading the TOC
#defineTRY_DELAY        100             // Delay between attempts
#define MAX_TOC_SIZE    (2352)          // Max. TOC size

main(int argc, char **argv)
{
        long a, real_len, try = 1;          // Main variables
        unsigned char TOC[MAX_TOC_SIZE];    // The TOC will be read here
        unsigned char CDB[ATAPI_CDB_SIZE];  // SCSI CDB block for SCSI/ATAPI devices

        // TITLE
        fprintf(stderr,"crackme 9822C095 by Kris Kaspersky\n");

        if (argc <2)
        {
                fprintf(stderr, "USAGE:crackme.9822C095h.exe drive\n");
                fprintf(stderr, "\tdrive — \\\\.\\X: or Trg.Lun\n");
                return -1;
        }

        // Buffer initialization
        memset(CDB, 0, ATAPI_CDB_SIZE); memset(TOC, 0, MAX_TOC_SIZE);

        // Preparing the CDB block
        CDB[0] = 0x43;                  // READ TOC
        CDB[2] = 0x2;                   // RAW TOC
        CDB[6] = 0;                     // Number of the first session
        CDB[7] = HIBYTE(MAX_TOC_SIZE); // Size...
        CDB[8] = LOBYTE(MAX_TOC_SIZE); //        ...of the buffer

                                        // Reading the TOC
```

```
while(1)
{
        // Sending CDB block to SCSI/ATAPI device
        a = SEND_SCSI_CMD(argv[1], CDB, ATAPI_CDB_SIZE, NO_SENSE,
                          TOC, MAX_TOC_SIZE, SCSI_DATA_IN);
        if (a == SCSI_OK) break;         // TOC successfully read, exiting

        // An error occurred. Is the drive ready?
        Sleep(TRY_DELAY);                // Pausing
        if (try++ == MAX_TRY)            // Is the max. number of attempts
  // exceeded?
                { fprintf(stderr, "-ERR: can not read TOC\x7\n"); return -1;}
}

// TOC read, starting its analysis
//---------------------------------------

// Checking the number of sessions
if ((TOC[3] - TOC[2]) != (_N_SESSION-1))
                {fprintf(stderr, "-ERR: not original CD\n"); return -1;}

// Checking starting LBA address of the _TRACK track
//---------------------------------------------------
real_len = TOC[0]*0x100L+TOC[1];        // Determining the actual TOC length
for (a = 4; a < real_len; a+=11)        // Testing all entries
{
        if (TOC[a+3] == _TRACK)         // Is this our track?
            if ((((TOC[a+4]*60L)+TOC[a+5])*75L)+TOC[a+6] != _TRACK_LBA)
                {fprintf(stderr, "-ERR: not original LBA\n"); return -1;}
        Else
            break;
}

// This is original disk!
printf("Hello, original CD\n");
}
```

The suggested protection is not copied by Clone CD (since it creates only one session instead of the expected two). However, it can be bypassed easily by Alcohol 120%, because, although it places garbage in the first session, this program quite correctly recreates the original TOC.

To strengthen this protection, we can try not only to check for the existence of both sessions, but also check the integrity of their contents. Naturally, it is not necessary to dig up each session entirely. It is enough to choose some key sectors, preferably having unique contents. Wait! Didn't the author warn us about the consequences of a check like this? No one can guarantee that these sectors will be read on the user's equipment! Well, my answer is that it is actually not recommended to rely on the *readability* of sectors. However, it is not only possible, but even recommended, to check the sectors that were *successfully read*. This means that, if key sectors cannot be read, everything is OK, and there is no reason to consider the disk to be an unauthorized copy. This simply means that this effect is due to specific features of the user's equipment (I mean, that it is incorrect and non-compliant with standards). It is another matter if the sectors were read without errors and contain something absolutely different than the key data. This means that the problem is caused by the disk, not by the equipment.

The strengthened variant of protection cannot be copied by Alcohol 120% (in fact, instead of the original content of the first session, Alcohol 120% burns some horrible garbage onto the disc). However, it can be copied manually, according to the technique described above. Furthermore, binding to an incorrect TOC can be cracked easily using debugger/disassembler. How? I'll answer this question very soon. Thus, further improvement of protection of this type is absolutely senseless. After all, we have already protected the disk against ordinary users. With regard to hackers, it is impossible to protect anything against them anyway (or, at least, not using this method). Either way, advanced protection mechanisms are the topic for a separate discussion.

Complete Neutralization of the Protection

Obtaining a workable copy of a protected disc is only half of our job. Accomplishing the cracking goal implies at least the recovery of the incorrect TOC and unbinding the protection from the disc. In other words, it must be possible to copy a disc that has been correctly cracked on any equipment, using any standard copier, and without any conflicts.

The process of removing protection usually starts with an analysis of the disc geometry, in order to detect the sessions/sectors that are actually used. Incorrect sessions usually do not contain any useful information, because the mere fact of their existence is the thing that really matters for the protection. Their contents, which might even be unavailable on some drives, are of no importance. What methods are there for checking for the existence of these sections? At the hardware level, there is only one method — the computer sends the READ TOC SCSI/ATAPI command to the drive, and, in response, gets the full listing of the directory contents. At the software level, access to the hardware is most often gained using the ASPI/SPTI interface, or, less often, directly via I/O ports. Some types of protection prefer to work via the CD-ROM driver, considering this method more civilized and less dangerous.

Anyway, a hacker usually has two options, from which to choose. The first is to localize the command for reading the TOC in machine code (this is usually done by setting the breakpoint to the `SendASPI32Command` function) and then trying to re-write the program code in such a way as to ensure its correct operation with any TOC. The second is to intercept the `CreateFile/DeviceIoControl` function and implant a spy tracing the entire flow of SCSI/ATAPI commands passing through it. In case when an attempt at reading the TOC of a protected disc is made, the implanted code would return fake data to the protection. The first approach is more reliable, and therefore, more practical. Let's consider it in more detail.

Fictitious Track in the Genuine Track

> Those who go off the deep end have a greater chance to drown.
>
> *Folklore*

The fact that data discs are addressed exclusively at the sector level provides wider possibilities for playing tricks with placement of tracks — neither the drive itself nor the operating system pay any attention to this. However, it can confuse the over-whelming majority of copiers, including protected CD copiers that try to copy discs track by track, rather than sector by sector. Placing fictitious tracks in service areas that can't be copied by the drive at all or are bound to little-known and rarely used struc-tures that copiers prefer to ignore is even more efficient. To begin with, however, let us first examine how standard tracks are organized and operate.

For the sake of space economy, the control structures of CDs contain the mini-mum of required information, and track length is not stored anywhere explicitly. Roughly, it is computed by means of subtracting the starting address of the current track from the starting address of the next track (or the starting address of the Lead-out area, if the current track is the last within the session). Starting addresses are stored in the disc's TOC.

Listing 6.9. An example of a raw disc TOC with comments

```
session number
 | ADR/control
 |  | TNO
 |  |  | point
 |  |  |  | AM:AS:AF
 |  |  |  |  |  |  | zero
 |  |  |  |  |  |  |  | PM:PS:PF
01 14 00 A0 00 00 00 00 01 00 00 ← Number of the 1st track of the 1st session
01 14 00 A1 00 00 00 00 02 00 00 ← Number of the last track of the 1st session
01 14 00 A2 00 00 00 00 00 1D 21 ← Lead-out address of the 1st session
```

```
01 14 00 01 00 00 00 00 00 02 00  ← Starting address of track N1
01 14 00 02 00 00 00 00 00 11 00  ← Starting address of track N2
02 14 00 A0 00 00 00 00 03 00 00  ← Number of the 1st track of the 2nd session
02 14 00 A1 00 00 00 00 03 00 00  ← Number of the last track of the 2nd session
02 14 00 A2 00 00 00 00 03 18 17  ← Lead-out address of the 2nd session
02 14 00 03 00 00 00 00 03 01 21  ← Starting address of track N3
```

Between the end of the Lead-in area and the starting address of the 1st track of each session there is a so-called *Pre-gap area* with a length of 150 sectors, formally belonging to the first track. According to the Red Book and Yellow Book standards (the basic standards for audio CDs and data CDs, respectively), this area doesn't contain any useful data. On standard CDs manufactured by stamper-injection molding, this area is usually filled with zeroes. The type of Pre-gap area coincides with the type of its related track. In fact, the Pre-gap area is designed in the image and likeness of the related track. This means that for tracks recorded in MODE1, MODE2 FORM1, and MODE2 FORM2, the Pre-gap area isn't blank. It contains, at least, the correct sector headers, and, at a maximum, the sector headers, checksum, Reed-Solomon codes, and other control information.

Listing 6.10. A sector from the Pre-gap area of an audio track (left) and data track (right)

```
00 00 00 00 00 00 00 00 00 00 00 00 00 00 00 00 | 00 FF FF FF FF FF FF FF FF FF FF 00 00 00 02 01
00 00 00 00 00 00 00 00 00 00 00 00 00 00 00 00 | 00 00 00 00 00 00 00 00 00 00 00 00 00 00 00 00
00 00 00 00 00 00 00 00 00 00 00 00 00 00 00 00 | 00 00 00 00 00 00 00 00 00 00 00 00 00 00 00 00
00 00 00 00 00 00 00 00 00 00 00 00 00 00 00 00 | 00 00 00 00 00 00 00 00 00 00 00 00 00 00 00 00
00 00 00 00 00 00 00 00 00 00 00 00 00 00 00 00 | 00 00 00 00 00 00 00 00 00 00 00 00 00 00 00 00
00 00 00 00 00 00 00 00 00 00 00 00 00 00 00 00 | 00 00 00 00 00 00 00 00 00 00 00 00 00 00 00 00
00 00 00 00 00 00 00 00 00 00 00 00 00 00 00 00 | 00 00 00 00 00 00 00 00 00 00 00 00 00 00 00 00
00 00 00 00 00 00 00 00 00 00 00 00 00 00 00 00 | 00 00 00 00 00 00 00 00 00 00 00 00 00 00 00 00
00 00 00 00 00 00 00 00 00 00 00 00 00 00 00 00 | 00 00 00 00 00 00 00 00 00 00 00 00 00 00 00 00
00 00 00 00 00 00 00 00 00 00 00 00 00 00 00 00 | 00 00 00 00 00 00 00 00 00 00 00 00 00 00 00 00
00 00 00 00 00 00 00 00 00 00 00 00 00 00 00 00 | 00 00 00 00 00 00 00 00 00 00 00 00 00 00 00 00
00 00 00 00 00 00 00 00 00 00 00 00 00 00 00 00 | 00 00 00 00 00 00 00 00 00 00 00 00 00 00 00 00
00 00 00 00 00 00 00 00 00 00 00 00 00 00 00 00 | 00 00 00 00 00 00 00 00 00 00 00 00 00 00 00 00
00 00 00 00 00 00 00 00 00 00 00 00 00 00 00 00 | 00 00 00 00 00 00 00 00 00 00 00 00 00 00 00 00
00 00 00 00 00 00 00 00 00 00 00 00 00 00 00 00 | 00 00 00 00 00 00 00 00 00 00 00 00 00 00 00 00
00 00 00 00 00 00 00 00 00 00 00 00 00 00 00 00 | 00 00 00 00 00 00 00 00 00 00 00 00 00 00 00 00
...                                             | ...
00 00 00 00 00 00 00 00 00 00 00 00 00 00 00 00 | 69 A0 A7 82 CA 8A 00 00 00 00 00 00 00 00 00 00
00 00 00 00 00 00 00 00 00 00 00 00 00 00 00 00 | 00 00 00 00 00 00 CA 65 65 BC AF D9 00 00 00 00
00 00 00 00 00 00 00 00 00 00 00 00 00 00 00 00 | 00 00 00 00 00 00 00 00 00 00 00 00 00 00 00 00
00 00 00 00 00 00 00 00 00 00 00 00 00 00 00 00 | 00 00 A7 5B BD 72 88 0A 92 23 00 00 00 00 00 00
00 00 00 00 00 00 00 00 00 00 00 00 00 00 00 00 | 00 00 00 00 00 00 00 00 00 00 3D 90 90 48 AD D8
```

Between the end of the last track and Lead-out area of each session, there is the Post-gap area with a length of 150 or more sectors. Formally, it belongs to the last track. Similar to Pre-gap, it usually doesn't contain any data. The type of the Post-gap area is the same as that of the track that precedes it.

If a track of one type is followed one of another (for example, MODE1 is changed to MODE2 or audio tracks are interleaved with data tracks), these tracks are separated by a transition area with a length of at least 350 sectors. The first 150 sectors are taken up by the Post-gap area of the preceding track, while the remaining 200 sectors belong to the extended Pre-gap area of the next track. The extended Pre-gap area comprises two parts, of 50 and 150 sectors, respectively. The first 50 sectors retain the type of track that preceded them, while the remaining 150 sectors are from the normal Post-gap area.

Data tracks of an identical type can be located either right beside each another or can be separated by transition areas. However, some copiers (Ahead Nero, in particular) erroneously assume that transition areas between adjacent tracks are always present. Therefore, they skip about the last 350 sectors of each track on their own. Therefore, discs without transition areas (or with shortened transition areas) are copied incorrectly by these copiers, despite their full correspondence with the standard.

Note that the sizes of the transition areas specified above are the minimum allowed by the standard. Their maximum length is practically unlimited. The size of the transition area is not stored anywhere in an explicit form, and, in order to determine their boundaries, it is necessary to analyze subchannel data. To be more precise, we have to analyze the contents of the INDEX field of the Q subcode channel. A zero value corresponds to a Pre-gap (or a pause, when dealing with audio discs), while any other value corresponds to the actual track sector or to the Post-gap area. Thus, the Post-gap area is no different from the track preceding it, and the copier cannot determine its length. The presence of the Post-gap can only be detected implicitly, namely, by the lack of information in the user data about the last sectors of the track. A properly designed copier should copy the contents of all of the disc sessions in their entirety, from the first to the last sector belonging to them, without making any attempts to analyze the track layout, as it can be changed arbitrarily. The addressing of data discs is carried out exclusively at the sector level, so the tracks are not involved at all. Therefore, the tweaking of their attributes is tolerated by the operating system. Unfortunately, most copiers (including protected-disc copiers) rely implicitly on the standard sizes of Post-gap areas, and, consequently, are very sensitive to their modifications.

Listing 6.11. Defining the length of the Pre-gap area by subchannel data

---

```
                    ++- Track number
                    !! ++- Index
03CC:00 15 00 0C 01 14 01 01 00 00 03 CC 00 00 03 CC
03CD:00 15 00 0C 01 14 01 01 00 00 03 CD 00 00 03 CD
```

```
03CE:00 15 00 0C 01 14 01 01 00 00 03 CE 00 00 03 CE ← Post-gap end of the 1st track
03CF:00 15 00 0C 01 14 02 00 00 00 03 CF 00 00 00 96 ← Pre-gap start of the 2nd track
03D0:00 15 00 0C 01 14 02 00 00 00 03 D0 00 00 00 95
03D1:00 15 00 0C 01 14 02 00 00 00 03 D1 00 00 00 94

...

0462:00 15 00 0C 01 14 02 00 00 00 04 62 00 00 00 03
0463:00 15 00 0C 01 14 02 00 00 00 04 63 00 00 00 02
0464:00 15 00 0C 01 14 02 00 00 00 04 64 00 00 00 01 ← Pre-gap end of the 2nd track
0465:00 15 00 0C 01 14 02 01 00 00 04 65 00 00 00 00 ← Start of the 2nd track
0466:00 15 00 0C 01 14 02 01 00 00 04 66 00 00 00 01
0467:00 15 00 0C 01 14 02 01 00 00 04 67 00 00 00 02
```

In Listing 6.11, note that the second track starts from the address 465h, which corresponds to the absolute address 00:11:00 (see Listing 6.9). The starting address of the Pre-gap is 3CFh. It is 96h (150) sectors from the starting address of the track. Consequently, this Pre-gap corresponds fully to the standard.

CD-R and CD-RW discs use Pre-gap for storing an exotic and little-known data structure known as *TDB* (*Track Descriptor Block*). This data structure contains information about the recording mode, packet size, and so on. The standard requires that the track description block be burned in the batch writing mode and in the TAO (Track At Once) mode. Most burners (including the above-mentioned Ahead Nero), however, burn TDB in all available modes, including DAO. An example of a TDB from a disc burnt using Nero (recording of the disc was carried out in XA MODE2 FORM1. Therefore, the first byte of user information starts from offset 17h instead of offset 10h, as is the case in MODE1) is shown in Listing 6.12. The TDT explanation is as follows: Pre-gap length — 150 sectors, this TDB relates only to the first track, TDT is directly followed by a single TDU, describing the current track; TDU is as follows: record type — continuous.

Listing 6.12. Example of a TDB from a disc burnt using Nero

```
000:00 FF FF FF FF FF FF FF FF FF FF 00 00 00 05 02...............♠● ; sector head
010:00 00 00 00 00 00 00 00 54 44 49 01 50 01 01 01..........TDI☺P☺☺☺ ; TDT-block \
020:01 80 FF FF FF 00 00 00 00 00 00 00 00 00 00 00.☺A............... ; TDU-block / TDB
030:00 00 00 00 00 00 00 00 00 00 00 00 00 00 00 00..................
040:00 00 00 00 00 00 00 00 00 00 00 00 00 00 00 00..................
050:00 00 00 00 00 00 00 00 00 00 00 00 00 00 00 00..................

...

810:00 00 00 00 00 00 00 00 C3 0C 2E 82 00 00 00 00........├♀.B..... ; Rc
```

```
820:00 00 00 00 00 00 00 00 93 78 85 F5 60 F5 F5 F5.........УхЕï`ïï ; E   o
830:F5 0B AA AA AA 00 00 00 00 00 00 00 00 00 00 00.ïσкκκ........... ; E   r
840:00 00 00 00 00 00 00 00 00 00 00 00 00 00 00 00................ ; D   e
850:00 00 00 00 00 00 00 00 00 00 00 00 00 00 00 00................ ; -   c
860:00 00 00 00 00 00 00 00 00 00 00 00 00 00 58 14..............X¶ ; S   t
870:72 9B 00 00 00 00 00 00 00 00 00 00 00 00 C7 3C.rы...........╟< ; O   i
880:CC F4 30 F4 F4 F4 F4 8B 55 55 55 00 00 00 00 00.╟ïоïïïïлиии..... ; L   o
890:00 00 00 00 00 00 00 00 00 00 00 00 00 00 00 00................ ; O   n
8A0:00 00 00 00 00 00 00 00 00 00 00 00 00 00 00 00................ ; M
8B0:00 00 00 00 00 00 00 00 00 00 00 00 00 00 00 00................ ; O   c
8C0:00 00 00 00 9B 18 5C 19 00 00 00 00 00 00 00 00.....ы↑\↓........ ; N   o
8D0:00 00 00 00 00 00 72 9B E5 94 71 47 E6 48 00 00.......rыхФqGцH.. ;     d
8E0:D1 00 F3 15 CC F5 2B 2C B1 AF F6 51 41 80 E0 F2.╤ е§╟ï+,▐пÿQAAрє ; e   e
8F0:23 40 00 00 00 00 00 00 00 00 00 00 00 00 00 00.#@.............. ; r   s
900:00 00 00 00 00 00 00 00 00 00 5C 19 54 03 75 4A..........\↓T♥uJ ; r
910:7D 50 00 00 7B 00 0C BF 93 AB D5 AD 24 2E 42 51.}P..{ ♀┐УЛ╠H$.BQ ; o
920:4E 0D 6E CF 77 04 00 00 00 00 00 00 00 00 00 00.N♪n═w♦.......... ; r
```

The track descriptor block occupies one sector. It starts from the first byte of its user-data part and is duplicated in all sectors of the second half of the Pre-gap of this track. At the structure level, it comprises two parts, called TDT (Track Descriptor Table) and TDU (Track Descriptor Unit).

The TDT starts with a special signature: "TDI" (54h 44h 49h), which stands for Track Descriptor Identification. The next two bytes store the declared length of the Pre-gap area, written in BCD format. The "type of Track Description Unit" field specifies the number of track description modules (*Track Description Unit*, or TDU, for short), starting directly after the end of the TDB block. A value set to 1 corresponds to the only module related to the current track. If the value is set to zero, this corresponds to a case where there are two modules, one directly following the other. The first of these describes the attributes of the preceding track, while the next track is specified by the second module.

The lowest and highest track fields written in BCD format contain the minimum and maximum track numbers described in the current TDB, respectively, and are used mainly in batch writing mode to define the preferred writing mode. In all other cases, it is unnecessary to trace the correctness of these fields.

The first byte of the TDU contains the BCD number of the track it describes. The next byte specifies the recording method and can take the following values:

❏ 00000000b: continuous recording (audio track)
❏ 10010000b: continuous recording (one packet)

❏   10010000b: incremental recording in packets of variable length

❏   10010001b: incremental recording in packets of fixed length

The Packet Size field is valid only in the mode of incremental recording in packets of fixed length. In this case, it contains the packet size specified in sectors. In all other cases, this field must contain FF FF FFh.

Table 6.1. The structure of a TDB terminating with one TDU

Byte	Contents
0	"T"
1	"D"
2	"I"
3	Pre-gap length
4	
5	Type of Track Description Unit
6	Lowest Track Number
7	Highest Track Number
8+00	Track Number
8+01	Write Method of the Track
8+02	Packet Size
8+03	
8+04	
8+05	Reserved
8+06	
8+07	
8+08	
8+09	
8+10	
8+11	
8+12	
8+13	
8+14	
8+15	
8+16	

Most copiers of protected discs (including Alcohol 120%/Clone CD) behave absolutely improperly in relation to transition areas. They never copy the Pre-gap of the first track and do not burn it at all either (Alcohol 120%), or fill it with zeroes (Clone CD). All further transition areas are copied normally.

All transition areas, with the exception of the Pre-gap or the first track of the first session of the disc, are freely available at the sector level and do not cause any problems with regard to reading. However, the Pre-gap of the first track of the first session is specific. Because the logical address of the first significant disc sector is taken to be zero (this is the address of the first sector of the first track), the Pre-gap area that precedes it lies entirely in the area of negative addresses. This does not present any difficulties for the READ CD MSF command, which receives absolute addresses as arguments. However, when using the READ CD command, an entirely different system of address translation is needed (the drive refuses to understand negative LBA addresses). This address-translation system is described in the standard. However, developers of CD-copying programs do not always pay attention to it. Perhaps, they are simply too lazy. Who can tell? Regardless, neither of the CD copying programs reads the first Pre-gap. This allows us to use this area for storing key information (on replicated CD-R/RW discs) or binding to specific TDB (on CD-R/RW discs).

According to the standard, the sector with the address 00:00:00 (the first Pre-gap sector) does not necessarily have to be read, since the drive does not have subchannel data yet. It must accumulate this over time. In practice, however, actual data reading from stampered CD-ROM and recorded CD-R discs, depending on their quality and on the drive model, starts approximately from second — tenth sector. Prior to these sectors, any attempt at reading the disc will result in an error. The situation is much worse with regard to rewritable discs, which often contain unreadable sectors even in the middle of the Pre-gap!

Thus, to protect a CD against unauthorized copying, we can use the following techniques:

❏ Place adjacent tracks close to one another, without transition areas (such a disc can't be copied using Ahead Nero. Alcohol 120% and Clone CD, however, successfully cope with this task).

❏ Place key information in the Pre-gap area of the first track of the disc (a disc where this has been done can be copied by Ahead Nero, but cannot be copied by Alcohol 120% or Clone CD).

❏ Create a fictitious track in the actual track or in the transition area of the natural track (such a disc cannot be copied by Ahead Nero. Clone CD, however, will copy it).

❏ Place the fictitious track in the Pre-gap of the first track (no CD-copying program is capable of copying such a disc).

Adding a fictitious track results in an incorrect length for the first track, because it now must be calculated by means of subtracting the starting address of the first (genuine) track from the starting address of the second (fictitious) track, minus the Post-gap size of the first track and the Pre-gap of the second (Fig. 6.4). Let's assume that we have a disc with a single track (Fig. 6.4, *a*). After that, we add a fictitious entry into the TOC specifying that there is another, actually non-existent track, on the disc. As a result, the length of the first track will be reduced by a value equal to the `sizeof(TRACK2) + sizeof(post-gap) + sizeof(pre-gap)`, and a "hole" equal in size to the `sizeof(post-gap) + sizeof(pre-gap)` bytes (Fig. 6.4, *b*) will be created between tracks. Such a disc will be impossible to copy using standard end-user CD copiers!

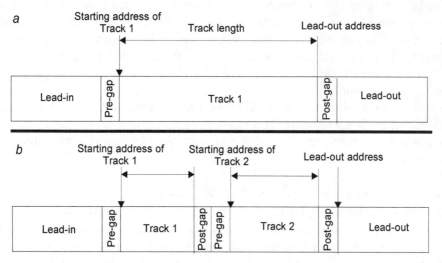

Fig. 6.4. Track length is determined as the difference between the starting address of the next track and the starting address of the current track, minus the size of the Post-gap area

Since track numbers are not taken into account when addressing data discs, including Pre/Post-gap areas formed at the boundary of genuine and fictitious tracks, such a disc will be read normally on any equipment functioning on any operating system. However, only copiers that copy the contents of both Pre- and Post-gap will be able to copy it. According to the standard, copiers aren't required to do this, because, from the official point of view, these areas do not contain anything of interest. Consequently, the copy will contain a 300-sector "hole," filled with zeroes. Such a "wound" can ruin any file, or even several files at once!

The creation of fictitious tracks in buffer Post- and Pre-gap areas is even more promising. The length of the resulting track computed according to the following algorithm: `PreGap_len = min(&Lead-Out, &NexTrack-150)- &MyTrack-150` becomes strongly negative. This will confuse copiers like Ahead Nero, CDRWin, Blind Write and Alcohol 120%. At the same time, in contrast to the first three copiers, which tactfully refuse to copy the protected disc and terminate their operation by displaying an error message, Alcohol 120% simply crashes.

As for Clone CD, it can properly copy discs of this type! At first glance, this renders this protection mechanism absolutely senseless (who needs protection that can't prevent the copying of a disc by at least one widely used and popular copier?). However, don't rush to a final conclusion. Protection mechanisms are different, and among them there are those that can be easily copied by Alcohol 120%, but cause Clone CD to crash. Combining several protection mechanisms on the same disc is similar to amalgamating several different states (counties or principalities) into a united and more powerful state that is certainly more capable of resisting invasion. Taking this into consideration, all intentionally introduced errors involving the placing of fictitious tracks in Pre- and Post-gap areas represent rather promising protection technology, even more so that it is conflict-free. Therefore, this protection technology is likely to become widespread.

Thus, the minimal task is to add another track to the IMAGE.CCD file, and correct all related fields accordingly. This mission, at first glance rather elementary, actually requires the introduction of massive changes to the file. It is, at a minimum, necessary to do the following:

❒ The number of `TocEntries` must be increased by 1.

❒ The `PMin` field belonging to `point 0A1h` also must be increased by 1.

❒ A new entry specifying a false track must be added (for simplicity, you can copy the entry of the actual track and slightly change its starting address).

❒ The numbers of all tracks that follow must be increased by 1 (which means that all further points like `64h > point > 00h` must be renumbered. At the same time, note that the disc is assumed to contain less than `63h` tracks, because the maximum track number has a strict upper limit).

❒ The numbers of all further entries must be increased by one.

❒ If the disc contains more than one session, then the numbers of tracks and points `A0h/A1h` of further sessions must be increased by 1 (point `A0h` of the first session doesn't have to be increased).

❒ A false track must be added into the track map, and all further tracks must be renumbered.

To correspond better with the standard, it would be useful to correct the subchannel data of the false track by increasing the values of the `TNO` (Track Number) fields by one for each of them. This information is contained in the Q subcode channel, which, along with all other channels, is contained in the IMAGE.SUB file. Each 0Dh + 60h * N byte of the file contains the TNO field of sector N (strictly speaking, there is no rigid correspondence between subchannel data and sectors. Therefore, this formula is approximate). After introducing all of the required changes, the checksum of each 16-byte subchannel section must be recalculated. Otherwise, the disc being protected will cease to operate. To achieve this, it is possible to use the CalcSubChannelCRC function from the newtrf.dll library included with the Ahead Nero burner.

Listing 6.13. An example of a subchannel data section. The field highlighted in bold contains the number of the current track

---

```
0003060C:   41 02 01 00 00 06 00 03 | 01 39 63 8A 00 00 00 00....A●☺......♠...♥☺9cK....
```

If you are too lazy to mess with subchannel data, don't do anything and leave everything "as is." In the course of reading the data disc, track numbers are not used in any way. The situation is different with audio discs. On these, the TNO field is used for indicating the track that is currently being played, and, sometimes, for switching between tracks.

On the other hand, the presence of an incorrect TNO considerably strengthens disc protection, since not every copier is capable to copy subchannel data. Those that do possess this ability are few, and, moreover, they do not have this option enabled by default (for example, in Clone CD this option is disabled).

Fictitious Track in the Data Area of a Genuine Track

The simplest (and, from the compatibility point of view, the most reliable) approach is to place the fictitious track in the data area of a genuine track by choosing the starting address of the fictitious track in such a way as to ensure that the number of sectors remaining before the starting point of the next track is no less than 350. These sectors will be required for Post-gap/Pre-gap (for the last track of the session, it is enough to have 150 sectors, since there is no need here to provide sectors for a Pre-gap). Between the starting address of the genuine track and starting address of the fictitious track, there must also be no less than 350 sectors available for the Post-gap of the genuine track and the Pre-gap of the fictitious track. Violation of this rule strengthens the protection, but creates some side effects, which we will discuss later.

For the moment, the main problem for us is that of how to add a new entry into the IMAGE.CCD without damaging its ability to operate properly. The algorithm for creating a fictitious track covered in detail in the previous section is a theoretical possibility, but is still far from actual practice. In the course of implementing our ideas, we can encounter various difficulties that we'll have to overcome or simply bypass.

Let's consider the most difficult case, that is, we have a multisession disc. Professional ethics oblige us to correct not only the contents of the session, to which we are adding a new track, but also the attributes of all other sessions. This is necessary because of the pass-through numbering of all tracks on the disc. The common error of most beginners is renumbering all of the tracks, but forgetting to reset the pointers to the first and the last track of each session. As a result, the protected disc becomes absolutely unreadable or is read incorrectly (the specific behavior depends on the drive, into which the disc is inserted).

Listing 6.14 shows a practical example of adding a new track to an existing one. Of course, it isn't too illustrative (after all, a printed book lacks the illustrative capabilities of, for example, WinDiff utility). However, it is still better than nothing. The first and the third columns (filled by gray) contain the original values from the file being edited, while the second and the fourth columns contain the modified values. The modified values themselves are in bold.

Listing 6.14. Creating a fictitious track — track 2. All changes are in bold, and contents of original fields is shown in odd columns

[CloneCD]	[CloneCD]	[Entry 6]	**[Entry 7]**
Version=3	Version=3	Session=1	Session=1
		Point=0xc1	Point=0xc1
[Disc]	[Disc]	ADR=0x05	ADR=0x05
TocEntries=12	**TocEntries=13**	Control=0x04	Control=0x04
Sessions=2	Sessions=2	TrackNo=0	TrackNo=0
DataTracksScrambled=0	DataTracksScrambled=0	AMin=4	AMin=4
CDTextLength=0	CDTextLength=0	ASec=120	ASec=120
		AFrame=96	AFrame=96
[Session 1]	[Session 1]	ALBA=26946	ALBA=26946
PreGapMode=1	PreGapMode=1	Zero=0	Zero=0
PreGapSubC=0	PreGapSubC=0	PMin=0	PMin=0
		PSec=0	PSec=0
[Session 2]	[Session 2]	PFrame=0	PFrame=0
PreGapMode=1	PreGapMode=1	PLBA=-150	PLBA=-150
PreGapSubC=0	PreGapSubC=0		
[Entry 0]	[Entry 0]	[Entry 7]	**[Entry 8]**
Session=1	Session=1	Session=2	Session=2
Point=0xa0	Point=0xa0	Point=0xa0	Point=0xa0
ADR=0x01	ADR=0x01	ADR=0x01	ADR=0x01
Control=0x04	Control=0x04	Control=0x04	Control=0x04
TrackNo=0	TrackNo=0	TrackNo=0	TrackNo=0
AMin=0	AMin=0	AMin=0	AMin=0

```
ASec=0              ASec=0              ASec=0              ASec=0
AFrame=0            AFrame=0            AFrame=0            AFrame=0
ALBA=-150           ALBA=-150           ALBA=-150           ALBA=-150
Zero=0              Zero=0              Zero=0              Zero=0
PMin=1              PMin=1              PMin=2              PMin=3
PSec=0              PSec=0              PSec=0              PSec=0
PFrame=0            PFrame=0            PFrame=0            PFrame=0
PLBA=4350           PLBA=4350           PLBA=8850           PLBA=-1


[Entry 0]           [Entry 0]           [Entry 8]           [Entry 9]
Session=1           Session=1           Session=2           Session=2
Point=0xa0          Point=0xa0          Point=0xa1          Point=0xa1
ADR=0x01            ADR=0x01            ADR=0x01            ADR=0x01
Control=0x04        Control=0x04        Control=0x04        Control=0x04
TrackNo=0           TrackNo=0           TrackNo=0           TrackNo=0
AMin=0              AMin=0              AMin=0              AMin=0
ASec=0              ASec=0              ASec=0              ASec=0
AFrame=0            AFrame=0            AFrame=0            AFrame=0
ALBA=-150           ALBA=-150           ALBA=-150           ALBA=-150
Zero=0              Zero=0              Zero=0              Zero=0
PMin=1              PMin=1              PMin=2              PMin=3
PSec=0              PSec=0              PSec=0              PSec=0
PFrame=0            PFrame=0            PFrame=0            PFrame=0
PLBA=4350           PLBA=4350           PLBA=8850           PLBA=-1


[Entry 1]           [Entry 1]           [Entry 9]           [Entry 10]
Session=1           Session=1           Session=2           Session=2
Point=0xa1          Point=0xa1          Point=0xa2          Point=0xa2
ADR=0x01            ADR=0x01            ADR=0x01            ADR=0x01
Control=0x04        Control=0x04        Control=0x04        Control=0x04
TrackNo=0           TrackNo=0           TrackNo=0           TrackNo=0
AMin=0              AMin=0              AMin=0              AMin=0
ASec=0              ASec=0              ASec=0              ASec=0
AFrame=0            AFrame=0            AFrame=0            AFrame=0
ALBA=-150           ALBA=-150           ALBA=-150           ALBA=-150
Zero=0              Zero=0              Zero=0              Zero=0
PMin=1              PMin=2              PMin=3              PMin=3
PSec=0              PSec=0              PSec=24             PSec=24
PFrame=0            PFrame=0            PFrame=23           PFrame=23
PLBA=4350           PLBA=-1             PLBA=15173          PLBA=15173


[Entry 2]           [Entry 2]           [Entry 10]          [Entry 11]
Session=1           Session=1           Session=2           Session=2
```

Point=0xa2
ADR=0x01
Control=0x04
TrackNo=0
AMin=0
ASec=0
AFrame=0
ALBA=-150
Zero=0
PMin=0
PSec=29
PFrame=33
PLBA=2058

[Entry 3]
Session=1
Point=0x01
ADR=0x01
Control=0x04
TrackNo=0
AMin=0
ASec=0
AFrame=0
ALBA=-150
Zero=0
PMin=0
PSec=2
PFrame=0
PLBA=0

Point=0xa2
ADR=0x01
Control=0x04
TrackNo=0
AMin=0
ASec=0
AFrame=0
ALBA=-150
Zero=0
PMin=0
PSec=29
PFrame=33
PLBA=2058

[Entry 3]
Session=1
Point=0x01
ADR=0x01
Control=0x04
TrackNo=0
AMin=0
ASec=0
AFrame=0
ALBA=-150
Zero=0
PMin=0
PSec=2
PFrame=0
PLBA=0

[Entry 4]
Session=1
Point=0x02
ADR=0x01
Control=0x04
TrackNo=0
AMin=0
ASec=0
AFrame=0
ALBA=-150
Zero=0
PMin=22
PSec=0

Point=0x02
ADR=0x01
Control=0x04
TrackNo=0
AMin=0
ASec=0
AFrame=0
ALBA=-150
Zero=0
PMin=3
PSec=1
PFrame=33
PLBA=13458

[Entry 11]
Session=2
Point=0xb0
ADR=0x05
Control=0x04
TrackNo=0
AMin=4
ASec=54
AFrame=23
ALBA=21923
Zero=1
PMin=22
PSec=14
PFrame=34
PLBA=99934

[Entry 5]
Session=1
Point=0xc0
ADR=0x05
Control=0x04
TrackNo=0
AMin=162
ASec=128
AFrame=140
ALBA=288590
Zero=0
PMin=97
PSec=27

Point=0x03
ADR=0x01
Control=0x04
TrackNo=0
AMin=0
ASec=0
AFrame=0
ALBA=-150
Zero=0
PMin=3
PSec=1
PFrame=33
PLBA=13458

[Entry 12]
Session=2
Point=0xb0
ADR=0x05
Control=0x04
TrackNo=0
AMin=4
ASec=54
AFrame=23
ALBA=21923
Zero=1
PMin=22
PSec=14
PFrame=34
PLBA=99934

[Entry 6]
Session=1
Point=0xc0
ADR=0x05
Control=0x04
TrackNo=0
TrackNo=0
ASec=128
AFrame=140
ALBA=288590
Zero=0
PMin=97
PSec=27

	PFrame=0	PFrame=21	PFrame=21
	PLBA=-1	PLBA=-11604	PLBA=-11604
[Entry 4]	[Entry 5]	[TRACK 1]	[TRACK 1]
Session=1	Session=1	MODE=1	MODE=1
Point=0xb0	Point=0xb0	INDEX 1=0	INDEX 1=0
ADR=0x05	ADR=0x05		
Control=0x04	Control=0x04		[TRACK 2]
TrackNo=0	TrackNo=0		MODE=1
AMin=2	AMin=2		INDEX 1=0
ASec=59	ASec=59		
AFrame=33	AFrame=33	[TRACK 2]	[TRACK 3]
ALBA=13308	ALBA=13308	MODE=1	MODE=1
Zero=3	Zero=3	INDEX 1=0	INDEX 1=0
PMin=22	PMin=22		
PSec=14	PSec=14		
PFrame=34	PFrame=34		
PLBA=99934	PLBA=99934		

Having saved the edited IMAGE.CCD file to the disc, burn the resulting image onto the CD using Clone CD or Alcohol 120%. Make sure that the protected disc is processed normally by the operating system and that another track has been added to the two existing tracks (Fig. 6.5).

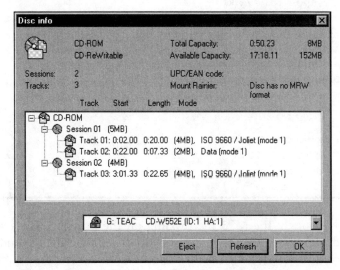

Fig. 6.5. First session contains two tracks, the first of which is quite normal and genuine, while the other is the fictitious track created manually

An attempt at copying the protected disc using standard, end-user copiers (for instance, Stomp Record Now! or Ahead Nero) seems to be successful at first glance. However, as you investigate the copy more carefully, you'll notice that there is a "hole" consisting of 300 sectors filled with zeroes between the first and the second track. This result was predictable! User copiers understand the standard too literally. And the standard states that neither the Post-gap nor the Pre-gap contain any data.

Subchannel information is also gets changed. Copiers that instead of actually reading the Q subcode channel of the disc being copied restore this data on their own, duly marking subchannel data with the ordinal numbers of their corresponding tracks, which allows us to easily distinguish a rough copy from the original.

Listing 6.15. A demonstration of the changes of subchannel information in the course of disc copying

```
# Reading the protected disc's TOC to determine the starting address of the 2nd track
$toc TEAC 0
00 14 01 00 00 00 00 00
00 14 02 00 00 00 02 A3 # Starting address of the 2nd track is 2A3h, or 675 (decimal)
00 14 03 00 00 00 34 92
00 14 AA 00 00 00 3B 45

# Reading subchannel data from the 2nd track of the protected disc
$seek_and_Q TEAC 675
seek CD-ROM & read Q-subcode by KK
LBA - 02A3: 00 15 00 0C 01 14 01 01 00 00 02 A3 00 00 02 A3
# TNO field of the 2nd track contains ^^ number one

# Copying the disc using Ahead Nero/Easy CD Creator/Record Now!
# or Clone CD/Alcohol without reading subchannel data

#  Reading subchannel data from the 2nd track of the copy
$seek_and_Q TEAC 675
seek CD-ROM & read Q-subcode by KK
LBA - 02A3: 00 15 00 0C 01 14 02 01 00 00 02 A3 00 00 00 00
# TNO field of the 2nd track contains ^^ number 2
# Subchannel data has changed!
```

Strangely enough, the MP3 file residing on the original disc is played normally, even if the disc is severely damaged. It only produces a gurgling sound when the damaged location is encountered, which, of course, is unpleasant, but can be tolerated. Of course, the more fictitious tracks are contained on the protected disc and the closer they are located to each other, the more considerable will be the difference of the unauthorized copy from the original. The copy of the disc stuffed with the fictitious track — instead of playing music — hisses, scratches and gurgles, thus driving pirates to a form of madness mixed with confusion. This is the origin of the legend about inevitable quality degradation in the course of CD copying. Naturally, this is only true for discs containing MP3 files or video. Data CDs are much more vulnerable, and if the "hole" left by the copier matches an executable file and/or archive, this file will almost certainly be corrupted irrecoverably.

Still, the strength of this form of protection is virtually insignificant. Discs of this type can be successfully copied by Alcohol 120% and Clone CD (provided, of course, that the subchannel data reading option is enabled). Apparently, these copiers ignore the starting addresses of the tracks altogether and read the entire readable area of each session from the end of the Lead-in to the beginning of the Lead-out. Hmmm! So much the worse for those who use this protection to complicate the copying of their programs. With regard to the celebrated Blind Write, it refuses to copy these discs altogether, and exits by the exception generated by "read engine." What it finds wrong with the fictitious track is a mystery.

Fictitious Track in the Post-Gap of the Genuine Track

Placing a fictitious track in the middle of a genuine one (as was shown in Fig.6.4) is not of much interest. It is much better to place the fictitious track entirely in the Post-gap area of a genuine track. In this case, all copiers will go crazy when attempting to compute the number of the fictitious track. Recall, that, according to the standard, the length of any normal track is equal to: `min(&Lead-Out, &NexTrack − 150) − &MyTrack − 150`. If the track start is located so that `min(&Lead-Out, &NexTrack − 150) < (&MyTrack − 150)`, its computed length will be negative, and most copiers won't even understand what to do with such a track. Furthermore, most copiers store the length of the tracks in variables of the `unsigned long` type. Therefore, a negative value with a small absolute value, erroneously interpreted by the processor as unsigned, will turn into a very large positive value. In this case, writing the "contents" of a fictitious track will require about 4 GB of disk space on the hard disk, and the same amount of space on the CD to be burnt.

Let's access `point A2h`, storing the Lead-out area address, and copy its `PMin`, `PSec` and `PFrame` fields into the appropriate fields of the fictitious sector, reducing its `PFrame` value by a certain value (this technique was discussed in detail in the previous two sections).

Fictitious Track in the Pre-Gap of a Genuine Track

Placing a fictitious track in the Pre-gap area of the first genuine track produces rather interesting results, which deserve a separate chapter. At first glance, this protection is absolutely similar to that discussed in the preceding section, with the only difference being that now the address of the *first* track will be changed, instead of that of the *second* track. This is, actually, only partially true! The Pre-gap of the first track is a special case. Aside from the fact that, according to the standard, it is unavailable for reading (although, some drives still manage to read it), the LBA address of its starting point is a negative number! Let's recall that LBA addresses are related to the absolute addresses by the following formula: LBA = ((Min * 60) + Sec) * 75 + Frame − 150, where 150 equals to sizeof(pre-gap).

According to the standard, the absolute starting address of the first normal track must be 00:02:00 (which corresponds to the LBA address 0h), and the absolute starting address of the first Pre-gap is 00:00:00 (which corresponds to LBA address -96h, or 150 in decimal notation). Even if the developer of the copier used signed variables for storing addresses, this doesn't change anything, because the arguments of the READ and READ CD commands are always unsigned numbers! Moreover, placing the second track in the Post-gap of the first one results in the fact that the starting address of the second track becomes smaller than the starting address of the first track. Most copiers are not prepared for such a situation.

It is impossible to copy the contents of the first Pre-gap (where the fictitious track resides), and, in fact, this isn't necessary. Does, however, every copier know about it? If only the developers didn't make provisions for handling such a situation, the copier, depending on the type of addressing that it uses, would either report a read error (absolute addressing), or move the head very far away to an unreal LBA address (LBA addressing without checking for correctness of addresses). Another variant is that it will be blinded because it won't know what to do with a negative address (LBA addressing with checking for address correctness). Looking a bit ahead, let's note that only Clone CD is capable of coping with protection of this type (codename Jackal).

Using the IMAGE.CCD file that remained from the previous experiments, let's move the starting point of the fictitious track to the 00:01:00 absolute address, as shown below:

Listing 6.16. A fictitious track in the Post-gap of the genuine track, located by the address 00:01:00

```
[Entry 4]
Session=1
Point=0x02
ADR=0x01
Control=0x04
TrackNo=0
AMin=0
ASec=0
AFrame=0
```

```
ALBA=-150
Zero=0
PMin=00
PSec=01
PFrame=0
PLBA=-1
```

When you open the modified IMAGE.CCD file, the Clone CD copier will incorrectly compute the length of the first track (see Listing 6.17). However, this has no influence on the process of burning a CD.

Listing 6.17. Clone CD displays incorrect information about the length of the first track

```
SESSION 1 INFORMATION:
Session size: 4726 Kbytes
Number of tracks: 2
Track 1: Data Mode 1, size: 4.294.967.124 Kbytes
Track 2: Data Mode 1, size: 4899 Kbytes

SESSION 2 INFORMATION 2:
Session size: 3939 Kbytes
Number of tracks: 1
Track 3: Data, size: 3939 Kbytes
```

The check shows that the disc protected using this method is read normally in NEC and TEAC drives, while ASUS "sees" only the first track of the first session of the disk. Therefore, it is not wise to rely on the second or following sessions. It also isn't safe for your reputation, because irritated users will certainly complain.

When attempting to copy a protected disc using end-user copiers, they behave quite strangely. Stomp Record Now!, and Ahead Nero refuse to read the disc altogether, complaining of `Invalid Disk` and `Invalid Track Mode`, respectively.

Having encountered a fictitious track in the Pre-gap area, Ahead Nero becomes totally disoriented, and starts to make blunders when trying to determine the disc geometry (Fig. 6.9). Well, it is no wonder that the length of the first track is determined incorrectly. Why, however, was the copier unable to determine the attributes of all other tracks? The starting address of the second track, which is `3728:17:16`, obviously specifies that Ahead Nero uses unsigned LBA addresses as a base address method, and converts them into MSF, when needed, on the fly. Since the unsigned LBA address of the starting point of the second track is a very large positive number, the difference between the starting Lead-out address and the starting address of the fictitious track becomes negative. This reduces Ahead Nero to absolute confusion, leading it to produce a catastrophically incorrect result. We can only guess the reasons why the third track also was determined incorrectly. Possibly, this was in some way related to the incorrect number of sessions: Ahead Nero has detected only one of the two sessions. Why did this happen? I suggest that you to contact technical support and inform them about the bugs in their program. Let them fix the bugs instead of taking on a job for the sake of quick and easy money.

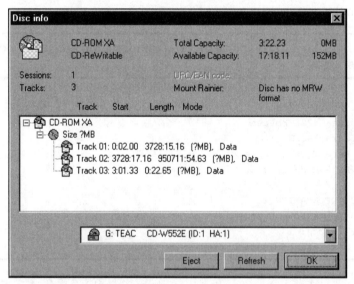

Fig. 6.6. Ahead Nero, having encountered a fictitious track in the Pre-gap area of the genuine track, becomes so confused that it cannot correctly determine the length of all tracks. The address of the second (fictitious) track is also determined incorrectly

An attempt to scan the disc surface using the Ahead Nero CD Speed utility for finding damaged sectors (~**Extra** → **ScanDisk**) results in the program terminating abnormally. Tests such as CPU Usage, Spin Up/Down also stop and report an error. Thus, *placing a fictitious track in the Post-gap of the genuine track can serve as an efficient means for counteracting utilities defining the disc quality, thus allowing the sale of faulty discs having physical defects as flawless ones.* No, this is not advice to use this approach with this goal (actually, anyone behaving like this deserves a beating). On the contrary, it is statement of the sad fact that our world is far from ideal, and no information or individuals should be trusted. But enough lyricism. Let's try to copy the protected disc using Alcohol 120%.

If the **Ignore read errors** checkbox hasn't been set beforehand, Alcohol 120% will interrupt the disc reading process after having read about 13%, display the unintelligible error message `Illegal Mode For This Track`, and prompt you to delete incomplete files. Certainly, we are dealing with a trend.

Disc reading with errors ignored doesn't produce a desirable result either. Having reached sector 2056 (the next to last sector in the Post-gap of a genuine track), Alcohol 120% encounters the Lead-out and also stops copying.

Fictitious Track in the Lead-Out Area

A fictitious track located in the Lead-out area doesn't prevent normal reading of the disc. It does, however, complicate the operations of end-user copiers quite seriously. First, the length of this fictitious track computed as the difference between the starting addresses of the Lead-out area and this track minus `sizeof(post-gap)`, in this case is expressed by a negative value. We already know of the complications created by any negative value for any standard copier! Second, the contents of the Lead-out area, because of its unavailability at the sector level, can easily be confused with the bad sectors, bringing all of the possible consequence of such an error. Third, the next to last sector of the Post-gap area of the genuine track (conventionally called X-sector), for some unknown reason is not processed either by the `READ CD` command or by the `SEEK` or `READ HEADER` commands.

Let's consider point `A2h`, which stored the address of the Lead-out area, and copy its values for `PMin`, `PSec` and `PFrame` into the corresponding fields of the fictitious sector, increasing the `PSec` value of the latter by one or any other value that doesn't go beyond the Lead-out limits.

Having skipped the traditional error message from Clone CD complaining about the abnormal length of the second track, burn the modified image on a CD-R/CD-RW disc. As in the previous example, NEC and TEAC drives "see" all of the available sessions, while ASUS notices only the first. Therefore, we can't rely on the second or any further sessions.

Copiers such as Stomp Record Now! and Ahead Nero will refuse to copy such a disc. The **Disk Info** window returned by the latter will be incorrect (Fig. 6.7). Thus, Ahead Nero cannot determine the mode and length of the third track. This is strange, because the third track has no relation to the first two and to determine its attributes, it is sufficient to read the TOC.

An attempt to copy the protected disc using the Alcohol 120% doesn't produce any positive results either. If the **Skip read errors** option was disabled, then the program will display the error message: `Error: [05/64/00] — Illegal Mode For This Track`, and the process of image creation will stop abnormally.

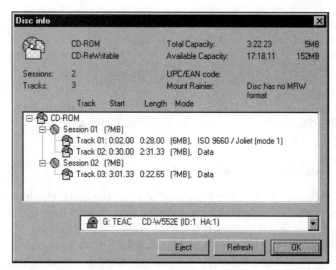

Fig. 6.7. Ahead Nero incorrectly determined the length of the second (fictitious) track. Strangely enough, it couldn't correctly determine the length and mode of the third track, which belongs to another session

Listing 6.18. The reaction of Alcohol 120% to the fictitious track in the Lead-Out area (the error-skipping option is disabled)

```
01:25:17 Processor information: Pentium III (0.18 um) 256KB OnDie L2 Cache (736MHz)

01:25:17 Disc dump: (G:) TEAC CD-W552E (1:1)

01:25:18 Read mode: RAW

01:25:18 Source information:  Session: 2, Track: 3, Length: 29.6 MB / 003:22:23

01:25:18 Image file: L:\CD-hack\030713_1649.img

01:25:20 Disc read error: 2048

01:25:20 There was an error when creating disc dump!

01:25:20 Error:  [05/64/00] - Illegal Mode For This Track

01:25:20 L:\CD-hack\030713_1649.ccd: Image file creation canceled!
```

If the error-skipping option was enabled, the image creation seems to be successful (although not without a large number of bad sectors, starting from address 2058 and terminating with address 2172). Obviously, these sectors belong to the Pre-gap/Post-gap area of the fictitious track checked in vain by Alcohol 120%).

Listing 6.19. The Alcohol 120% reaction to a fictitious track in Lead-out (the error-skipping option was enabled)

```
01:32:11 Processor information: Pentium III (0.18 um)
         With 256 KB On-Die L2 Cache   (736MHz)
 01:32:11 Disc dump: (G:) TEAC CD-W552E (1:1)
 01:32:12 Read mode: RAW, Error skipping enabled
 01:32:12 Source information:  Session: 2, Track: 3, Length: 29.6 MB / 003:22:23
 01:32:12 Writing dump file: L:\CD-hack\030713_1649.img
 01:32:21 Disc read error: 2056
 01:32:21 Disc read error: 2058
 01:32:21 Disc read error: 2059
 01:32:21 Disc read error: 2060
 ...
 01:32:22 Disc read error: 2169
 01:32:22 Disc read error: 2170
 01:32:22 Disc read error: 2171
 01:32:22 Disc read error: 2172
 01:32:32 L:\CD-hack\030713_1649.ccd: Image file creation completed!
 01:32:32 Disc dump completed!
```

What Alcohol 120% was hoping for is a mystery. The newly-created image is useless and produces an error like Sector not found. Cannot read folder contents (Fig. 6.8):

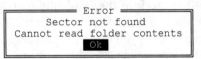

```
============= Error =============
       Sector not found
  Cannot read folder contents
             Ok
```

Fig. 6.8. Disc copied by Alcohol 120% is unreadable. When attempting to view its contents, the operating system displays an error message

Clone CD, on the contrary, copies the disc without any errors, and the resulting duplicate is usable. However, it still differs from the original. Reading the X-sector using the READ CD command still returns an error, but head positioning using the SEEK command and reading the header using the READ HEADER command are carried out normally (recall that the X-sector of the original disc couldn't be processed by either of these commands).

Listing 6.20. An attempt at reading the X-sector of the original disc using the READ CD command results in the following error: Sense Key == 3 MEDIUM ERROR (left), disc duplicated obtained using Clone CD behaves similarly (right)

```
>cd_raw_read.exe 1.1 2056 1              >cd_raw_read.exe 1.1 2056 1
-ERR:F0 00 03 00 00 00 00 0A 00 00 00 00 11 00  -ERR:F0 00 03 00 00 00 00 0A 00 00 00 00 11 00
```

Listing 6.21. An attempt at reading the header of the original disc using the READ HEADER command results in the following error: Sense Key == 5 ILLEGAL REQUEST (left), but the copy obtained using Clone CD is processed normally (right)

```
>read.header.exe 1.1 2056 2056           >read.header.exe 1.1 2056 2056
READ HEADER (44h) SCSI/ATAPI commad demo by KK   READ HEADER (44h) SCSI/ATAPI commad demo by KK
-ERR:f0 00 05 00 00 00 00 0a 00 00 00 00 64 00   LBA:0808h --> MSF:00:1D:1F (MODE-1 [L-EC symb])
```

Listing 6.22. An attempt at positioning on the X-sector of the original disc using the SEEK command with subsequent reading of subchannel information using the READ SUBCHANNEL command results in an interesting effect: the drive doesn't diagnose an error, but it also doesn't move the optical head and, after issuing the READ SUBCHANNEL command, it returns subchannel data from its previous location (left). A disc duplicate obtained using Clone CD, on the contrary, doesn't prevent head positioning on the X-sector and returns successfully its subchannel data (right)

```
>seek_and_Q.exe 1.1 2056                 >seek_and_Q.exe 1.1 2056
seek CD-ROM & read Q-subcode by KK       seek CD-ROM & read Q-subcode by KK
00 15 00 0C 01 14 01 01 00 00 05 83 00 00 05 83   00 15 00 0C 01 14 01 01 00 00 08 08 00 00 08 08
```

Thus, placing a fictitious track in the Lead-out area, along with processing of the X-sector using READ HEADER and SEEK/READ SUBCHANNEL commands, allows us to distinguish original disc from its copy reliably (this protection has the codename "Wolf").

How can we copy a disc protected using the "wolf" protection? When writing the edited image to the disc, Clone CD will display the following information on its geometry:

Listing 6.23. Having encountered a disc with fictitious track in the Post-gap area, Clone CD incorrectly computes its length (in bold and gray)

```
SESSION 1 INFORMATION:
Session size: 4726 Kbytes
Number of tracks: 2
Track 1: Data Mode 1, size: 299397 Kbytes
Track 2: Data Mode 1, size: 4294672626 Kbytes
```

According to Clone CD, the length of the second track is 4,294,672,626 Kbytes, or *4 Tb*! Fortunately, this in no way prevents disc burning. If everything was done correctly, the protected disc will be processed normally by the operating system.

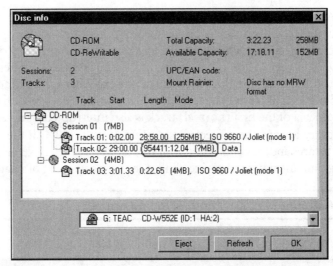

Fig. 6.9. Information displayed by Ahead Nero when analyzing the geometry of the protected disc. A monstrous error in determining the length of the fictitious track prevents it from being copied normally

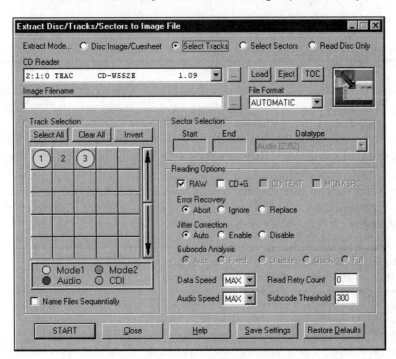

Fig. 6.10. CDRWin refuses to determine the type of the fictitious track

As for Ahead Nero (and the overwhelming majority of other copiers), it will behave differently. It will refuse to process a fictitious track and stop abnormally, returning an error message such as `illegal track mode` or something of the sort.

The CDRWin copier, for some unknown reason, refuses to determine the type of fictitious track (although the track type is written explicitly in the headers of each of its sectors) and prevents it from being selected. Without being selected, the track cannot be retrieved. Retrieval of the first (normal) track is also interrupted by an error message.

Now, let's try to copy the protected disc using Alcohol 120%. If the **Skip** errors option was not set beforehand, Alcohol 120% will display the `Illegal Mode for this track` error message and interrupt the disc reading at the very beginning of image creation:

Listing 6.24. Alcohol 120% without skipping errors

```
02:40:38 Information on the processor: Pentium III (0.18um) 256KB OnDie L2Cache (736MHz)
02:40:38 Disc dump: (G:) TEAC CD-W552E (1:1)
02:40:46 Read mode: RAW
02:40:46 Source information:  Session: 2, Track: 3, Length: 29.6 MB / 003:22:23
02:40:53 Image file: L:\CD-hack\030713_1649.img
02:40:58 Disc read error: 2048
02:40:58 An error has occurred in the course of dump creation!
02:40:58 Error:  [05/64/00] - Illegal Mode For This Track
02:40:58 L:\CD-hack\030713_1649.ccd: Writing image file was cancelled!
```

Well, let's set the **Skip read errors** checkbox and try to copy the protected disc once again. Having reached the X-sector (with the LBA address of 2056), Alcohol 120% will display a read error message and bump into the Lead-out area, pouring out a bunch of bad sectors. Having reached 100 percent, for some unknown reason it continues the reading process. Then, most likely to make sure that the user gets the point, it locks the **Cancel** button and freezes. To be more accurate, it doesn't freeze completely, since it continues to pour out the bad sectors. It is impossible to stop this alcoholic-induced brawl. Anybody who likes to talk about "programming culture" should stop and take a look at this raging alcoholic!

Listing 6.25. Alcohol 120% with error-skipping enabled. Having reached 100 percent, it freezes, but continues to report bad sectors

```
09:52:22 Information on the processor: Pentium III (0.18 um) 256KB OnDie L2 Cache (736MHz)
09:52:22 Disc dump: (G:) TEAC CD-W552E (1:1)
09:52:29 Read mode: RAW , Read error skipping enabled
09:52:29 Source information:  Session: 2, Track: 3, Length: 29.6 MB / 003:22:23
09:52:38 Disc read error: 0
```

```
09:52:39 Image file: L:\CD-hack\030713_1649.img
09:52:53 Disc read error: 2056
09:52:57 Disc read error: 2057
09:52:57 Disc read error: 2058
...
09:53:01 Disc read error: 2707
09:53:01 L:\CD-hack\030713_1649.ccd: Image file cancelled!
09:53:01 Disc dump cancelled!
```

The third attempt to copy the protected disc begins with the restarting Alcohol 120% and setting the **Fast bad block skipping** option. This time, Alcohol 120% does not freeze... but it doesn't copy either, refusing to read the entire disc. According to the Alcohol 120%, the bad sectors begin with the first (i.e., zero) LBA address and continue up to the last. Wonderful, isn't it?

Listing 6.26. Alcohol 120% with fast error skipping

```
02:52:18 Processor information: Pentium III (0.18 um) With 256 KB On-Die L2 Cache  (736MHz)
02:52:18 Disc dump: (G:) TEAC CD-W552E (1:1)
02:52:25 Read mode: RAW , Fast skipping of bad sectors
02:52:25 Source information:  Session: 2, Track: 3, Length: 29.6 MB / 003:22:23
02:52:25 Disc read error: 0
02:52:26 Disc read error: 1
02:52:26 Disc read error: 2
02:52:26 Disc read error: 3
```

Fictitious Track Coinciding with the Genuine Track

Creating a fictitious track combined with the genuine track results in the length of the first track becoming zero. Why does it become zero instead of a negative number? After all, the length of the genuine track is this case is: &Track2 − &Track1 − sizeof(post-gap) − sizeof(pre-gap), which, in actual values appears as follows: 00:02:00 − 00:02:00 − 00:02:00 − 00:02:00 == −00:04:00, or −300 in LBA addresses.

The point is that address 00:02:00 is special. The track starting from this address doesn't have a Pre-gap (or, to be more precise, doesn't allow us to process its Pre-gap in a normal manner). Therefore, the actual length of such track is computed in a special branch of the program, which is clever enough not to subtract sizeof(post-gap) from zero. The particular features of operation of individual copiers are not of interest for the moment. It is enough to know that most of them compute the length of the first and all further tracks correctly (although, this doesn't solve all of our problems with regard to copying protected discs).

Introducing an X-sector into the genuine track (see "Jackal") results in the following side effect: an attempt to read the X-sector using the READ CD command returns an error, the positioning of the head to the X-sector using the SEEK command is carried out without errors; without, however, moving the head itself. Reading the header of the X-sector using the READ HEADER command once again returns an error. Running a few steps forward, note that the disc copy obtained using Clone CD reads the header and positions the head without errors (and the head actually moves), thanks to which the duplicate can easily be distinguished from the original.

When opening the original image of the protected disc, Clone CD finds only the second (fictitious) track in the first session, and refuses to detect the genuine track (see Listing 6.27). Fortunately, disc burning is carried out successfully despite this fact.

Listing 6.27. Clone CDs reaction to a fictitious track coinciding with the genuine track

```
SESSION 1 INFORMATION:

Session size: 4726 Kbytes
Number of tracks: 2
Track 2: Data Mode 1, size: 4726 Kbytes

SESSION 2 INFORMATION:
Session size: 3939 Kbytes
Number of tracks: 1
Track 3: Data Mode 1, size: 3939 Kbytes
```

Viewing the disc geometry confirms the existence of two tracks with the same starting addresses, the length of the first track actually being equal to zero instead of a negative number (Fig. 6.11). What's even more interesting is that the type of the first track is determined to be "ISO 9660/Joliet", which, to put it mildly, is very far from the truth. The identifier of the ISO 9660 file system is contained in the 16th sector of the track, and Joliet in the 17th sector. Provided that the track length is equal to zero (which is true), a natural question arises: What relation is there between these sectors and the first track? It seems to me that the file system identification procedure doesn't check the range of available addresses at all...

NEC and TEAC drives were smart enough to read such a disc. ASUS, on the contrary, was able to see only the first session. Consequently, you should not rely on the second or all following sessions.

An attempt to copy the protected disc using Alcohol 120%, according to tradition, fails (if the **Skip read errors** mode is not enabled, Alcohol will refuse to copy the disc at all, and if this mode is enabled, it will bump into the Lead-out, fall into an endless loop, and cannot be terminated by any other method than killing the process). Clone CD, as was mentioned before, processes the fictitious track normally. However, it removes the "Jackal" from the Post-gap, as a result of which the duplicate can be easily distinguished from the original.

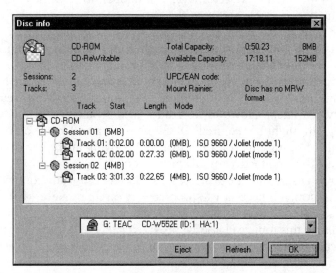

Fig. 6.11. The first and the second tracks have identical starting addresses and, as a result, the length of the first track turns to zero

Invalidating Track Numbering

According to the ECMA-130 standard, information tracks must be numbered sequentially, starting from 1 and finishing with the last track of the disc ("*Track Numbers 01 to 99 shall be those of the Information Tracks in the User Data area. Consecutive Information Tracks shall be numbered consecutively. The first Information Track of the user Data area of a disk shall have Track Number 01*"). The common sense possessed by hardware and software developers leads them to hold the same opinion. Therefore, there is agreement that every operating system can rely on track number one being followed either by track number two or by the Lead-out (track number AAh). However, track numbering can easily be modified so that the first track is followed either by, for instance, track number 9, or even by another track "number 1"!

Tests have shown that the vast majority of drives and copiers react inadequately to modified track numbering. Sometimes, they refuse to recognize such discs at all. Sometimes, they display the data track as audio. No wonder the copying of modified discs of this type causes serious problems. Even advanced tools like Clone CD and

Alcohol 120% are unable to grasp the numbering of the protected disc. Consequently, the copies are either horribly disfigured or completely unusable.

Theoretically, a disc with invalid track numbering should be copied without problems, because track numbers are not considered in absolute addressing. Thus, when working with the disc at the sector level, it is enough to read the entire contents of the disc from the first readable sector to the last, without even suspecting of the existence of tracks. In practice, however, the situation is different, and the vast majority of copiers copy discs by tracks, not sectors. At the same time, algorithms used for TOC analysis are horribly stupid and can't even handle obvious errors. Any deviations of the track numbering from the norm can be successfully written to the disc using Clone CD (except for the track starting from number zero. More details on this topic will be provided later). However, to read a disc invalidated in this way, a more advanced program might be required. Of all the programs I know of, only my own copier is capable of doing this (or a manual disc copying at the sector level). Therefore, this technique is very effective for CD protection!

In order to ensure that the protected disc doesn't cause any conflicts with the equipment of legal users, it is necessary to proceed very carefully. Never change the numbering of the tracks of the first session, because this often renders the disc absolutely unreadable (more details on this topic will also be provided later). A pleasant exception is the creation of a fictitious track with the number of the genuine track. Protection in this form doesn't conflict with any equipment that I have at my disposal. For all appearances, it shouldn't conflict with any equipment at all. I can't, however, say with 100-percent certainty that this is actually the case. The numbering of the tracks of the second session can be changed more or less painlessly. In the worst case, the drive simply won't see the tracks of the second session, The first session, however, will be fully available.

To change the track numbering, it is enough to change the number of the point corresponding to the original number of the track that you are going to change and correct the value of the PMin field of point A1h, which stores the number of the last disc track (if we do not do this, we will end up with protection of the `Incorrect last track number` type). It is also necessary to change the track's layout, which is contained in the end of the CCD file. The following example demonstrates how to create a gap between the first and the third tracks by increasing the number of the latter from three to nine:

**Listing 6.28. Creating a gap between the second and the third track.
Odd columns, filled with gray, contain the original contents of the CCD file.
Even columns show the modified values (modifications are in bold)**

[Entry 8]	[Entry 8]	[Entry 11]	[Entry 11]	[TRACK 1]	[TRACK 1]	
Session=2	Session=2	Session=2	Session=2	MODE=1		MODE=1
Point=0xa1	Point=0xa1	Point=0x03 →	**Point=0x09**	INDEX 1=0	INDEX 1=0	
ADR=0x01	ADR=0x01	ADR=0x01	ADR=0x01			

Control=0x04	Control=0x04	Control=0x04	Control=0x04	[TRACK 2]	[TRACK 2]			
TrackNo=0	TrackNo=0	TrackNo=0	TrackNo=0	MODE=1		MODE=1		
AMin=0		AMin=0		AMin=0		AMin=0	INDEX 1=0	INDEX 1=0
ASec=0		ASec=0		ASec=0		ASec=0		
AFrame=0	AFrame=0	AFrame=0	AFrame=0	[TRACK 3] →	[TRACK 9]			
ALBA=-150	ALBA=-150	ALBA=-150	ALBA=-150	MODE=1		MODE=1		
Zero=0		Zero=0		Zero=0		Zero=0	INDEX 1=0	INDEX 1=0
PMin=3	→	PMin=9		PMin=3		PMin=3		
PSec=0		PSec=0		PSec=1		PSec=1		
PFrame=0	PFrame=0	PFrame=33	PFrame=33					
PLBA=8850	PLBA=-1		PLBA=13458	PLBA=13458				

Because most data CDs have only one track per session, to renumber tracks within the limits of one session, it is necessary to create a fictitious track within the genuine track. This technique was already covered above.

Incorrect Starting Number for the First Track

Changing the starting number of the first track is a strong and honest-enough method of protection. The vast majority of drives reliably recognize discs, in which track numbering starts from a number other than one. For instance, let us assume that the disc starts from track number two…

Let's return to the original image of the disc being protected and edit the IMAGE.CCD by shifting numbers of all of the tracks by one, without forgetting that the numbers of the first and the last track of each session are stored in `points 0xA0` and `0xA1`, respectively. For proper disc protection, they also must be modified.

Listing 6.29. Changing the number of the first track. Original values are in the columns marked in black, while modified values are shown in the columns marked in gray. The modified values are set out in bold and marked with arrows.

[Entry 0]	[Entry 0]	[Entry 1]	[Entry 1]	[Entry 3]	[Entry 3]
Session=1	Session=1	Session=1	Session=1	Session=1	Session=1
Point=0xa0	Point=0xa0	Point=0xa1	Point=0xa1	Point=0x1 ⇒	Point=0x2
...	...	...	...	...	...
PMin=1 ⇒	PMin=2	PMin=1 ⇒	PMin=2	PMin=0	PMin=0
PSec=0	PSec=0	PSec=0	PSec=0	PSec=2	PSec=2
PFrame=0	PFrame=0	PFrame=0	PFrame=0	PFrame=0	PFrame=0

Listing 6.30. Changing the number of the second track

```
[Entry 7]        [Entry 7]        [Entry 8]        [Entry 8]        [Entry 10]       [Entry 10]
Session=2        Session=2        Session=2        Session=2        Session=2        Session=2
Point=0xa0       Point=0xa0       Point=0xa1       Point=0xa1       Point=0x2  ⇒     Point=0x3
.                ..               .                ..               .                ..
PMin=2  ⇒        PMin=3           PMin=2  ⇒        PMin=3           PMin=0           PMin=0
PSec=0           PSec=0           PSec=0           PSec=0           PSec=2           PSec=2
PFrame=0         PFrame=0         PFrame=0         PFrame=0         PFrame=0         PFrame=0
```

Listing 6.31. Changing the map

```
[TRACK 1] ⇒   [TRACK 2]   [TRACK 2] ⇒   [TRACK 3]
MODE=1        MODE=1      MODE=1        MODE=1
INDEX 1=0     INDEX 1=0   INDEX 1=0     INDEX 1=0
```

Let's write the modified image to the disc (Attention: the **Do not restore subchannel data** option in the profile parameters must be set. Otherwise, the data on the track number in the Q subcode channel won't correspond to the TOC, which will have a negative effect on the compatibility). The recorder produces a nice protected disc, in which track numbering starts with 2 (Fig. 6.12). Drives like ASUS or TEAC will show all its tracks and display the disc TOC normally, using the operating system's built-in tools. Even more so, they will agree to work with protection at the sector level without any doubts. However, NEC fails to work with such a disc, because after the first attempts at access (regardless of whether or not this attempt was undertaken at the sector level), the drive issues low clicking sounds and falls into a stupor that can be interrupted only by the EJECT button. Alas, but protection mechanisms of this type are characterized by compatibility with non-standard equipment, which is very far from perfect.

Now let's see how well this mechanism protects against copying. Standard copiers, such as Stomp Record Now! and Ahead Nero, refuse to view this disc as a proper one, and won't even try to start copying! Alcohol 120%, because of some internal error, simply spits out message about a critical access error and passes into another world, refusing to react to the keyboard or mouse. Clone CD, on the other hand, copies such a disc quite successfully (although, for some unknown reason, it skips `point 0xC1`, which stores the ATIP copy. This circumstance can easily be used for binding to the original disc).

The fact that this protection cannot be copied by current versions of Alcohol 120% is no cause for feelings of self-satisfaction, because in this case, we are dealing with an annoying programming error, and not with a conceptual architectural limitation on the part of the copier. This error might be fixed any moment, meaning that our protection would no longer perform its function. To strengthen this protection, we will have to wander considerable distance from the letter of the law in the standard. To do this, we will have to create a mismatch between the number of each track and the numbers of points 0xA0 and 0xA1. Let points 0xA0/0xA1 of the first session point to 1, and points 0xA0/0xA1 of the second session to 2, while the numbering of the tracks themselves starts with 2.

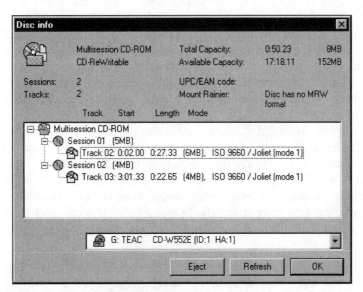

Fig. 6.12. Track numbering starts from 2

At the higher level, no drive of which I am aware is able to read such a disc (even ASUS can only see the first session). It is, however, still possible to work with it at the sector level (except for on the NEC drive). Therefore, this method of protection is only suitable for two-disc programs, in which the first disc is a normal one, the second disc is protected, and the data contained on it are read directly by applications at the sector level.

Protected CD copiers cannot bypass this kind of protection: Both Alcohol 120% and Clone CD interpret the disc as being absolutely empty. Alcohol 120% doesn't see any of the sessions, while Clone CD admits that:

```
INFORMATION ON THE CD IN DRIVE:
No information on the CD is available.  Disc empty?
```

However, we know that the disc is not blank! Its copying must be possible. Provided that the drive you are using supports discs of this type, it is enough to analyze the TOC, which, as was mentioned several times before, can be read using the READ TOC (opcode: 0x43; format 0x2) command and grab the contents of all of the tracks at the sector level. After this, all that remains is to form the image for disc burning. In fact, it is quite surprising that protected-CD copiers are still unable to copy these discs automatically. There is really nothing too difficult here.

Two Identical Tracks

This is a reliable, easy-to-implement protection mechanism that is compatible with practically all equipment. At the same time, this protection is quite elegant. All we need to do is change the number of the second track to one. As a result, the disc will contain two tracks with identical numbers but absolutely different contents (do not forget to correct the `points 0xA0/0xA1` and forcibly disable the recovery of subchannel data).

The protected disc can be read normally on all drives known to me. It cannot, however, be copied by any of the copiers available to me (except, naturally, for those that I wrote myself). The first two tracks look quite strange (Fig. 6.13) and do not create any problems for the drive itself or for the operating system. The drive firmware usually searches only for the first track (which, according to the naive assumptions by some developers, always bears the number 1), and ignores the numbers of all other tracks. The operating system (or, to be more precise, the file system of CDs) also addresses tracks by absolute sector addresses instead of track numbers. Therefore, the numbers of all tracks, except for the first ones, fall out of touch with the operating system. Naturally, all of the above-mentioned relates only to data discs.

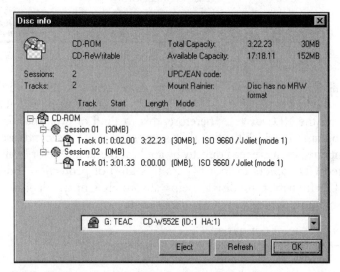

Fig. 6.13. Protected disc containing two tracks with the number one

In theory, copying such discs shouldn't cause any problems. Actually, the track contents are wonderfully readable at the sector level and track numbers do not take part in absolute addressing. Therefore, a well-designed copier has only to read the TOC and retrieve the contents of all its tracks without taking into account their numbers. Of course, if a short-sighted developer has decided to place the data of track *N* of the array with index *N*, then the presence of two (or more) tracks with identical numbers will break this weak algorithm easily.

Standard copiers refuse to copy discs of this sort, displaying the error messages. Alcohol 120% correctly analyzes the disc geometry (see the listing below), but, even in this case, two problems still remain.

Listing 6.32. The data on the protected disc (left) and data on the disc image created by Alcohol 120% (right)

```
IMAGE FILE INFORMATION:                  IMAGE FILE INFORMATION:

Sessions: 2                              Sessions: 2
Used space: 34850 Kbytes                 Used space: 34850 Kbytes
Sectors: 15173                           Sectors: 15173
Time: 03:22:23 (Min:Sec:Frames)          Time: 03:22:23 (Min:Sec:Frames)

SESSION 1 INFORMATION:                    SESSION 1 INFORMATION:
Session size: 4726 Kbytes                Session size: 4726 Kbytes
Tracks: 1                                Tracks: 1
Track 1: Data Mode 1, size: 4726 Kbytes  Track 1: Data Mode 1, size: 4726 Kbytes

SESSION 2 INFORMATION:                    SESSION 2 INFORMATION:
Session size: 3939 Kbytes                Session size: 3939 Kbytes
Tracks: 1                                Tracks: 1
Track 1: Data Mode 1, size: 3939 Kbytes  Track 1: Data Mode 1, size: 3939 Kbytes
```

First, the map of tracks created by Alcohol 120% contains errors all over it, so it turns out to be a horrible blunder. Instead of two tracks, Alcohol 120% has placed only one track, but, at the same time, duplicated indexes, making a mess of their numbers and values.

Listing 6.33. A map of the protected disc tracks (left) and disc map created by Alcohol 120% (right)

```
[TRACK 1]                [TRACK 1]
MODE=1                    MODE=1
INDEX 1=0                 INDEX 0=-13608
                         INDEX 1=-13458
[TRACK 1]
MODE=1
INDEX 1=0
```

Second, the burning of the protected disc image is carried out in unusual way. The progress indicator, having reached the 100-percent mark, doesn't stop. Instead of this, it continues its steady advance. Then, as if it has suddenly recalled something, Alcohol 120% resets the progress to zero, and restarts the burning process (probably, because it is beginning to process the second track number 1). When this process comes close to its end, the drive starts to produce some lamentable sounds. Nevertheless, the burning process is completed without errors. An attempt, however, to read the TOC of the burnt disc freezes the drive and causes it to produce an entire symphony of squeaking sounds. To put it simply, Alcohol 120% in this case produces a 120% failure.

Clone CD already begins producing absolute garbage at the stage of analyzing the protected disc, losing both the second track and its session. Besides this, for some unknown reason, Clone CD reduces the size of used disc space by 3 Kbytes (30,911 Kbytes instead of 34,850 Kbytes), reducing the number of sectors accordingly. Despite the fact that the protected CD uses all 15,173 sectors, Clone CD sees only 13,458. Where the remaining 1,688 sectors are is a mystery. Note that this information is received by means of TOC analysis, which reported the original size and original number of sectors honestly! And, besides this, the disc size has not been reduced by the size of the lost track (this, after all, has a reasonable explanation)! On the contrary, the disc size has been reduced by an absolutely arbitrary value! See for yourself...

Listing 6.34. The data for the protected disc (left) and information taken from its image created by Clone CD (right)

```
INFORMATION ON THE CD IN THE DRIVE:          INFORMATION ON THE IMAGE FILE

Sessions: 2                                  Sessions: 1
Used space: 34850 Kbytes                     Used space: 30911 Kbytes
Sectors: 15173                               Sectors: 13458
Time: 03:22:23 (Min:Sec:Frame)               Time: 02:59:33 (Min:Sec:Frame)

INFORMATION ABOUT SESSION 1:                 INFORMATION ABOUT SESSION 1:
Session size: 4726 Kbytes                    Sessions size: 30911 Kbytes
Tracks: 1                                    Tracks: 1
Track 1: Data 1, size: 4726 Kbytes           Track 1:Data Mode 1, size:30911 Kbytes
INFORMATION ON SESSION 2:
Session size: 3939 Kbytes
Tracks: 1
Track 1: Data Mode 1, size: 3939 Kbytes
```

This is nothing, however, compared with what is to come. When attempting to copy the disc, Clone CD actually reads the first 15 percent, and then encounters a vast array of unreadable (from its viewpoint) sectors. The starting point of this array (or, so to speak, an entire continent of unknown lands) matches exactly the Lead-out address, written directly and openly in the TOC. Why in the world did Clone CD need to read the Lead-out? An hour goes by, and then another, but Clone CD continues on with its vain attempt to read the unreadable Lead-out sectors and is unlikely to give up on this total waste of time.

Well! Neither Clone CD, nor Alcohol 120% managed to bypass the disc protection. However, what if we use them in combination? Perhaps this symbiosis will produce at least something? Recall that Alcohol 120% has successfully produced a correct image of the CD to be copied. It only failed with burning this image on a CD. Clone CD, on the contrary, burns these images with enthusiasm (after all, it was Clone CD that we used to created this protected disc), but fails to create a correct disc image. What if we create the disc image using Alcohol 120% and pass it furtively to Clone CD for burning? When doing so, it is necessary to remember to correct the track map to the original version, which, because of its simplicity, can be restored easily. You can skip this, however, because the attempt will fail anyway. Clone CD will certainly burn the image created by Alcohol 120%, but reading is a different matter. After dragging the head for a long time, accompanied by the strained roar of the motors, the drive will display only the contents of the first session. Where, you might ask, is the second? To understand this, it is enough to view the image file formed by Alcohol 120%. A byte-by-byte comparison of the sectors of both tracks shows that their contents are identical, which means that the second track overwrites the first!

Thus, the suggested protection actually cannot be copied by the most common protected-CD copiers. This doesn't, however, mean that it cannot, in principle, be copied. Actually, copying here is possible! To do this, let's use any of the available utilities or reading sectors at the raw level. Proceeding this way, retrieve the contents of the second track and write it into the image file (to find the starting point of the second track, analyze the absolute addresses in its header). Just open the file in any HEX editor and find the following sequence: "00 FF FF FF FF FF FF FF FF FF FF 00 00 02 00", i.e., the sync group plus address of the first sector (00:02:00). Note that the first occurrence will correspond to the first track, while the second occurrence will correspond to the second track overwritten by the first.

The check shows that the copied disc is absolutely usable this time. Therefore, the protection mechanism is not as strong as the developers of licensed programs would like to believe. Nevertheless, this protection is strong enough for the users armed with typical hacking tools. Because its compatibility with various equipment is rather good, it may become rather popular with time.

Incorrect Number for the Last Track

Most drives are oversensitive to an incorrect number for the last track (the A1h pointer in TOC). This protection technique, therefore, is only of interest from an academic point of view. From the practical point of view, it is of little interest (and it is not recommended to protect your discs in this way). Nevertheless, provided that the necessary precautions have been observed, this technique can still be used.

Open the IMAGE.CCD file mentioned above, find the `Point=0xA1` string located in session 1, and change the `PMin` field from 1 to 2. Thus, you'll make the drive consider the number of the last track of the first session to be equal to 2 instead of 1, as is the case in reality.

```
[Entry 1]              [Entry 1]
    Session=1              Session=1
    Point=0xa1            Point=0xa1
    ...              ...
    PMin=1                PMin=2
    PSec=0                PSec=0
    PFrame=0              PFrame=0
```

After burning the changed image on a CD, Clone CD will produce correct information about the track number, which serves as an indirect indication that it doesn't analyze the values of the `A1h` pointer, and that the number of the last track is determined by means of analyzing the `01h` — `99h` pointers. The last encountered pointer will be the last track number in the current session (Attention: The point with the largest number is not necessarily the last track, because track numbering can be intentionally modified in order to complicate disc copying).

A disc protected in such a way (or, to be more precise, disfigured in such a way) displays only its first session when it is read on the ASUS drive. NEC sees both tracks. However, because of the rich imagination of its electronic circuitry, it erroneously determines their type as AUDIO. The fact that, all the same, it refuses to play this as audio denies us the pleasure of hearing a unique symphony of noise and grinding. The TEAC drive doesn't recognize the disc at all. In brief, it appears that the firmware of most drives behaves differently from Clone CD. Instead of counting the tracks, it reads the contents of the A1h pointer directly. If this pointer is incorrect, the drive begins to behave inadequately. In general, this form of protection is poor, so we won't consider it further.

Most drives, however, are much more tolerant to an incorrect number for the last track of the second session (which means that the disfigured second session doesn't prevent the first session from being read). Let's try an experiment. Open the original copy of the IMAGE.CCD file and perform the following "surgery" on it: Change the contents of the `PMin` field belonging to point A1h of the second session from 2 to 1, thus attempting to assure the drive that the number of the last track of the second session terminates with 1 (although you can choose any other value, for instance, 3 or 8):

```
[Entry 8]              [Entry 8]
    Session=2              Session=2
```

```
Point=0xa1              Point=0xa1
...                     ...
PMin=2                  PMin=1
PSec=0                  PSec=0
PFrame=0                PFrame=0
```

ASUS and TEAC drives display only the first session of the disc, while the second session is not available even at the sector level. The NEC drive also sees only the first session. It, however, kindly allows us to read the second session at the sector level. Nevertheless, you should not rely on this kindness, because most drives are not as generous as NEC.

Let's try to copy the protected disc, previously having studied its geometry using a suitable program (Ahead Nero, for example). As shown in Fig. 6.14, Nero sees both tracks. However, the second, incorrect, track is interpreted as absolutely empty (which, by the way, is not too far from truth, because this track is not available at the sector level). An attempt to copy this disc using Nero results only in the copying of the first session. Although a disc copied in such a way is, formally, usable, the protection still can detect the forgery by means of elementary TOC analysis. It is enough to check the number of sessions present on the disc and the attributes of the second track. Naturally, they won't match for the copy produced by Nero.

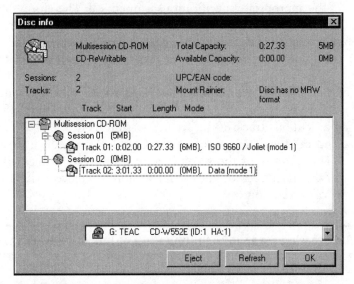

Fig. 6.14. Nero's response to the incorrect number of the last track

Clone CD also fails to copy such a CD. First, it becomes unable to recognize the session limits correctly, and, when the end of the first session is reached, obstinately tries to read the Lead-out contents at the sector level. Of course, the process of "grinding" defective sectors is relatively fast, so the user won't have time to get bored. Naturally, the second session is not copied, and Clone CD corrects the TOC by removing any mention of the second session. As a result, the TOC of the copied disc will be radically different from that of the original. Therefore, the protection mechanism won't have to expend a significant effort to detect the unauthorized copy. Alcohol 120% also copies only the first session.

Is it possible to copy such a disc manually? Of course! It is enough to create an exact copy of the original TOC without introducing any changes, and burn the contents of the first session to the CD.

Gap in Track Numbering of the First Session

We will cover this flaky protection mechanism only theoretically — just in case you encounter a disc, on which the first session has been broken by some morally depraved person, and because of the conflict with your equipment, it is read incorrectly (or, more probably, is absolutely unreadable). The criminal codes of most countries contain clauses covering acts of sabotage to cover occurrences of this nature. From the point of view of consumer rights, selling goods that certainly don't match the requirements of the appropriate specifications is unethical. Therefore, the neutralization of this kind of "protection" can't really be considered to be cracking from a legal point of view. On the contrary, it is simply the repair of goods the purchaser makes on his or her own and at his or her expense. So, every ugly protection is just waiting for a hacker to crack it.

In order to study this protection, let's create a kind of a "laboratory rat" or test bench (whichever you prefer). Retrieve the CCD file that remained after experiments with creating a fictitious track in the second session from the archive (I assume that you archive and carefully store all of your CCD files) and edit it as shown below in Listing 6.35. The number of the second track is replaced with 9, and, accordingly, the number of the third track of the second session is replaced with 10 to ensure correct "docking" of two sessions.

Listing 6.35. Creating a gap in the numbering of tracks of the first session

```
[Entry 1]       [Entry 1]       [Entry 3]       [Entry 3]       [Entry 8]       [Entry 8]
Session=1       Session=1       Session=1       Session=1       Session=2       Session=2
Point=0xa1      Point=0xa1      Point=0x02 →    Point=0x09      Point=0xa0      Point=0xa0
ADR=0x01        ADR=0x01        ADR=0x01        ADR=0x01        ADR=0x01        ADR=0x01
Control=0x04    Control=0x04    Control=0x04    Control=0x04    Control=0x4     Control=0x4
TrackNo=0       TrackNo=0       TrackNo=0       TrackNo=0       TrackNo=0       TrackNo=0
```

AMin=0	AMin=0	AMin=0	AMin=0	AMin=0	AMin=0
ASec=0	ASec=0	ASec=0	ASec=0	ASec=0	ASec=0
AFrame=0	AFrame=0	AFrame=0	AFrame=0	AFrame=0	AFrame=0
ALBA=-150	ALBA=-150	ALBA=-150	ALBA=-150	ALBA=-150	ALBA=-150
Zero=0	Zero=0	Zero=0	Zero=0	Zero=0	Zero=0
PMin=2 →	**PMin=9**	PMin=3	PMin=3	PMin=3 →	**PMin=10**
PSec=0	PSec=0	PSec=1	PSec=1	PSec=0	PSec=0
PFrame=0	PFrame=0	PFrame=33	PFrame=33	PFrame=0	PFrame=0
PLBA=8850	**PLBA=-1**	PLBA=13458	PLBA=13458	PLBA=8850	**PLBA=-1**
[Entry 9]	[Entry 9]	[Entry 11]	[Entry 11]	[TRACK 1]	[TRACK 1]
Session=1	Session=1	Session=1	Session=1	MODE=1	MODE=1
Point=0xa1	Point=0xa1	Point=0x03 →	**Point=0x010**	INDEX 1=0	INDEX 1=0
ADR=0x01	ADR=0x01	ADR=0x01	ADR=0x01		
Control=0x04	Control=0x04	Control=0x04	Control=0x04	TRACK 2]	**[TRACK 9]**
TrackNo=0	TrackNo=0	TrackNo=0	TrackNo=0	MODE=1	MODE=1
AMin=0	AMin=0	AMin=0	AMin=0	INDEX 1=0	INDEX 1=0
ASec=0	ASec=0	ASec=0	ASec=0		
AFrame=0	AFrame=0	AFrame=0	AFrame=0	[TRACK 3] →	**[TRACK 10]**
ALBA=-150	ALBA=-150	ALBA=-150	ALBA=-150	MODE=1	MODE=1
Zero=0	Zero=0	Zero=0	Zero=0	INDEX 1=0	INDEX 1=0
PMin=3 →	**PMin=10**	PMin=6	PMin=6		
PSec=0	PSec=0	PSec=1	PSec=1		
PFrame=0	PFrame=0	PFrame=33	PFrame=33		
PLBA=8850	**PLBA=-1**	PLBA=26958	PLBA=26958		

Problems will already arise when burning the tweaked image. Besides incorrectly determining the length of the second track (which now became the 9th track), which is not surprising for us after all of our experiments, Clone CD has also incorrectly interpreted the Lead-out area of the first session. In fact, it has taken it to be a stand-alone data track with the number 170 (AAh). What is most interesting here is that the point referring to the Lead-out is not explicitly stored in the TOC. This means that track number 170 is not present in the disc TOC, and the only way of retrieving it is by reading the Q subcode channel from the Lead-out! However, if Clone CD explicitly accesses the Lead-out, why does it take it for a stand-alone track?

Nevertheless, this strange bug doesn't influence the burning quality, and, therefore, we can ignore it with clear conscience.

Listing 6.36. Clone CD has inadequately reacted to the gap in the track numbering

```
SESSION 1 INFORMATION:
Session size: 4726 Kbytes
Tracks: 9
Track 1: Data Mode 1, size: 4823 Kbytes
Track 9: Data, size: 4294967200 Kbytes
Track 170: Data, size: 4294962570 Kbytes


SESSION 2 INFORMATION:
Session size: 3939 Kbytes
Tracks: 1
Track 10: Data, size: 3939 Kbytes
```

In fact, it has gone so crazy that it interpreted the Lead-out track (AAh or 170 in decimal notation) as a data track, and the size of the 9th and 170th tracks has grown to unimaginable values. A disc "protected" in this way is not recognized by the TEAC drive. Following a long period, during which the blinking of the activity indicator is accompanied by strained grinding sounds, the drive stops the motor and informs us that it hasn't found any CD. On the other hand, NEC detects nine audio tracks. Any attempts at playing them, however, result in the displaying of a message informing the user that there is no disc in the drive. The ASUS drive produced the best results. Although it lost the second session, it at least processed the contents of the first one normally.

Is it possible to read such a disc without having ASUS or any other similar drive at your disposal? Yes. To achieve this, it is enough to feed the drive a disc with an absolutely correct TOC, and, after this disc has been recognized, immediately hot-swap the disc on the fly. Such a technique allows us to copy the disc contents, but not its TOC. To read the TOC, we will have to use ASUS or any other drive that is capable of recognizing incorrect discs and doesn't prevent working with them at the sector level. Even if you do not have ASUS at your disposal, don't fall into despair, since reading the TOC is an absolutely senseless operation. We can restore the boundaries of the tracks and sessions without it. (Have you forgotten about the existence of the Q subcode channel?) With regard to the incorrect track numbers, this is not a problem, because cracking of this "protection" assumes the restoration of correct track numbering that is recognizable by all drives, without exception. Therefore, track number 1 must be followed by track number 2, which, in turn, must be followed by the track number 3, and so on. Thus, the trash written in the TOC is of no importance! Not all information can be trusted. However, the protection mechanism can be bound to the TOC by reading its contents and comparing them to the original! If this is so (and, most often, this is exactly the case), we must intercept the call to the READ TOC command (opcode 43h) and modify the code that carries out this comparison so that it will not carry out comparison any more. Further details on this topic are provided in my book *"Hacker Disassembling Uncovered"*.

Gap in Track Numbering in the Second Session

Hacking the track numbering of the first session is a nasty and ugly technique. Most drives, however, react more adequately to incorrect track numbering in the second session. Provided that all of the necessary precautions have been taken, the probability of conflicts with user equipment will be reduced to a reasonable minimum. This means that the damage from unauthorized copying of unprotected CDs is considerably lower than financial losses resulting from returning "unreadable" discs. Moreover, there are users who tend to bring manufacturers to court for every conflicting CD.

Based on the experience gained in the course of previous experiments, we can easily break the second session by changing the number of the third track to 9 (naturally, you can choose any other number; however, remember that superstitious people believe that even numbers can bring misfortune).

When burning the tweaked image, Clone CD incorrectly determines the number of the last track of the broken session by erroneously interpreting the Lead-out as a stand-alone track. However, this has no effect on the burning quality.

Listing 6.37. Clone CD has incorrectly determined the number of tracks to be eight tracks (actually, there are two)

```
SESSION 1 INFORMATION:

Session size: 4726 Kbytes
Tracks: 1
Track 1: Data Mode 1, size: 4726 Kbytes

SESSION 2 INFORMATION:

Session size: 3939 Kbytes
Tracks: 8
Track 2: Data Mode 1, size: 1722 Kbytes
Track 9: Data Mode 1, size: 2216 Kbytes
Track 170: Data, size: 4294932446 Kbytes
```

Furthermore, track with the number 170 is actually the Lead-out track erroneously interpreted as data track (combined tracks).

Field tests of the protected disc have revealed the following results. NEC and TEAC drives see only the first session of the disc, while the second session is unavailable even at the sector level. However, such commands as SEEK, READ SUBCHANNEL, and READ HEADER are executed successfully. If all other drives behaved similarly, then the protection developers would feel free to place a key mark in the Q subcode channel or simply check the Q subcode channel of the "broken" session for readability. Copiers such as Alcohol 120% and Clone CD won't notice the broken session. Even if they do, they won't be able to copy its contents, which, as was already mentioned, are returned together with the main data flow instead of by a separate channel. Provided that the broken session is not available at the sector level (and this is actually the case), it will be missing on unauthorized copies. Consequently, commands like SEEK, READ SUBCHANNEL, and READ HEADER will return an error, thus allowing us to distinguish an unauthorized copy from the original.

Unfortunately, some drives (ASUS in particular) do not provide any access to the broken session. Because of this, the original disc will be erroneously interpreted by the protection as an unauthorized copy. Therefore, you should not rely on the second session! Nevertheless, this precaution does not really weaken the protection, since the entire session of this disc cannot even be copied.

Viewing disc geometry with the Ahead Nero copier shows that the latter is not only unable to determine the length of the tracks of the broken sessions correctly (according to it, their length is zero), but also incorrectly displays their numbers to a catastrophic degree. Actual track numbers written in the TOC are not displayed at all. On the contrary, they are replaced by sequential ordinal numbers (Fig. 6.15). Thus, track 9 is represented as track 3. In a certain sense, this might be correct. However, to copy the protected disc correctly, ordinal numbers are not sufficient.

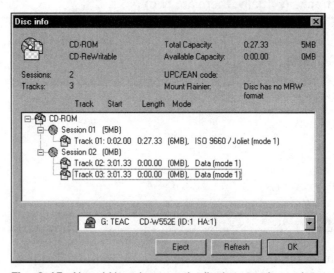

Fig. 6.15. Ahead Nero incorrectly displays track numbers

Clone CD sees only the first session of the protected disc, and, it would seem, doesn't even suspect the existence of the second session (see Listing 6.38). As a result, the broken session is not copied at all, and the TOC of the resulting copy lacks any mention of it. Thus, the protection mechanism only needs to read the TOC and compare it to the reference TOC of the original to discover that it is an unauthorized copy.

Listing 6.38. Clone CD incorrectly displays track numbers

```
INFORMATION ABOUT THE CD IN THE DRIVE:
Sessions: 1
Used space: 30911 Kbytes
Sectors: 13458
Time: 02:59:33 (Min:Sec:Frame)

SESSION 1 INFORMATION:
Session size: 30911 Kbytes
Tracks: 3
Track 1: Data Mode 1, size: 30911 Kbytes
```

With regard to the broken session, everything is more or less clear. The developers of Clone CD didn't expect to encounter perversions of this type. They simply didn't foresee that the track numbering could be cunningly tweaked. Well, everyone makes mistakes sometimes. However, the first session of the protected disc was also copied incorrectly!

Listing 6.39. TOC contents of the original disc (left) and that of the copy produced by Clone CD (right)

```
[Entry 2]      [Entry 2]      ; The Lead-out address of the first session was
Session=1      Session=1      ; determined incorrectly! Clone CD has set it
Point=0xa2     Point=0xa2     ; to the address of the starting point of track 2
ADR=0x01       ADR=0x01       ; (the first track of the second session), which has resulted
Control=0x04   Control=0x04   ; in an incorrect length for the first track and
TrackNo=0      TrackNo=0      ; generated lots of unreadable sectors in
AMin=0         AMin=0         ; Lead-in/Lead-out. Thus, to check if the disc
ASec=0         ASec=0         ; is a legal copy, it is not necessary to read the TOC.
AFrame=0       AFrame=0       ; It is enough to determine the full disc capacity,
ALBA=-150      ALBA=-150      ; which can be done using the built-in OS
Zero=0         Zero=0         ; functions, without needing to use the
```

```
PMin=3 →        PMin=0          ; ASPI/SPTI interfaces.
PSec=1 →        PSec=29         ; An alternative is to read the TOC contents
PFrame=33       PFrame=33       ; with the IOCTL_CDROM_READ_TOC command, which also
PLBA=13458 →    PLBA=2058       ; doesn't require the use of ASPI/SPTI.

[Entry 10]      [Entry 4]       ; Track number 2, belonging to the second session,
Session=2       Session=1       ; was stuffed into the end of the first session.
Point=0x02      Point=0x02      ; Clone CD didn't even try to compare its starting
ADR=0x01        ADR=0x01        ; address to the starting address of the Lead-out of
Control=0x04    Control=0x04    ; the first session. "Magically", they coincide, and
TrackNo=0       TrackNo=0       ; this is probably why Lead-out is erroneously taken for
AMin=0          AMin=0          ; a stand-alone track. An attempt at reading the second
ASec=0          ASec=0          ; track doesn't produce any result, and the third
AFrame=0        AFrame=0        ; (i.e., 9th) track was lost altogether. Therefore,
ALBA=-150       ALBA=-150       ; the copy produced by Clone CD differs from the original
Zero=3          Zero=3          ; and the protection will easily detect unauthorized copy
PMin=3          PMin=3          ; without even accessing the second session.
PSec=1          PSec=1          ; Here is the fabulous Clone CD! And note that it
PFrame=33       PFrame=33       ; pretends to deserve the proud name of
PLBA=13458      PLBA=13458      ; protected CD copier!
```

Alcohol 120% copes much better with the task of copying a disc of this type. However, the copy produced by it also bears at least one considerable difference from the original. The number of the broken track is arbitrarily changed from nine to three, which means that Alcohol 120% automatically restores the correct track numbering. However, it is incorrect track numbering that we need! The protection mechanism that binds to the TOC will refuse to work with such a disc, because it will identify it as an unauthorized copy. (Curiously enough, the contents of point A1h, specifying the number of the last track of the disc, remain unchanged, which means that Alcohol 120% recovered the TOC incorrectly.)

Thus, for binding to the original TOC, the protection mechanism doesn't need to read its original contents in the raw form. It is enough to use the standard built-in functionality of the operating system, because the changes introduced by protected CD copiers in the TOC are so significant that they can be noticed immediately, even by the naked eye.

Nevertheless, protection mechanisms of this type are not very strong. The hacker can edit the disc imaged produced by Alcohol 120% manually and return the track number to its initial value of nine or any other number (the required value can be determined easily using the CD_READ_TOC or any other similar utility).

Discs That Start from a Track With a Number Other Than One

"Your queries are exceedingly demanding..." –

Said the database, before freezing totally.

The requirement in the standard that track numbering starts from one, as well as point A0h stores the number of the first track being present, seems a bit strange, if not excessive. Of course, it is possible to argue that point A0h has special meaning for the second and all following sessions. My answer, however, would be that, first, the number of the first track of each session is equal to point A1h of the previous session plus one, and, second, that the number of the first track of each session is the smallest track number of all tracks belonging to this session. Thus, points A0h and A1h are redundant anyway, and are intended exclusively to allow us quickly to determine the first and last track numbers without analyzing the entire TOC. This task was necessary for the weak processors of the first audio players.

The really interesting question here is as follows: Do contemporary CD drives analyze these points or silently and blindly rely on the default number of the first track (the standard, by the way, doesn't prohibit this)? Let's try to find the answer by creating a disc, on which the first track bears a number other than one (for example, let's suppose that the disc starts immediately from track 2). Based on all previous experience, this can be done easily. It is enough to change point 0x01 to point 0x02, and number the points of all remaining tracks (if there are any) accordingly, change [TRACK 1] to [TRACK 2] and renumber all remaining tracks (if, again, there are any), and, finally, increase point A1h of the first session and points A0h/A1h of all remaining sessions by one. If you forget to do this and leave all points with their default values, the disc will be totally unreadable by an NEC drive. For a TEAC drive, the disc will be accessible only at the sector level, and even ASUS will see only the first session. And this will only happen after some lengthy dragging by the reading head. Thus, while ASUS is an excellent drive, in some respects it behaves quite nervously. If you attempt to copy a disc of this type using Clone CD, the latter will declare that the disc is blank (even though this is not the case). Clone CD only discovers that the disc is not empty when it tries to clear it. Alcohol 120% will not see anything on the disc either. Like Clone CD, it won't copy anything. If you are not sure that the drives your users have at their disposal are capable of reading these discs at least at the sector level, it will be easy to create practically crack-proof protection that will never be copied by any copier (except for the one that I have developed on my own, because my copier never looks at the TOC). However, because of possible conflicts, I wouldn't advise this.

Discs starting from tracks numbered other than one, but with points A0h and A1h set properly, are readable by practically all of the drives that I have at my disposal. Only the NEC drives produce soft clicking sounds and freeze so badly that you end up having to hit the eject button. Thus, this protection is far from perfect. This is even more the case when you consider that Clone CD cracks it easily by creating a correct and usable copy. Alcohol 120% behaves differently, because it displays an "access violation" error message and terminates abnormally.

Thus, ASUS and TEAC actively use points A0h and A1h, and NEC, to all appearances, relies on the assumption that track numbering must necessarily start from 1. While, on the one hand, this isn't contradictory to the standard, on the other, it does not exactly fully correspond to it either, since the presence of point A0h is justified. Consequently, ignoring it won't do us any good.

The situation with Alcohol 120% is not fully clarified yet. Access violation is the consequence of severe algorithmic blunders and design bugs. In all likelihood, Alcohol 120% reads the TOC into the buffer and scans it sequentially to find track number one, forgetting to check the situations where the buffer limits are exceeded.

Clone CD interprets the standard literally, thanks to which it can copy protected discs by storm (although, for the sake of accuracy, such behavior is more an exception than the rule). As we have seen, discs with incorrect TOCs that can be copied correctly are very rare.

Disc with Track Number Zero

Did you ever think about the following question: Why does track numbering on CDs start from one and not from zero? After all, to distinguish a programmer from a plain user, it is enough to give the military "Number off!" command. The normal reaction would simply be for the first individual in line to yell out "First". In its way, this is correct. A programmer, however, will first ask, in which notation (binary, octal, or hexadecimal) to count, and then will proudly shout out "Zeroth"! Some people might object that CDs were developed specially for the users, who are bound to feel more comfortable with decimal notation and numbering that starts from one.

However, despite the persuasive nature of this argument, it's faulty. Track counting for any disc starts from zero instead of one. In fact, the number zero is reserved for the service track (disc Lead-in area) and its content is not available at the interface level. This, however, doesn't change anything! The TNO (Track Number) field of the Q subcode channel of the Lead-in disc area is equal to zero, which means that, *from the drive's point of view, every disc starts from track number zero*. The electronic circuitry of the drive reads and addresses track zero in absolutely the same way as any other disc track. This allows it to preserve transparency and order in the numbering system. From the standpoint of system programmers that develop CD drive firmware, track numbering always starts from zero. As for end users, they think that track numbering starts from one. In other words, both parties are free to maintain their own point of view.

The attributes of track number zero are missing from the TOC because this is the track that is used for storing the TOC itself. Let's consider what happens if one of the points of an actual or fictitious track is assigned the value zero. In other words, what will happen if we create another track number zero in the user area of the disc?

If, besides entering fictitious data in the TOC, we also correct the contents of the Q subcode channel by filling the TNO field with zeros, then, from the drive's point of view, such a track will be indistinguishable from the disc Lead-in area. Any attempt at reading this track sector-by-sector will fail (although some drives can cope even with the worse situations). The subchannel data of track number zero, theoretically, must be available for reading by commands such as SEEK/READ SUBCHANNEL. However, there is no guarantee of this, because the presence of two sequential Lead-in areas causes the drive to behave nervously and unpredictably. Abandoning the restoration of sub-channel data doesn't change the situation considerably. The presence of the zero point in the TOC is an unusual event in itself.

Most drives will go a little crazy and will refuse to process such a disc, reading its TOC in an unpredictable way. For example, NEC returns an error when executing the READ TOC command, while ASUS interprets track number zero as an indicator of TOC termination. TEAC, having encountered track number zero, starts to behave nervously, and instead of the attributes of all further tracks "spits out" the contents of all its internal buffers along with the garbage that remained from the TOC of the previous disc. In brief, *the presence of track number zero makes the CD practically unreadable.*

We could, actually, halt our discussion at this point. After all, who needs conflict-prone protection that works exclusively under lab conditions but is unusable in practice? However, there is one factor in favor of this type of protection. Because CD costs are dropping rapidly, these discs can be used not only for storing information, but also as a kind of key.

The point is that the presence of track number zero does not prevent the reading of the subchannel data of the spiral track, but most copiers (including Alcohol 120% and Clone CD) are more likely to freeze than to copy such a disc! Thus, the algorithm of the protection mechanism consists of the "manual" reading of the TOC using SEEK/READ SUBCHANNEL commands and checking it further for the presence of track number zero.

Although the key disc cannot contain any other data except the TOC being checked, this is not a problem. In a certain sense, this is even an advantage. For example, suppose that the first CD, which is not protected against copying in any way, contains the demo version of some program freely available for downloading from the Internet. To turn this demo version into a fully functional one, the user must insert the key disc into the drive. The key disc can be obtained either from the regional dealer or sent to the user by mail. It is not actually necessary to keep the key disc in the drive constantly, because the protection can remember the registration flag, store it in the system registry and request the key disc only from time to time — just in case the user decides to lend it to someone. No one would argue that this isn't much more reliable than the key file or registration number. Most users actually share them with friends or even publish them on the Internet. Taking into account that subchannel data of the disc can store not only the key, but also executable (or interpreted) code that ensures the full functionality of the registered program, it becomes clear that if the hacker has not got a single copy of the fully functional program of the protected application, it will be unrealistic to crack this program within a reasonable time. However, let us proceed with our goal and try to create an image of the protected disc containing a track number zero on it. As we will see quite soon, this task is not an easy one!

If we simply reset the point of the first track to zero, Clone CD will refuse to open this image because of an analysis error. There are actually at least two such errors. First, Clone CD is unaware of the possible existence of tracks with numbers equal to zero. It can't even spot these tracks when looking right at them. Second, Clone CD is inexcusably optimistic, because it relies on the assumption that every session must contain at least one track (which is only an assumption).

Alcohol 120% is more tolerant of sessions containing only track number zero: It opens the image of the protected disc successfully, and correctly displays the track number (Listing 6.40). Yet the track length is determined incorrectly. When attempting to burn such an image, the "access violation" error message appears, and the copier freezes totally, without even attempting to terminate abnormally (Fig. 6.16). Calling Task Manager and killing the process doesn't solve the problem, because the disc tray will become locked, and the user will have to run the CD.lock.exe utility (see the companion CD) for decreasing the lock counter by one.

Listing 6.40. How Alcohol 120% opens the image of the protected disc

---

```
Type:   CloneCD image file
Path:   L:\CD-hack\
Name:   IMAGE.CCD
        IMAGE.img
        IMAGE.sub
Size:   8.81 MB
Sessions:  2
Tracks:    2


Session 01:
    Track 00: Mode 1, Length: 000000(0 Byte), Address: 000000
Session 02:
    Track 01: Mode 1, Length: 000000(0 Byte), Address: 013458
```

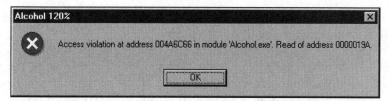

Fig. 6.16. Response of Alcohol 120% to an attempt of burn the CD image
with only track number zero inside the first session

But wait: This is actually a gold mine! The disc with only track number zero within the first session cannot be copied, and it also cannot be burnt! Even if a hacker manages to make a correct dump of a protected disc through some innovative or highly scientific method, there will be no tool capable of burning it! To be absolutely fair, it is necessary to mention that the developer of the application being protected will find him or herself in a similar situation. They also will have no tools for burning the key disc if they don't undertake the task of writing a custom burner. Naturally, manufacturing a stampered CD with track number zero is not a problem. Not everyone, however, can afford this (or certainly at least not freelance programmers).

A compromise variant of protection here is to add at least one track with a non-zero number to the sessions being tweaked. It is possible to prepare such a disc using Clone CD. In this case, the programmer doesn't have to undertake the tedious job of writing a custom burner, which certainly is an advantage. On the other hand, because the original disc is created using a widely known utility, the process of creating unauthorized duplicates is also simplified considerably. In this case, the hacker must only make a correct dump of the protected disc, and all the other tasks can be delegated to Clone CD. There is no need to write specialized cracking software. In other words, everything that is easy to protect can also easily be cracked. But qualified hackers are not numerous; therefore, to prevent the leaking of your information and unauthorized copying of your programs, it is enough to create a key disc that cannot be copied by widely used copiers in automatic mode. As we will see later, protection mechanisms of this type satisfy this requirement.

The process of creating a protected disc is without certain refinements. While the creation of a fictitious track number zero doesn't create special complications on its own, it does raise one question: Where do we put it? Would it be best to put it in the first session, or, instead, in the second? Also, should it precede or follow a genuine track? Because the Lead-in area of the first session is not available for reading at the subchannel level, it is impossible to read the TOC of the first session manually. Furthermore, you can't rely on the READ TOC command, because as was mentioned earlier, there is no guarantee that it will execute correctly. The Lead-in areas of the second and all following sessions are available at the subchannel level, and manual reading of their TOCs is still possible. The specific position of track number zero within the session doesn't play any special role. Track number zero can be placed either before or after a non-zero track with equal success.

Don't forget the need to correct point A0h, storing the number of the "first" track of any session. If this value remains unchanged, Clone CD will write the disc image without any complications. However, the TOC of the burnt CD won't contain any mention of track zero. Alcohol 120% behaves similarly. To avoid this, the value of point A0h of the session, to which you add track zero, must be reset to zero.

A fragment of the edited CCD file is provided below:

Listing 6.41. A fragment of a CCD file with track number zero added.

```
TocEntries=13   TocEntries=14   ; Correcting the number of TOC entries
[Entry 8]       [Entry 8]       ; This must not necessarily have to
                                ; be entry number 8.

Session=2       Session=2       ; The main point here is to ensure that
                                ; Session == 2 and Point == A0h

Point=0xa0      Point=0xa0      ; This point corresponds to the
                                ; number of the first track.

ADR=0x01        ADR=0x01        ; These are ADR/Control fields describing
Control=0x04    Control=0x04    ; the processing mode of this track (data track)
TrackNo=0       TrackNo=0       ; TNO = 0 - this is a Lead-in area
AMin=0          AMin=0          ; \
ASec=0          ASec=0          ; +- Current absolute address
AFrame=0        AFrame=0        ; /
ALBA=-150       ALBA=-150       ; Current LBA address
Zero=0          Zero=0          ; This field is always zero.
PMin=2  →       PMin=0          ; Correcting the number of the "first" track
PSec=0          PSec=0          ; These fields have no actual sense and
PFrame=0        PFrame=0        ; must be equal to zero.
PLBA=8850       PLBA=8850       ; LBA address of the number of the "first" track

                [Entry 11]      ; Adding another Entry, describing track 0
                Session=2       ; Track number 0 must not be in the first session.
                Point=0x00      ; Track number is zero.
                ADR=0x01        ; Subchannel Q encodes current position data
                Control=0x04    ; Data track
                TrackNo=0       ; This is the Lead-in area.
                AMin=0          ; \
                ASec=0          ; + - Conventional absolute Lead-In address
                AFrame=0        ; /
                ALBA=-150       ; Conventional LBA address of Lead-In
                Zero=0          ; This field must be equal to zero.
```

```
PMin=3          ; \
PSec=1          ;  + - Absolute starting address of track 0
PFrame=66       ; /
PLBA=13458      ; LBA address of track 0
```

When viewing the geometry of a disc protected in this way, Ahead Nero displays approximately[i] the information show in Fig. 6.17. The fact that it interpreted the second session as open (*"Session is open"*) has a reasonable explanation, in that the track number 0 that we have created was erroneously interpreted by Nero as the Lead-in. As a result, the shaky equilibrium between the Lead-in and Lead-out areas has been disturbed. The second session of the disc, by the way, is closed, and TOC analysis confirms this. To remain unaware of the fact that Lead-in areas are never mentioned in the TOC is a mistake. It is a little more difficult to understand why the second track was incorrectly identified as belonging to the first session. This appears to be an algorithmic blunder that doesn't do anything to increase our faith in Nero or its developers.

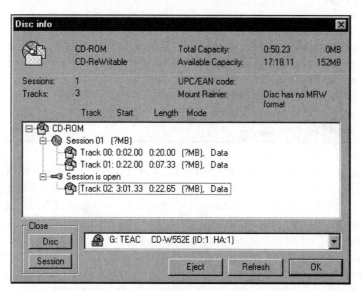

Fig. 6.17. Presence of track number 0 confuses Nero with regard to the status of the last session of the disc. Nero thinks that the second session is open, although this is actually not the case

Clone CD behaves similarly. When attempting to copy the protected disc on drives such as ASUS and TEAC, it runs into the Lead-out area of the first disc session right

---

[i] "Approximately" means that on some drives, Nero doesn't produce any information at all.

away. As a result of algorithmic blunders, it loses track of the second session (the one that contains track 0) completely. As a consequence, the TOC of the copied disc will never mention it. The starting address of the Lead-out area of the first session is also determined incorrectly (Clone CD sets it to the starting address of track 0 of the second session). Points B0h (the starting address of the next position for further writing) and C0h (the starting address of the first Lead-in area of the disc) are also lost. In other words, the TOC of the copied disc considerably differs from the TOC of the original disc. Thus, determining that this is unauthorized copy is simple. Just compare for yourself the TOC of the original key disc with track 0 in the second session and the TOC of its copy obtained using Clone CD. All mismatches are in bold.

Listing 6.42. The original TOC (left; attributes of track 0 are marked by gray shading) and its copy obtained by Clone CD (right)

```
01 14 00 A0 00 00 00 00 01 00 00         01 14 00 A0 00 00 00 00 01 00 00
01 14 00 A1 00 00 00 00 01 00 00         01 14 00 A1 00 00 00 00 01 00 00
01 14 00 A2 00 00 00 00 00 1D 21         01 14 00 A2 00 00 00 00 03 01 42
01 14 00 01 00 00 00 00 00 02 00         01 14 00 01 00 00 00 00 00 02 00
01 54 00 B0 02 3B 21 03 16 0E 22
01 54 00 C0 A2 C8 E0 00 61 1B 15
02 14 00 A0 00 00 00 00 02 00 00
02 14 00 A1 00 00 00 00 00 00 00
02 14 00 A2 00 00 00 00 03 18 17
02 14 00 00 00 00 00 00 03 01 42
```

When attempting to copy the protected disc on a NEC drive (which, as was mentioned earlier, refuses to read a TOC containing track 0), Clone CD surprisingly sends out a "disc empty?" query. No matter what answer we give, Clone CD will make no effort to start copying, thus annoying, perhaps even enraging, the hacker.

Alcohol 120% freezes when attempting to copy the protected disc. It barely manages to find enough time to spit out the "access violation" exception before it "dies." It also locks the drive's tray so that, in order to remove the disc from the drive, the user has to either decrement the lock counter or reboot the system.

Overall (at least from the pirate's point of view, naturally), things look pretty bad. We now have the right to consider the procedure of creating a key disc that essentially can't be copied as having been successfully completed. Now, it would be nice to be able to understand how to work with the obtained disc and how the protection mechanism will be able to distinguish the copy from the original.

The first idea that comes to mind is to read the raw TOC using the READ TOC command and check for the presence of track 0 and its attributes (just to be on the safe side). If track 0 is actually present in TOC and its attributes (i.e., the Session, ADR, Control, and PMin:PSec:Pfarme fields) correspond completely to the reference values, then we are dealing with an original disc. Otherwise, the disc is an unauthorized copy. The advantage of this algorithm is that it is easy to implement. In fact, its implementation requires only about ten lines of code. The drawback, on the other hand, is the instability of key disc recognition on certain drive models. The drive might refuse to read the TOC, and our protection mechanism must be prepared for this situation. Let's do the following: If the READ TOC command returns an error message, but the disc is present in the drive and does not prevent the execution of the SEEK command, then it is the original disc. Naturally, such heuristic assumptions considerably weaken the protection. However, for most applications, it will still remain sufficiently strong.

However, error-free execution of the READ CD command cannot be considered as evidence of the fact that it has actually been completed successfully. Although there are drives capable of reading a TOC containing track number 0, I do not know of a single drive that does this correctly. Therefore, the protection must take into account the nature of possible TOC errors beforehand, and take adequate counter-measures.

For example, let us consider the result returned by the TEAC drive as shown in Listing 6.43. Track 0 is marked by gray shading, and the garbage that follows it is in bold.

Listing 6.43. Contents of the TOC of an original key disc returned by the TEAC drive

```
Session number
|  ADR/Control
|  |  TNO
|  |  |  Point
|  |  |  |  AM:AS:AF PM:PS:PF
|  |  |  |  |   |  |  |   |  |
01 14 00 A0 00 00 00 00 01 00 00 ; point A0 — first track of session 1 in PM
01 14 00 A1 00 00 00 00 01 00 00 ; point A1 — last track of session 1 in PM
01 14 00 A2 00 00 00 00 00 1D 21 ; point A2 — Lead-out address of session 1 in PM:PS:PF
01 14 00 01 00 00 00 00 00 02 00 ; point 01 — starting address of track 1 in PM:PS:PF
01 54 00 B0 02 3B 21 03 16 0E 22 ; point B0 — position for further writing in AM:AS:AF
01 54 00 C0 A2 C8 F0 00 61 1B 15 ; point C0   lead In starting address in PM:PS:PF /tweaked
02 14 00 A0 00 00 00 00 02 00 00 ; point A0 — first track of session 1 in PM
02 14 00 A1 00 00 00 00 00 00 00 ; point A1 — last track of session 2 in PM
02 14 00 A2 00 00 00 00 03 18 17 ; point A2 — Lead-out address of session 2 in PM:PS:PF
02 14 00 00 00 00 00 00 03 01 42 ; point 00 — starting address of track 0 in PM:PS:PF
FB FD 00 FB F4 FB 7A FF FD FD FF ; \              | As you can see, TEAC, having encountered
FB DF 00 FA FD F5 FF BF FB FE FF ; + - garbage | track 0 starts to spit out garbage
FE F7 00 FB FF FD FB FF FF F7 FF ; /              | instead of useful data.
```

Look at the suspicious garbage that follows immediately after track 0. This is the content of the internal buffers of the drive, which is present here as a result of a programming mistake in the drive's firmware (by the way, I used the newest firmware version available at the moment of writing — version 1.09). A basic investigation shows that this garbage is not arbitrary and represents the "tail" of the TOC of the previous disc.

For example, let us load a disc into the drive (in my experiment, this was the *"Soul Ballet Hit Collection"*), then replace it with the key disc and see what comes out.

Listing 6.44. The TOC of the Soul Ballet Hit Collection disc (left) and the TOC of the key disc (right), returned by the TEAC drive

```
01 10 00 A0 00 00 00 00 01 00 00        01 14 00 A0 00 00 00 00 01 00 00
01 10 00 A1 00 00 00 00 10 00 00        01 14 00 A1 00 00 00 00 01 00 00
01 10 00 A2 00 00 00 00 48 1C 05        01 14 00 A2 00 00 00 00 00 1D 21
01 10 00 01 00 00 00 00 00 02 00        01 14 00 01 00 00 00 00 00 03 00
01 10 00 02 00 00 00 00 03 35 40        01 54 00 B0 02 3B 21 03 16 0E 22
01 10 00 03 00 00 00 00 08 14 33        01 54 00 C0 A2 C8 E0 00 61 1B 15
01 10 00 04 00 00 00 00 0C 21 0D        02 14 00 A0 00 00 00 00 02 00 00
01 10 00 05 00 00 00 00 10 3A 2D        02 14 00 A1 00 00 00 00 00 00 00
01 10 00 06 00 00 00 00 16 23 19        02 14 00 A2 00 00 00 00 03 18 17
01 10 00 07 00 00 00 00 1C 1B 0C        02 14 00 00 00 00 00 00 03 01 42
01 10 00 08 00 00 00 00 21 07 49        09 25 00 1F 00 00 00 00 19 01 10
01 10 00 09 00 00 00 00 25 1F 19        0A 2A 00 01 00 00 00 00 06 01 10
01 10 00 0A 00 00 00 00 2A 01 06        0B 2D 00 2D 00 00 00 00 00 01 10
01 10 00 0B 00 00 00 00 2D 2D 00        0C 33 00 29 00 00 00 00 02 01 10
01 10 00 0C 00 00 00 00 33 29 02        0D 39 00 08 00 00 00 00 45 01 10
01 10 00 0D 00 00 00 00 39 08 45        0E 3F 00 1E 00 00 00 00 27 01 10
01 10 00 0E 00 00 00 00 3F 1E 27        0F 43 00 1E 00 00 00 00 29 01 10
01 10 00 0F 00 00 00 00 43 1E 29        10 44 00 03 00 00 00 00 15 FF FF
01 10 00 10 00 00 00 00 44 03 15
```

Look at this! Now, the TOC contents of the key disc have changed considerably. Maybe not entirely, but the tail has clearly changed. Note that the sequence of bytes in the "tail" of the key disc corresponds to the sequence of bytes of the *"Soul Ballet"* CD. Well, although "...09 00 00 00 00 25 1F 19..." is not absolutely the same as "...09 25 00 1F 00 00 19...", if we remove the parasitic zeros, we end up with "...09 25 1F 19..." and "...09 25 1F 19...", which are absolutely identical. Thus, we are actually dealing with a firmware error. This is not exactly an endorsement for the drive or to its developers.

ASUS behaves more correctly, by simply "cutting off" the TOC by track 0, even if track 0 is not the last track of the disc. This is also a firmware error, although not as blatant as the one above.

Listing 6.45. The TOC of the key disc returned by the ASUS drive

```
01 14 00 A0 00 00 00 00 01 00 00
01 14 00 A1 00 00 00 00 01 00 00
01 14 00 A2 00 00 00 00 00 1D 21
01 14 00 01 00 00 00 00 00 03 00
01 54 00 B0 02 3B 21 03 16 0E 22
01 54 00 C0 A2 C8 E0 00 61 1B 15
02 14 00 A0 00 00 00 00 02 00 00
02 14 00 A1 00 00 00 00 00 00 00
02 14 00 A2 00 00 00 00 03 18 17
02 14 00 00 00 00 00 00 03 01 42
```

As mentioned before, NEC does not produce anything except errors, which the protection mechanism must interpret as an indication of a genuine disc. Otherwise, its developer will have to deal with complaints from legal users trying to "feed" this disc to an "incorrect" drive (from the protection's point of view).

Nevertheless, intentionally weakening the protection mechanism is not the optimal solution. It is much better to try to read the TOC manually. Of course, it is hard to implement programmatically. On the bright side, it is even harder to crack! Although it is easy to emulate the READ TOC command, the task of reproducing specific features of subchannel data processing is unrealistic. Thanks to this, the improved protection variant will easily bypass all copiers that emulate virtual discs.

At the risk of cooling down your programming zeal, I should mention that reading subchannel data correctly is not as easy a task as it might appear at first. Official specifications are not sufficient to implement an effective protection mechanism correctly, because they do not reflect even the most minor of the cranky features inherent in various drives, something that you will encounter in practice.

First and foremost, absolute sector addresses are in no way related to their "corresponding" subchannel data. This is because one section of subchannel data is "spread" over several sectors. Furthermore, as a result of certain design features, the processing of subchannel data is separate from the processing of the main data flow. Because of this, the positioning of the head to sector X, followed by a call to the READ SUBCHANNEL command, will produce subchannel data of a sector other than X. It will be sector Y located somewhere "nearby" to sector X. At the same time, every manufacturer has its own idea of what "nearby" means, and in some cases you'll find yourself hundreds of sectors ahead of the one required.

Second, the combination of commands SEEK/READ SUBCHANNEL is *unstable,* and its reproducibility is very poor. This means that there is no guarantees that positioning the head to sector X+k will result in the reading of the subchannel data for sector Y+k. The drive might return the data from sector Y, but, with equal probability, it might return data from sector Y+i. Also, there are no guarantees that the repeated positioning of the head to sector X will return subchannel data from sector Y once again. *By the way, do not forget to pause for at least 1 second between two sequential calls to the SEEK command. Otherwise, the head won't have enough time to move to another location, and the drive will return subchannel data from the previous location, which has already been cached.* All that remains is to rely on the current sector addresses returned in subchannel information itself (the *"Absolute CD Address"* field). Having encountered the address of the required sector in this field, we can be absolutely sure that the subchannel information belongs to that sector, and not to any other.

Listing 6.46. A correct interpretation of subchannel information

```
LBA - 10D4:00 15 00 0C 01 14 00  A0  00 00 22 92  00 00 11 6D
^^^^^^^^^^^                       ^  ^^^^^^^^^^^^  ^^^^^^^^^^^
     |                            |       |             |
LBA address of the sector to      | Point attributes  LBA address of the sector whose
which the head was positioned     |                   subchannel data was returned by the drive
using the SEEK command          Point
```

Third, the specific format of the subchannel information is not defined by the standard. On the contrary, it depends on the drive itself, and varies significantly from model to model. Lead-in and Lead-out areas of discs are the most inconsistent in this respect. The standard doesn't say anything about the possibility of reading them at the subchannel level, silently assuming that no one will ever need this. Consequently, manufacturers implement the drives at their own discretion. Fields of absolute and relative addresses can be swapped without notification, and addresses themselves can be specified in any format, M:S:F or LBA. The values of points A0h, A1h, and A2h (the number of the first track, the number of the last track, and the Lead-out address) can be replaced by the values 64h, 65h and 66h, respectively. Finally, non-standard points (including zero points) are often missing from subchannel data. If this is the case, the data from either the preceding or following sections are returned instead!

All of these factors significantly complicate the interpretation of subchannel data and searching in them for track number 0. Consequently, we have to proceed as follows: Sequentially read the subchannel data of different disc sectors, and wait until the track numbers change first to AAh, then to 00h, which corresponds to the head movement from Lead-out area of the first session to the Lead-in area of the second session.

Continuing to read the Lead-in, we are trying to detect the pattern, according to which the values of absolute and relative address fields are changing, as well as their format (LBA or M:S:F). The representation format can actually be detected quite easily. If the least significant byte of the address takes a values larger than 75 (4Bh), this means that we are dealing with LBA, if not, then it is M:S:F. Further on, since the relative address fields in the Lead-in area of the disc are used for storing attributes of the "own" point, they considerably differ from the current sector addresses (i.e., the ones, to which the head was positioned). On the contrary, the fields of absolute addresses must be sufficiently close to the current addresses.

Now, only one problem remains — what should we do if the subchannel data of the Lead-in area do not contain track 0? Don't rush to conclude that the disc is an unauthorized copy, because, as already mentioned, some drives do not return nonstandard points. At the same time, the *absolute addresses of sectors storing subchannel attributes of track 0 will not be present in the TOC that has been read*. A disc copy obtained using any of the copiers available at the current moment, according to these absolute addresses, will contain attributes of other tracks, which the drive will correctly read and return, or will simply refuse to position the head to this area, returning an error message of some sort.

So, folks, are we still going to implement this? To simplify the perception of this material, some listings will be provided below, containing subchannel information of the key disc returned by several different drives. They are supplied with comments that, as I hope, will help you to understand the idea.

Listing 6.47. The result of reading subchannel information from the Lead-in on the TEAC drive; track 0 is clearly visible

```
            +internal+  Format
            | | | | |  ADR/Control
            | | | | |  | TNO
            | | | | |  | | Point
            | | | | |  | | | +- PLBA -+  +- ALBA -+
            | | | | |  | | | | | | | | | | | | | |

LBA - 10D4:00 15 00 0C 01 14 00 A0 00 00 22 92 00 00 11 6D ; LBA 10D4 → 11CD
LBA - 10D5:00 15 00 0C 01 14 00 A0 00 00 22 92 00 00 11 6D ; LBA 10D5 → 116D
LBA - 10D6:00 15 00 0C 01 14 00 A0 00 00 22 92 00 00 11 6E ; LBA 10D5 → 116E
LBA - 10D7:00 15 00 0C 01 14 00 A0 00 00 22 92 00 00 11 6D ; LBA 10D7 → 116D (!)
LBA - 10D8:00 15 00 0C 01 14 00 A0 00 00 22 92 00 00 11 6E ; (head "beat")
LBA - 10D9:00 15 00 0C 01 14 00 A0 00 00 22 92 00 00 11 6E ; LBA 2292 = 02:00:00 M:S:F

LBA - 10DA:00 15 00 0C 01 14 00 A1 00 FF FF 6A 00 00 11 73 ; LBA FFh - 6Ah = 95h (149)
LBA - 10DB:00 15 00 0C 01 14 00 A1 00 FF FF 6A 00 00 11 73 ; LBA 149 == MSF 0:0:1
```

```
LBA - 10DC:00 15 00 0C 01 14 00 A1 00 FF FF 6A 00 00 11 74 ; Curious, because the number
LBA - 10DD:00 15 00 0C 01 14 00 A1 00 FF FF 6A 00 00 11 75 ; of the last track must be
LBA - 10DE:00 15 00 0C 01 14 00 A1 00 FF FF 6A 00 00 11 74 ; in PM, not in PF.
LBA - 10DF:00 15 00 0C 01 14 00 A1 00 FF FF 6A 00 00 11 74 ; Take this into account!
LBA - 10E0:00 15 00 0C 01 14 00 A2 00 00 3B 45 00 00 11 79 ; Head beat continues.
LBA - 10E1:00 15 00 0C 01 14 00 A2 00 00 3B 45 00 00 11 79 ; Sectors are out of order:
LBA - 10E2:00 15 00 0C 01 14 00 A2 00 00 3B 45 00 00 11 7B ; 1179, 1179, 117B, 1179, 117A,
LBA - 10E3:00 15 00 0C 01 14 00 A2 00 00 3B 45 00 00 11 79 ; 117A, and there are no
LBA - 10E4:00 15 00 0C 01 14 00 A2 00 00 3B 45 00 00 11 7A ; sectors 1176, 1177,
LBA - 10E5:00 15 00 0C 01 14 00 A2 00 00 3B 45 00 00 11 7A ; and 178.
LBA - 10E6:00 15 00 0C 01 14 00 02 00 00 34 92 00 00 11 80 ;
LBA - 10E7:00 15 00 0C 01 14 00 02 00 00 34 92 00 00 11 80 ;
LBA - 10E8:00 15 00 0C 01 14 00 02 00 00 34 92 00 00 11 80 ; Head beat
LBA - 10E9:00 15 00 0C 01 14 00 02 00 00 34 92 00 00 11 7F ;          continues.
LBA - 10EA:00 15 00 0C 01 14 00 02 00 00 34 92 00 00 11 80 ;
LBA - 10EB:00 15 00 0C 01 14 00 02 00 00 34 92 00 00 11 81 ;
LBA - 10EC:00 15 00 0C 01 14 00 00 00 00 34 B3 00 00 11 85 ; Here is track 0, it
LBA - 10ED:00 15 00 0C 01 14 00 00 00 00 34 B3 00 00 11 85 ; is located in sectors
LBA - 10EE:00 15 00 0C 01 14 00 00 00 00 34 B3 00 00 11 86 ; 1185 and 1186 - let's
LBA - 10EF:00 15 00 0C 01 14 00 00 00 00 34 B3 00 00 11 85 ; memorize this!
LBA - 10F0:00 15 00 0C 01 14 00 A0 00 00 22 92 00 00 11 8C ; Point A0 repeats...
LBA - 10F1:00 15 00 0C 01 14 00 A0 00 00 22 92 00 00 11 8C ; and all other points are
LBA - 10F2:00 15 00 0C 01 14 00 A0 00 00 22 92 00 00 11 8B ; repeated with it. By reading
LBA - 10F3:00 15 00 0C 01 14 00 A0 00 00 22 92 00 00 11 8B ; subchannel data further,
LBA - 10F4:00 15 00 0C 01 14 00 A0 00 00 22 92 00 00 11 8C ; we will encounter track 0
LBA - 10F5:00 15 00 0C 01 14 00 A0 00 00 22 92 00 00 11 8B ; once again, but already
LBA - 10F6:00 15 00 0C 01 14 00 A0 00 00 22 92 00 00 11 8B ; in other sectors. Let's
LBA - 10F7:00 15 00 0C 01 14 00 A0 00 00 22 92 00 00 11 8B ; memorize them too.
```

Here, the absolute addresses are represented in LBA format. The discrepancy between the address, to which the head is positioned, and the address whose subchannel data are read is about 400 sectors. However, the pattern is quite regular, and the absolute addresses fall in a closely-grouped bunch, although TEAC is not quite perfect, and faults such as 11:6D, 11:6E, 11:6D, 11:6E occur frequently. The attributes of track 0 are present in an explicit form, which is very good.

With regard to the ASUS drive, its behavior is a little more disordered.

Listing 6.48. The result of reading Lead-in subchannel information on the ASUS drive

```
+internal+ Format
|  |  |  |  |  ADR/Control
|  |  |  |  |  |  TNO
|  |  |  |  |  |  |  Point
|  |  |  |  |  |  |  |  +- PLBA -+  +- ALBA -+
|  |  |  |  |  |  |  |  |  |  |  |  |  |  |  |  |
```

```
LBA - 10D3:00 15 00 0C 01 14 00 A0 00 00 22 92 00 00 11 6F ; Here, subchannel data are returned
LBA - 10D4:00 15 00 0C 01 14 00 A1 00 FF FF 6A 00 00 11 73 ; in a more disorderly fashion,
LBA - 10D5:00 15 00 0C 01 14 00 A1 00 FF FF 6A 00 00 11 73 ; therefore it is already
LBA - 10D6:00 15 00 0C 01 14 00 A1 00 FF FF 6A 00 00 11 73 ; impossible to distinguish
LBA - 10D7:00 15 00 0C 01 14 00 A1 00 FF FF 6A 00 00 11 73 ; neighboring points from
LBA - 10D8:00 15 00 0C 01 14 00 A0 00 00 22 92 00 00 11 6F ; each other. Nevertheless,
LBA - 10D9:00 15 00 0C 01 14 00 A0 00 00 22 92 00 00 11 6F ; they are located by the same
LBA - 10DA:00 15 00 0C 01 14 00 A0 00 00 22 92 00 00 11 6F ; ALBA addresses as in the
LBA - 10DB:00 15 00 0C 01 14 00 A0 00 00 22 92 00 00 11 6F ; previous case. Therefore,
LBA - 10DC:00 15 00 0C 01 14 00 A1 00 FF FF 6A 00 00 11 73 ; ALBA addresses can serve
LBA - 10DD:00 15 00 0C 01 14 00 A0 00 00 22 92 00 00 11 6F ; as a solid helper
LBA - 10DE:00 15 00 0C 01 14 00 A1 00 FF FF 6A 00 00 11 73 ; in identifying points
LBA - 10DF:00 15 00 0C 01 14 00 A1 00 FF FF 6A 00 00 11 73 ; independently from the mood,
LBA - 10E0:00 15 00 0C 01 14 00 A2 00 00 3B 45 00 00 11 79 ; age, or design features
LBA - 10E1:00 15 00 0C 01 14 00 A2 00 00 3B 45 00 00 11 79 ; of specific drive models.
LBA - 10E2:00 15 00 0C 01 14 00 A2 00 00 3B 45 00 00 11 79 ; This considerably
LBA - 10E3:00 15 00 0C 01 14 00 A1 00 FF FF 6A 00 00 11 75 ; simplifies the procedure
LBA - 10E4:00 15 00 0C 01 14 00 A2 00 00 3B 45 00 00 11 7A ; for checking
LBA - 10E5:00 15 00 0C 01 14 00 A1 00 FF FF 6A 00 00 11 75 ; whether the disc is genuine
LBA - 10E6:00 15 00 0C 01 14 00 02 00 00 34 92 00 00 11 80 ; or an unauthorized copy.
LBA - 10E7:00 15 00 0C 01 14 00 02 00 00 34 92 00 00 11 81
LBA - 10E8:00 15 00 0C 01 14 00 A1 00 FF FF 6A 00 00 11 75
LBA - 10E9:00 15 00 0C 01 14 00 A2 00 00 3B 45 00 00 11 7B
LBA - 10EA:00 15 00 0C 01 14 00 00 00 00 34 B3 00 00 11 85 ; Track 0 attributes
LBA - 10EB:00 15 00 0C 01 14 00 02 00 00 34 92 00 00 11 81
LBA - 10EC:00 15 00 0C 01 14 00 A2 00 00 3B 45 00 00 11 7B
LBA - 10ED:00 15 00 0C 01 14 00 00 00 00 34 B3 00 00 11 85 ; Note that they are located
LBA - 10EE:00 15 00 0C 01 14 00 02 00 00 34 92 00 00 11 81
LBA - 10EF:00 15 00 0C 01 14 00 00 00 00 34 B3 00 00 11 86 ; at the same LBA addresses:
LBA - 10F0:00 15 00 0C 01 14 00 A0 00 00 22 92 00 00 11 8B
LBA - 10F1:00 15 00 0C 01 14 00 00 00 00 34 B3 00 00 11 85 ; 1185h и 1186!
LBA - 10F2:00 15 00 0C 01 14 00 A0 00 00 22 92 00 00 11 8B
```

Here, absolute addresses are also presented in the LBA format, and the delta is again about 400 sectors. However, the level of disorder in the information being returned is considerably higher, and sector numbers start to drift (see the ALBA field).

Listing 6.49. The result of reading the subchannel information from the Lead-In area by a NEC drive

```
    +internal+  Format
    | | | | |  ADR/Control
    | | | | |  | TNO
    | | | | |  | | Point
    | | | | |  | | |  +- ALBA -+  +- PLBA -+
    | | | | |  | | |  | | | |  | | | |
```

```
LBA - 1171:00 15 00 0C 01 14 00 64 00 00 11 6E 00 02 00 00 ; Point 64 is actually
LBA - 1172:00 15 00 0C 01 14 00 64 00 00 11 6E 00 02 00 00 ; point A0 (first track number).
LBA - 1173:00 15 00 0C 01 14 00 64 00 00 11 6E 00 02 00 00 ; The less-than-clever drive has
LBA - 1174:00 15 00 0C 01 14 00 64 00 00 11 6E 00 02 00 00 ; clumsily invalidated it.
LBA - 1175:00 15 00 0C 01 14 00 64 00 00 11 6E 00 02 00 00 ; Also note that all addresses go
LBA - 1176:00 15 00 0C 01 14 00 64 00 00 11 6E 00 02 00 00 ; to sector 116E!
LBA - 1177:00 15 00 0C 01 14 00 64 00 00 11 6E 00 02 00 00 ;
```
```
LBA - 1178:00 15 00 0C 01 14 00 65 00 00 11 74 00 00 00 00 ; Sharp move of addresses
LBA - 1179:00 15 00 0C 01 14 00 64 00 00 11 6E 00 02 00 00 ; from 116E to 1174 (+6).
LBA - 117A:00 15 00 0C 01 14 00 65 00 00 11 74 00 00 00 00 ; This is the discontinuity
LBA - 117B:00 15 00 0C 01 14 00 65 00 00 11 74 00 00 00 00 ; of the SEEK on NEC drive!
LBA - 117C:00 15 00 0C 01 14 00 65 00 00 11 74 00 00 00 00
LBA - 117D:00 15 00 0C 01 14 00 65 00 00 11 74 00 00 00 00
LBA - 117E:00 15 00 0C 01 14 00 65 00 00 11 74 00 00 00 00
LBA - 117F:00 15 00 0C 01 14 00 65 00 00 11 74 00 00 00 00
LBA - 1180:00 15 00 0C 01 14 00 65 00 00 11 74 00 00 00 00
```
```
LBA - 1181:00 15 00 0C 01 14 00 66 00 00 11 7A 00 00 3B 45
LBA - 1182:00 15 00 0C 01 14 00 66 00 00 11 7A 00 00 3B 45
LBA - 1183:00 15 00 0C 01 14 00 02 00 00 11 7F 00 00 34 92 ; 117F - …
LBA - 1184:00 15 00 0C 01 14 00 66 00 00 11 7A 00 00 3B 45
LBA - 1185:00 15 00 0C 01 14 00 66 00 00 11 7A 00 00 3B 45
LBA - 1186:00 15 00 0C 01 14 00 66 00 00 11 7A 00 00 3B 45
```
```
LBA - 1187:00 15 00 0C 01 14 00 02 00 00 11 81 00 00 34 92 ; 117F - 1181 is the range
LBA - 1188:00 15 00 0C 01 14 00 02 00 00 11 7F 00 00 34 92 ; of addresses taken by
LBA - 1189:00 15 00 0C 01 14 00 02 00 00 11 7F 00 00 34 92 ; subchannel information for
LBA - 118A:00 15 00 0C 01 14 00 02 00 00 11 81 00 00 34 92 ; point = 2
LBA - 118B:00 15 00 0C 01 14 00 02 00 00 11 80 00 00 34 92
LBA - 118C:00 15 00 0C 01 14 00 02 00 00 11 81 00 00 34 92
LBA - 118D:00 15 00 0C 01 14 00 66 00 00 11 7A 00 00 3B 45
```
```
LBA - 118E:00 15 00 0C 01 14 00 64 00 00 11 8B 00 02 00 00 ; Look! Here is a sharp move
LBA - 118F:00 15 00 0C 01 14 00 64 00 00 11 8B 00 02 00 00 ; from address 1181 to address
LBA - 1190:00 15 00 0C 01 14 00 64 00 00 11 8B 00 02 00 00 ; 118B - 10 sectors are omitted.
LBA - 1191:00 15 00 0C 01 14 00 64 00 00 11 8B 00 02 00 00 ; This is not simply the head
LBA - 1192:00 15 00 0C 01 14 00 64 00 00 11 8B 00 02 00 00 ; beat, since these sectors
LBA - 1193:00 15 00 0C 01 14 00 64 00 00 11 8D 00 02 00 00 ; are missing from
LBA - 1194:00 15 00 0C 01 14 00 64 00 00 11 8D 00 02 00 00 ; subchannel data! And they
LBA - 1195:00 15 00 0C 01 14 00 64 00 00 11 8B 00 02 00 00 ; are exactly the ones that
LBA - 1196:00 15 00 0C 01 14 00 65 00 00 11 92 00 00 00 00 ; contain the attributes of track 0.
LBA - 1197:00 15 00 0C 01 14 00 65 00 00 11 92 00 00 00 00 ; Consequently, track 0 is still
LBA - 1198:00 15 00 0C 01 14 00 65 00 00 11 92 00 00 00 00 ; present on the disc (otherwise,
LBA - 1199:00 15 00 0C 01 14 00 65 00 00 11 92 00 00 00 00 ; these sectors would be returned).
```

Here, the "drift" is about 10 sectors or, sometimes, even smaller. However, the sectors themselves are absolutely out of order, and there are no zero points. Sectors with addresses 1185h and 1186h (where the attributes of tracks 0 are actually stored) are missing altogether. Instead, the drive has positioned the head to addresses 118Bh and 118Dh, as a result of which the number of points 64h (points A0h before invalidation) has grown outrageously. In addition to all this, the absolute sector addresses, for some unknown reason, moved to the field of relative addresses. If our protection tries to analyze the subchannel information in accordance with the standard, it would certainly go at least a little crazy.

Thus, despite of the awkwardness and difficulties involved in implementing such a protection mechanism, it can still be done so as to ensure that the key disc is recognized with confidence on all existing drive models. Is it, however, worth implementing? In other words, how can we crack a disc protected in such a way?

Well, in this case cracking is a tough job. In principle, a disc of this type can be copied. However, neither Clone CD nor Alcohol 120% are enough for this purpose, and not every drive model will be able to tackle the problem. Only those drive models that read the TOC with confidence and return the attributes of non-standard points are suitable for cracking, because the protection mechanism can be bound either to the TOC or to nonstandard point attributes. But wait, you might say. The protection can't rely on the TOC availability and attributes of a zero point. This will render the program unusable on some drive models! True enough. However, if the drive agrees to read the TOC, why don't we do this?

If the drive used for cracking doesn't allow for the reading of the TOC contents, the hacker won't be able to restore the original TOC (unless he or she decides to disassemble the entire protection mechanism). Therefore, the copied disc will be usable only on the hacker's own drive!

Provided that the qualified hacker has a drive capable of reading TOC, however, he or she can easily copy the protected disc. It is enough to read the TOC (using the READ TOC command), and then read the disc contents at the subchannel level (using the SEEK/READ SUBCHANNEL commands) and the contents of the main channel (the READ CD command). After this, all that remains is to form CCD, IMG, and SUB files, and, using Clone CD, burn them into the disc. This, however, is easier said than done. Not every hacker, let alone normal users, can carry out this task successfully.

Track with Non-Standard Number

Implanting fictitious tracks with non-standard numbers into the TOC ensures the creation of a strong, elegant, and non-conflicting form of protection. We'll discuss everything in due order. According to the standard, the numbers of normal tracks can take values ranging from 1 to 99 (4Bh) inclusively. Track 0 belongs to the disc Lead-in and is never explicitly mentioned in the TOC (see the *"Disc with Track Number Zero"* albums, photos, or video clips are not encrypted and are stored in the WAV/BMP/AVI formats, respectively. Even a beginner can easily extract whatever files from the disc and do with them whatever he or she pleases!

Hence, the conclusion is straightforward: Do not confuse CD protection and that of its *contents*. To protect a CD's contents, a large variety of methods are available...

Invalid File Sizes

By the time of the arrival of monochrome terminals and 133" diskettes[i], there was already an ugly, but very easy protection technique to prevent media from being copied at the file level. By means of changing file structures, protection developers could "ruin" a diskette to that point that working with it was only possible provided that the introduced changes were taken into account. The protection program, being aware of the file-system errors, could operate with it without encountering any problems. Standard OS built-in utilities, on the other hand, failed to do so. Note that, at that time, there were not yet widely available "hacking" copiers...

For instance, the protection often consisted of several files referring to common clusters. In this case, writing data into the same file resulted in their immediate appearance in another, which the protection mechanism could use to achieve its purposes. Naturally, after copying the files to another disk, the common clusters were written to different locations and the cunning mechanism of implicit data exchange ceased to operate. The protected program also ceased to operate. This, of course, only happened provided that the user managed to copy the disc contents at all... Copying files with overlapping clusters resulted in their multiple replication in each copied file. Because of this, the file size grew to such an extent that the capacity of the entire hard disk was insufficient to store it! If the last cluster of the file happened to be "glued" to its starting point (i.e., the file got looped), both its size and the time required for its copying immediately became infinite... Naturally, "disk doctors" were already available by that time, but they failed to produce the desired result, since correction of the file system rendered the protection system unusable (for example, in the above-considered case with the file looping, if the protection relied on the fact that the file start follows after its end, this technique became inapplicable after processing the disc with the "disc doctor" utility, with all the resulting consequences).

---

[i] No, this is not a joke or misprint. Such diskettes actually existed before even the earliest 8" diskettes designed by IBM in 1971. They were so large that not every door was wide enough to let the programmer carrying such a diskette easily go through it. I cannot exactly recall their capacity, but this was something about several tens of Kilobytes. The most interesting fact about it is that they already contained a file system, although the concept of files was non-existent by that time...

section of this chapter). Track AAh (170) belongs to the disc Lead-out area and also is never present in the TOC. Tracks with numbers A0h, A1h, A2h, B0h, B1h, B2h, B3h, B4h, C1h, and C2h are used for storing control information and are interpreted in a special way, specific to each number. In particular, the starting address of track A1h contains the number of the last track of the current session, stored in the PMin field.

According to the standard, the drive is not allowed to process tracks with non-standard numbers, and these tracks must be ignored. Thus, when creating a track with a non-standard number, we can be absolutely sure that it won't drive your CD-ROM drive crazy and won't impair disc readability. There is a certain probability, though, that the non-standard track number that we have chosen, with time, will pass into the group of standard numbers, making drive behavior unpredictable. This risk, however, is negligible, because the format of the CD-ROM storage media doesn't change every day and already contains everything that could be needed. Thus, it is unlikely that the developers will add new points there, or that these points will match the one that we have chosen. Therefore, the protection mechanism that is proposed in this section corresponds both to the spirit and letter of the standard.

However, if the protected disc is correctly processed by the drive, what are the problems associated with its copying? The point is that there is no easy way for the copier to become aware of the existence of nonstandard tracks. *Even when reading the raw TOC (using the READ TOC command in format 2), the drive does not return the attributes of nonstandard tracks*, so the "raw mode" is questionable. Getting your hands on tracks of this type is possible only at the subchannel level by reading the contents of the Lead-in area using the SEEK/READ SUBCHANNEL commands (remember that tracks with non-standard numbers must be placed into sessions other than the first, because the Lead-in area of the first session is not available at the interface level).

For the protection mechanism, it will be enough to scan the Lead-in area of the appropriate session to check for the presence of specific predefined track numbers. If tracks with predefined numbers happen to be missing, then we are dealing with an unauthorized copy instead of the original. Reading the subchannel data of the Lead-in areas of the second and all following sessions can be carried out by any drive, although some do this awkwardly. For instance, non-standard number X can be replaced by the number 64h + (X - A0h). The NEC drive, for example, interprets the number ABh as 6Fh. Consequently, it is necessary to impose certain limitations on the choice of non-standard track numbers. For example, for reasons of compatibility and eliminating conflicts, it is no recommended to choose numbers 65h...9Fh, because the drive might erroneously interpret the non-standard track number as being standard. Suppose, for instance, that you have chosen the 66h track number, then 64h + 66h - A0h == 2Ah (42 in decimal notation). And track 42 is a standard track number.

Now, let's proceed with our traditional experiments. Open the CCD image that remains from our previous experiments with track 0, change the string "Point = 0x00" to "`Point = 0xAB`" (naturally, instead of 0xAB, you can choose any other value, though taking into account the above-mentioned limitations for non-standard track numbers). If you haven't got a CCD image, proceed as follows:

1. Using your favorite burner, prepare a CD containing two sessions, each containing one track.
2. Create a disc image in the Clone CD format. Note that any other compatible copier (Alcohol 120%, for example) can be used for this purpose.
3. Open the CCD file in any text editor (for example, you can use Windows Notepad, or simply press <F4> in FAR Manager).
4. Increase the value of the `TocEntries` field by one.
5. Directly after track 2 (`Session = 2`, `Point = 2`), add another entry, which will have a `Point` equal to `ABh` or any other non-standard value of your choice. The contents of the other fields of this entry are of no importance, and you can use them for storing the key information.
6. To preserve the consistency of the chosen numbering system, increase the values of all further entries by one.
7. Save the changes in the edited file. For this purpose, you can press <F2> or <Ctrl>+<S> (Attention: The notepad version built into Windows 9x doesn't react to this keyboard shortcut. Notepad built into Windows NT/2000 will, however).

Proceeding one way or another, you should obtain approximately the following result (because of limited space in this book, Listing 6.50 only contains a fragment of the resulting file):

Listing 6.50. A fragment of the CCD file containing a non-standard track number

```
[Entry 12]
Session=2
Point=0xAB
ADR=0x01
Control=0x04
TrackNo=0
AMin=0
ASec=0
AFrame=0
ALBA=-150
Zero=0
PMin=3
PSec=1
PFrame=66
PLBA=13458
```

Having burnt the resulting image onto a CD, make sure that it is correctly readable by all drives that you have at your disposal. Make sure that it also doesn't conflict with anything. Now, read the TOC contents and check to see whether our non-standard track number is present there:

Listing 6.51. The raw TOC contents with a missing non-standard track

```
KPNC$F:\.PHCK3\src\etc\RAW.CD.READ>CD_RAW_TOC_READ.exe 1.1
RAW TOC READER by Kris Kaspersky
* * * TOC * * *
session number
 | ADR/control
 |   | TNO
 |   |   | point
 |   |   |   | AM:AS:AF
 |   |   |   |   |   |   | zero
 |   |   |   |   |   |   |   | PM:PS:PF
01 14 00 A0 00 00 00 00 01 00 00
01 14 00 A1 00 00 00 00 01 00 00
01 14 00 A2 00 00 00 00 00 1D 21
01 14 00 01 00 00 00 00 00 02 00
01 54 00 B0 02 3B 21 03 16 0E 22
01 54 00 C0 A2 C8 E0 00 61 1B 15
02 14 00 A0 00 00 00 00 02 00 00
02 14 00 A1 00 00 00 00 02 00 00
02 14 00 A2 00 00 00 00 03 18 17
02 14 00 02 00 00 00 00 03 01 21
02 54 00 B0 04 36 17 01 16 0E 22
```

It appears that the non-standard track number was not written to the disc. In reality, however, this assumption is incorrect. The non-standard track number was written, but it is unlikely that it was read by the drive. Actually, the drive has simply refused to return the attributes of the non-standard track, pretending that no such track was there at all. At the same time, this is not a defect of a specific drive model. All drives (or, at least, all of those available to me) behave in this way! Now, let's look at the results from reading the Lead-in area of the second session at the subchannel level. Naturally, to read the subchannel data of the Lead-in area, we must know its starting address. How do we determine it? Actually, this is an easy task. Open the CCD file and find an entry, for which the session is 1 and the point is A2h (it contains the starting address of the Lead-out area of the first session).

Listing 6.52. The starting address of the Lead-out area of the first session

---

```
[Entry 2]
Session=1
Point=0xa2
ADR=0x01
Control=0x04
TrackNo=0
AMin=0
ASec=0
AFrame=0
ALBA=-150
Zero=0
PMin=0
PSec=29
PFrame=33
PLBA=2058
```

It can be seen clearly that the absolute address of the Lead-out area of the first session is `00:29:33` (or 2,058 in the LBA format). Increase it by the length of the Lead-out area (*30 seconds or 2,250 in the LBA format*), and you will obtain the absolute address of the Lead-in area of the second session, which, in this case, is `00:59:33` (or 4,308 in the LBA format).

Now all that remains is to start the `seek_and_Q.exe` utility (see the companion CD) and analyze the displayed result.

Listing 6.53. The contents of the TOC read at the subchannel level on the TEAC drive contains a non-standard track number

---

```
KPNC$F:\.PHCK3\src\etc\RAW.CD.READ>seek_and_Q.exe 1.1 4308 4444
seek CD-ROM & read Q-subcode by KK
LBA - 10D4:00 15 00 0C 01 14 00 A0 00 00 22 92 00 00 11 6E
...
LBA - 10E9:00 15 00 0C 01 14 00 02 00 00 34 92 00 00 11 7F
LBA - 10EA:00 15 00 0C 01 14 00 AB 00 00 34 B3 00 00 11 85
LBA - 10EB:00 15 00 0C 01 14 00 02 00 00 34 92 00 00 11 81
LBA - 10EC:00 15 00 0C 01 14 00 AB 00 00 34 B3 00 00 11 85
LBA - 10ED:00 15 00 0C 01 14 00 AB 00 00 34 B3 00 00 11 85
LBA - 10EE:00 15 00 0C 01 14 00 AB 00 00 34 B3 00 00 11 86
LBA - 10EF:00 15 00 0C 01 14 00 A0 00 00 22 92 00 00 11 8B
LBA - 10F0:00 15 00 0C 01 14 00 AB 00 00 34 B3 00 00 11 86
LBA - 10F1:00 15 00 0C 01 14 00 A0 00 00 22 92 00 00 11 8B
LBA - 10F2:00 15 00 0C 01 14 00 A0 00 00 22 92 00 00 11 8B
```

That's it — non-standard track numbers are present in the TOC. Let's take a look at how other drive models behave. The most interesting result is that generated by the NEC drive, which is the most capricious in this respect.

Listing 6.54. The TOC contents read at the subchannel level on the NEC drive also contain the non-standard track number

```
LBA - 1188:00 15 00 0C 01 14 00 66 00 00 11 7A 00 00 3B 45
LBA - 1189:00 15 00 0C 01 14 00 6F 00 00 11 86 00 00 34 B3
LBA - 118A:00 15 00 0C 01 14 00 6F 00 00 11 87 00 00 34 B3
LBA - 118B:00 15 00 0C 01 14 00 6F 00 00 11 85 00 00 34 B3
LBA - 118C:00 15 00 0C 01 14 00 6F 00 00 11 87 00 00 34 B3
LBA - 118D:00 15 00 0C 01 14 00 6F 00 00 11 85 00 00 34 B3
LBA - 118E:00 15 00 0C 01 14 00 02 00 00 11 80 00 00 34 92
```

Although there is no track with the number ABh, there is still a track with the number 6Fh, which, taking into account the formula provided above, means: A0h + 6Fh - 64h == ABh, i.e., exactly the result that we need.

Apparently, copying the protected disc using Alcohol 120% or Clone CD goes normally (the system doesn't freeze and there are no explosions or smoke). However, after closer investigation, you'll discover no non-standard track numbers in the subchannel data of the second session. These absolute addresses will contain attributes of different tracks. Look for yourself:

Listing 6.55. A copy of the protected disc won't contain any non-standard tracks

```
LBA - 10EB:00 15 00 0C 01 14 00 02 00 00 34 92 00 00 11 7F
LBA - 10EC:00 15 00 0C 01 14 00 A0 00 00 22 92 00 00 11 86
LBA - 10ED:00 15 00 0C 01 14 00 A0 00 00 22 92 00 00 11 86
LBA - 10EE:00 15 00 0C 01 14 00 A0 00 00 22 92 00 00 11 86
LBA - 10EF:00 15 00 0C 01 14 00 A0 00 00 22 92 00 00 11 87
```

Proceeding according to the method described above, the protection mechanism will easily distinguish the original disc from its unauthorized copy. At the same time, replication of the original discs doesn't require any special equipment and can be easily carried out on standard equipment (a normal recorder and Clone CD/Alcohol 120% are all that you'll need). This protection will be no less successful when manufacturing printed CDs — a topic, however, which deserves a separate discussion.

Now, let's continue with practical examples, i.e., with cracking. Although this protection is strong and can withstand attacks carried out using the automatic copiers in existence at the time of writing, an experienced hacker must be capable of copying the original disc. It is enough to start an analyzer of subchannel data (the `seek_and_Q` utility is suitable for this purpose) and read the raw TOCs of the second and all following sessions of the disc (if there are any). There, along with other information, we will discover the non-standard track number:

Listing 6.56. Identification of the protected disc

```
                        ADR/Control
                        | TNO
                        | | Point
                        | | |  +   PLBA   +   +current address+
                        | | |  |        |  |           |
LBA - 10EB:00 15 00 0C 01 14 00 02 00 00 34 92 00 00 11 81
LBA - 10EC:00 15 00 0C 01 14 00 AB 00 00 34 B3 00 00 11 85
LBA - 10EF:00 15 00 0C 01 14 00 A0 00 00 22 92 00 00 11 8B
```

Now all that remains is to open the CCD image of the original disc created using Clone CD and add an entry carrying the track with a non-standard number. However, this is easier said than done... As soon as you attempt to do this, a large number of questions arise. How can we transform subchannel data into a format understandable by Clone CD? Where in the CCD file should we add the new entry? Let's start by answering the second question. When viewing the subchannel information from the original disc, it is easy to see that the track with the non-standard number ABh follows track 02h and precedes track A0h (see Listing 6.56). On old drives with loose heads, this pattern is harder to detect, because the subchannel data are returned chaotically, and, therefore, instead of the addresses, to which the head was positioned, we have to rely on the absolute addresses returned in the subchannel information, as already mentioned. Open the CCD image and find a location between tracks 02h and A0h... What? If we believe the information for the CCD file (or, to be more precise, the information returned by the drive in response to the READ TOC command, on the basis of which the CCD file is created), then the entry with track 02h is followed by the entry with track B0h (the starting address for further writing), and the entry with track A0h (the number of the first track of the current session) is the first entry of the current session! How should we interpret this? The fact is that the starting address for further writing is not stored in subchannel data. Because of this, there is no track B0h present in these data. Furthermore, because the TOC of each session is duplicated in the sub-channel data many times, it becomes clear why track ABh is followed by track A0h — after all, the TOC is "looped" and simply has to "catch itself by the tail" to satisfy considerations of reliability and fault tolerance.

Thus, we must find the entry with track 02h and add a new entry with track ABh immediately after it. The `Session` field must be set to 2 (because we were reading the Lead-in area of the second session), the ADR field is equal to the four most significant bits of the ADR/Control field, and after Control — four least significant bits. In our case ADR/Control == 14h, consequently, ADR = 1, and Control = 4. TrackNo = 0, because we are in the Lead-in area (the control track with number 0). Theoretically, the fields AMin, ASec, AFrame must contain the addresses of the subchannel data corresponding to them. However, according to common agreement, they are considered to be equal to zero, which corresponds to the ALBA address equal to –150 (minus one hundred and fifty). The Zero field is equal to zero, as its name implies, and the fields PMin:PSec:PFrame are equal to the PLBA fields corresponding to them, represented in the M:S:F format. You should remember that some drives tend to swap PLBA and ALBA fields. In our case, the PLBA field of the subchannel data is 34B3h, which corresponds to the 03:01:66 absolute address.

That's all. Having generalized all this material, we will obtain a nice entry that looks approximately as follows:

Listing 6.57. Forming an entry for copying protected discs

```
[Entry 12]
Session=2
Point=0xAB
ADR=0x01
Control=0x04
TrackNo=0
AMin=0
ASec=0
AFrame=0
ALBA=-150
Zero=0
PMin=3
PSec=1
PFrame=66
PLBA=13458
```

Now increase the contents of the TocEntries field by one and renumber all trailing Entries so that the newly added entry doesn't disrupt their consistent numbering, then burn the edited image to a new disc (do *not* add the [TRACK AB] field).

If everything has been done correctly, the newly-burnt disc will represent an undistinguishable copy of the original and the protection will fail to recognize it as a copy. However, not everyone is capable of doing this. As we have already seen, to crack this protection successfully, the hacker must have fairly impressive knowledge in the field of CD organization and know specific features of their processing by various drive models.

Data Track Disguised as Audio

What is the difference between audio tracks and data tracks? What will happen if we label a data track as an audio track? At first glance, nothing extraordinary will happen, and the test track will be easily readable using the READ CD command. The only difference will be that automatic correction of the Q- and P-level errors won't be carried out by the drive. However, bad sectors can be corrected manually. The protection mechanism, knowing the true format of the sectors being read, can carry out this correction without difficulty. However, this is not true for software copiers. Therefore, if the disc is copied many times, the number of read errors will grow constantly. At some point, the error-correcting capabilities of the Reed-Solomon codes will become insufficient, and the next copy will be unusable. However, with the quality of optical media today (especially provided that they are handled carefully), the number of Q- and P-level errors is negligible. Therefore, the copies of at least the first three generations are guaranteed to be readable even by old, loose, no-name drives. Therefore, this approach doesn't promise dependable protection.

This type of reasoning is typical for second-rate specialists that consider data tracks to differ from audio tracks only in a single bit of the ADR/Control bit (this is the third bit, counting from zero), and, at the same time, wonder why their drives don't quite grab audio tracks correctly. Experts, after digging through the specifications and having disassembled a couple more CD-drive firmware versions, will discover at least five conceptual differences between the processing of audio tracks and data tracks. Here they are:

❑ Exact positioning to the specified audio sector is virtually impossible, because the addresses of the sectors that currently float over the optical head are not stored in the sector itself, but rather reside in the Q subcode channel that is spread over the spiral track. Simply speaking, subchannel data from 748 frames or 8 sectors (the more correct name is "block") are joined into *packets*. Each packet contains four reference points, which, in the ideal case, correspond to the error of ±1 sector. In practice, this error is usually larger. The standard sets the maximum allowed level of error equal to ±1 second (or ± 75 sectors). Some drive models, however, deliver considerably worse results. For example, my TEAC drifts forward by about 500 sectors! And there is practically no possibility to read a sector with the address specified beforehand. This situation, which satisfies the requirements of audio tracks, is absolutely unacceptable for data tracks. Therefore, data tracks are forced to supply a special field containing their own address in their header. Rough positioning to the sector is carried out on the basis of subchannel data. Fine positioning, on the other hand, is carried out on the basis of their headers. As a result, the drive always reads the exact sector that was requested.

❑ The concept of the "sector" is absolutely inapplicable to audio tracks. The do not contain any sectors as such. Instead, they contain so-called "blocks," which consist of the sequences of unnumbered frames. At the same time, block boundaries are not strictly fixed, and the block can start from any frame, for which the drive has a fancy and which is located within the positioning limits. Therefore, when reading a data track in the audio mode, we cannot be sure that the sectors being read start from the head, and not from the tail.

❏ In contrast to audio blocks, data sectors are scrambled. The need for scrambling depends not on the type of the current track, but on the presence of a sync group and correct Mode value in its header. *A data track written as audio track is forcibly scrambled in the course of writing (which ruins the Mode), but is not descrambled when reading.* In other words, when reading a disc, the drive reads information different from that was written to it.

❏ Some drives (Plextor, for example) carry out forcible audio correction of the data being written, explaining this by their yearning to ensure better sound quality. No wonder that an attempt at writing a data track in the audio mode ruins it totally.

❏ As already mentioned above, audio tracks do not contain Q- and P- correction codes. Therefore, the drive doesn't correct them, which results in error accumulation, although the copies of the first three to five generations are readable even without error-correcting codes.

Now, it becomes clear why the task of retrieving exact copies of audio tracks is so difficult (if even possible). However, can we use this in practice? Let's write a data track as an audio track and experiment with it. This will help us to answer our question.

Naturally, this task cannot be accomplished directly using standard burners. They won't understand our cunning plan. In the best case, they will display something like "Illegal mode for this track", and in the worst case, even swear at us, so to speak. Well, let's try to outflank them. Using Ahead Nero, Stomp Record Now!, or any similar program, create a normal CD containing one or more data tracks. Then, using Clone CD or Alcohol 120%, create a disc image and tweak its CCD file. All that we need is to find an entry with a point equal to the number of our track and change the contents of the Control field to 0 or 2 (which corresponds to an audio track without copyright protection and audio track with copyright protection, respectively). Then change the track MODE from 1 to 0 (wee the [TRACK] section).

Listing 6.58. Creating a protected disc image

```
[Entry 11]        [Entry 11]        [TRACK 1]        [TRACK 1]
Session=2         Session=2         MODE=1           MODE=1
Point=0x02        Point=0x02
ADR=0x01          ADR=0x01          [TRACK 2]        [TRACK 2]
Control=0x04      Control=0x02      MODE=1           MODE=0
TrackNo=0         TrackNo=0         INDEX 1=0        INDEX 1=0
```

```
AMin=0            AMin=0
ASec=0            ASec=0
AFrame=0          AFrame=0
ALBA=-150         ALBA=-150
Zero=0            Zero=0
PMin=3            PMin=3
PSec=1            PSec=1
PFrame=33         PFrame=33
PLBA=13458        PLBA=13458
```

It is not necessary to correct subchannel data. On the contrary, it is recommended to leave them unchanged. This will rule out playback of this track in the audio mode and relieve you (and your users) from the serious psychological shock caused by listening to a "symphony" of data, disguised as audio. What will happen if you correct the subchannel data and try to play back this "audio track" on a normal audio player or PC CD-ROM drive? Well, actually, nothing too horrible, except for a cacophony of noise. If you have ever loaded software from a magnetic tape for tape recorders into computers like ZX-Spectrum, and have left the modem's speaker on during data transmission, then you can imagine the sound that your poor users will hear after they load a disc like this into the drive. It is possible to become a stutterer, especially if the volume is set to maximum (by the way, some specialists say that it is possible even to damage the amplifier output and speakers. In my opinion, these rumors are groundless. Neither the maximum allowed level of the output signal nor the allowed frequency spectrum can be exceeded in this case, and a properly designed amplifier, or speakers, won't suffer any damage).

Nevertheless, if you use the "digital playback" mode of tracks, for which Windows 2000 provides built-in support, then, independently on the contents of the subcode channel, data tracks labeled as audio tracks will still be played as audio! And certain drives (such as NEC, for example) will also play these tracks back in audio mode. So what? Let them do it! To all of the indignant cries and screams of surprised users, we will simply answer that the program loads itself through the audio channel, as it was long ago. Isn't it the perfect remedy against nostalgia?

Now let's read the image of the disc with the audio track and compare its contents to the original. I assure you that the result will exceed all of your expectations! Let's start with a byte-by byte comparison of the IMG files that carry the data of the main channel. For this purpose, you can use any comparison utility (either fc.exe supplied with Windows, or my favorite — c2u from Professor Nimnul). Start it in approximately the following way: "`FC.EXE IMAGE.IMG IMAGE_T.IMG /B > IMAGE.DIF`", where `IMAGE.IMG` is the image taken from a "normal" disc, and `IMAGE_T.IMG` is the image taken from the disc with the "audio" track.

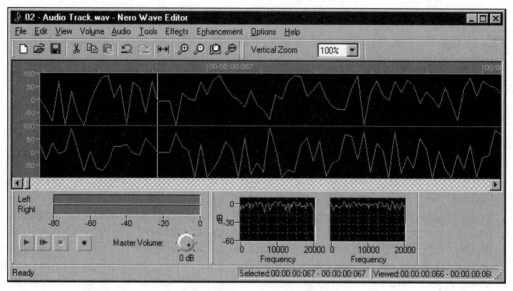

Fig. 6.18. A data track disguised as audio

After several minutes of waiting (in contrast to c2u, the FC utility is very slow), a file named IMAGE.DIF will appear on your hard disc, with a size of about 50 MB. This means that there actually are differences between the copy and the original, and these differences are not just numerous, but large in the extreme!

Listing 6.59. A fragment of the original disc

```
0049D2B0:  00 FF FF FF FF FF FF FF | FF FF FF 00 00 29 32 01................)2☺
0049D2C0:  00 00 00 00 00 00 00 00 | 00 00 00 00 00 00 00 00................
...
0049DBE0:  00 FF FF FF FF FF FF FF | FF FF FF 00 03 01 33 01...............♥☺3☺
0049DBF0:  00 00 00 00 00 00 00 00 | 00 00 00 00 00 00 00 00................
0049DC00:  00 00 00 00 00 00 00 00 | 00 00 00 00 00 00 00 00................
0049DC10:  00 00 00 00 00 00 00 00 | 00 00 00 00 00 00 00 00................
0049DC20:  00 00 00 00 00 00 00 00 | 00 00 00 00 00 00 00 00................
0049DC30:  00 00 00 00 00 00 00 00 | 00 00 00 00 00 00 00 00................
0049DC40:  00 00 00 00 00 00 00 00 | 00 00 00 00 00 00 00 00................
0049DC50:  00 00 00 00 00 00 00 00 | 00 00 00 00 00 00 00 00................
```

Listing 6.60. A fragment of the copied disc

```
0049D2B0:  00 FF FF FF-FF FF FF FF-FF FF FF 00-00 29 32 01   yyyyyyyyyy...)2☺
0049D2C0:  00 00 00 00-00 00 00 00-00 00 00 00-00 00 00 00   ................
...
```

```
0049DBE0:  00 FF FF FF-FF FF FF FF-FF FF FF 00-02 81 33 61   .yyyyyyyyy.●?3a
0049DBF0:  00 28 00 1E-80 08 60 06-A8 02 FE 81-80 60 60 28   .(…▲Иロ`♠?●??И``(
0049DC00:  28 1E 9E 88-68 66 AE AA-FC 7F 01 E0-00 48 00 36   (▲z?hfo?u△◎a…H…6
0049DC10:  80 16 E0 0E-C8 04 56 83-7E E1 E0 48-48 36 B6 96   И—aЛE♦V?~aaHH6╢Ц
0049DC20:  F6 EE C6 CC-52 D5 FD 9F-01 A8 00 7E-80 20 60 18   oi?IROyY◎?.~И.`↑
0049DC30:  28 0A 9E 87-28 62 9E A9-A8 7E FE A0-40 78 30 22   (■z3(bzй?~?a@x0"
0049DC40:  94 19 AF 4A-FC 37 01 D6-80 5E E0 38-48 12 B6 8D   Φ↓?Ju7◎ОИ^a8H↨╢?
0049DC50:  B6 E5 B6 CB-36 D7 56 DE-BE D8 70 5A-A4 3B 3B 53   ╢a╢E6?V??OpZд;;S
```

The first thing that catches our eye is that the Pre-gap area of the second track, which earlier was filled with zeros, is now stuffed with data, looking very much like garbage and not corresponding to any of the data on the source data track. Let's choose any sequence, such as "1E 9E 88 68 66 AE AA" (in the listing, it is in bold) and try to find it in the source IMAGE.IMG file. There won't be anything of the sort here!

The absolute sector address placed into its header (in the listing, it is framed) also bears a resemblance to the ravings of a madman. Look: The A-SEC field takes an outrageously high value, as high as 81h, which certainly is a mistake. At maximum, this field should contain the value not exceeding 59h. The Mode field, which in this case contains 61h, is also invalid.

Perhaps, this is simply a minor error? No. After reviewing sector headers, you'll discover that they all are like this:

Listing 6.61. Invalid sector headers

```
0049DBE0:  00 FF FF FF-FF FF FF FF-FF FF FF 00-02 81 33 61   yyyyyyyyyy ●?3a
0049E510:  00 FF FF FF-FF FF FF FF-FF FF FF 00-02 81 34 61   yyyyyyyyyy ●?4a
0049EE40:  00 FF FF FF-FF FF FF FF-FF FF FF 00-02 81 35 61   yyyyyyyyyy ●?5a
0049F770:  00 FF FF FF-FF FF FF FF-FF FF FF 00-02 81 36 61   yyyyyyyyyy ●?6a
004A00A0:  00 FF FF FF-FF FF FF FF-FF FF FF 00-02 81 37 61   yyyyyyyyyy ●?7a
```

There you are. Well, to hell sector headers! For the moment, we have to deal with a more urgent question: Where are our source data, and what is this garbage that is read from the audio track? What, or who, is responsible for all this — disc failures, audio correction or scrambling?

The right answer is scrambling. Having detected a sync group signature 00 FF FF FF FF FF FF FF FF FF FF 00 in the header along with MODE set to 1, the drive ignored the track type specified in the TOC and interpreted this sector as data. Based on this result, it scrambled all of the bytes in this sector, from 12 to 2,351, inclusively. Not only the user data area, but also the MODE field were scrambled. Consequently, further reading of this sector belonging to the data sectors wasn't obvious enough, and the drive, having looked into the TOC, decided that it deals with "audio" sector, which doesn't need to be descrambled. As a result, we have obtained scrambled data in the output that were not recovered.

This "feature" of drive behavior is not authorized by the standard. On the contrary, the standard describes all of these aspects too ambiguously and obscurely and, therefore, most drives (the vast majority) forcibly scramble the "audio" data being written. Some drives write them "as is." To tell the truth, the possibility of reading non-scrambled sectors is not guaranteed, because they might contain regular data sequences that confuse the read head, leading to errors (see *"Weak Sectors"*). Therefore, it is recommended first to work with drives that forcibly scramble sectors, such as NEC and TEAC.

Having passed the read data through a descrambler, which can be borrowed from the ElbyECC.dll library supplied as part of Clone CD, we will recover the sectors mangled by the scrambler in their initial form, with which our program will be able to work. Individual errors due to disc failures can be eliminated manually, because we have error-correcting codes at our disposal. If you decide to write your own Reed-Solomon decoder, you can use the above-mentioned ElbyECC.dll (don't forget, however, that if you distribute it as part of your product, you'll violate the copyright of its developers).

It would appear, then, that we have discovered a real gold mine! Since the contents of a data track labeled as an audio track are forcibly scrambled in the course of recording, an attempt to copy such a disc will result in its being scrambled once again. As a result, we will get absolutely different data (strictly speaking, this won't be "different" data, because repeated scrambling is the same thing as descrambling, and the source "audio" track will be completely restored. However, since the protection mechanism also descrambles the data, it will be able to work only with its "own" disc. However, a copy of a copy will also produce the desired result. This idea, however, will not occur to every user).

Alas! Because the MODE field is also scrambled, the sector read from the protected disc will no longer be recognized by the drive as a data sector. Therefore, it won't be forcibly scrambled, because of which the "protected" disc is copied quite normally. However, we have gone too far for us to surrender now, haven't we?

If we record "audio" tracks on a drive that doesn't carry out automatic scrambling, and then try to copy them on any other drive model, these attempts will inevitably fail. This is because such drives carry out scrambling, which will irreversibly ruin the sector contents. It will be impossible to recover the sectors, even by creating a copy of copy. The only way out is to find a non-scrambling drive (which will be a difficult task in itself). For instance, all of my attempts at doing so failed. Therefore, I simply patched the firmware of my CD recorder in such a way as to allow me to enable or disable sector scrambling at will. Any drive that can be patched is suitable for this purpose

(TEAC, for example). Download the newest firmware version from the manufacturer's site, then start the disassembler that understands the "language" of this processor and analyze the firmware operating algorithm. Remember that incorrectly patched firmware may render your drive totally unusable, because the patching procedure is contained in the firmware. If the latter ceases to operate, you can kiss your drive good-bye, because all of its circuitry will also cease to operate. Although the firmware patching is a realistic task, it requires fairly qualified hands to carry it out.

Unfortunately, the developers of the protected application are in no better situation, because in order to record original discs, they will require a similar drive, which is very hard to find on the market and no easier to create on one's own. On the other hand, if you are strongly motivated, you'll always find a way to implement your ideas! This protection mechanism is, however, wonderfully suitable for printed CDs, for which there are no limitations imposed on their logical structure. The task of copying a disc protected on the basis of this technology is practically unrealistic. Now let's proceed with weak sectors, i.e., the sectors containing sequences unfavorable from the drive's point of view. One of such sequence appears as follows — ...04 B9 04 B9 04 B9.... The unscrambled sector that contains this sequence in its body will be written without any problems. However, due to some design limitations, even the best drives will be unable to ensure its reading stability. Most drives will be unable to read it at all. This is because the physical representation of this sequence results in the creation of long chains of lands or pits, and a constantly changing HF signal is vitally important for correct drive operation. In other words, the drive is unable to read homogeneous areas of the spiral track. More detailed information on weak sectors is provided in *Chapter 1*. Currently, the most important fact is that some drives are still capable of managing to find a way out by simply changing the starting position of the sector in the frame, which results in massive changes at the physical level of information representation. Consequently, a weak sequence ceases to be weak, and becomes normally readable by all drives. However, to copy such a disc, it is necessary to have a drive that effectively recognizes and correctly processes weak sequences (for instance, Plextor. For a complete list of models suitable for this purpose, see Clone CD Help system).

On the other hand, drives that record weak sequences "as is" are very useful for the high-quality simulation of the bad sectors, because sectors that contain weak sequences are not readable at the physical level. This is better approach than trivial invalidation of the EDC/ECC fields, which is easily detectable by protection mechanisms by means of reading sectors in raw mode. Beside this, weak sectors cause the drive to reduce speed and drag the read head for some time, thus creating a certain time delay that is caused by actual defective sectors (and most protection mechanisms rely on this). A sector with a tweaked EDC/ECC field, on the contrary, is read almost instantly, thus giving itself away. In other words, weak sectors are useful not only for protection.

They provide rich opportunities for hackers and crackers as well. I hope that you have no objections to experimenting with them.

So let's open our old image of the original file (this must be the image taken from a normal disc, not the image of the protected disc damaged by scrambling). Change the data track attributes to audio, as we have done before. However, in addition to this, tweak the Sync and/or MODE fields of several sectors with addresses known beforehand. Burn the image to the CD to make sure that the contents of sectors are now no longer scrambled, and the data read from the disc is exactly the data that were read to it (although, if the sector contains regular sequences, it might be unreadable, because scrambling was actually needed for data sectors).

Now, fill these sectors with the sequence ...04 B9 04 B9 04 B9... and burn them once again. If your drive is not clever enough to choose the starting position of the sector in the frame, our sectors will be written in the most unfavorable way, and attempts at reading them will result in errors! By the way, if you stuff the disc with faulty sectors, its copying will be exceedingly complicated, especially if you place weak sectors in groups, ranging in size from 9 to 99 sectors, followed by a single key sector (i.e., a normal sector containing the key information). The point is that advanced protected disc copiers (Clone CD or Alcohol 120%), having detected that the disc contains lots of defective sectors that require a long time to read, allow the user to enable the mode, in which bad sectors are quickly skipped. In this case, having encountered a bad sector, the copier will skip the next 100 sectors, thus saving time on attempts at reading them. Protection mechanisms that bind to actual physical defects of the disc surface are easily deceived by this trick, because defects tend to accumulate and grow with the time. Therefore, implanting key information near the defective area is dangerous. Weak sectors, however, are not defective in the literal sense of the word. Therefore, they don't prevent reading of the adjacent sectors. Because of this, we can easily rely on their existence! The copying of the protected disc in the fast skipping mode will skip not only weak sectors, but also key labels. The copying process in normal mode will take several hours (or more), the reasons for which we will discuss later.

Incorrect Run-out as Protection Tool or X-Sector

From the hacker's point of view, Stomp Record Now! is interesting because it is practically the only utility that secretly writes a special label to each disc being burnt. This label is a kind of a "watermark," the existence of which is not known to most users, and which obviously violates their privacy. However, let's proceed in due order.

The Randomly Writable mode in CD-RW discs is implemented using the Run-in/ Run-out blocks mechanism, closely related to the packet writing mode. Each packet starts from four Run-in blocks (three such blocks on DDCD media) and is terminated by two Run-out blocks (on DDCD media, there are three such blocks). Run-in/Run-out blocks are normal sectors, but having an unusual value for the MODE field in their headers (see Listing 6.62). Depending on the addressing mode, Run-in/Run-out blocks are either addressed as all the other sectors, or are excluded from the address space. Except for the packet-writing mode, Run-in/Run-out blocks are not used anywhere, however...

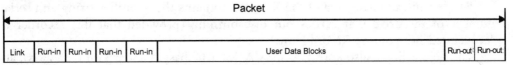

Fig. 6.19. Run-in/Run-out blocks

Listing 6.62. Extended interpretation of the MODE field

```
Bits 7, 6, 5 = 000 - User Data block
= 001 - Fourth Run-in block
= 010 - Third Run-in block
= 011 - Second Run-in block
= 100 - First Run-in block
= 101 - Link block. Physical linking of EFM data
= 110 - Second Run-out block
= 111 - First Run-out block
Bits 4, 3, 2 = 000 - Reserved
Bits 1, 0 = 00 Mode 0 Data
= 01 - Mode 1 Data
= 10 - Mode 2 Data
= 11 - Reserved
```

The Stomp Record Now! program has an interesting feature for supporting Run-out blocks secretly implanted into the end of each data track, or, to be more precise, into the next-to-last sector of its Post-gap area, the header of which is slightly modified.

Because there is only one Run-out block (although, according to the Orange Book, there must be at least two), and there are no Run-in blocks, in this case we are dealing with a standard violation. Whether it is intentional or not, remains a secret. Most likely, this is a kind of developer's watermark or "Easter egg," which complicates the copying of the original disc (in this section, we will use the term "original disc" to mean the disc created using the Stomp Record Now! program, and the next-to-last sector of the Post-gap area as a watermark sector or X-sector).

The MODE field of the X-sector, specifying the type of the track, instead of the actual track, is replaced by the "watermark" constant E1h (or, rarely, E2h), which corresponds to the qualifier of the first Run-out block (see Listing 6.62). The three most significant bits define the specific block qualifier, while the two least significant bits specify the track type. Thus, the "watermark" number in the general case is: `Water Mark Value (WMV) == E0h | Track MODE`, accordingly: `Track MODE == MODE & 3`, where `Track MODE` is the track type and `MODE` is the value of the appropriate field of the sector header.

Besides this, the data area of the X-sector contains the identifier string and serial number of the drive that carries out disc burning (provided that this recorder is "acquainted" with Stomp Record Now!).

The Yellow Book, also known as ECMA-130 (the basic standard for data CDs), allowed for only three types of tracks: MODE 0, MODE 1, and MODE 2, and interpreted all the others as errors. Applications designed in full accordance to the ECMA-130 standard are unable to determine the actual type of the X-sector, because they "do not know" that the six most significant bits of the `MODE` field must be reset to zero. Such a sector cannot be discarded, but at the same time, it is impossible to pass it through Reed-Solomon decoder, because it is not known beforehand whether or not `EDC/ECC` codes are present there.

According to the standard, Pre-gap and Post-gap areas are intended exclusively for the positioning of the optical head[i] and don't contain user data. In normal operating mode, these sectors are never accessed (the standard allows us to rely only on sub-channel data), thanks to which the watermarks (like Run-in/Run-out blocks) have no effect on the drive's operation. The drive doesn't notice them at all. At the same time, the contents of the Pre-gap and Post-gap areas are actively used by various protection mechanisms for storing key marks, operating according to approximately the same principle as key marks written into the engineering sectors of hard disks (71 and/or 72 tracks of the diskette). It is not unlikely that an unexpected conflict could arise between watermarks and key marks, rendering one of these parties fully or partially unusable. Therefore, it is not recommended to make excessive use of this technique.

To discover if watermarks are present on the disc being investigated, we must read the next-to-last sectors of all of the Post-gaps in raw mode. For this purpose, it is possible to use the `CD_RAW_SECTOR_READ` utility of any other similar tool (for instance, Clone CD is very well suited for this). Now it remains to determine the absolute addresses of the Post-gap ends for all tracks. This is easy. The absolute address of the last sector of the Post-gap area is equal to the starting address of the next track, minus `sizeof(pre-gap)` (starting address of the Lead-out area, if this track is the last one)

---

[i] Ancient drives were too primitive, and for decoding subchannel information (which, by the way, is spread over a large disc surface), they required a certain time, during which the optical head moved long ahead over the spiral track. Therefore, when attempting at positioning the head to the starting point of the track, a certain number of sectors was inevitably skipped. Therefore, the developers had to add several turns of "blank" information to the starting point of every track, to compensate for drop-out of sectors with meaningful information.

minus one. Accordingly, to find the next-to-last sector, this value must be decreased by one. In other words: x-sector address = (next track != Lead-out) ?next track address – 3:lead out address – 2.

The starting addresses of all tracks are stored in points with numbers from 01 to 99 inclusively, and the starting address of the Lead-out area of the disc is stored in point A2h. Suppose that the disc being investigated contains only one track, and the starting address of the Lead-out area is 00:29:33 (see Listing 6.63). Then the address of the X-sector will be 00:29:31.

Listing 6.63. Determining the Lead-out address

```
[Entry 2]
Session=1
Point=0xa2
ADR=0x01
Control=0x04
TrackNo=0
AMin=0
ASec=0
AFrame=0
ALBA=-150
Zero=0
PMin=0
PSec=29
PFrame=33
PLBA=2058
```

Note that the absolute address 00:29:31 corresponds to LBA address 2056. Let's memorize this value, because it will be encountered several times in our further experiments. Having passed the obtained address to the CD_RAW_SECTOR_READ program, after a couple of seconds we will obtain its contents. Finding the "watermark sector" in the CD image created using Clone CD (or any other similar program) is slightly more difficult. It is, however, still possible. There are at least two methods of approaching this task: Knowing the size of one raw sector (2352 bytes) and the LBA address of the X-sector, we can compute the offset of the required sector in the file by simply multiplying both values (2352 * 2056 == 49C980h). Another approach is to open the image file using any HEX editor and carry out a context search for the following sequence: 00 FF FF FF FF FF FF FF FF FF FF 00 00 29 31, i.e., Sync + address.

No matter, which method we choose, the result will be the same.

Listing 6.64. Watermarks implanted into the next-to-last Post-gap sector by the Stomp Record Now! program: The incorrect track number in the sector header (E1h instead of 01h) is marked in bold and framed, and the identifier of the recorder, on which the disc was burnt, is marked in bold

```
0049C980:  00 FF FF FF FF FF FF FF | FF FF FF 00 00 29 31 E1 ................)1c
0049C990:  52 49 44 30 31 00 00 00 | 4E 45 43 00 00 00 00 00 ...RID01....NEC....
0049C9A0:  4E 52 31 31 00 00 00 00 | 02 58 56 00 00 00 00 00 ...NR11.....⊕XV....
0049C9B0:  4E 45 43 20 20 20 20 20 | 20 20 20 20 20 20 20 20 ...NEC.............
0049C9C0:  20 20 20 20 20 20 20 20 | 20 20 20 20 20 20 20 20 ..................
0049C9D0:  4E 52 2D 39 31 30 30 41 | 20 20 20 20 20 20 20 20 ...NR-9100A........
0049C9E0:  32 58 56 32 32 38 31 53 | 31 31 31 20 20 20 20 20 ...2XV2281S111.....
0049C9F0:  00 00 00 00 00 00 00 00 | 00 00 00 00 00 00 00 00 ..................
0049CA00:  00 00 00 00 00 00 00 00 | 00 00 00 00 00 00 00 00 ..................
```

Standard copiers (Ahead Nero, in particular) do not copy the contents of the Pre-gap and Post-gap areas. Therefore, watermarks will be missing on the copied discs! To distinguish the original disc from its copy, the protection mechanism must: *1)* using the READ TOC (format 0x2 — full TOC) command, read the disc TOC in the raw mode; *2)* read the Lead-out address of any session (for instance, that of the first session); *3)* determine the address of the X-sector, and, using the READ CD command, read it in raw mode; *4)* analyze the contents of the MODE field (15th byte of the sector header, counting from zero); if this value is larger than 2, then we are dealing with the original disc or a high-quality copy; *5)* for paranoids, it is recommended to read the contents of the user data area and compare this to the reference model. This won't make the protection mechanism any stronger, because if the copier is capable of copying the "watermark" into the MODE field, it will also copy the user data part of the sector. All the same, it might increase the developer's self-confidence.

The simplest example of protection-mechanism implementation is as shown below (naturally, nothing could be simpler than detecting and eliminating the conditional jump that carries out the comparison of the MODE field to the reference "watermark" constant. Therefore, in order actually to make the protection stronger, it is recommended to abandon using explicit checks and use the read sector header, for example, for decrypting critical sections of the code).

Listing 6.65. [crackme. 68E8B0Abh] Searching for watermarks implanted by Stomp Record NOW!

```
// VITAL CONSTANTS
#define _WATERMARK        0xE1  // watermark code
#define _A2           3    // offset of point A2h in TOC
#define _MODE        15    // offset of the MODE field
                           // in the sector header
#define _M           8     // offset of PMin    in TOC
```

```
#define _S            9    // Offset of PSec    in TOC
#define _F            10   // Offset of PFrame  in TOC

#define argCD argv[1]
main(int argc, char** argv)
{
    int      a, b, x_sec, LBA_lead_out = 0;
    unsigned char buf[RAW_SECTOR_SIZE*2];

    // TITLE
    fprintf(stderr,"crackme.68E8B0ABh Record NOW! watermark\n");

    // Help on command-line options
    if (argc != 2)    {
        printf("USAGE: crackme.68E8B0ABh.exe CD\n"); return -1;}

    // Reading TOC in raw mode
    a = cd_raw_toc_read(argCD, buf, RAW_SECTOR_SIZE, W_FULL_TOC);

    if (a != SCSI_OK) {    // Was the operation successful?
        fprintf(stderr, "-ERR: read TOC\x7\n"); return -1; }

    // Searching for point A2h storing the starting address of the Lead-out
    for (a = 4; a < buf[0]*0x100L+buf[1]; a+=11)
    {
        // Is this point A2?
        if (buf[a + _A2] == 0xA2)
        {
            // Point A2 found
            // Getting the Lead-out address of the first session
            // and exiting
            LBA_lead_out=((buf[a+_M]*60+buf[a+_S])*75+buf[a+_F])-150; break;
        }
    }

    // Was the search of Lead-out address successful?
    if (LBA_lead_out == 0) {
        fprintf(stderr, "-ERR: find A2h point\x7\n"); return -1;}

    // Computing X-sector address, where the watermark is stored
    x_sec = LBA_lead_out - 2;

    // Reading the sector containing the watermark in raw mode
    a = cd_raw_sector_read(argCD, buf, RAW_SECTOR_SIZE*2, x_sec, 1, 0xF8);

    if (a != SCSI_OK) {    // Was the read operation successful?
        fprintf(stderr, "-ERR: read X-sector\x7\n"); return -1; }

    // Checking for the watermark presence
    if (buf[_MODE] != _WATERMARK)
    {
        // This is not an original disc.
```

```
        fprintf(stderr, "hello, hacker!\x7\n");   return 0;
    }

    // This is the original disc.
    printf("hello, legal user!\n");
}
```

Testing protected CD copiers shows that watermarks are not copied by Clone CD, which refuses to process such "incorrect" (from its point of view) sectors and silently corrects them to appear more decent. To do so, it corrects the value of the MODE field and destroys all identification information. As a result, the copied sector appears as follows:

Listing 6.66. In the copy of the original disc obtained using Clone CD, watermarks disappear, and the MODE field is "corrected" in such a way that the program being protected can easily distinguish original disc from its unauthorized copy

```
0049C980:   00 FF FF FF FF FF FF FF | FF FF FF 00 00 29 31 01 ...........♥$.☺..
0049C990:   00 00 00 00 00 00 00 00 | 00 00 00 00 00 00 00 00 ................
0049C9A0:   00 00 00 00 00 00 00 00 | 00 00 00 00 00 00 00 00 ................
0049C9B0:   00 00 00 00 00 00 00 00 | 00 00 00 00 00 00 00 00 ................
0049C9C0:   00 00 00 00 00 00 00 00 | 00 00 00 00 00 00 00 00 ................
0049C9D0:   00 00 00 00 00 00 00 00 | 00 00 00 00 00 00 00 00 ................
0049C9E0:   00 00 00 00 00 00 00 00 | 00 00 00 00 00 00 00 00 ................
```

In some other cases, the copied X-sector is unreadable, and the READ CD command persistently returns uninformative error messages such as MEDIUM ERROR. Why this happens is not absolutely clear. Perhaps, Clone CD attempts to emulate the bad sector, erroneously assuming that the X-sector is defective. This might also due to an incorrect call to the recorder (if Track MODE > 2, then, theoretically, the sector being recorded in raw mode is not scrambled, and unfavorable regular sequences appear on the disc, so the drive encounters difficulties in reading them due to design limitations).

Nevertheless, for some reason, Clone CD simply destroys all watermarks, and a copy of the protected disc becomes unusable. Naturally, in future versions of Clone CD, the situation may change (support for X-sectors doesn't require radical code redesigning, and may be implemented any time). In this case, it will become too easy to overcome protection based on watermarks. Furthermore, Alcohol 120% and (presumably) CDRWin successfully copy X-sectors. Therefore, watermarks in their canonic form do not provide efficient protection. To strengthen this protection, it is recommended to combine watermarks with other types of protection (an incorrect starting address for the first track, track 0 present on the disc, a fictitious track in the Post-gap of the key track, etc.). Such combined protection mechanisms are strong enough and there are, at present, no tools for copying them.

The concept of X-sector: The phenomenon of X-sectors was discovered accidentally. In the course of the development of protection mechanisms based on non-standard disc formats, the author tried to invent "irregularities" that would be correctly processed by all drive models, but which would be impossible to copy with any of the existing protected CD copiers. Experiments were going on with different levels of success, and many of the protection mechanisms that I invented were, sadly, forced to drop out of the race because they could not withstand the horrible cruelty of my experiments. Some of them found too many faults with respect to equipment. On some drives, protected discs were fully or partially unreadable. Other protection mechanisms were too weak and could be copied easily by common copiers such as Alcohol 120% and Clone CD...

Often, one or two faulty sectors would appear of the disc being protected, which I initially attributed to physical defects in the media. However, I had to abandon this explanation, because faulty sectors appeared in a strictly predefined position, which, after closer investigation, proved to be the next-to-last sector of the Post-gap area of any track. It was exactly that sector where the header was invalid!

Copying X-sectors: In theory, there is nothing especially difficult in copying X-sectors. It is enough to choose contemporary CD reading and recording software, designed in accordance with Orange Book requirements and aware of the existence of the Run-in/Run-out blocks (i.e., resetting the sector type by the two least significant bits, instead of the entire MODE field). Besides this, the copier must carefully and accurately copy the contents of Pre-gap and Post-gap areas from the original to the copy. It must ignore the good-natured growling of the standard related to the fact that there are no user data there anyway.

As already mentioned, Clone CD doesn't meet this requirement. The dump of the protected disc that it produces is quite correct. However, it is unable to burn this dump onto the copy. Alcohol 120% carries out a correct dump and burns a usable duplicate. Naturally, in this case, I mean only the copying of the watermarks in their pure form. Even the simplest complication of the protection mechanism drives both copiers crazy and causes both of them freeze.

Because Clone CD is more competent than Alcohol 120% in creating dumps, it is recommended to use Clone CD for creating dumps, and burn discs using CDRWin/Alcohol 120%. If this doesn't help, the hacker will have to develop a custom copier and crack the protection mechanism itself.

Experiments with X-sector. An interesting side effect is the unreadability of the next-to-last sector, which earlier belonged to the Post-gap of the genuine track (its absolute address is &Lead-Out - 2), which is known as X-sector. An attempt to read this sector using the READ CD command results in returning non-standard error messages, which are typical for each specific drive model. Provided below is SENSE INFO for the ASUS, NEC and TEAC drives. The SENSE-INFO returned by the ASUS drive is the most interesting. The drive reports a read error, but cannot provide an understandable explanation of its cause. The first byte of SENSE-INFO equal to zero proudly affirms that there are no errors here!

Listing 6.67. ASUS drive SENSE-INFO

```
-ERR:00 00 00 00 00 00 00 00 00 00 00 00 00 00
```

The SENSE-INFO returned by the NEC drive is more informative, because SENSE KEY equal to three specifies a "MEDIUM ERROR". The values of other fields are non-standard (this is indicated by the first byte, which is equal to F0h). Alas, specifications that I have at my disposal do not allow me to decode the meaning of these values.

Listing 6.68. NEC drive SENSE-INFO

```
-ERR:F0 00 03 00 00 00 12 0A 00 00 00 00 02 00
```

The SENSE-INFO returned by the TEAC drive also specifies that there was a "MEDIUM ERROR", but doesn't provide any other details.

Listing 6.69. TEAC drive SENSE-INFO

```
-ERR:F0 00 03 00 00 00 00 0A 00 00 00 00 11 00
```

On the other hand, positioning the head to X-sector using the SEEK (2Bh) command with further reading of the contents of the Q subcode channel using the READ SUBCHANNEL (42h) command was successful on all drives available to me.

Although all copiers, of which I am aware (including programs such as Clone CD and Alcohol 120%), always read subchannel information in the common data flow (i.e., they obtain this information using the READ CD), they are unable to read the subchannel information of the unreadable X-sector! Thus, by placing a key mark in the Q subcode channel of the X-sector, we will be able to distinguish the original disc from a copy.

The procedure for preparing the image of the protected disc is as follows. Start any HEX editor (for example, HIEW), open the IMAGE.SUB file containing subchannel information, and find there the absolute address of the X-sector (in our case, it is 00:29:31). Make sure that it is actually an absolute address, and not the checksum field (all absolute address fields are located in the IMAGE.SUB file at the offset 0xxxxxx0Ch). Change one of the fields of the Q subcode channel of this sector, and then correct its checksum accordingly. The easiest way is to swap the contents of Q subcode channels of the neighboring sectors. For example, let's swap sectors 00:29:31 and 00:29:32.

Listing 6.70. The contents of the original IMAGE.SUB file (the location where the mark will be implanted is in bold)

```
0003030C:  41 01 01 00 27 31 00 00 | 29 31 8F AA 00 00 00 00   A@@.'1..)1Пк
0003036C:  41 01 01 00 27 32 00 00 | 29 32 51 1B 00 00 00 00   A@@.'2..)2Q←
```

Listing 6.71. The contents of the "marked" IMAGE.SUB (the mark is in bold)

```
0003030C:  41 01 01 00 27 32 00 00 | 29 32 51 1B 00 00 00 00   A@@.'2..)2Q←
0003036C:  41 01 01 00 27 31 00 00 | 29 31 8F AA 00 00 00 00   A@@.'1..)1_Є
```

Now burn the modified image and make sure that the subchannel mark is actually present.

Listing 6.72. The key mark in the Q subcode channel of X-sector (left) and the unprotected disc (right)

```
>seek_and_Q.exe 1.1 2056              >seek_and_Q.exe 1.1 2056
seek CD-ROM & read Q-subcode by KK    seek CD-ROM & read Q-subcode by KK
00 15 00 0C 01 14 01 01 00 00 08 09 00 00 08 09   00 15 00 0C 01 14 01 01 00 00 08 09 00 00 08 08
```

Look, the subchannel information of sector 2056 (808h in hex) states that the LBA address of this sector is equal to 809h (2057 in decimal notation), i.e., that subchannel information is actually modified! For comparison, take any unprotected disc, and make sure that its subcode channel information is correct.

As was already mentioned before, Clone CD does not use the READ SUBCHANNEL command, but instead, receives subchannel information in the main data flow. Having encountered an unreadable X-sector, Clone CD, on its own initiative, restores its subchannel information in the form that it (according to its opinion) must have. In other words, when copying the protected disc using Clone CD, our key mark will be lost, and the Q subcode channel of the X-sector will contain the "correct" data. See for yourself!

Listing 6.73. Subchannel information of the X-sector of the original disc (left) and its copy, obtained using Clone CD (right)

```
>seek_and_Q.exe 1.1 2056              >seek_and_Q.exe 1.1 2056
seek CD-ROM & read Q-subcode by KK    seek CD-ROM & read Q-subcode by KK
00 15 00 0C 01 14 01 01 00 00 08 09 00 00 08 09   00 15 00 0C 01 14 01 01 00 00 08 09 00 00 08 08
```

To obtain more detailed information, start Clone CD, make sure that the protected disc is still in the drive, and let's read a CD into the image file. Subchannel information obtained by Clone CD significantly varies from drive to drive. It is, however, in all cases incorrect (compare it to subchannel information provided in Listing 6.71).

An ASUS drive that does not support the mode for returning subchannel data in the common data flow has made Clone CD recover this data on its own, using information from the sector headers for this purpose. Consequently, it will be as if there was never any key mark.

Listing 6.74. Contents of X-sector returned by ASUS

```
000302AC:   41 01 01 00 27 31 00 00 | 29 31 8F AA 00 00 00 00...A☺☺.'1..)1Пк...
0003030C:   41 01 01 00 27 32 00 00 | 29 32 51 1B 00 00 00 00...A☺☺.'2..)2Q←...
```

The NEC drive has actually gone crazy with such a disc and, instead of subchannel data, has returned senseless garbage

Listing 6.75. Contents of X-sector returned by NEC

```
000302AC:   01 01 01 00 00 00 00 00 | 02 00 5A 28 00 00 00 00...☺☺☺.....●.Z(....
0003030C:   01 01 01 00 00 00 00 00 | 02 00 5A 28 00 00 00 00...☺☺☺.....●.Z(....
```

TEAC has correctly returned the subchannel information of the sector that directly follows the X-sector, but the subchannel information of the X-sector itself was still incorrect!

Listing 6.76. Contents of X-sector returned by TEAC

```
0003030C:   41 01 01 00 27 31 00 00 | 29 31 8F AA 00 00 00 00...A☺☺.'1..)1Пк....
0003030C:   41 01 01 00 27 31 00 00 | 29 31 8F AA 00 00 00 00...A☺☺.'1..)1Пк....
```

Thus, the protection mechanism based on *the fictitious track in the Post-gap of the genuine track with the mark in Q subcode channel of the next to last sector in Post-gap* (codename *"Fox"*) cannot be copied by any protected CD copier known to me. At the same time, it doesn't conflict with any other equipment known to me (and it shouldn't conflict with anything). Because of this, it is possible to call the "fox" a sufficiently strong and high-quality protection mechanism.

Nevertheless, do not overestimate its strength. It can be cracked easily! Let's use a pair of SEEK and READ SUBCHANNEL commands, read the subchannel information of the entire disc, and compare it to the contents of the IMAGE.SUB file created by Clone CD or any other similar copier. It is, actually, not necessary to read all of the subchannel information, as it is enough to check only how correct the faulty sectors (i.e., the ones that Clone CD could not read) are... Having detected a key mark here, simply correct the appropriate fields in the IMAGE.SUB file and burn the modified image to a CD-R/CD-RW disc. That's all. Now, from the protection point of view, the copy and original will be identical.

Chapter 7: Protection Mechanisms for Preventing Playback in PC CD-ROM

Low-end CD players are considerably less intellectual than PC CD-ROM drives. Most of them do not support multisession discs and tolerate incorrect TOCs, because they ignore most part of the TOC fields. Thus, by introducing minor errors into the TOC, it is possible to make the disc look OK for CD players, but, at the same time, unreadable for PC CD-ROM drives.

This idea has numerous applications. For example, instead of high-quality music, the vendor might try to palm off a data session created specially for PC CD-ROM and containing heavily compressed MP3 files. Another trick that developers of this kind of protection can play is correcting the pointer to the Lead-out area so as to force the PC CD-ROM to interrupt playback several seconds after it starts. A variant of this is to alter the starting address of the first track so that its LBA address takes a negative value. In all of the cases listed above, normal playback of the disc on a PC CD-ROM drive is impossible. However, an invalid TOC on a protected disc can be easily corrected (I'll show you how a little bit later).

Protection mechanisms based on the introduction of irrecoverable C1/C2-level errors are considerably harder to overcome in this respect. To crack this type of protection, you'll need a drive capable not only of detecting such errors, but also able to specify their location.

Audio Overlapped by Data

Let's consider a multisession CD containing two sessions — an audio session and a data session. When browsing such disc using built-in Windows tools, we'll see only the data session. On the other hand, low-end audio players will play back the audio session, without even picking up that the data session exists (for compatibility with CD players, the session containing audio tracks must come first). Theoretically, it is possible to play back audio tracks by manually starting the CD-player application. However, in practice, attempts to do this usually fail, because the protection mechanism uses additional levels of defence (for instance, a "castrated" Lead-in, the introduction of irrecoverable CIRC errors, etc.), which prevent such an easy method of "cracking."

Visually, these discs can be recognized by their characteristic Lead-out area located near the outside disc edge (Fig. 7.1). This is the barrier that separates the audio session from the data session. Naturally, the presence of an "extra" Lead-out area in itself is not an evidence of the presence of protection. This can also be found on so-called CD-Enhanced discs, i.e., mixed-type discs (audio plus data), which are compatible with contemporary drives and operating systems. However, its presence is, all the same, a disturbing symptom. Unless it is necessary for some reason, it is better not to purchase this type of disc (don't worry if you have, however, as that protection can be easily bypassed). The glittering ring of a Lead-out area near the external edge of a disc, easily noticeable in reflected light, isn't yet evidence of the presence of protection against playback. However, the probability that it is present is pretty high.

Fig. 7.1. Disc displayed in this photo is protected by Cactus Shield 2.00, which currently is the most popular protection against the digital copying of audio discs

The data session can include practically anything (it can even be, sometimes, absolutely empty). As a rule, however, it contains heavily compressed audio in the MP3 format. At the same time, this MP3 audio is not recorded as individual files that can be copied from the disc and uploaded onto the Internet. Instead, this audio information is usually "rolled up" into an executable shell that can be started only from the original CD! Naturally, this executable file can only run under Windows, so the only thing that remains to UNIX/Mac users is either to lick their lips or... crack this protection! By the way, the procedure of recovering an incorrectly written CD by a user on their own and at their own expense must not be considered *cracking*.

If no provision for additional levels of protection has been made, the content of the audio session can easily be grabbed into MP3/WMA format. Most end-user programs for burning CD-R/RWs allow you to view the contents of all disc sessions, including the first one. You can use Roxio Easy CD Creator, Stomp Record Now!, or any similar program. To do this using Easy CD Creator, select the **CD Information** command from the **CD** menu, and choose one or more audio tracks from the first session. Then, click **Convert Audio** and enjoy high-quality music grabbed into your favorite format (the Easy CD Creator version supplied with the PHILIPS recorder provides only two variants, from which the user can choose: WMA and WAV, and doesn't support MP3).

Another variation is to create a corrected copy of the protected disc by removing a data session. The Clone CD program can do this automatically. To achieve this, find the **Audio read parameters** tab in the **Profile parameters** window, set the **Read first session only** checkbox, and click **OK**. Disc copying will proceed in a normal mode. As a result, you'll get a normal audio CD with all of the garbage thrown out.

Alcohol 120% doesn't support this capability. It does, however, allow you to achieve the same result manually. This can be done as follows: First, create the disc image recorded in the Clone CD format (Alcohol 120% allows you to do this). Then, edit the CCD file by removing from it any references to the data session(s). Second, it is necessary to decrease the value of the Sessions field from 2 to 1. Then, remove from the file all entries, for which the Session value is more than 1. Next, decrease the value of the TocEntries field by the number of removed entries. Now, all that remains is to delete the one or more data tracks that go last. Pass-through numbering of tracks slightly complicates this task, which, at first glance, appears to be an easy one. The difficulty is that we cannot easily discover, which track belongs to which session. Therefore, we have to either calculate the number of tracks manually (this corresponds to the number of Point fields having a value greater than 0, but smaller than 0x64), or remove all tracks, for which the Mode value is not zero. An example of practical work with the CCD file is shown in Listing 7.1.

Listing 7.1. Correcting the CCD to crack a protected disc

```
[CloneCD]                          [CloneCD]
Version=3                          Version=3
[Disc]                             [Disc]
TocEntries=24                          TocEntries=20
Sessions=2                         Sessions=1
DataTracksScrambled=0                      DataTracksScrambled=0
CDTextLength=0                         CDTextLength=0
[Session 1]                        CDTextLength=0
PreGapMode=0                           PreGapMode=0
PreGapSubC=0                           PreGapSubC=0
[Session 2]                        [Session 2]
PreGapMode=2                           PreGapMode=2
PreGapSubC=0                           PreGapSubC=0
[Entry 0]                          [Entry 0]
Session=1                          Session=1
Point=0xa0                         Point=0xa0
ADR=0x01                           ADR=0x01
Control=0x00                           Control=0x00
TrackNo=0                          TrackNo=0
AMin=97                            AMin=97
ASec=26                            ASec=26
AFrame=66                          AFrame=66
ALBA=-11634                        ALBA=-11634
Zero=0                             Zero=0
PMin=1                             PMin=1
PSec=32                            PSec=32
PFrame=0                           PFrame=0
PLBA=6750                          PLBA=6750
...
[Entry 20]                         [Entry 20]
Session=2                          Session=2
Point=0xa0                         Point=0xa0
ADR=0x01                           ADR=0x01
Control=0x04                           Control=0x04
TrackNo=0                          TrackNo=0
AMin=72                            AMin=72
ASec=22                            ASec=22
AFrame=38                          AFrame=38
ALBA=325538                        ALBA=325538
Zero=0                             Zero=0
PMin=16                            PMin=16
PSec=32                            PSec=32
```

```
PFrame=0                        PFrame=0
PLBA=74250                      PLBA=74250
...
[Entry 23]                      [Entry 23]
Session=2                       Session=2
Point=0x10                      Point=0x10
ADR=0x01                        ADR=0x01
Control=0x04                        Control=0x04
TrackNo=0                       TrackNo=0
AMin=72                         AMin=72
ASec=23                         ASec=23
AFrame=17                       AFrame=17
ALBA=325592                     ALBA=325592
Zero=0                          Zero=0
PMin=73                         PMin=73
PSec=54                         PSec=54
PFrame=38                       PFrame=38
PLBA=332438                     PLBA=332438
[TRACK 1]                       [TRACK 1]
MODE=0                          MODE=0
FLAGS= DCP                      FLAGS= DCP
INDEX 1=0                       INDEX 1=0
[TRACK 2]                       [TRACK 2]
MODE=0                          MODE=0
FLAGS= DCP                      FLAGS= DCP
INDEX 1=19173                       INDEX 1=19173
...
[TRACK 16]                      [TRACK 16]
MODE=2                          MODE=2
INDEX 1=0                       INDEX 1=0
```

Some discs contain a nasty program that starts automatically when the disc is loaded into the drive and secretly loads itself into the RAM. Its main goal is to protect audio tracks against digital grabbing. The specific approaches of this kind of "guard" may differ. For example, it is possible to scan the list of top-level windows periodically (see descriptions of FindWindows or EnumWindows function in Platform SDK) to search for the headers of the most popular grabbers. Really good programs for working with digital audio are few. Therefore, being able to recognize them all is not unrealistic. If a window of one of these programs is found, the protection mechanism can do whatever it likes to this window. For instance, in order to forcibly close the application, it is enough to send it the WM_DESTROY message.

Castrated Lead-Out

Another popular method of preventing the playback of Audio CDs in PC CD-ROM drives is invalidating the TOC contents in such a way as to make the pointer to the Lead-out area point to locations closer to the disc's beginning than the actual Lead-out. The overwhelming majority of low-end CD players ignore the value of this field, since they don't need it. PC CD-ROM drives, on the other hand, behave less predictably when encountering an invalid Lead-out. Some of them obediently stop the playback after the time specified by the TOC elapses. Some drives simply freeze, vainly trying to find the fictitious Lead-out in a location where there isn't anything of the sort (this may even happen before the start of playback, that is, immediately after loading the disc into the drive). Although some drives are intelligent enough to "guess" that the TOC has been purposefully disfigured (or, perhaps, they simply ignore it) and successfully bypass this protection, but this is something that you can't count on.

To create a protected disc, you'll need any normal audio CD (which we are going to protect) and any protected CD copier (such as Alcohol 120% or Clone CD). The CD recorder doesn't necessarily need to support RAW DAO mode.

Having created the image of the disc that you are going to protect, open the CCD-file created by the copier and find the following text string: `point=0xa2`. This is the entry that points to the Lead-out area, the address for which is stored in the `PMin`, `PSec`, and `PFrame` fields, containing the values in minutes, seconds, and frames, respectively. Reduce the absolute address to a reasonable value (28 seconds, for instance), save the changes, and burn the edited image onto a CD-R/CD-RW disc. Wait some time for the burnt disc to cool down (just kidding!), remove it from the drive and insert it into any low-end CD player. The protected disc will play normally in almost all cases; although, some chance of running into problems remains. Now, insert the test specimen into a PC CD-ROM. The drive will obediently stop the playback at the 28th second.

In practice, this type of protection can easily be bypassed. Create a disc image using Clone CD, and edit the TOC by restoring the correct Lead-out position. To determine the correct value for the Lead-out pointer, manually view the content of the Q subcode channel. Find the track with the `TNO` field containing the value `0xAA`. Note that Clone CD can remove such protection on its own.

Negative Starting Address of the First Audio Track

Here is another dirty trick: To protect audio CD against copying, edit the TOC by setting the address of the first audio track so that it points to the area preceding the Lead-in. In other words, assign it a negative offset (Fig. 7.2).

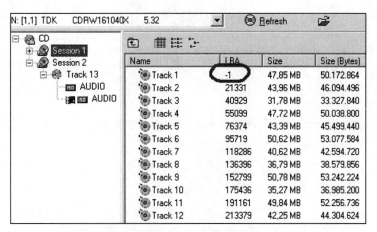

Fig. 7.2. The negative starting address of the first audio track
prevents disc playback on PC CD-ROM

This protection is cracked in a way similar to those considered before. Therefore, we won't concentrate here on a detailed discussion.

Chapter 8: Protection against File-by-File Disc Copying

High-quality and properly designed protection mechanisms usually contain two independent levels of protection, operating at the sector and file levels, respectively. Sector-level protection mechanisms are oriented towards protection against sector-level copiers, which copy the entire disc. These copiers create an exact copy of the disc. File-level protection mechanisms prevent file-by-file copying of the entire disc, as well as the extraction of individual files.

It may seem that when high-quality sector-level protection is present, file-level protection is absolutely useless (especially since all file-level protection mechanisms can easily be bypassed even by end-user copiers such as Roxio CD Copier. This isn't true, however! Impossibility to create an exact disc copy doesn't necessarily mean that it is impossible to grab at least *part* of its contents. Of course, while it's clear that a part still isn't the whole, it is still better than nothing at all. Here is an example. Protection mechanisms for most multimedia encyclopedias (for example, such Russian multimedia products as "Nautilus Pompilius — Diving" and "Agatha Christie — Virtual Concert") operate only at the sector level, but do not prevent you from file-by-file copying of a CD's contents to the hard disk or to another CD. Naturally, the resulting "copy" is unusable and, when starting the multimedia shell, the protection mechanism refuses to work with the illegal copy and terminates its operation abnormally. Nevertheless, it is still possible to operate with both discs without the shell, because all

The file systems of CDs, naturally, are very different from those used on diskettes. The general principles of introducing errors, however, are very similar. By increasing the fictitious lengths of the protected files ten times or more, the developer of a protection mechanism can raise their total size up to hundreds of gigabytes. Thus, in order to copy a protected disc, you'd need a stack of DVDs or a large hard drive. A protection mechanism that "remembers" the original lengths of all files can operate with them without encountering any problems. However, most file copiers won't understand this humor, and, consequently, will go crazy.

Going outside of the file limits, in principle, shouldn't cause any problems. CD file systems are very easy. CDs do not support file fragmentation, and, consequently, don't require FAT. All files take a continuous sequence of sectors, and only the two most important characteristics are related to any file: the *number of the first sector* of the file specified in the LBA (Logical Block Address) format and its *length,* specified in bytes. All other attributes, such as file name and its creation time, are of no importance, because we are currently speaking only about sectors.

An increase in the file length results in the "capturing" of a number of sectors adjacent to its tail. Provided that the number of the last sector belonging to the file doesn't exceed the number of the last sector of the disc, file copying, in principle, will be carried out normally. By "in principle" we mean that all of the other files that are encountered in the copying process will be included into the copy. If the number of the last sector of our file goes beyond the limits of the disc, the CD-ROM drive reports an error and stops reading. Standard copiers built into the operating system, as well as most third-party tools, automatically remove the "tail" of the incompletely copied file from the disk. As a result, the user achieves no result at all. Of course, it isn't too difficult to write a custom copier. However, how do we know what number of bytes we actually need to copy? How can we determine where the useful information is and where the over-end garbage begins? This is exactly the problem that we are now going to solve!

However, not everyone has CDs protected using this method. Therefore, we are going to create one right now! Let's take any unprotected disc and protect it on our own (the title of this book is, after all, *"Protecting against Unsanctioned CD Copying,"* not *"Protection cracking").* The first task we must accomplish is obtaining an image of the disc that we are going to protect. The best way of doing this is using *Roxio Easy CD Creator* or any other similar program. *Clone CD* is not suitable here, since it refuses to carry out short sector read (i.e., user data only) and always processes entire sectors by forcibly adding the checksum and error-correction codes to the end of each sector. As a result, none of our manipulations will produce any effect. They will, on the contrary, be corrected automatically on the fly by the drive's firmware. It is possible, of course, to compute a new checksum and error-correction codes after entering the required changes, but why complicate our life unnecessarily?

If you do not have Easy CD Creator, take *Alcohol 120%*, and choose the **Standard ISO images** option.

OK, now let's assume that the CD image has been successfully saved in the trask.iso file, with which we are going to work now. Open this file using HIEW or any other HEX editor and find the sector that contains the TOC. A pretty business! How can we find it? To do so, we need at least to view the Joliet/ISO-9660 file system specification or exert a bit of mental effort. Since the file size is specified in bytes, not in sectors (it just can't be specified in sectors, file systems that measure files in blocks became obsolete long time ago), then we can find the required field using a trivial context search. Choose the file the length of which we are going to measure, and convert it to a hex. For instance, let it be the file named "01 - Personal Jesus.mp3" having the length of 3,591,523 bytes. In hex notation, taking into account the inverse byte order, this value will appear as follows: 63 CD 36 00. Press <F7> and enter the sequence that we are looking for…

Listing 8.1. The first occurrence of the desired sequence in the disc image

```
0000CBD0:   07 06 14 38 16 0C 02 00 | 00 01 00 00 01 01 01 30   •♠¶8—♀●…☺…☺☺☺0.
0000CBE0:   00 91 01 00 00 00 00 01 | 91 63 CD 36 00 00 36 CD   .C☺…☺Cc=6…6=…..
0000CBF0:   63 67 06 1D 17 0D 0A 28 | 0C 00 00 00 01 00 00 01   cg♠↔↕♪■(♀…☺…☺..
0000CC00:   0E 30 31 30 5F 30 30 30 | 31 2E 4D 50 33 3B 31 00   ♫010_0001.MP3;1
```

Listing 8.2. The second occurrence of the desired sequence in the disc image

```
00010370:   01 00 00 00 00 01 91 63 | CD 36 00 00 36 CD 63 67   ☺…☺Cc=6…6=cg…..
00010380:   06 1D 17 0D 0A 28 0C 00 | 00 00 01 00 00 01 32 00   ♠↔↕♪■(♀…☺…☺2…..
00010390:   30 00 31 00 20 00 2D 00 | 20 00 50 00 65 00 72 00   0 1…-…P e r….
000103A0:   73 00 6F 00 6E 00 61 00 | 6C 00 20 00 4A 00 65 00   s…o…n…a…l … J…e
000103B0:   73 00 75 00 73 00 2E 00 | 6D 00 70 00 33 00 3B 00   s…u…s…. m…p…3…;
```

The desired value is actually present in the disc image. In fact, there are not one, or even two, but *four* such occurrences! No, this isn't some kind of devilry — in fact, this is how it should be. Contemporary CDs contain two file systems: one of them, *ISO-9660*, is written to the disc exclusively for compatibility with obsolete software, limiting the maximum length of a file name to 11 characters (eight for the name itself, and the remaining three for the filename extension). Contemporary software operates with more advanced file systems, including Joliet, developed by Microsoft. If you think that all we need now is Romeo, strangely enough, there is a file system by that name! It was developed by Adaptec, but, unfortunately, didn't become widespread and passed away quite soon. Joliet, therefore, will remain alone.

Enough of romance, let's get back to business. Generally, it isn't necessary to worry about synchronization of the two file systems, because Windows "sees" only Joliet and ignores ISO-9660, while MS-DOS does exactly the opposite. Therefore, if we increase the file length in Joliet, but "forget" about doing the same in ISO-9660 (this is the particular trick that some developers of protection mechanisms play), Windows will never even have a shadow of suspicion that some deception is taking place. However, the question is different with hackers! The original length of files left without changes in ISO-9660 will considerably simplify the task of the cracker. Consequently, it isn't recommended to leave them as they are! Besides this, there are several drivers that allow you to manually choose, which of the two file systems you wish to mount. Don't be lazy, therefore, and correct both values simultaneously by changing the two most significant bytes from `36 00` to `FF 66` (you may, of course, prefer another value). When doing this, pay special attention to the double word `00 36 CD 63`. This also is the file length, written, however, in the inverse order, which is unnatural for IBM PC. Here, the least significant byte is located at the *higher* address. The address of the starting sector of the file is also written in two variants. Such a scheme of information representation has obviously been chosen on the basis of considerations of compatibility. Every platform is free to choose the byte order that is natural for it. There is no guarantee, however, that Windows will choose the "less significant byte by lower address" variant. Everything depends on the file system driver, which, in turn, depending on the specific features of its implementation, can work with any of these two fields. Therefore, both fields must always be coordinated.

Now the modified (I mean, invalidated) ISO image can be burnt onto a CD-R/CD-RW or mounted to a virtual CD drive (for this purpose, you'll need Alcohol 120% or any similar program). Issue the `dir` command, and you'll see the following:

Listing 8.3. The size of the "Personal Jesus.mp3" file is modified on purpose

```
> dir N:\Depeche Mode
Volume in drive N has label 030706_2038
Volume serial number is 61A1-A7EE

Directory of N:\Depeche Mode

06.07.2003  21:56       <DIR>          .
06.07.2003  21:56       <DIR>          ..
01.01.1601  04:00       1 728 040 291 01 - Personal Jesus.mp3
30.06.2003  00:11         3 574 805 02 - See You.mp3
30.06.2003  00:12         3 472 405 03 - Strangerlove.mp3
30.06.2003  00:12         3 718 165 04 - Enjoy The Silence.mp3
30.06.2003  00:13         2 956 643 05 - The Meaning Of Love.mp3
30.06.2003  00:14         3 820 565 06 - Master and Servant.mp3
```

```
30.06.2003    00:15              3 066 149 07 - Never Let Me Down Again.mp3
30.06.2003    00:16              3 806 772 08 - Its Called a Heart.mp3
30.06.2003    00:16              3 813 460 09 - Little 15.mp3
30.06.2003    00:17              3 574 805 10 - Everything Counts.mp3
30.06.2003    00:18              3 687 236 11 - People Are People.mp3
30.06.2003    00:19              4 916 036 12 - The Thing You Said.mp3
30.06.2003    00:20              4 182 100 13 - Agent Orange.mp3
30.06.2003    00:21              4 585 012 14 - World in my Eyes.mp3
30.06.2003    00:22              3 646 276 15 - Behind The Wheel.mp3
30.06.2003    00:22              3 049 012 16 - Black Celebration (live).mp3
30.06.2003    00:23              3 800 085 17 - Nothing.mp3
30.06.2003    00:25              7 151 700 18 - Bonus (unnamed).mp3
                   18 files   1 794 861 517 bytes
                    2 folders               0 bytes free
```

Well! The file size has increased to 1,728,040,291 bytes (see the string highlighted in bold), which is more than twice the volume of the entire CD. And they have the gall to say that one part cannot be larger than the whole! Naturally, any attempt to copy this file to the hard disk will fail. Therefore, we must look for a way to bypass this. Let's focus on the fact that files on the CD are placed sequentially, which means that the last sector of the current file is directly followed by the starting sector of the next file. Because we know the starting sectors of all files, determining the position of the terminating sectors, except for the last, shouldn't present any problem.

Let's copy the ISO image of the protected disc into a file and consider its directory once again:

Listing 8.4. A fragment of the file image under consideration

```
0000E040:  00 01 01 01 54 00 94 01 | 00 00 00 00 01 91 63 CD    .☺☺☺T...Φ♦..☺Cc=..
0000E050:  FF 66 66 FF CD 63 00 00 | 00 00 00 00 00 00 00 00    .ff...=c........
0000E060:  01 00 00 01 32 00 30 00 | 31 00 20 00 2D 00 20 00    ☺..☺2...0...1...-.....
0000E070:  50 00 65 00 72 00 73 00 | 6F 00 6E 00 61 00 6C 00    P...e...r...s...o...n...a...l
0000E080:  20 00 4A 00 65 00 73 00 | 75 00 73 00 2E 00 6D 00    ..J...e...s...u...s......m
0000E090:  70 00 33 00 3B 00 31 00 | 46 00 6B 08 00 00 00 00    p...3...;...1...F...k■...
0000E0A0:  08 6B 15 8C 99 00 00 99 | 8C 15 67 06 1D 17 0B 1C    ■k$MⅡ..ⅢM$g♠↔↕♂L
0000E0B0:  0C 00 00 00 01 00 00 01 | 24 00 30 00 32 00 20 00    ♀...☺...☺$...0...2.....
0000E0C0:  2D 00 20 00 53 00 65 00 | 65 00 20 00 59 00 6F 00    -...S...e...e...Y...o....
0000E0D0:  75 00 2E 00 6D 00 70 00 | 33 00 3B 00 31 00 50 00    u...m...p...3...;...1...P
```

The smallest number of the file's starting sector, after sector 0191h, is 086Bh. Thus, the "01 - Personal Jesus.mp3" file cannot contain more than 086Bh - 0191h == 6DAh sectors or 1754 * 2048 == 3,592,192 bytes. Naturally, this is a somewhat excessive value, and the actual file is 1.5 K shorter. This difference, however, is already of no importance. Most multimedia files will be processed correctly, even with the presence of a certain amount of irrelevant garbage at the tail. Having corrected the file image, let's write it to the disc or simply shorten the file to the required length using any available program, such as "Pinch of file."

What should you do if you are not satisfied with such a low level of reliability from this protection? There is, in fact, something that can be done. For example, it is possible to reduce the numbers of starting sectors of several files, which allows you to kill two birds with one stone. First, the file with an incorrectly specified sector definitely won't be processed correctly by an associated application (which isn't surprising, since after this kind of manipulation, the actual starting point of the file will be somewhere in its middle). Second, the algorithm used to determine original file lengths from the difference of the neighboring starting sector addresses is sure to produce an incorrect result, according to which the restored file will be cut off.

A protection mechanism that knows the actual offset of the file's starting sector in relation to its real starting point must either shift the file pointer by means of calling the SetFilePointer function or "swallow" the garbage data using the ReadFile function. Both methods are equally effective, and each of them has its strong and weak points. SetFilePointer operates considerably faster. However, it is easily recognizable (especially to hackers). When encountering the ReadFile call, on the contrary, it is necessary to find out what kind of data it actually reads — useful information or simply garbage.

Let's study how the cracking process appears in practice. Writing a fully functional MP3 player just for the sake of illustration isn't a rational approach (besides which, it would take a lot of space). Therefore, all of the data processing in this demo example consists of displaying the original file contents on the screen. Before starting this program the first time, the starting sector number of the protected file must be decreased by the _NSEC_ value, and the size must be increased by at least 2048*_NSEC_ bytes. There is no limitation on the maximum length (which means that you can use all 32 bits of the length field).

Listing 8.5. [crackme.27AF7A2Dh] A demo example illustrating the processing of files with incorrect attributes for starting sector and length

```
/*-----------------------------------------------------------------------
 *
 *          crack me 27AF7A2D
 *
 *          =================
 *
 *
 *   A demo example illustrating the processing of files with an intentionally
 * decreased number for the starting sector and an increased length; positioning of the file
 * pointer is carried out by a call to the fseek function, therefore this crackme
```

```
* is very easy to crack.
*
* Build 0x001 @ 02.07.2003
----------------------------------------------------------------------------*/
#include <stdio.h>

// Program settings
// ===================
// Name of the file to be opened
// If protection resides on the CD, then there is no need to specify
// full pathname.
#define _FN_         "M:\\Depeche Mode\\01 - Personal Jesus.mp3"

// The number of sectors by which the starting point of the file is offset
#define _NSEC_          4

// Original file size
#define _FSIZ_          3591523

// User data size
#define SECTOR_SIZE     2048

// Screen width in characters (needed to display a dump)
#define _SCREEN_LEN_ 80

// Size of the block being processed
#define BLOCK_SIZE   0x666

// Finding the minimum of two numbers
#define _MIN(a,b)   ((a<b)?a:b)

// DISPLAYING HEX DUMP
//-------------------------
// src - Pointer to the data being output
// n   - Number of bytes displayed on the screen
print_hex(unsigned char *src, int n)
{
 int a; static p = 1;
 for (a=1; a <= n; a++)
     printf("%02x%s", src[a-1], (p++%(_SCREEN_LEN_/3-1)) ? " ":"\n");
}

main()
```

```
{
int   a;
FILE *f;
long p = _FSIZ_;
char buf[BLOCK_SIZE];

// TITLE
fprintf(stderr, "crackme 27af7a2d by Kris Kaspersky\n");

// Trying to open the file
if ((f = fopen(_FN_, "rb")) == 0)
{
    fprintf(stderr, "-ERR: can not open %s\n",_FN_); return -1;
}

// Skipping _NSEC_ extra sectors in the beginning of the file
fseek(f, _NSEC_*SECTOR_SIZE, SEEK_SET);

// Reading file by blocks, taking care that we don't go
// beyond the limits of its original size
while(p)
{
    // Attention: Don't use the fgetc function for processing files with an
    // incorrect size, since in most of implementations
    // this function processes files in blocks instead of bytes.
    // Block size isn't known beforehand. This means that
    // the fgetc function carries out transparent input buffering,
    // based on the specified file size as a reference.
    // If this value is incorrect, there is no guarantee
    // that the fgetc function will remain within the disc size limits.
    // The consequences of the function's going beyond these limits
    // are unpredictable (this is particularly probable
    // if the file being processed is the last file on the CD).
    // Therefore, use fread, or better still, ReadFile,
    // which certainly won't end up running ahead of the hounds.
    // Reading the next block
    fread(buf, 1, a = _MIN(p,BLOCK_SIZE), f);
    print_hex(buf,a); p-= a          // Displaying it on the screen
}
}
```

Having discovered that the main file attributes are incorrect (which means that this file is unreadable), the hacker will certainly want to determine the offset of the first actual byte and original file size.

Listing 8.6. Soft-ice log file

```
:bpx CreateFileA         ; Set the breakpoint to CreateFileA
:x               ; Exit the Ice
...
Break due to BPX KERNEL32!CreateFileA (ET=3.37 seconds)
; The debugger pops up, which means that someone has called the CreateFileA function.
; But who ? Let's try to determine this by the name of the opened file.

:d esp->4        ; Viewing the first argument passed to the function
0010:0040706C 4D 3A 5C 44 65 70 65 63-68 65 20 4D 6F 64 65 5C   M:\Depeche Mode\
0010:0040707C 30 31 20 2D 20 50 65 72-73 6F 6E 61 6C 20 4A 65   01 - Personal Je
0010:0040708C 73 75 73 2E 6D 70 33 00-4D 3A 5C 44 65 70 65 63   sus.mp3.M:\Depec
; That's it! It is exactly what we need!

:p ret           ; Exiting the function
:? eax           ; Viewing the value of the file descriptor
00000030  0000000048  "0"    ; The descriptor is 0x30 (or 48 in decimal notation).

:bpx SetFilePointer  if (esp->4 == 0x30);
:bpx ReadFile        if (esp->4 == 0x30)
; Setting the breakpoints to the main file functions, SetFilePointer and ReadFile,
; thus making the debugger show up only when "our" descriptor is passed to these
; functions (special note for developers of protection mechanisms: ladies and gentlemen,
; don't let the hackers to deceive you so easily! Open the file several times
; and work with it using various descriptors, changing them from time to time,
; as this will seriously complicate the analysis)

:x               ; Exiting the debugger
...
Break due to BPX KERNEL32!SetFilePointer  IF ((ESP->4)==0x30)  (ET=76.19 microseconds)
; This was our breakpoint set to the SetFilePointer function, now we need to view
; the offset value, by which the pointer has been shifted,
; and the origin - to determine,
; in relation to which part of the file the count is carried out.

:? esp->8        ; Viewing the second argument of the function
00002000  0000008192  "  "    ;   The pointer is moved 0x2000 bytes from..
```

```
:? esp->0C             ; Viewing the third argument of the function
00000000  0000000000  " "   ;   ...the starting point of the file (SEEK_SET)

:p ret                 ; Exiting the debugger

...
```

; The SetFilePointer function isn't called any more. However,
; there are multiple calls to the ReadFile function.
; We won't issue the P RET command for analysis of the protection code
; (in contrast to some hacking recommendations). After all, ReadFile
; is most likely called from some library wrapper, instead of direct calls,
; and analysis of this wrapper is unlikely to produce any valuable result.
; Instead of this, let us view the calls stack...

...

```
:stack                 ; Viewing the calls stack
12F8C8   401E1C     KERNEL32!ReadFile
12F8F8   4010E5     crackme!.text+0E1C
12FFC0   77E87903crackme!.text+00E5
12FFF0   0          KERNEL32!SetUnhandledExceptionFilter+005C
```
; Obviously, the address 55E87903h belongs to some OS internals.
; Therefore, it is of no interest to us, as well as address 401E1Ch
; (the return address from ReadFile),
; since as was already mentioned before, it is most likely that it belongs to some
; library wrapper. As relates to the address 4010E5h, it is worth investigating:

```
:u 4010E5
001B:00401072   mov   edi, 36CD63      ; EDI := 36CD63
001B:004010C8   cmp   edi, 00000666    ; \                              ← (1)
001B:004010CE   mov   esi, edi         ;  +- ESI := _min(0x666, EDI)
001B:004010D0   jl    004010D7         ;  +
001B:004010D2   mov   esi, 00000666    ; /
001B:004010D7   push  ebx              ; ...
001B:004010D8   push  esi              ; Number of elements being read
001B:004010D9   lea   eax, [esp+14]    ; Getting the pointer to a buffer
001B:004010DD   push  01               ; Size of a single element
001B:004010DF   push  eax              ; Passing the pointer to buffer
001B:004010E0   call  00401141         ; This function calls ReadFile
001B:004010E5   lea   ecx, [esp+1C]    ; Getting the pointer to the buffer
001B:004010E9   push  esi              ; ...
001B:004010EA   push  ecx              ; ...
001B:004010EB   call  00401000         ; Processing the data that has been read
001B:004010F0   add   esp, 18          ; Removing unneeded arguments from the stack
```

```
001B:004010F3    sub    edi, esi      ; EDI := EDI - _min(0x666, EDI)
001B:004010F5    jnz    004010C8      ; Looping, until there is anything to process
001B:004010F7    pop    esi           ; …
; Studying the environment of the 4010E5 address allows us
; to restore the file processing algorithm in a matter of seconds.
; The file is being read in 0x666-byte blocks
; until there are exactly 0x36CD63 (or 3,591,523 in decimal notation)
```

Thus, after the file is opened, its pointer is moved 0x2000 bytes (4 sectors) forward, then 3,591,523 data bytes are read, after which its processing stops. Consequently, it is possible to restore the protected file as follows…

Try to play it using any available MP3 player. If everything was done correctly, you'll enjoy the Depeche Mode no longer spoiled by any protection mechanism! By the way, this music is especially suitable as background music to make the work of improving protection mechanisms more pleasant. In fact, there are a lot of things that need improvement!

"Cunning" processing of protected files assumes the use of at least three descriptors for each file: two are actually used for data processing, while the third descriptor dances wildly over the entire file, reading senseless garbage. This garbage is passed to a bulky and horribly complicated procedure that carries out sophisticated computations, which are never used in practice. "Feeding" this procedure by the first _NSEC_ sectors of the protected file, we'll create a false impression that file processing begins from the start of the file (well, practically from the start, because protection developers can easily move the pointer to whatever position he or she likes).

Descriptors that are actually used must be opened after returning a false one, since most crackers trace only the first call to CreateFileA, which opens the specified file, ignoring all further calls to that function. Actually, most crackers don't even guess that the same file can be opened more than once.

For positioning on the first byte of the useful data, it is better to read the garbage and imitate its processing instead of calling the SetFilePointer function. In a well-designed protection mechanism, it is very difficult to determine where the garbage ends and the actual data begins. However, the implementation of such a protection is very difficult (and remember that along with implementing the code, you'll have to debug it). Therefore, for simplicity's sake, it is possible to limit the protection by ensuring that the starting point of useful data coincides with the first byte of the next block being read.

It is extremely undesirable to store the original file length in the form of a constant, because all constants are immediately revealed in the course of analysis. In fact, the required value can quickly be found by using the brute force approach. This is because in most programs, there aren't too many constants with values comparable with the lengths of files being processed. Therefore, instead of file length, it is recommended to store the length of its "tail", i.e., the remainder from the division of the original length by the size of processed blocks. Naturally, block size and the number of blocks also must be stored somewhere, but analysis of the relationship between three constants is much more difficult than finding a single constant!

Taking into account all of the above-mentioned considerations, we can improve our protection mechanism significantly. One of the possible variants of its implementation could appear as follows:

Listing 8.7. [crackme.CEE99D84h.c] Software implementation of a protection mechanism based on an invalid disc TOC

```
// Size of the "tail" of the last block
#define TAIL_SIZE        (_FSIZ_ % BLOCK_SIZE)

// Number of whole blocks
#define N_BLOCKS        (_FSIZ_ / BLOCK_SIZE /2)

// FALSE DATA PROCESSING
// ------------------------
// It is best to make this function as bulky and complicated
// as possible, so that its activities (thrashing, in fact)
// won't be self-evident.
thrashing(unsigned char *src, int n)
{
    int a, sum = 0;for (a = 0; a< n; a++) sum += src[a]; return sum;
}

main()
{
    int  a = 0;
    long p = _FSIZ_;
    FILE *f_even, *f_uneven, *f_thrashing;
    char buf[BLOCK_SIZE + (_NSEC_*SECTOR_SIZE)];

    // TITLE
    fprintf(stderr, "crackme 27af7a2d by Kris Kaspersky\n");

    // Trying to open the file
    // The best practice is to open f_thrashing first, because
    // the first call to CreateFileA encountered by a cracker
    // must return a "false" descriptor.
    if ( ((f_thrashing = fopen(_FN_, "rb")) == 0) ||
        ((f_even   = fopen(_FN_, "rb")) == 0) ||
        ((f_uneven = fopen(_FN_, "rb")) == 0))
```

```
                { fprintf(stderr, "-ERR: cannot open %s\n",_FN_); return -1;}

        // Setting f_even
        fread(buf, 1, _NSEC_*SECTOR_SIZE, f_even);

        // Imitating the skipping of NSEC*SECOR_SIZE/2 bytes
        // (hoping that this will deceive the cracker)
        // Actually, all NSEC*SECTOR_SIZE starting bytes of
        // the file go to dev/null
        thrashing(buf + _NSEC_*SECTOR_SIZE/2,_NSEC_*SECTOR_SIZE/2);

        // Setting f_uneven
        fread(buf, 1, _NSEC_*SECTOR_SIZE+BLOCK_SIZE, f_uneven);

        // Imitating the skipping of NSEC*SECOR_SIZE/3 bytes
        thrashing(buf + _NSEC_*SECTOR_SIZE/3, 2*_NSEC_*SECTOR_SIZE/3+BLOCK_SIZE);

        // Setting thrashing, thus directing the cracker by false trace
        fseek(f_thrashing,_NSEC_*SECTOR_SIZE/4,SEEK_SET);

        // Reading the file in blocks, making sure that we do not go
        // beyond the limits of its original size

        for (a=0; a < N_BLOCKS; a++)
        {
            // Reading trash data
            fread(buf, 1, BLOCK_SIZE, f_thrashing);threshing(buf,BLOCK_SIZE);

            // Reading the even block with actual data
            fread(buf, 1, BLOCK_SIZE, f_even);      print_hex(buf,BLOCK_SIZE);

            // Skipping uneven block for f_even descriptor
            fread(buf, 1, BLOCK_SIZE, f_even);      threshing(buf,BLOCK_SIZE);

            // Reading uneven block of actual data
            fread(buf, 1, BLOCK_SIZE, f_uneven);        print_hex(buf,BLOCK_SIZE);

// Skipping the even block for f_uneneven descriptor
            fread(buf, 1, BLOCK_SIZE, f_uneven);        threshing(buf,BLOCK_SIZE);
        }
        // Reading the tail
        fread(buf, 1, TAIL_SIZE, f_even); print_hex(buf, TAIL_SIZE);
}
```

Try to crack this protection. Did you succeed? An attempt at tracing calls to SetFilePoiner and ReadFile functions doesn't produce any result, because the manner of data read is highly non-linear, and there is no efficient method to distinguish trash from useful data quickly. These protection mechanisms shouldn't be cracked using only a debugger. In this case, you'll require a disassembler. Not even this, however, will guarantee that you'll succeed quickly. The complexity and intricacies of the data processing algorithm considerably complicate program analysis. With regard to determining the actual boundaries of the protected file, even professionals might end up spending several hours (or sometimes even *days*). Because of the space limitations, disassembled listings and a description of the cracking process won't be provided in this book. They don't, in fact, contain anything interesting — just routine operations. The only clue in this case is the thrashing function that imitates the data processing. As soon as the hacker understands that the results of its operation are not used by the program in any way, he or she will have made a considerable advance in cracking activities. Breakpoints set to memory read/write operations will allow him or her to quickly and elegantly determine if specified memory cells are actually accessed. In other words, there are no secrets that cannot be revealed using Soft-Ice and IDA…

File Encryption

To prevent file-by-file copying, it would be ideal to use *custom non-standard data formats*, which wouldn't be possible to view or play by bypassing the shell program. However, the development of a custom file format requires considerable investment, which is unjustified, because long before the program can make a worthwhile return on this investment, hackers will "unbind" it from the disc by cracking the protection at the sector level and, thus, be able to engage in disc replication.

Developers of protection mechanisms, therefore, prefer to base them upon existing formats (such as MP3), and simply *encrypt the files before writing them to the master disc*, then decrypting the CD contents on the fly when playing back. The drawback of this approach is that protection mechanisms based on it are very easy to crack. To do this, it is enough to set the breakpoint to the CreateFile function, wait until the required file is opened, and then trace the EAX register value at the instance of exiting from the function. This value will be the descriptor of the opened file. After that, all that remains is to set the breakpoints to the SetFilePointer/ReadFile functions to make the debugger show up only in cases when "our" descriptor is passed. The breakpoint set to the memory area containing the data read from the CD will lead the hacker directly to the decryption procedure. Having analyzed its algorithm, the hacker will be able to write a custom decrypting procedure!

If the encryption algorithm is just a trivial XOR (which is most often the case), the disc contents can be cracked even faster! In practice, all non-standard file formats contain a certain volume of more or less predictable information, and, therefore, can be decrypted by an attack based on plain text. For example, AVI, MP2/MP3, WMA, and ASF files contain long chains of consecutive zeros (and/or characters with the code FF).

The encryption key, therefore, is detected by trivially viewing the contents of the protected file in any HEX editor.

Consider the following example. Assume that you have a multimedia CD "The Best of Depeche Mode," and the contents of one of its files looks as follows:

Listing 8.8. The hex dump of the header of the file being investigated

```
K:\sex\1\03 - Strangerlove.dat                    DOS    3472405
00000000:  9D 9A F0 39 62 61 60 3A | 65 A4 8B F0 52 C1 01 98   ЭЪЁ9ba`:едЛЁR⌐©Ш
00000010:  BA DB 03 5A 54 27 A6 4C | 43 ED 46 1D 8B 21 ED 9A   ‖♥ZT'жLCэF↵Л!эЪ
00000020:  D3 C7 7B 58 4B A6 78 5D | F6 FA F0 A9 55 63 66 A8   ╙╟{XKжx]ў·ЁйUcfи
00000030:  7E 6A 5A 79 61 68 E8 7B | 69 47 F9 7B 60 22 E3 88   ~jZyahш{iG·{`"уИ
00000040:  61 E2 67 98 E0 E2 2D ED | 13 AD E3 38 C5 A5 71 FB   aтgШрт-э‼ну8┤eq√
00000050:  1A 01 C0 B6 85 77 5A 49 | 46 4F 93 7B BF 30 A5 9D   →☺╚╢EwZIFOУ{┐0eЭ
```

This dump doesn't look like MP3 (MP3 files start with the FF FB signature, which isn't always located in the beginning of the file, however). It doesn't appear as a WAV, either (because WAV files start with the RIFF signature). It doesn't look like a RealAudio file (RealAudio files start with .RMF), but these files are played in some way or another! Also, at the same time, it is unlikely that the developers of this multimedia CD have designed a custom file format. In all likelihood, this file is encrypted. If this is the case, it is possible to decrypt it!

Let's scroll the HEX editor window down until we encounter the regular sequence shown in Listing 8.9.

Listing 8.9. A regular sequence detected inside the file being investigated

```
K:\sex\1\03 - Strangerlove.dat                    DOS    3472405
000001E0:  C3 5A AF F8 70 4A D8 83 | 5D 9E 9D 86 9D 9E 9D 86   ├Zп°pJ╪Г]ЮЭЖЭЮЭЖ
000001F0:  9D 9E 9D 86 9D 9E 9D 86 | 9D 9E 9D 86 9D 9E 9D 86   ЭЮЭЖЭЮЭЖЭЮЭЖЭЮЭЖ
00000200:  9D 9E 9D 86 9D 9E 9D 86 | 9D 9E 9D 86 9D 9E 9D 86   ЭЮЭЖЭЮЭЖЭЮЭЖЭЮЭЖ
00000210:  9D 9E 9D 86 AA C2 62 79 | 62 B4 C0 6A 9D 9E 9D 86   ЭЮЭЖк┬byb┤╚jЭЮЭЖ
00000220:  9D 9E 9D 86 9D 9E 9D 86 | 9D 9E 9D 86 9D 9E 9D 86   ЭЮЭЖЭЮЭЖЭЮЭЖЭЮЭЖ
00000230:  9D 9E 9D 86 9D 9E 9D 86 | 9D 9E 9D 86 9D 9E 9D 86   ЭЮЭЖЭЮЭЖЭЮЭЖЭЮЭЖ
00000240:  9D 9E 9D 86 9D 9E 9D 86 | 70 B8 46 0B 3B 61 63 30   ЭЮЭЖЭЮЭЖp╕F♂;ac0
```

It is highly probable that in this position, the original file contained a chain of bytes having identical values, for instance, it might be a sequence of zeros or FF bytes, which were XOR'ed using a four-byte key.

Since XOR is a symmetric operation, ((A XOR B) XOR A) == B, this means that repeated encryption of the file with its original contents will produce the key. Supposing that there were zeros in this position, the encryption key will be "...9E 9D 86 9D...".

The dots on each side of the key mean that, for the moment, we are not ready to separate the start and end of the regular sequence. Actually, it may be both 9E 9D 86 9D, and 9D 86 9E 9D, or even 86 9D 9E 9D or 9D 9E 9D 86. However, instead of blindly trying all four variants, let's note that the length of the regular sequence is four. Consequently, the first byte of each "period" must be located at an offset that is a multiple of four. Hence, the required sequence must be 9D 9E 9D 86, and because they are located at invalid addresses, all other variants are incorrect. Since the starting addresses of HEX strings displayed by the editor are aligned by the 0x10 bytes boundary (and 0x10 is a multiple of 4), then the first byte of the key must match the starting address of any string.

Now, let us assume that in this position of the original file there was a chain of zeros. Then the encryption key should be as follows: 9D 9E 9D 86 (because (A XOR 0) == A). Start HIEW, press <Enter> to switch to the hex mode, and press <F3> to activate the edit mode. Then press <F8> to open the **Enter XOR mask** dialog, and enter the hex sequence. After that, you can place something heavy on the <F8> key and go somewhere to relax for a while, because HIEW will take a long time to decrypt the file. As a result, there's nothing else to do other than to take your favorite compiler and write the decryption program yourself. The listing provided below isn't a masterpiece of programming art, but it will do as a working variant developed to quckly close the problem.

Listing 8.10. [/etc/DeXOR.c] A demo example of a simple decryptor

```
/*-------------------------------------------------------------------------
 *
 *       XORs THE FILE CONTENTS BY ARBITRARY MASK
 *       ========================================
 *
 * Build 0x001 @ 09.07.2003
-------------------------------------------------------------------------*/
#include <stdio.h>

#define MAX_LEN  666         // Max. mask length
#define MAX_BUF_SIZE (100*1024)  // Read buffer size
#define FDECODE  "decrypt.dat"      // Name of decrypted file

main(int argc, char **argv)
{
long a, b;
long key_len;
FILE *fin, *fout;
long buf_size, real_size;
unsigned char key[MAX_LEN];
```

```
unsigned char buf[MAX_BUF_SIZE];

if (argc<3)      // HELP on the command-line options
{
    fprintf(stderr,"USAGE: DeXOR.exe file_name AA BB CC DD EE...\n");
    return 0;
}

// Finding the key length and setting the buffer size
// equal to its multiple
key_len = argc - 2; buf_size = MAX_BUF_SIZE - (MAX_BUF_SIZE % key_len);

// Retrieving keys from the command line into the key array
for(a = 0; a < key_len; a++)
{
    // Converting from HEX-ASCII to long
    b = strtol(argv[a+2], &" ", 16);

    if (b > 0xFF)       // Check for maximum allowed value
        {fprintf(stderr, "-ERR: val %x  not a byte\x7\n", b); return -1;}

    key[a] = b;      // Storing the value of the next byte of the key
}

printf("build a key:"); // Displaying the key (for control)
for(a=0; a < key_len; a++) printf("%02X", key[a]); printf("\n");

// Opening the file for reading or writing
fin = fopen(argv[1], "rb"); fout=fopen(FDECODE, "wb");
if ((fin==0) || (fout==0))
    { fprintf(stderr, "-ERR: file open error\x7\n"); return -1; }

// Main processing loop
while(real_size=fread(buf, 1, buf_size, fin))
{
    // Loop by the buffer
    for (a = 0; a < real_size; a+=key_len)
    {
        // Loop by the key
        for(b=0; b < key_len; b++)
            buf[a+b] ^= key[b];
    }

    // Flushing the encrypted (decrypted) buffer to disk
```

```
    if (0 == fwrite(buf, 1, real_size, fout))
    {
        fprintf(stderr, "-ERR: file write error\x7\n");
        return -1;
    }
}
// Exiting
}
```

Let's compile this program and start it: `"DeXOR.c "03 — Strangerlove.dat"`
`9D 9E 9D 86`. It would appear that we have failed! The decrypted file doesn't look like
an MP3 or a file of any other format. However, this simply means that this wasn't
a chain of zeros. Instead, it was something else — a sequence of FF characters, for instance. To test our assumption, let's XOR the `9D9E9D86h` regular sequence by the number FFFFFFh. If we are lucky, we will get the original key as a result of this operation.
To do this, we will once again need HIEW, or even the built-in Windows Calculator.
Start Windows Calculator, and select the **Scientific** option from the **View** menu. Then
set the **Hex** radio button (or press <F5>, as alternative). Enter the value `9D9E9D86`,
then click the **XOR** button and enter FFFFFFFF. Then press <Enter>. The calculator
will reply with `62616279`. This is the key for which we are looking. Enter it into the
DeXOR program (separate bytes by blanks), and…

…after renaming the file Strangerlove.dat with the name Strangerlove.mp3, it can
be played using any MP3 player. Files of other formats contained on the protected
CD can be decrypted in a similar way (naturally, they will have different decryption
keys, but the method of finding the keys will be the same).

What conclusions can we draw from this discussion? If you are going to encrypt
files with predictable contents, choose an encryption-key length that is comparable to
the lengths of predictable sequences, or, better still, a key length that exceeds this
length by a number of times. As an alternative, you can use more advanced encryption
algorithms instead of XOR (if, that is, you aren't too lazy to implement them).

The task of obtaining a long non-periodic encryption key can actually be elegantly
carried out using a random (or, more precisely, a *pseudo-random*) number generator.
As you probably remember, the pseudo-random sequence generated by the `rand()`
library function is constant at each program start. Therefore, it is an excellent but,
at the same time, not self-evident key! The program provided below does exactly this.

Listing 8.11. [crackme.765B98ECh.c] Using rand() for storing the encryption key

```
/*-------------------------------------------------------------------------
 *
 *        IMPLICIT GENERATION OF THE DECRYPTION KEY USING RAND()
 *
 *        =========================================================
 *
```

```
 *
 * Encrypts and decrypts files using the rand() function
 * for generating the key; since rand() generates the same sequence any time
 * the program is started, specified by srand(), we get a very long
 * non-periodic encryption key, "blinding" plain-text attacks.
 * Besides, if we modify the rand() code slightly, IDA will be unable
 * to detect it. This won't seriously complicate an attempt at cracking, however,
 * since rand() implementation is strangely primitive in most cases.
 *         Additional protection levels are ensured by complicating the
 * data-processing algorithm (for example, it is possible to create the entire
 * series of decryptors, only one of which would produce useful data,
 * while others will return senseless garbage).
 *
 *         NOTE: To encrypt the original file, start the program
 * with the "-crypt" command-line option. You only need to do this once
 * (the file available on the companion CD is already encrypted, and an attempt
 * to encrypt it will produce the opposite result — the file will be decrypted
 * and saved to the disk in decrypted form).
 *
 * Build 0x001 09.07.2003
-----------------------------------------------------------------------------*/

#include <stdio.h>
#include <math.h>

#define FNAME      "file.dat"     // The name of the file to be encrypted or decrypted
#define MAX_SIZE   (100*1024)     // Max. possible file size

#define SEED       0x666   // Setting the rand() sequence
                           // This can be any number.
                           // It simply has to be present!

//--[crypt]-------------------------------------------------------------
// fname   -     - file name
// buf         - pointer to the buffer to which the decrypted data must be loaded
// buf_size    - buffer size
// need_store  - is it necessary to store encrypted or decrypted file on the disk?
//        :0 — do not write, != 0 - write
//---------------------------------------------------------------------
crypt(char *fname, char *buf, int buf_size, int need_store)
{
    FILE *f;
```

```
    long a, b;

    // Do not forget to initialize the random number generator explicitly.
    // If other branches of the program also use rand(),
    // the decryption result will "float".
    srand(SEED);

    // Opening the decrypted file
    f=fopen(fname, "rb"); if (f==0) return -1;

    // Loading data into the buffer
    a = fread(buf, 1, buf_size, f); if (!a || (a == buf_size)) return -1;

    // (En|de)crypt the buffer contents using the key
    // generated on the fly by the rand() function
    for (b = 0; b < a; b++) buf[b] ^= (rand() % 255); fclose(f);

    // Debugging for automatic file encryption
    if (need_store)
    {
        f=fopen(fname, "wb"); if (f==0)  return -1;
        fwrite(buf, 1, a, f); fclose(f); return -1;
    }
    return a;
}

main(int argc, char** argv)
{
    long  a, x;
    long  need_store = 0;
    unsigned char buf[MAX_SIZE];

    // TITLE
    fprintf(srderr, "crackme 765b98ec by Kris Kaspersky\n");

    // If there is the debug key -crypt encrypt
    if ((argc > 1) && !strcmp(argv[1], "-crypt")) need_store++;

    // Load the FNAME file, decrypt and display its contents.
    if ((x=Crypt(FNAME, buf, MAX_SIZE, need_store))!=-1)
        for (a = 0; a < x; a++) printf("%c", buf[a]);
}
```

Chapter 9: Protection Mechanisms Based on Binding to Storage Media

That a properly produced digital copy is absolutely identical to the original seems to be a broadly held view at present, thanks to which consumers are often of the opinion that the only difference between the two options lies in the question of their price. In actuality, this isn't the case, as no two CDs are absolutely identical to each other. In fact, each CD is characterized by a set of unique parameters that differentiate it from all other CDs. These unique characteristics (later on, we'll call them *marks*) can be used by protection mechanisms for the identification of original media and weeding out unauthorized copies.

Professional ethics oblige protection developers to use only the marks that satisfy the following (rather stringent) requirements as means for this type of identification:

❐ The mark must be detected without errors by all existing drives.
❐ The mark mustn't be reproducible by any copier.
❐ The mark stability against any external influence (scratches or the natural aging of the disc) mustn't be lower than that of other data written using a standard method.

Unfortunately, a protection mechanism that can satisfy all of the above-listed requirements has yet to be invented. Quite often, customers encounter the situation where a program legally purchased erroneously considers itself to be a counterfeit copy and refuses to run. What are chosen as the key characteristics by protection developers? An analysis of existing protection mechanisms shows that they include, first, physical media flaws (both natural and those purposely introduced); second, the timing characteristics for reading sector groups; third, reading stability; and finally, the information reported by the storage medium itself (ATIP, in particular).

Putting Marks vs. Dynamic Binding

The introduction on purpose of unique marks to the storage medium is a simple task in itself, and is widely used. Those whose financial resources are limited simply scratch the disc with a sharp needle. Those with access to more cash can afford to disfigure it with a laser. More sophisticated systems of protection use pits of non-standard shapes, or carry out complicated manipulations of the density and/or pattern of the spiral track. None of these methods, however, are without their own drawbacks. First, they require specialized equipment. Second, unique characteristics of the storage medium are considered as such because they can't just be reproduced on demand. On the contrary, they are formed in process of medium creation. This means that, at present, when the disc is removed from the burner, the protection mechanism doesn't know the medium characteristics, to which it is bound. When the burning process has been completed, it's already too late to report these characteristics to the protection, since the disc is already burnt and CD-ROM drives do not support the writing of additional information. In theory, encoded marks can be placed into the diskette supplied along with the protected CD-ROM. Users, however, are unlikely to be enthusiastic about this approach. Finally, these "unique" marks that are placed on the master copy of the CD are useless against the CD fabrication plants that prefer to steal part of the printed lot.

Therefore, it is much better not to introduce any marks to the disc. A much better approach is to use those that already exist and try to detect their uniqueness on the fly. Is this possible? Actually, it's easy! The protection mechanism measures the disc characteristic that is most vulnerable to the maximum scatter from one medium instance to another (as a rule, this is the read timing characteristic). Then, according to a specially designed algorithm, this characteristic is converted into a certain code, which is reported to the disc owner. The owner passes this code to the program developer and receives (naturally, at a price) the registration number derived from this code (for the sake of simplicity, let's assume that the registration code is equal to the disc characteristic code multiplied by 0x666). After the user enters the registration number, the protection mechanism carries out an inverse operation over this code and compares the result to the code of the disc characteristic (as a variant, the protection can compute the appropriate registration code for the code of the disc characteristic on its own, and then compare it to the registration number entered by the user). If the results match, then everything is OK. If not, the program refuses to operate[i].

The first advantage of this mechanism is that the creation of a protected disc does not require any specialized equipment. Any CD recorder is suitable for this purpose. The copying of a protected disc is accomplished without any problems. All duplicates, however, automatically lose their registration status, because the code of the disc characteristic changes. These duplicate copies can be registered legally, however, if the user contacts the program developer. This is the second advantage!

Naturally, the algorithm used for generating the registration number must be chosen in such a way as to ensure that no dependence between the registration number and the characteristic code can be traced. Furthermore, the procedure itself must complicate its investigation using disassemblers and debuggers as much as possible. Otherwise, the protection mechanism can be cracked easily and efficiently.

Protection Mechanisms Based on Physical Defects

The idea of protection mechanisms of this type lies in intentionally damaging disc surface in one or more locations. When the drive attempts to read sectors located in the damaged area, it will drag the read head for a while and then, after several failed reading attempts, return an error message. Most end-user copiers will be unable to copy such a disc, and will terminate their operation abnormally after encountering the first damaged sector. More advanced copiers capable of skipping damaged sectors, will succeed in copying all of the readable information on a defect-free disc. However, in this case, absolutely normal and readable sectors will be located in positions occupied by damaged areas (such sectors, however, will contain irrelevant garbage, since the copier failed to copy these them).

The protection mechanism will check the storage medium for the presence of physically damaged sectors in the predefined locations, and, if the sectors with predefined numbers can be read without a problem, the protection will conclude that it is dealing with an unauthorized copy of the original disc.

As a rule, the physical defects, to which protection mechanisms bind, are tiny spots (approximately one or two millimeters in diameter) burnt on the disc surface by a laser. They can easily be located visually when viewing the disc in reflected light (see Fig. 9.1). At first glance, it seems that we'd be able to reproduce an identical damage on the copied medium by precisely measuring their geometric coordinates (using a palette, for instance). Practice, however, shows that this isn't the case. This is because sector numbers are not in any way bound to their physical location. Depending on the

---

[i] Some programs react rudely to the failed attempts at their cracking. For example, Alcohol 120% displays messages with obscene words ;).

width of the spiral track, the size of the Lead-in area and the lengths of the pits and lands, the same geometric area of the disc can contain sectors with different numbers! The probability of the fact that these sectors will coincide for two irrelevant lots of discs is negligible. Therefore, any attempt at blindly copying such a disc will fail.

Under such conditions, we'll have to play another trick, and imitate the read failure programmatically. The first idea that comes to mind is creating a simple CD-ROM emulator that would report read error, when an attempt is made to access sectors that are checked by the protection. This will deceive the protection mechanism. At the same time, both the emulator itself and the image of the original CD can be easily burnt into a CD-R disc, using the over-burn method. Another technique of cracking consists in the implementation of a resident program that intercepts all attempts at accessing CD-ROM and returns read error messages when checking specific CD sectors.

Both methods were already widely used by the time of MS-DOS and 5" diskettes, so it is a tried and true technology. Clearly, a CD isn't the same thing as a diskette, but the techniques for working with them are generally the same. The only problem is that Windows NT requires administrative privileges for installing a disc emulator, and not every user has been granted such privileges. With these considerations in mind, using the "interceptor" might be the better option, since no special privileges are required for intercepting API calls. All you have to do is to correct the import table! As a variant, it is possible to set breakpoints to API functions or set hooks on them. Which functions are to be intercepted will be covered later in this chapter.

One positive difference in favor of CDs when compared with diskettes is that they allow for the emulation of physical defects at the logical layer. Do you recall the error-correction codes located in the end of each sector? Now imagine what will happen if they are purposefully modified so that an irrecoverable error is reported even in cases where a sector was read successfully (an error that can't be corrected even by means of redundancy). The drive's firmware, having carefully analyzed the situation, even having attempted to read the sector several times, will finally cease these vain attempts to position the read and return an error message. However, we aren't going to clarify whether this was a physical or a logical error. This means that the software will consider both physical and logical errors as absolutely the same! In general, the protection might ask you to return the contents of the damaged sector in a RAW format. In this case, if the disc surface isn't physically damaged, this sector will be read successfully. If this is the case, we are dealing with a copy. However, not all drives support RAW reading. Therefore, most legal users will blame protection developers for any attempt at industrial use of this type of check. These complaints are caused by hardware incompatibilities, so this approach isn't recommended. However, developers of protection mechanisms can — to borrow a term from chess — play a knight's move. If the drive doesn't support RAW reading, then the protection relies on the information that is supplied to it. Otherwise, an additional check must be carried out. The copy will be usable only when inserted into the drives that do not support RAW reading.

Finally, it is possible to load the protection into disassembler/debugger, locate the procedure that checks for damaged sectors, and then crack it! Naturally, for this it is necessary to know how such a check is carried out, to which facts it is necessary to pay attention, and what to search for (don't even suggest a full analysis of the protection code).

Operating systems of the Windows family are surprisingly rich with the tools for working with CDs at the sector level. Besides the obvious `CreateFile/DeviceIoControl`, there are ASPI (Windows 9*x*/NT) and SPTI (Windows NT only). There is also a wide variety of other interfaces. When working under Windows 9*x*, you can directly call on the CDFS driver through the `ABSOLUTE_READ`[i] function — `INT 2Fh` (or, to be more precise, through the 16-bit DLL stub, calling the Simulate Real Mode Interrupt DPMI function[ii]). More detailed information on this topic is provided in the *Q137813 "How Win32 Applications Can Read CD-ROM Sectors in Windows 95"* technical note, which is supplied as part of Knowledge Base, accompanying the Microsoft Visual Studio product. There is also the source code of the function for working with the CD-ROM at the sector level.

Under Windows NT, reading/writing sectors is even easier. It is enough to open the disc in the cooked-mode[iii], after which it will be possible to work with it at the logical level. Figuratively speaking, the entire contents of the CD will be interpreted as one large file. A detailed description of this process can be found in the Q138434 *"How Win32-Based Applications Read CD-ROM Sectors in Windows NT"* technical note, which is part of the Microsoft Knowledge Base.

By the way, to check the disc for the existence of a physical defect, it isn't necessary to go to the raw sector level. File exchange is a tool that is just as efficient. Obviously, a file that contains at least one damaged sector can't be read, and any attempt at doing so will produce an error! The main advantage of this method is that it can be implemented using any language and operating with only standard capabilities. There is no need for API calls and a monstrous `IOTCL`. Calls to `fopen/fread` functions will be enough!

Thus, there are many different methods of binding to the disc, and locating the protection mechanism in the code of the application being cracked is a tedious job. If setting breakpoints to the `DeviceIoControl` function do not produce a result (which is rare), then you'll have a tough time. You might end up spending all night cracking this protection. Let API spy and context search help you. While you probably agree that everything is clear with the spy, you may ask, why do we need context search? Knowing the numbers of bad sectors, you can try to locate the corresponding con-

---

[i] `EAX := 1508h`, see *Interrupt List* by Ralf Braun.
[ii] This, by the way, is a very useful function, which allows win32 applications do whatever things that are allowed to MS-DOS applications (free access to the hardware, working with interrupts, and so on).
[iii] The disc can be opened in cooked mode by means of the `CreateFile` function called as follows: `hCD = CreateFile ("\\\\.\\X:", GENERIC_READ,FILE_SHARE_READ| FILE_SHARE_WRITE,NULL, OPEN_EXISTING, FILE_ATTRIBUTE_NORMAL, NULL)`; where X stands for the drive letter.

stants in the body of the program. If the developer of the protection mechanism hasn't used any other additional tricks, the numbers of the sectors being controlled are written in the program code "as is." In this case, all that remains to do is to set a breakpoint to the corresponding memory cell and wait until that cell is accessed. Naturally, if you are investigating the program on a disassembler instead of a debugger, you'll need to use cross-references instead of breakpoints.

If, despite all your efforts, you still cannot crack the protection, try to use Clone CD and/or Alcohol 120%. Both utilities recognize bad sectors and simulate them at the logical level. Clone CD does this using error-correction codes, while Alcohol 120% achieves the same goal using error-correction codes and virtual disc! As practice has shown, there is no need to use virtual disc in most cases. Protection mechanisms in most cases are very credulous, and can be deceived easily by changing the checksum of a sector.

Fig. 9.1. Disc with an intentionally damaged sector (a small "volcano" a little below
the middle of the screen). Using specialized equipment allows you to burn
the surface exactly in the center of the spiral track

Thus, the reliability of protection mechanisms based on this approach is unsatisfactory. You'll have to carefully weigh all of the pros and cons before you decide to implement this kind of protection in your programs. Any advanced user who has some experience in working with Clone CD, will copy such a disc easily — and you'll find yourself out of job. Furthermore, to create physical defects with the required precision and quality ("high-quality physical defect" is certainly an interesting phrase!), you'll require expensive equipment, something not available to every freelance programmer. With regard to scratching the disc with a needle, this is not an option. First, this method is unreliable, bad for the health of CD-ROM drives, and finally, not particularly aesthetically pleasing.

If you still decide to opt for this type of protection, bear in mind a few pieces of advice. First, introduce the damage on the side of protective layer, not on the side of the polycarbonate base. In other words, this should be done on the top side of the disc. When damaging the disc, remember that an attempt to create a deep radial scratch usually produces a very poor result. The disc loses its mechanical strength, which means that sooner or later, it will be torn to pieces by the centrifugal forces. This almost always means curtains for the CD-ROM drive. It is better to create a small pinhole in the reflective layer. This will be enough to make one or more sectors unreadable. This can be achieved using a normal sewing needle.

Now, let's discuss the question of how to avoid damaging useful data when introducing physical defects. Scratching the unwritten area of a CD is practically useless, because it won't be read. For this reason, as an experiment, write something useless to the test disc (something that you won't mind losing). One possible algorithm is as follows.

1. Take a new CD-R disc and burn to it all of the files of your program, except for the information contained in the protection mechanism that binds to the disc. As a rule, this will be the main executable file of your program, although the protection mechanism may be located in one of the DLLs or even implanted into a data file (although this, of course, is an exaggeration).

2. Press the <EJECT> button and, using any method, mark the location of the last written track (for instance, you can just measure the diameter of the burnt area using a ruler).

3. Once again, return the disc to the drive and write approximately 150 MB of garbage there. This trash will serve as the testing material for scratching. Don't close the session yet!

4. Now, introduce one or more physical defects to the disc. You can do this by prodding the area of the last written track with a sharp needle.

5. Start any disc doctor and register the positions of all of the bad sectors.

6. "Hard-encode" the numbers of bad sectors into the program that you are going to protect and burn the protection module to the CD-R, closing all sessions.

7. That's all! Your protection is ready for use.

Protection Mechanisms Based on the Read Timing Characteristics

A *read timing diagram* is probably the most easily measured but, at the same time, unique disc characteristic. It varies considerably from disc to disc. Let's carry out an easy experiment: Take any CD, create its copy, and then compare the read timing diagram of the copy to that of original. The result that the author obtained is illustrated by the two diagrams provided below (Fig. 9.2). (An "Agatha Christie" disc served as the test example and PHILIPS CDRW 24000 was the test burner. Disc copying and creating the graphs was carried out using Alcohol 120% and the copying was carried out on an IMATION 48x disc).

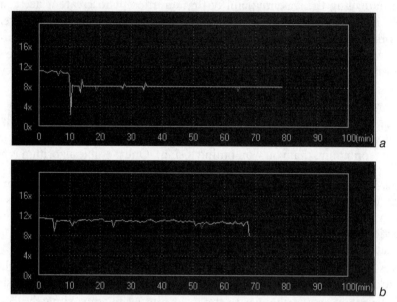

Fig. 9.2. Read timing diagrams of the original disc (*a*) and its copy (*b*)

Just look at the difference! All discs are not the same. They differ *so significantly* that this can be noticed with the naked eye! How can we use this difference for protecting programs? Identify some *node points* on the timing curve, which correspond to the "peaks," "dips" — or lack of either — in the specified section. Then convert them into the characteristic code, bearing in mind that the curve profile will change in the course of using the disc (and, besides, that it will vary from drive to drive). Some ruptures might appear, while others might disappear. Therefore, for disc identification, it will be necessary to use the fuzzy comparison algorithm, which means that under conditions where several nodal points match, the disc is considered to be original. Of course, the softer the selection criteria, the greater is the probability that the copyleft will be considered to be copyright. Excessively stringent criteria will engender excessive complaints from those users who own older drives that distort the timing curve in such a way that an original and legally purchased CD suddenly ceases to be recognized as such. According to the author's experience, a good balance between reliability and stability is ensured by the 3:10 ratio, which means that if at least three nodal points out of ten are recognized, the disc must be considered original. In the long run, it would be much better if the protection doesn't notice its presence than to swear at legal users.

We should mention that, for building a timing diagram, it isn't necessary to work with the disc at the sector level. Measuring read-timing characteristics for individual files produces an equivalent result. For this purpose, you can read using any standard means, such as, for instance, the `fread` built-in C function. Naturally, the files chosen for testing must be large. They must be large enough to guarantee that they don't fit into the cache memory and make the operating system access the hard disk instead of retrieving these files from the RAM. The drawback of this approach is that for building the timing curve, you'll have to read at least half of the entire disc (and this takes time), because the "resolution" capability of the file "measurer" is too low. On the other hand, won't you have to read the data written to the hard disc anyway? If so, why not combine the useful with the pleasant?!

If you are going to write a couple of small utilities to the disc, it is much better to measure the reading time of individual sectors for binding to the disc. Since the sector lengths "drift" within a wide range because of technology imperfection, the time required for the drive to read them also drifts, because the disc rotation speed is constant! Well… practically constant. CDs, being self-synchronizing devices by their nature, do not impose stringent requirements on the drive-rotation speed. The main thing here is that the speed gradient must be considerably lower than the frequency of changes from pits to lands (because the generator is self-tuning when crossing their boundaries). It isn't difficult to show that if the angular rotation speed of the disc is constant, its linear speed along the spiral track inevitably grows. If no additional measures are taken, the pits on the external sectors of the disc will sweep by with such speed that the laser head won't have time to read them. To prevent this, special mechanisms for dynamic regulation are used in CD-ROM drives to keep the linear-rotation speed within *predefined limits*. Besides, the specific values of linear and angular rotation speeds are unknown, and we cannot measure them with the necessary precision. If the disc-rotation speed is unknown, how can we measure the sector length?

Let's base our examination on the fact that for the short section of the spiral track disc rotation speed will remain more or less constant. By comparing the read times of the neighboring sectors, we'll be able to determine the approximate relation between their lengths. If there is a short sector between two long sectors, there will be a peak on the graph. On the other hand, if the lengths of three or more sectors are more or less identical, there will be a long "plateau" on the graph.

The results of investigating one of my own discs are shown in Fig. 9.3. This dull pattern, somewhat similar to a two-handled saw, is very capricious by its nature. Repeated runs of the program with the same disc will repeatedly produce different results. Nevertheless, most peaks and pits coincide, and it is still possible to identify the original disc.

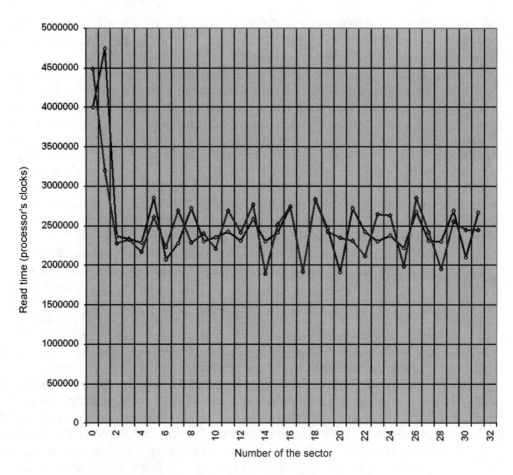

Fig. 9.3. Nodal profiles obtained from two runs of the same disc

Now let's copy the disc and try to compare the obtained copy to the original. The pattern has changed! The relief has changed to a degree that makes it unrecognizable. First, the tops of peaks do not match. Second, the number of "pits" on the duplicate is surprisingly low (perhaps, it was a good disc specimen). Finally, instead of the large "trident" between the 14th and 22nd sectors that was present in the original, there is a large plateau sloping downward on the copy.

Thus, measuring relative sector read times allows us to distinguish the original disc from its replica unambiguously. At the same time, such measurements can be easily carried out using the operating system's built-in tools and is compatible with practically all drive models.

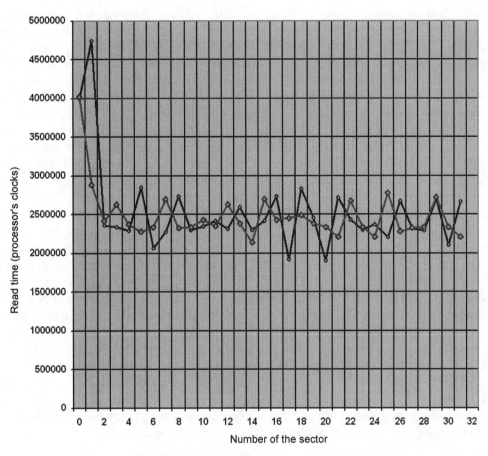

Fig. 9.4. Nodal profiles of two different discs

Measuring Angles between Sectors

Having heard that some protection mechanisms measure the angle between the first and the last logical blocks on the CD, I began to wonder how they actually do this? Because I didn't have programs protected using this method, and developers, naturally, do not disclose the technical details of its implementation, I had to use logical deduction and confirm them through practical experiments. Having ruined a pack of CD-R discs and spent an entire day, I managed to discover the secret method and created a functional protection system. Let's proceed step by step.

As a matter of fact, CDs are sequential-access devices with accelerated rewinding, which is carried out by means of radial movement of the optical head along the spiral track. Having moved along the track a certain distance, the head positions itself to a new track and waits for the arrival of the nearest sync group, which marks the start of each sector. Having read the address contained in its header, the head compares the current address with that which is required and, if necessary, moves forward or backward. This process is repeated until the head comes sufficiently close to the required sector (within the range of a single disc turn). Now the head stops fussing about and waits until the sector reaches its field of sight.

Let's assume that searching for the required track always takes the same time. Although this is not exactly soo the case, this assumption will do as the starting point for our discussion, since the positioning of the head to sectors located on adjacent spiral turns is carried out by means of head deflection by a magnetic field. This means that it takes place practically instantly. The head is moved in "slides" by a special drive mechanism, which operates at snail speed only in cases of positioning the head to remote sectors. Based on our assumption, the full access time to the sector will depend directly on the angle between the current sector and the sector that was read last (Fig. 9.5). Accordingly, having measured the access time, we will be able to measure the angle. The only problem consists in determining the head-positioning time. Since it varies significantly from drive to drive, we cannot rely on the absolute access time. However, relative changes are clearly discernible. Sequentially moving the head between sector 0 and sectors X, $X + 1$, $X + 2$, $X + 3$ we will observe "wave-like" fluctuations in the full access time. Wave crests correspond to the maximum angle between these sectors, while wave troughs correspond to the minimum angle (in this case, the required sector is encountered immediately after the positioning process is completed). Having registered sector combinations corresponding to the minimum and the maximum, let's try to compare this combination to the same combination obtained for the disc duplicate.

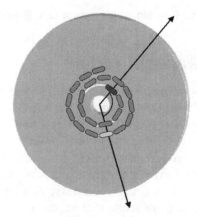

Fig. 9.5. Measuring the angle between sectors

Have we succeeded? Actually, different lots of CD-R discs are formatted differently, and the density of their spiral tracks is also different. Because of this, the angle between our sectors is also not the same, and these differences grow sharply with the growth of the distance between sectors. Let's assume that the difference between the average sector length on the original and duplicate is 0.01 percent. Then, provided that full disc capacity is about 350,000 sectors, the change of the angle between the first and the last disc sector will be 3.5%, which is a measurable value. In practice, the declared formatting precision is never observable. When copying a model disc to media from other manufacturers, angular differences sometimes are as high as 180 degrees!

Specially for this purpose, I have developed a program, which I called CD-physical pattern detector. Because of the limited volume of this book, I won't provide its listing here, because it is quite large, and, anyway, the source code of this program can be found on the companion CD. Two screenshots illustrating its operation are shown in Figs. 9.6 and 9.7. Having started it for execution and after allowing the CD-ROM drive to move its head for some time (the protection mechanism is actually recognized by these movements), we will discover that the access time to sectors with different numbers is measured in an interesting way (Fig. 9.6). Four or five neighboring sectors are read with approximately the same speed, then the curve bends sharply, almost doubling the access time. After one or more sectors, the access time changes stepwise once again. The alternation of peaks and pits is strictly periodical, deviating from the average position by only several sectors, which is probably caused by the variable time of the optical head's moves. Naturally, the older the drive is, the lower is the measurement precision. However, if we have a large sample of measurements (Fig. 9.7), the measurement error will be relatively low.

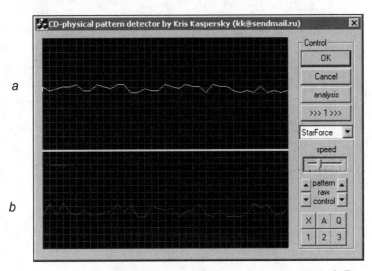

Fig. 9.6. CD-physical pattern detector: *a*— unprotected disc,
b — disc protected by StarForce

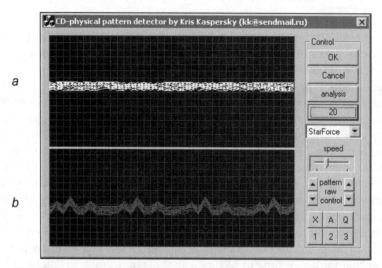

Fig. 9.7. CD-physical pattern detector at work: *a* — unprotected disc, *b* — disc protected by StarForce. The program actually allows to see the pattern! Provided that we have a large sample of measurements, the measurement error will be relatively low

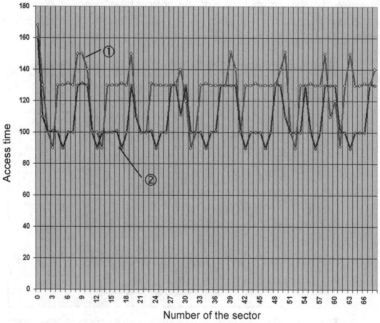

Fig. 9.8. The spiral track profile for IMATION (1) and TDK (2) discs

Fig. 9.8 shows profiles of spiral tracks created for two different discs. The first curve (1) corresponds to the disc produced by IMATION, while the second one (2) relates to a disc from TDK. Notice the difference between the two graphs!

Protection Mechanisms Based on Weak Sectors

I had already had plenty of hacking experience when I first encountered these protection mechanisms, but I was greatly impressed by them all the same — anybody would be! Consider for yourself — copying of the protected disc takes place normally and without error. However, when the copy is checked, this check reveals numerous bad sectors, which show up even when the contents of the original disc are copied to the hard disk file by file and then burnt onto the CD-R from there. What causes this effect? Is it a hardware malfunction or, possibly, the result of operations by some intricate driver, secretly installed by the protection during the first run of the protected program? The answer is no.. All of the equipment is operating normally and there is no stealth driver lurking. Bad sectors appear even when the disc is copied on a brand new computer with a freshly installed OS.

Investigating the files being copied using debugger (HEX editor, disassembler) doesn't reveal anything unusual either. If we crack the protection based on binding to the CD (provided that it is present there), then the protected application will start successfully from a hard disk (or Zip drive). It will, however, still be impossible to burn it onto the CD-R. If the protected files are corrected in some way (for example, by being compressed using any archiver), they will be copied to CD-R successfully and without errors. This, however, isn't exactly what we are after.

Thus, the reason for the strange behavior on the part of the protection must lie at the physical, and not the software level. This is the most cunning anti-debugging technique that I have ever encountered! Actually, from the point of view of a hacker without access to sophisticated measurement equipment at his disposal, a CD-ROM drive is a "black box," operating according to approximately the same principle as any other storage media. Even if we open it, we won't see anything other than a mess of wires and chips. The only thing that remains is to read the standards carefully. After all, if the protection mechanism works on all (or at least on the overwhelming majority of) CD-ROM models, it must be based on standard properties, features or characteristics.

Here is one part of the standard: *"A regular bit pattern fed into the EFM encoder can cause large values for the Digital Sum Value in cases where the merging bits cannot reduce this value (see annex E). The scrambler* reduces this risk *by converting the bits in bytes from 12 to 2, 351 of a Sector in a prescribed way"*. If you still think that CD-ROMs are the ideal storage media for executable files and databases, you are sadly mistaken. CDs were initially developed for storage and playback of music. Only after considerable efforts and wondrous advances in engineering theory did they agree to store binary data.

Note the non-itatlicized words in the quotation above. Scrambler does not guarantee that the data being written will be readable. It simply reduces the risk of encountering unfavorable (from the drive's point of view) sequences to an acceptable level. Nevertheless, with enough effort, it is quite possible to create a couple of files stuffed with such unfavorable sequences. Theoretically, these files will be readable, but only CD-ROM models of the highest quality will be able to cope with this task, while all others will fail and return an error message.

Let's consider the following combination: 04 B9 04 B9 04 B9... Having revised the EFM encoding table, we will find out that 04 is converted to 01000100000000, and B9 to 10000000001001. Now let us try to write them together: 01000100000000 xxx 10000000001001 yyy 01000100000000, where xxx and yyy are merging bits. Since 04 has eight trailing zeros, and B9 starts with 1, the only possible combination for the first set of merging bits will be 100. Accordingly, because B9 is terminated by 1 and 04 has only one starting zero, the only possible combination for the second set of merging bits will be 000.

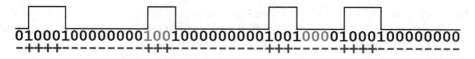

Fig. 9.9. Physical representation of the 04 B9 04 sequence

Look at the effect that this sequence will produce (Fig. 9.9). The DSV value is sharply negative! This means that pits dominate over lands and disc surface becomes very dark. Consequently, the tracking device will lose the track because of insufficient brightness of the light falling into the photoelectric receptor. Most interesting here is the fact that, according to the standard, such bit combinations are not obliged to be readable (although some drive models cope with this task successfully). Would anyone still cling to the fallacy that CDs represent a reliable storage medium?

If, of course, we simply create a file stuffed with \x04\xB9\x04\xB9..., the process of its recording and subsequent reading will take place without problems, because the data flow being recorded is scrambled previously! A scrambling algorithm chosen on the basis of expertise shouldn't allow for effective conversion. Otherwise, the hacker can pass the most unfavorable regular sequences through an "anti-scrambler," and then, after repeated scrambling, they will be written to the disc in their initial form. So here's a complaint — the scrambling algorithm used by the CD-ROM allows for this kind of reversible conversion! All you'll need for the writing of an anti-scrambler is a couple of free evenings and the text of the ECMA-120 standard. Since the scrambling algorithm is based on the XOR function, repeated scrambling of the data already processed by the scrambler converts this data back to its initial form. Thanks to this, we can get by with just one function — that of the scrambler.

Having passed the protected files through the scrambler, we will discover that they contain at least one very unfavorable sequence, for which the DSV is strongly negative (or on rare occasions, strongly positive). Generally speaking, it is considerably different from zero. Having complemented the scrambler with the function for computing DSV (details of its implementation are described in ECMA-120), we will get an automatic scanner for protection mechanisms based on weak sectors. Wow! Isn't this great?! If particular unfavorable sequences are discovered in the protected files, don't even try to copy them to CD-R — you'll fail.

But how can we explain the fact that these same unfavorable sequences are successfully read from the original disc?! To answer this question, we'll have to go deep into the maze of CD spiral tracks. This travel will be long and full of dangers. People will try to warn you and talk you out of it. For instance, here is a quotation from the work of some anonymous author: *"...actually, things are even more interesting, since, in addition to sectors, there are also sections of the same effective size, but having mismatching boundaries, part of the addresses being sector addresses and part being section addresses. However, it is better to forget about it immediately;)"*. The smiley sign terminating this phrase stimulates your curiosity and leads you to reread the standard repeatedly (because, unfortunately, there is nothing more informative at hand). One way or another (see the forum on **http://club.cdfreaks.com**), we will discover that boundaries of sectors and frames may or may not coincide. The sector can start from 0, 4, 8, 12, 16, or the 20th byte! Changing the starting point inevitably changes the DSV of the first frame and the most interesting facts begin here. If the number of binary ones of the frame is odd, then the second frame is inverted (which means that the pits and lands exchange positions). Otherwise, the next frame appears "as is." Thanks to this, it becomes possible to compose a regular sequence that will be quite favorable for one of the entry points and very unfavorable for all others.

Unfortunately, recorders still do not allow you to choose the entry point arbitrarily, and set it on by themselves and at their own discretion. Good recorders (like Plextor) choose the entry point so as to minimize the absolute value of the sector DSV (because of this, they allow for the copying of protected discs without problems). Unfortunately, the vast majority of other models aren't this clever, and cannot cope with the task of DSV minimization. Either they don't try to compute the correct entry point or they compute it incorrectly. Consequently, errors appear when trying to read the copies of protected discs.

Nevertheless, advanced copiers (Clone CD, for example) have long ago bypassed protections of this type. How did they manage this ? Having prepared the sector image for burning in the raw mode, they slightly disfigure its contents, thus breaking the unfavorable sequences (the inversion of a single data bit of the source data will dramatically change the data after scrambling). Error correction codes (prepared beforehand for the source data) *are not changed*. As a result, writing the sector written using this method will produce an error, and the drive will have to correct it on the basis of redundant information contained in the error-correction codes. After correction, the sector is returned to its initial state.

The advantage of this approach is that the copy of the protected disc contains a weakened protection mechanism that can be freely duplicated in raw mode. Standard copying will result in error, though, because honest copiers place "corrected" sectors on the CD. On the other hand, copiers writing sectors "as is" cannot differentiate intentionally introduced errors from physical read errors. Writing the uncorrected sector will result in the growth of the number of errors. Consequently, when attempting to make a copy of a copy, we may receive an unreadable duplicate (a considerable drawback). Is there any way out? Read the sector, correct it, pass it through the scanner, and, if any unfavorable sequence is detected there, intentionally invert one or more bits there. Copying errors will then cease to accumulate!

Chapter 10: Data Recovery from CDs

CD-R and CD-RW discs represent ideal backup media for saving moderate amounts of information (and any serious programmer carries out periodical backups of the information entrusted to him or her). Unfortunately, no one is perfect, and no job can be completed without some danger of errors (ERRARE HUMANUM EST "To err is human", as the ancients said). Therefore, the accidental deletion of files from CD-R/CD-RW discs, as well as the clearing of these disks, sometimes happens. Experience, in fact, suggests that this happens far too often.

To our knowledge, special utilities for restoring lost information from CDs have yet to be developed (or, at least, be widely available on the market), therefore, recovering information from corrupted CDs is something you will have to tackle on your own. In this chapter, we'll try to explain what can be done in this case and how to accomplish this task.

Restoring Deleted Files from CD-R/CD-RW

Having announced their support for multisession CDs, Microsoft's operating systems, including Windows 9*x* and all versions of Windows NT (up to W2K) have maintained their silence about the fact that this support is only partial. Each session is a standalone volume (a logical disk, according to Windows terminology), which has its own file system and its own files. Thanks to the pass-trough numbering of CD sectors, the file system of one session can reference files physically located in any other session. In order to ensure the possibility to work with the disk in the same way as with a unified volume, the file system of the last session must include the contents of the file systems of all previous sessions. If this condition isn't met, then the TOCs of all other sessions will be lost when viewing the disk using standard equipment. This is the case because Windows mounts only the last session of the disk and ignores all the others. Programs for burning CD-R/CD-RW discs, by default, add the contents of the file systems from the previous sessions to the current one. However, this doesn't necessarily mean that the last session *always* contains everything that was present in the previous sessions.

For example, let's look at how files are deleted from CD-R/CD-RW disks. No, this isn't a misprint (or an error, or a joke)! The contents of CD-R disks can, in principle, be deleted, despite the impossibility of re-writing them. To imitate file deletion, CD burners simply do not include a reference to the file that has to be "deleted" into the file system of the last session[i]. Consequently, although the "deleted" file is still present on the disk (it is physically present, since it takes up some disk space[ii]), this file won't be displayed in the directory when viewing the disk contents using Windows' built-in tools. So what is the meaning of "deleting" files from the CD-R if the available disk space isn't increased, but, on the contrary, *is reduced*?! In fact, the actual sense of this operation (if, of course, we can use the term "sense") lies in hiding the "deleted" files from normal users. Since deleted files aren't visible when viewing the disk contents using standard tools, they are formally unavailable to the normal user. As a result, they are not available for Windows standard built-in tools. On the other hand, Macintosh allows the user to mount any disk session as a separate volume, thanks to which all "deleted" files immediately reveal themselves when viewing multisession discs under Mac OS.

The situation is similar when deleting information from CD-RW discs. Despite the theoretical possibility of physically destroying their contents, most programs for writing disks support only a function for clearing the entire disk, and are unable to delete

---

[i] However, not all programs are capable of doing so. For example, Roxio Easy CD Creator provides this possibility, while Stomp Record Now! doesn't.

[ii] The reduction of available free space is explained by the fact that each newly opened session requires some space. However, if deletion of some files is accompanied by writing another files, it is necessary to open a new session, anyway, and in this case the deletion overhead is not present.

individual files. Thus, all that was said above about CD-R discs is equally applicable to CD-RWs.

Therefore, *if you write information to a disc in order to pass it to a third party, never use discs that have contained confidential data.* The "deletion" of data previously written to a disk doesn't mean complete removal!

Viewing the contents of a CD that you have received from a friend or colleague, or even just recovered from the garbage, it makes sense to try viewing previous sessions. Sometimes, it is possible to find a lot of hidden information. As experience has shown that there is often much of interest to be found. On the other hand, you might need to restore incidentally deleted files from your own disk, or even recover an entire session that has been destroyed by accident. (Some programs for writing CDs allow users to choose: they can either add a file system from the previous session when creating a new session, or include only new files in the new session. Choosing incorrect settings when preparing to write a CD will result in the loss of the contents of all of the previous sessions. Fortunately, however, this loss is reversible.)

The lack of standard tools for the selective mounting of sessions seriously complicates the life of all Windows users, leaving them to search for ways to bypass this problem. Ideally, it is best to implement a custom CDFS driver providing the required minimum of functional capabilities. However, this task is not simple and involves serious labor. This undertaking only makes sense in cases where you need to recover accidentally deleted files several times a day. Writing a set of utilities for working directly with the disc at the physical level is much simpler. In this case, all that you need is a display of the contents of the file system in a readable form. We are particularly interested in the following information: the file name and its starting address and length. Knowing these three important attributes, you can "grab" the file to the hard disk with ease and then do whatever you need with it. This technique is ideal for recovering small amounts of deleted (overwritten) files from any sessions. However, it is not practical in those situations where it is necessary to recover the entire session. In such cases, it makes more sense to copy the sessions being recovered to a separate CD-R/CD-RW disc.

Getting Access to Deleted Files

Before we start recovering deleted files, let's recall the main principles of ISO 9660 (Joliet) file system organization. The 16th sector of the first track of each session is strictly bound to the primary volume descriptor. This is easily recognized by the CD001 signature, which is stored in the sector by offset 1. If this is really the case (suppose that we have a disc without a file system, such as an Audio CD), then at the offset 156 of this sector you'll find the *Directory Record* of the root directory. Above all, the following fields of this record are of the highest importance: the length of the Directory

Record itself (the byte at offset 0), the starting LBA address of a file/subdirectory (double word; in low-endian format, by offset 2), the length of file/subdirectory (double word; in low-endian format, by offset 10), the file attributes (byte by offset 25), the length of the name of the file/subdirectory (byte at the offset 32) and, finally, the file-name itself (the chain of bytes starting at the offset 33). The Joliet file system is organized in a similar manner. Its corresponding volume descriptor, however, is located in sector 17, instead of sector 16.

If the first bit, counting from zero, is set to 1, then we are dealing with a subdirectory. Otherwise, the object in question represents a file. Nested directories (subdirectories) represent sets of Directory Records, each of which points either to a file or to another subdirectory.

Therefore, in order to view the contents of an arbitrary session, we need only know the starting address of its first track. This information can be obtained easily by reading the TOC at the raw level (command: 43h, format: 02h). Besides this, it is possible to use any CD-burning utility that is able to display information about the disc geometry (for instance, utilities such as Roxio Easy CD Creator, Stomp Record Now!, Ahead Nero — Burning Rom, and many other tools, are capable of doing this). Having increased the starting address of the first track by 16 (when working with ISO 9660) or 17 sectors (for working with Joliet), we will find the volume descriptor, i.e., the root directory. After that, recursive traversing of the directory tree will function as a well-lubricated mechanism. While running Windows, there is not even the need to worry about stack overflow, provided, of course, that the file system doesn't contain severe errors that will result in a fall into infinite loops (by the way, these types of tricks are frequently used in protection mechanisms).

Now, all that is left is to view the directories of all of the disk sessions in order to find the files that are missing from the directory of the last session. When doing so, it is necessary to pay attention not only to file names, but also to their starting addresses. Files having identical names, but different starting addresses, are different files! For example, if you periodically save your entire current project to CD, always writing it with the same name, then all previous versions of this file will be lost for the built-in Windows tools. However, a "manual" investigation of the contents of all of the sessions will allow you to recover any of the file versions that were earlier saved on the CD! By the way, in practice, this need arises frequently, so this skill is always useful.

For further experiments, we will need the ISO9660.dir utility, which was can be found on the companion CD. Using any CD burning program, let's write three sessions on CD-RW/CD-R so that the first or the second session will contain some "deleted" files that we actually need to find.

Let's assume that the starting addresses of the disk sessions are located as shown below.

Listing 10.1. The starting addresses of the first tracks of each of the three disk sessions (track number AA is the Lead-out area and doesn't present any interest to us)

```
> ISO9660.dir.exe 1.1
track |  Start LBA
------+-----------
   1  |         0
   2  |     13335
   3  |     22162
  AA  |     24039
```

Now, let's call the ISO9660.dir.exe utility consecutively, specifying for it the following starting addresses: 0, 13335 and 22162. Having done so, we'll see the contents of the first, second, and third sessions, respectively. For convenience of comparison, the result is presented in the form of a horizontal table:

Listing 10.2. A comparison of the contents of the directories of three sessions shows that the second session contains the deleted file, "See You.mp3" (in this listing, in bold), which is missing from the third session

```
>ISO9660.dir 1.1 0 -Joliet
start|size    |name
-----+-------+-----------------
22   |2048   |.
22   |2048   |..
25   |3591523|PersonalJesus.mp3


>ISO9660.dir 1.1 13335 -Joliet
start|size    |name
-----+-------+-----------------
13357|2048   |.
13357|2048   |..
25   |3591523|PersonalJesus.mp3
13360|3574805|See You.mp3


>ISO9660.dir 1.1 22162 -Joliet
start|size    |name
-----+-------+-----------------
22184|2048   |.
22184|2048   |..
25   |3591523|PersonalJesus.mp3
22187|3472405|Strangerlove.mp3
```

As you can see, the second session contains the "See You.mp3" file, which is missing from the TOC of the third session. This means that this file is practically unavailable to built-in OS tools! In fact, the `dir` command shows only two files:

Listing 10.3. The operating system views the disc contents as shown in this listing. However, we aren't so easily deceived! We know that there is one deleted file

---

```
The volume in drive G has the NEW label.
 Volume serial number: 4171-70DC


 Contents of the G:\ directory

30.06.2003  00:10          3 591 523 01 — Personal Jesus.mp3
30.06.2003  00:12          3 472 405 03 — Strangerlove.mp3
2 files         7 063 928 bytes
                0 folders     0 bytes free
```

In order to restore this file, it is enough to run our utility with the following command-line options: `ISO9660.dir.exe 1.1 "See You.mp3" 13360 3574805` or to use any program capable of grabbing disc sectors (in this case, however, we'll have to "cut off" the tail of the last sector by the required value manually). Briefly speaking, we must read 3,574,805 bytes, starting from sector 13,360, up to the last sector of the file (because of the lack of sector fragmentation, sectors belonging to the file are always located sequentially).

If everything has been done correctly, a new See You.mp3 file will appear on the hard disk, which you can play using any mp3-player. It is also possible to use any CD-burning program to write the restored file to the same CD by adding another session to it. Of course, this is not the optimal solution, since the recovered file will now be written twice. Unfortunately, however, none of the burner utilities with which I am familiar allows for interfering with the process of file system generation or for the manual creation of links to files from previous sessions.

Now let's prepare the disc so that we can test the recovery procedures. Write a file to CD. Then, after modifying its contents slightly, write the file to the same disc under the same name one or more times. Make sure that when you are viewing the disc contents using built-in standard Windows tools you can see only one file — namely, the one that was written last. Now imagine that it is of critical importance to gain access to one of the earlier versions. No problem! Start `ISO9660.dir`, and you'll see that the disc contains the sessions shown in Listing 10.4.

Listing 10.4. The disk being recovered has two sessions with starting addresses equal to 0 and 12,000, respectively

```
>ISO9660.dir.exe 1.1
track |  Start LBA
------+-----------
   1  |         0
   2  |     12000
  AA  |     12600
```

By consecutively starting the ISO9660.dir utility with the 0 and 12.000 command-line options, you'll find that... Well, don't rush forward. Now you'll see everything for yourself.

Listing 10.5. Both sessions contain the same file, asm.drf.zip; however, the starting addresses of the file don't match, and their lengths are also different

```
>  ISO9660.dir.exe 1.1 0 -Joliet      >  ISO9660.dir.exe 1.1 12000 -Joliet
 start   | size   | name              start   | size   | name
 --------+--------+-----------        --------+--------+-----------
 22      |2048    |.                  12022   |2048    |.
 22      |2048    |..                 12022   |2048    |..
 25      |38189   |asm.drf.zip        12025   |354533  |asm.drf.zip
```

At first glance, everything appears to be OK. The asm.drf.zip file is present in both sessions, and if you aren't careful enough, it could seem to you that you are dealing with the same file in both cases. However, a closer investigation shows that starting addresses of the files do not match. Therefore, we are dealing with two different files! The file lengths are also different and, to all appearances, the last file represents a newer version. To retrieve the previous version of the file, issue the following command: ISO9660.dir.exe 1.1 asm.drf.zip 25 38189. It really works!

The ISO9660.dir.exe utility is, unfortunately, terribly inconvenient for practical use. But don't judge it too severely. After all, it is only a demo example. In an attempt to stimulate the reader's creativity, I suggest that you implement all of the missing functionality on your own. Task number would be the development of a convenient GUI for the program, or, even better, the rewriting of it as a console application. For example, you can write a plug-in for FAR Manager displaying the contents of the chosen session in a pane. This is considerably simpler to do than to program a fully-functional disk driver. From the end-user point of view, however, the effect will be the same. The task of comparing file names and starting addresses should be automated, since manual searches for deleted or overwritten files are extremely inefficient. In fact, a typical CD-ROM contains thousands or even tens thousands of files distributed over a large tree-like hierarchy. Naturally, testing and analyzing them all is a tedious proposition!

Recovering Entire Sessions

An alternative method for the recovery of deleted files consists of the removal of one or more of the last sessions from the disc (we will refer to this method as "peeling the onion"). When proceeding in this manner, you expose each previous "layer," which now becomes the most recent and, consequently, the one accessible by the operating system's standard tools. Naturally, physically removing sessions from CD-R discs is virtually impossible (the removal of sessions from CD-RW discs is theoretically possible. The problem here, however, lies in the lack of required software). However, nothing prevents us from saving a disk image as a file, process the created file appropriately, and then burn it again. (In the case of a CD-RW, the same disc can be used. In the case of CD-R's, we need a new disc.) No one would argue that this method isn't long and tedious, but no more so than writing a custom burning program.

So let's start to prepare an experimental disk. Write one or two sessions on the test CD, instructing the burning program to join the file system of the new session with that of all previous ones (this usually takes place by default). Then, let's add another session, this time separate from all of the others. To do this, in Ahead Nero, you have to choose the **Start Multisession disk** menu item, instead of **Continue Multisession**. In Stomp Record Now!, it is necessary to select the **New Volume** option, instead of **Load Last Track**. When you start the recorder to burn a CD, you will notice that the contents of all previous sessions have been lost. For the sake of accuracy, we should point out that, for instance, Stomp Record Now! allows you to recover the "ruined" disk easily. To do this, simply choose the **Load Track 1** item from the **Mutlisession** drop-down list and write any file to the disc. This is necessary in order to initiate the recording process. After this, the contents of session 1 will appear, while that of the session 2 will disappear into thin air. Is this a problem? Let's change the option from **Load Track 1** to **Load Track 2** and initiate recording once again. This time the contents of the first two sessions will reappear, plus some files that we were forced to record in order to get Stomp Record Now! to agree and start burning.

Ahead Nero, when the **Continue Multisession** option has been selected, automatically requests that the user specify the session which holds the contents that it should use. Unfortunately, current versions of this program do not allow for the merging of the TOCs of two or more sessions. If there is, however, such a need, it is possible to use the sequential "cascading" method described above.

If you do not have Stomp Record Now! (or a similar program) at your disposal, it will be necessary to recover the overwritten sessions manually, i.e., using programs such as Clone CD or Alcohol 120%. Let's create one more test disc, the last session of which overwrites all of those before it. Then use Clone CD to create a disc image, and then the only thing left to do is to discard all references to the last session from the IMAGE.CCD file. The contents of the Sessions field must first be decreased by one.

Then, it is necessary to discard all [Entry] sections, for which the Session value was the latest. Then subtract the number of the deleted [Entry] sessions from the value of the TocEntries field, and, finally, remove the last [TRACK] section. Now, the edited image can be written to a new CD and there will be no last session — just as if it had never been present!

Beginners' Errors, or What You Should Never Do

You will sometimes hear the suggestion that grabbing one of the sessions of the disc being recovered, turning it into an ISO image and, then, mounting it to a virtual CD-ROM drive (or burning it to a physical disc) will make it possible to access its contents. In this way, we'll be able to quickly view the contents of all required sessions.

You'll be able to access the deleted files and do whatever you want with them. Be careful! When viewing the contents of the grabbed session, always bear in mind that: First, files belonging physically to other sessions will be still not available from the current session, despite abundant references to these files. When referencing a file that doesn't really exist, you'll either be confronted with some senseless garbage or an error message. Your system may also end up freezing. If this happens, simply press the <EJECT> button. Windows will immediately wake up and joyfully display a Device not ready message. Second, because of the pass-through sector addressing, each grabbed session must be written to the same disc location where it was located earlier, or all references to starting file addresses within that session will become invalid. Usually, the desired result can be achieved by means of changing the starting address of the first track. The method for doing this will be described in the next section, which is dedicated to restoring information from cleared CD-RW discs.

Restoring Cleared CD-RW Discs

There are two principally different methods of clearing CD-RW discs: *quick* and *full*. When carrying out quick erasing, only the TOC area is actually removed from the disc. As a result, the disc appears to be a "blank" one, even though its main contents remain intact. When carrying out full erasing, conversely, the laser "burns" the entire disc surface, from the first pit to the last. Naturally, this process takes time, with the full erasing of a disc taking about 10 minutes, while quick erasing can be done in just a couple.

The recovery of fully erased discs is possible only using special equipment that is capable of detecting even the slightest changes in the reflective character of the reflecting layer. Naturally, this kind of equipment is not available to most users. On the other hand, discs that have been erased using quick methods can be restored on a standard recorder, although not every model is suitable for this purpose.

We won't concentrate here on the ethical aspects of this problem. For simplicity, let us suppose that you need to recover your own CD-RW disc that you have accidentally erased. Or, suppose that this will be a perfectly legal operation requested by your employer. Bear in mind, however, that restoring confidential information from erased CD-RW discs belonging to someone else can be classified as unauthorized access to that information and can bring with it legal consequences. To carry out experiments related to the recovery of information from cleared CD-RW discs, you'll need the following:

❏ *A CD-RW drive* that doesn't keep the correctness of TOC contents too carefully, supporting the RAW DAO mode and capable of reading the Pre-gap content of the first track. Bear in mind that not every CD-RW drive is suitable for this purpose, therefore, be prepared to test a lot of different devices. For example, of the two devices that I have at my disposal, only the NEC drive is suitable for this purpose, while PHILIPS is unable to do this.

❏ *Recording software characterized by advanced capabilities*, allowing for the manipulation of the service areas of the disc as necessary. For instance, you can use Clone CD, CDRWin, Alcohol 120%, or any other similar utility of your choice. However, all of the material that follows is oriented exclusively towards use of Clone CD. Thus, if you choose another utility, you might encounter some problems. If you are not sure that you'll be able to solve these problems on your own, use Clone CD, and later on, as you acquire the required experience and professional skills, you'll become able to restore discs using other similar program.

❏ *Some tool for working with the disc at the sector level.* This must be a utility allowing you to read any specified sector (provided, of course, that this sector can be read by the drive equipment), which doesn't attempt to skip sectors that, according to its own reading, do not contain anything of interest. The copiers of protected discs listed above are not suitable for this purpose, since they refuse to read sectors that are "useless" from the program's point of view. There may be some copiers that behave differently, but I am unaware of any. Instead of testing one copier after another, I have written the required utility myself.

Before starting our experiments, let us try to understand why the disc becomes unreadable after being cleared. This question isn't as silly as it seems. After all, the information required for positioning the head and searching for the required sectors remains intact after fast disc clearing! Control information is distributed along the entire spiral track. Thus, for reading the disc at the sector level, TOC is not, generally speaking, required at all. While, admittedly, missing TOC significantly complicates the analysis of the disc geometry, and, in the general case, the drive has to read the entire disc in order to determine the number of disc tracks/sessions. However, when recovering the lost information, the time factor isn't the thing of primary importance, and can be neglected.

Nevertheless, after any attempt at reading any sector of the cleared disc, the drive persistently returns an error. Why is this? The answer is straightforward and easy. This is simply to protect against reading information that is certain to be incorrect. Not a single one of the drives with which I am familiar could read a single sector outside the Lead-out area (in fact, at the software level, the contents of Lead-in/Lead-out areas also is unavailable). Nevertheless, this isn't a principal or conceptual limitation. Removing "extra" checks from the drive firmware will allow us to read such disks easily. I'm not suggesting that you disassemble the firmware code. This is a difficult, labor-consuming task, that is, most of all, particularly safe. If you hack the firmware incorrectly, you'll ruin the entire drive, without hope of repairing it. We'll go about this another way!

The method for recovering information that I suggest is, generally, writing a fictitious TOC to the disc. The Lead-in and Lead-out addresses of this TOC must point to the first and the last sectors of the disc, respectively, and the starting address of the first track must coincide exactly with the end of the Pre-gap area, which, according to the standard, must occupy no less than 150 sectors (or 2 seconds, if converted to absolute addresses). After this easy operation, the drive will obediently read the original content of the cleared disc, provided, of course, that we manage to tune the CD burning software in such a way as to make no attempts at interpreting the pointers to Lead-in/Lead-Out areas supplied to it as an instruction to burn the entire disc surface after writing a fictitious TOC.

Experience has shown that Clone CD refuses to write such a TOC, complaining about the mismatched sizes of the disc and image file. Alcohol 120% carries out this task without any complaint, but does so in a manner that is not what we desire! Having stuffed the entire disc with unimaginable garbage, it informs us that write errors have occurred, and that, possibly, we must check the equipment usability.

Well, let's try another approach. Let's write one real track to the disc, taking up the maximum possible number of sectors (300, according to standards, although some drives are quite content with smaller values), but also extend the Pre-gap from two seconds to the entire drive! As a result, we'll lose only 300 trailing sectors, but, in exchange, we'll gain access to the entire remainder of the contents. Taking into account that that there are slightly above 300,000 such sectors on the disc, it isn't difficult to determine that the percentage of successfully recovered information will be about 99.999 percent of the total disc capacity, provided that the entire disc was filled with useful info (which is a rarity in itself). If you are not satisfied with this, it makes sense to develop a custom program that can correctly write a fictitious TOC. The TOC area is written by the drive itself on any occasion, however, it is possible to do without Lead-out if you carefully treat the disc. The main goal in this case is an attempt to correctly read the sectors that fall beyond the disc limits. Otherwise, the drive's behavior will become unpredictable. I should point out, however, that I have never encountered a situation where it was necessary to recover a completely filled disc.

The recovery procedure comprises three parts: Preparing the source image of the track with a normal Pre-gap; increasing the Pre-gap to the size of entire disc; and then, writing the corrected image to the disc that needs to be restored. The first two steps can be carried out in one operation, since the resulting image (we will call it the "correcting image" later on) can be used for all discs (or, to be more precise, *for all discs of the same capacity;* for obvious reasons, it will be impossible to recover a 23-minute disc correctly using an image intended for 80-minute disc, and vice versa).

To begin with, let us take a blank CD-RW disc. ("Blank" in this case doesn't mean "one that has been never written," but, on the contrary, one that has been cleared by means of quick or full erasing. CD-R discs are also suitable.) Use any standard utility for CD burning and write to it a file of a size not exceeding 500 K (larger files won't fit within the planned 300 sectors). It isn't necessary to finalize the disc.

Start Clone CD (or Alcohol 120%) and grab the disc image. After a couple of minutes, two files will appear on the hard disk: the file name.img and the file name.ccd (if you instruct Clone CD also to save subchannel information, there will be a third file — file name.sub. However, in this case subchannel information will be more of a bore than a help. Therefore, it is advisable either to disable the "read subchannel info from data tracks" or delete the file name.sub file from the disk. The "Cue-Sheet" that Clone CD proposes you to create for compatibility with other programs, specifically with CDRWin, is also unnecessary.

Open the file name.ccd file with any text editor (Notepad, for example), find the following strings (use the Point=0xa2 and Point=0x01 keywords for searching).

Listing 10.6. The original starting address of Lead-out (left) and starting address of the first track of the disc (left)

```
[Entry 2]        [Entry 3]  ; TOC entry
Session=1        Session=1  ; Session number
Point=0xa2       Point=0x01 ; point (A2h:leadout/01h:№ track)
ADR=0x01         ADR=0x01   ; data in q-subchannel positioned
Control=0x04        Control=0x04   ; data track
TrackNo=0        TrackNo=0  ; Lead-In track
AMin=0           AMin=0     ; \
ASec=0           ASec=0     ;  +- absolute address in M:S:F
AFrame=0         AFrame=0   ; /
ALBA=-150        ALBA=-150  ; — Absolute address in LBA [no corrupt
Zero=0           Zero=0     ; Reserved
PMin=0           PMin=0     ; \
PSec=29          PSec=1     ;  + — Relative address in M:S:F
PFrame=33        PFrame=0   ; /
PLBA=2058        PLBA=0     ; — Relative address in LBA
```

Let's change the `PMin:PSec:PFrame` fields belonging to point `A2h` so that they point to the end of the disc (`A2h` represents the Lead-out). The changed Lead-out may appear as follows: `74:30:00`. The Lead-out address must be chosen in such a way that a gap of at least 30 seconds remains between it and the external disc edge. It is even better if the width of Lead-out equals about 1 1/2 minutes. However, in this case the last tracks of the disc being restored will be lost.

The contents of the `PMin:PSec:PFrame` fields belonging to point `01h` (the starting address of the first track) must be increased by the same value that was added to the corresponding Lead-out fields. For example, the modified variant might appear as follows: `74:01:42`. (`74:30:00` /* new Lead-out address */ − `00:29:33` /* old Lead-Out address*/ + `00:01:00` /* old starting address of the first track */ == `74:01:42` /* new starting address of the first track */. Briefly speaking, the new version of the CCD file must appear as follows:

Listing 10.7. A key fragment of the "reanimating file" for 75-minute CD-RW discs

```
PMin=74          PMin=74
PSec=30          PSec=01
PFrame=00        PFrame=42
```

To be accurate, it would be desirable also to edit the `PLBA` fields (the LBA address is related to the absolute address by the following formula: `LBA == ((Min*60) + + Sec)*75 + Frame`. However, current versions of CD-burning software use only absolute addresses, ignoring LBA addresses. Now, everything that is located between the end of the Lead-in area and the starting point of the first sector will become the Pre-gap. In the course of CD burning, the Pre-gap area will remain intact, and later it will be possible to read it at the sector level — exactly what we need! Honestly speaking, an excessive increase in the size of the Pre-gap area of the first track is not the best idea, since not all drives are capable of reading a long Pre-gap. From the compatibility point of view, it would be better to increase the Pre-gap area of the *second* track. However, in this case we'll have to place the first track at the very beginning of the disc, in which case recoverable sectors will inevitably be lost from the body of the file. Although the fact that starting sectors are unlikely to contain anything valuable means that this doesn't present a big problem, it is still better to avoid using this approach unless absolutely necessary. In case of emergency, do the following: write two sessions to the disc, and instead of changing the point `01h` address, change the starting address of point `02h` (it will be located in the `session=2` section).

Now, let's clear our test disc and fill it with files of any type to the full capacity (text files are preferable for this purpose, since they will allow you to see immediately what you are restoring from the disc — garbage or some useful information). Having written these files to the disc, clear it immediately.

After making sure that the disc has actually been cleared and that its contents are no longer available, start Clone CD and write the "reanimator" image that we have just created. Writing should be carried out in the DAO mode. Otherwise, you'll fail to achieve anything useful. Therefore, before attempting to recover discs of any value on a drive, about which you have insufficient knowledge, first try to recover some test discs that hold nothing you are afraid of losing.

The moment will finally arrive when you are holding in your hands a newly recovered CD. But has it actually been restored? To find out, insert the CD "recovered from ashes" into the NEC drive and, with a sinking heart, arbitrarily pick any sector located somewhere in the middle of the disc to read (starting sectors are usually filled with zeroes and, furthermore, these sectors and the file system can easily appear to be useless garbage). Voila!!! The original content of the cleared disc is as readable as if it had never been erased!!! Still, when attempting to read the disc TOC using the standard tools in the operating system, your drive might go into a stupor very similar to the OS freezing (after all, the starting address of the first track is not located at the beginning of the disc, as might be expected, but in quite a different location). But this doesn't matter. The main thing is that the disc is still available at the sector level, although not on every drive. For instance, the ASUS drive simply refuses to read such a disc, returning an error message, while the PHILIPS drive reads only a garble (fortunately, this garble is easily clean up. All you need to do is carry out sector-level EFM re-encoding from a more "suitable" position. Since there are only 14 possible positions, testing all of them won't take long. Still, the best approach is to purchase a better-quality drive than making all of this effort.

All that remains is to bring the disc to a state that will be accepted without any problems by the OS (what's the sense of analyzing the disc at the low level?). Now, we read all of the disc sectors sequentially, and combine them into one IMG file, which, for the sake of clarity, we'll assign the recover.img name. The sectors that, even after multiple attempts, we couldn't manage to read will be skipped. Let's copy the "reanimator" CCD file to the recover.ccd file and return the starting address of the first track to its initial position. We will write the newly formed disc image to the new disc, and, if everything has been done correctly, any drive will read it without any problems. The test session of demo reanimation has been successfully completed. Now, having acquired the necessary experience, we can embark on much more serious tasks. For instance, start our own small business, dealing with the recovery of accidentally cleared CDs. Just kidding.

What should we do if the cleared disc was a multisession disc? After all, the above-described techniques were intended for working only with one session! Actually, multisession discs can also be restored and this task is only slightly more difficult.

To achieve this, however, we must first become acquainted with the other fields of the TOC. This topic will be covered in the next chapter.

But what if something was written to the disc after it was cleared? Is recovery possible in this case? It depends. Naturally, locations that were erased directly are lost. But the remaining information can still be restored. If it was a multisession disc before clearing, we won't even need to labor over the recovery of the file system, since the file system of each next session usually duplicates that of the previous one. "Usually" means "in all cases other than that of erased files". At the same time, the last disc session proves to be located far from the beginning of the disc. Consequently, the risk of erasing it is minimum (provided, of course, that you worry about this in due time and don't remember it suddenly after having rewritten the entire disc). The recovery of single-session discs with an erased file system is a much more difficult task, although it is also possible. First, a typical disc has two types of file systems: ISO-9660 and Joliet. Unfortunately, because of their close "geographical" location, both of them are ruined in the course of erasing the disc. Second, these file systems do not support fragmentation, and any file written to a CD represents a contiguous information block. All you need to do to restore it is determine its entry point and length. The entry point of the file always coincides with the starting point of the sector, and the vast majority of file types allow for identifying their headers by a unique signature (in particular, the following sequence is characteristic for ZIP files: 50 4B 03 04). The end of a file cannot be detected so definitely, and the only hook here is the structure of the file being restored. Nevertheless, most applications tolerate a collection of assorted garbage at the file trailer, so, in practice, the precision of 1 sector when determining the file length is sufficient. Since files reside on the disc sequentially and without gaps, the terminating sector of any file can be recognized reliably by decreasing the starting address of the next file by one.

Generally speaking, the technique for recovering CDs is considerably easier than the art of recovering their "relatives" — diskettes and hard disks. On the other hand, the proverb "measure seven times before cutting once" still applies. One of the most unpleasant specific features of working with CD-RW discs is that, in this case, you are unable to fully control the writing process in progress. Diskettes and hard disks are fully transparent in this respect — you get what you actually write. CD-RW disks, on the contrary, represent a kind of "black box." You can never be sure that a specific drive will correctly interpret the commands passed to it. The recovery of CD-RW discs is not a standard operation, and any non-standard manipulation can be interpreted differently by different drives. The only advice that can be given here, is as follows: Do not let things take their own course. Try, try, and try again. This will allow you to accumulate valuable experience that will sometimes be of inestimable help.

How to Recover Unreadable CDs?

CDs are not extremely reliable media. You can't insure against their surfaces becoming scratched or contaminated, even provided that you store them very carefully (sometimes, the CD drive itself scratches the media, and there is nothing you can do in order to prevent this). Even a disc that appears to be OK at first glance may have hidden flaws that render it totally or partially unreadable on standard drives. This problem is especially urgent for CD-R/CD-RW discs, whose manufacturing quality is still far from perfect, and the process of burning can be affected by various errors.

But even a disc that has physical defects of the surface can be read successfully, thanks to the excessive redundancy of the information that it stores. With the gradual increase of the number of defects, however, the correcting capabilities of Reed-Solomon codes suddenly cease to be sufficient. When this happens, the disc becomes unreadable for no visible reason. The drive can even sometimes refuse to recognize it.

Fortunately, in the vast majority of cases it is possible to recover the information stored on the disc even under these conditions. The next section will explain how to do this.

General Recommendations on Recovery

Not every CD that is unreadable (or is unstable) is actually defective. Most frequently, it is the operating system or the CD drive that is to blame. Before jumping to any conclusions, try to read the disc on all drives available to you that are installed on computers with newly installed operating systems. Many drives, even expensive brands, become extremely capricious after a short period of use. They often refuse to read discs that can be read without any problem on other drives. With regard to the operating system, it tends to catch various strange bugs as you install, reinstall, or remove various software. Sometimes, these bugs manifest themselves in unpredictable ways. For example, the TEAC drive installed in a system with a CDR4_2K.SYS driver inherited from PHILIPS conflicts with the CD Player, refusing to display the contents of data discs when that application is active. After removing the CDR4_2K.SYS driver, everything works without any problems.

Also, it mustn't be forgotten that the *corrective capabilities* of different drive models are very different. For example, correcting codes of C_1, C_2, Q-, and P- levels can be accomplished effectively by all drives with which I am familiar. Their corrective capabilities is up to two errors for each of the C_1 and C_2 levels, and up to 86 and 52 errors for the Q- and P- levels, respectively. To be honest, the number of detectable, but mathematically irrecoverable, errors is as high as to 4 errors for C_1 and C_2 levels and up to 172/104 errors per Q/P levels. But only the position of erroneous bytes in a frame or sector, and not their values, can be determined with any guarantee. Knowing the position of erroneous bytes and having at your disposal the source HF signal (e.g., *analog* signal taken directly from the read head), however, it is possible to recover some odds and ends of information — at least, theoretically. However, in my experience, the price of the drive is rather weakly correlated with its reading capabilities. For instance, relatively inexpensive ASUS drives read practically everything, while expensive PHILIPS drives recognize even their "native" discs with native drivers less consistently.

Another important characteristic is the *available range of read speeds*. In general, the lower the rotation speed of the disc, the lower the requirements on its quality. However, this relationship is not always linear. Most drives have one or more *preferred* rotation speeds, at which their reading capabilities are at a maximum. For instance, it is possible that a defective disc is readable without any problems at 8x, but is totally unreadable at any other speed. The optimal speed can be determined easily by experiment. All you have to do is test the full range of available speeds. When purchasing a CD-ROM drive, choose the device that has the widest range of speeds. For instance, the PHILIPS CDRW 2400 can operate only at the following speeds: 16x, 24x, 38x and 42x. The lack of speeds such as 4x and 8x limits the "ration" of this drive to high-quality discs only.

For some unknown reason, Windows built-in tools do not permit the control of disc-rotation speed. Therefore, to gain such control, it is necessary to use third-party utilities. Fortunately, there are a large number of these tools available. For example, you can use *Slow CD*, *Ahead Nero Drive Speed,* or any other similar tool. Generally speaking, most drives reduce the rotation speed on their own initiative if they encounter unreadable sectors. However, the quality of algorithms they implement for this purpose is still far from perfect, and user's control over the rotation speed provides considerably better results.

If the disc cannot be read on any drive available to you, it is possible to try polishing it with any polishing paste. The Internet provides a lot of information on polishing optical surfaces in general, and CD surfaces in particular. As a matter of fact, books on astronomy, especially those concentrating on the construction of telescopes, are the most useful in this respect. Because of the general availability of such information, I will cover this topic only briefly in this book. In the majority of cases, it is possible to polish a scratched disc. If done properly, it is highly likely that the information can be restored. However, a number of factors do limit the degree, to which this is true. First, polishing repairs only the scratches on the lower surface of the disc, and cannot deal with the destruction of the reflecting layer. Second, when removing scratches, you inevitably create new ones. Consequently, some CDs can become damaged even more badly after polishing. Third, it is impossible to acquire the skills of polishing CDs on your first try. To master this skill will take much time and a number of attempts. But we'll try another way!

What, in fact, is very good for your disc is sponging it with a special anti-static liquid (you can buy it in your local computer store). Before wiping the disc, blow off all dust particles from its surface, to avoid producing more scratches. Never wipe the disk with concentric circular motions! It is necessary to wipe the surface with radial movements, from the center to the edges, replacing the cloth with each pass.

The Disc Cannot Be Recognized by the Drive

You insert the disc into the drive. The drive starts to rotate the disc, with the activity LED blinking wildly, making sure that at the specified speed, the disc cannot be read. It then starts to reduce the rotation speed until it comes to a full stop. The "DISK IN" indicator (if it is present on the front panel of the drive), sadly, blinks and goes off, thus signaling you that the piece of plastic that you have inserted, from its point of view, is anything you want it to be except for a CD. An attempt to access the disc results in an error message informing you that there is no disc in the drive and prompting you to insert one.

The inability of the drive to recognize the disc is, in most cases, evidence of a malfunction in the CD-ROM. Cases where the problem is caused by a damaged CD are much more rare. Even if this disc was easily recognized yesterday, and even if the drive successfully recognizes all other discs, don't rush to assume that the drive is working properly. Try to read this disc on another drive. Worse comes to the worst, reduce the disc rotation speed down to minimum. Be prepared for the fact that the drive may not obey you. Most drives automatically reduce the previous rotation speed settings when replacing the disc and do not allow you to change the speed until the disc has been recognized successfully (in particular, this is particularly characteristic of TEAC drives, while ASUS drives usually behave less temperamentally).

If the disc being tested cannot be recognized by any of the drives available to you, the most likely cause is that the drives cannot read the disc's TOC, which is stored in the Lead-in area. Remove the disc from the drive and take a careful look at the narrow glittering ring located near the internal edge of the disc. This ring is the Lead-in. Make sure that it has no deep scratches or is not contaminated. If it is dirty, remove the dirt using a clean cloth (most individuals forget about the Lead-in area when cleaning the disc, probably taking it for some kind of useless decoration). Overcoming scratches is significantly more difficult. Without enough experience at polishing CDs, it is not advisable to attempt this. If this is the case, bring the disc to a center specializing in information recovery. However, these aren't always easy to locate and, further, this doesn't guarantee success. Finally, it is wise to consider confidentiality and the cost of the service, among other factors.

Is it possible to reanimate such a disc on your own? It is! However, in order to do this, you'll have to purchase certain equipment, at a cost of around $30. You will need a spare CD-ROM drive, with which you can experiment as you please and the loss of which won't be a problem. Low-speed drives left over from previous upgrades of your computer are the most suitable for this purpose.

The trick is that the TOC is not a must for working with CDs at the sector level, so you can do without it. In fact, this is not a hardware problem — it is the software problem. Having determined that irrecoverable errors have occurred in the course of reading the TOC, the drive firmware refuses to process the disc, despite the fact that TOC content is duplicated in the Q subcode channel and distributed over the entire spiral track. Furthermore, the drive actually only needs three main fields of the TOC: the *address of the disc Lead-out area* (in order to know, up to what position it is possible to move the head), the *starting address of the first track* (in order to know where to start reading the data) and the *address of the next Lead-in area* (only for multisession drives). The easiest task is dealing with the starting address of the first track — it is equal to 00:02:00 (which corresponds to the zero LBA address). The Lead-out address, directly dependent on the CD capacity, does not necessarily need to be specified with high precision. It is enough to choose it so that it is no less than the address of the current Lead-out. Otherwise, all of the sectors located beyond this boundary will become unavailable. By setting the Lead-out address to 80 — or even 90 — minutes, we can guarantee that the entire disc surface will be available to the drive. Briefly speaking, if we can get access to the internal structures of the drive firmware, the recovery of the corrupted TOC would be a trifling matter. For this purpose, I use specially modified firmware of a quite ordinary, old CD-ROM drive (this is an old 8x, no-name brand), which allows for the manipulation of any service data. Therefore, it reads everything that is physically readable.

If hacking microprocessor programs is too difficult for you, it is possible to proceed using another method. Carefully disassemble the CD-ROM drive and extract its internals from the case (the cheaper the spare drive, the better). Now, unscrew the bolts that fasten the metallic strap, on each a "plate" is fastened, that is pressed to the upper edge of the CD, to prevent it from sliding. Instead of this assembly, you can use a metallic ring, on any other heavy object. The main idea is to get free access to the CD, thus providing the possibility of "hot-swapping" it on the fly, without opening the tray.

Now, connect the drive to the computer, power it on, and proceeding in a normal way, insert a specially prepared disc into the drive. The Lead-out area of the disc must be located somewhere around 80 to 90 minutes (it is possible to insert any CD with the video, with the size starting from 700 MB). Make sure that the disc has been correctly recognized, and, without shutting the system down, remove it from the drive without opening the tray. Now insert into this drive the disc that you want to restore. Since the TOC of the previous disc is already loaded into the cache, and the drive is unable to detect disc replacement carried out in such a barbaric method, it will work with the new disc just the same way it would have with the old one. The only thing that you should not try to do is read the disc contents using the built-in operating-system tools. This won't produce any result. After all, the operating system also caches data. Therefore, you can click "Refresh" until you go crazy, but Windows will continue to display the previous contents. Instead of this, take any grabber that can read the disc at the sector level and doesn't ask any extra questions (for instance, you can use the free cd_raw_read utility by the author of this book) and copy the entire contents of the disc from the first sector to the last into an image file. Then, using any suitable CD-burning utility, write this image to CD-R or CD-RW. Although you won't recover the disc itself, you will at least save its contents! This method can be used both for audio and data discs with equal success.

As an alternative, instead of removing the pressure plate, you can find the sensor for disc replacement and temporarily remove it, thus preventing the drive from noticing that the disc being recovered has not been replaced. Cheap drives use simple mechanical sensors that can be found easily. More expensive models do not contain a separate sensor at all. In these, the act of pressing the <EJECT> button is considered an indication of disc replacement. If this is the case, you can use the hole for emergency disc ejection. However, bear in mind that ejecting a disc using this method on a running drive can ruin the mechanism altogether.

By the way, there are some drives that manage to read the disc even if the TOC has been completely destroyed. For instance, the list of these drives includes some MSI models. The lucky owners of these drives don't need to disassemble their devices, since they are capable of reading corrupted drives even without this operation.

When recovering multisession discs, it is possible to try to color the Lead-in disc area with black marker. The contents of the first session will be lost. All of the other sessions, however, will be read successfully by most drives. To do so, just recall that the Lead-in disc area looks like a glittering ring encircling the internal edge of the disc.

The Disc is Recognized by the Drive, but Not by the Operating System

You insert the disc into the drive. The drive starts to rotate it, and the DISK IN indicator (if there is one) goes on. However, any attempt to view the disc contents using standard OS tools results in various error messages. Scanning of the disc surface using Ahead Nero CD Speed (or any other similar utility) discovers one or two damaged sectors.

This is an obvious symptom of file-system corruption. To be more precise, this is the corruption of the root directory of the file system. If this happens, do not panic. Recovery of the CD root directory, in contrast to recovery of the root directories of hard disks and diskettes, doesn't present a serious problem. Most CDs contain not one, but two duplicate file systems — ISO 9660 and Joliet (this is true for all discs manufactured after 1995). The simultaneous corruption of both root directories is extremely unlikely. Besides this, due to the lack of fragmentation, subdirectories are not scattered over the entire CD surface. On the contrary, they are concentrated in a single location. Thanks to this, even if the root directory is totally destroyed, they can be recovered quite easily. Finally, each next session of a multisession disc includes the contents of the file systems of all previous sessions (excluding, naturally, the deleted files). Therefore, if the file system of the last session is destroyed, we can easily recover the contents of all of the previous sessions.

Unfortunately, built-in Windows tools do not allow you to selectively mount either the preferred file system or the preferred session. Instead, they force you to use the root directory of the Joliet file system of the last session. The simplest idea that comes to mind is to try to read the disc under pure MS-DOS with the MSCDEX driver, working exclusively with ISO 9660 and ignoring the existence of Joliet. Another variant is to use the ISO 9660.dir utility developed by the author specially for working with destroyed file systems and restoring practically everything that can be restored.

Naturally, since the maximum length of the file identifiers in the ISO 9660 systems is only 11 characters, long file names become irreversibly corrupted. However, you will probably agree, this is still better than nothing.

The Computer Freezes When Inserting the Disc into the Drive

You insert the disc into the drive, the drive starts rotating it, the activity indicator blinking intensely, and then it freezes. Quite often, it also freezes the operating system. In the best cases, the situation can be resolved by pressing the <EJECT> button. In the worst case, you'll have to press <RESET>.

Such behavior is typical for protected discs, the protection of which is based on a corrupted TOC. Most drives are loyal to corrupted TOC (although that depends on what exactly has been corrupted). However, one can run into devices that simply freeze after such a situation occurs. If it is still necessary to read the protected disc, try to change the drive.

Another possible variant is a looped file system. This happens frequently when burning CD-R/CD-RW discs using incorrectly written software. If this is the case, press and hold the <Shift> button during disc loading to prevent the operating system from reading its contents (or temporarily disable the AutoRun feature). Then, using utilities like ISO 9660.dir, copy everything that can be copied from the disc.

The Disc Is Read with Errors

If, despite all your efforts at decreasing the rotation speed or cleaning the disc surface, the disc is still read with errors, and corrupted sectors fall exactly to the area taken up by the most valuable files, then things have taken the worst turn. However, there is still some chance of successful data recovery, although very slim.

First and foremost, there are all kinds of errors. Cases where the entire sector is unreadable are rare. As a rule, the case in point is that one or two bytes belonging to that sector are unreadable. At the same time, the correcting capabilities of redundant codes are such that up to 392 corrupted bytes are corrected already in the first-level decoder (CIRC-decoder). P-codes are capable of correcting up to another 86 errors, and Q-codes can correct up to 52 errors. This means that, under favorable error distribution, it will be possible to recover up to 530 errors, or up to 25 percent of the total sector capacity. Only the horrible unreliability of optical media causes situations where even this vast data redundancy is sometimes unable to withstand failures.

Depending on the setup parameters, the drive, having detected an irrecoverable error, either returns the sector in the form, in which it managed to read it, or simply reports an error, leaving the contents of the output buffer in an undefined state. The idea of data recovery consists of making the drive return anything that it is capable to read. Naturally, corrupted bytes cannot be recovered. However, many file formats are quite tolerant to minor corruption. Music in the MP3/WMA format, video films and graphic images will be successfully recovered. Only in the exact place of the error will a click — sometimes louder than others — be audible, or some "artifact" will be noticeable. The case with archives is significantly worse. However, in most cases, only a single file will be lost, while the remaining contents of the archive will be unpacked normally (by the way, some archivers, such as RAR, support their own correcting codes, which provides for the restoration of corrupted archives with the expense of minimum redundancy).

"Wait!" — some readers will cry, — "This is not right!" In fact, we tried to recover unreadable discs with one or another utility. And what was the effect? The system refused to consider "reanimated" MPG or AVI as video files! However, I would object that these utilities simply discarded all of the sectors that they could not read, and as a result, the file size and relative offsets of all its structures have changed. Consequently, it is no wonder that the file cannot be played after such a "recovery."

Use any copier of protected discs that provides selective control over the error-processing mode and choose the 24h mode (the maximum possible error correction without interrupting data transmission in the case that an error encountered proves to be irrecoverable). Among all of the utilities suitable for this purpose, I recommend that you use the `cd_raw_read` utility developed by the author. As an alternative, it is possible to use Alcohol 120% and/or Clone CD.

What reasons can be behind the fact that the sector is unreadable? First of all, there could be deep and wide radial scratches on the upper part. After penetrating a thin barrier of protective coating, the scratches damage the reflective material directly, and with it, useful data are damaged.

Narrow scratches that are not too numerous generally are not too dangerous, since the sector contents are distributed along the spiral track. Therefore, the loss of several bytes can be easily compensated for by data redundancy. However, there is one "but." How does the drive get to know how many pits and lands have been omitted? Since pits and lands do not correspond to binary zeroes and ones directly, and a binary one is encoded by the transition from pit to land and vice versa, while zero is encoded by the lack of transitions at the given point, it becomes obvious that the disappearance of an odd number of pits/lands seems to "reverse" the entire frame trailer. In other words, it simply ruins it. Hence, even a single scratch can generate an entire cascade of errors that cannot be recovered using standard correcting codes. However, theoretically, such errors can be repaired manually. Manually? Well, not quite, since for this purpose, you'll need a special utility. An example of such a utility has already been written by the author and is now undergoing alpha-testing. It can successfully read discs that were not readable in a standard way. I hope that by the time that this book is published it will be ready for beta-testing and become available for free for all users who need it. However, since the length of one frame is only 24 bytes, the destruction of several sequential frames can be repaired even by standard correcting codes. Therefore, my utility will be needed only for recovering badly damaged discs with lots of scratches.

Wide scratches are a different matter. Not only do they "eat up" several frames entirely, they also send the optical head astray from the track. When the head falls into the hole created by a scratch, it becomes totally disoriented, since it simply has nothing to rely upon. After that, the head "flies out" and lands on one of the neighboring tracks. Intellectual drives detect such a situation and position the head to the required place. The drives that have no such intellectual functions, which, by the way, are the vast majority, self-confidently try to continue reading as if nothing has happened. As a result, the header of one sector is combined with the trailer of another one, and, naturally, any attempt to restore such a sector using standard correcting code will produce nothing but garbage. Consequently, the drive will report an irrecoverable error. The only way out is to read such a sector until the head falls into the same track, from which the reading of the sector was begun. The number of reading attempts in this case must be large enough (100 or more). After all, it is much easier to divert from the narrow spiral track than keep on following it!

Concentric scratches represent the most destructive type of damage that can only exist on CDs. The distribution of information along the spiral track is now unable to withstand the failure, since corruption influences the entire sector (in contrast to radial scratches that damage only a small part of the sector). Besides this, concentric scratches disorient the tracking system, since sensor lasers are slightly defocused, and, therefore, are very sensitive to such surface defects.

The scratches located at the lower side of the disc can in most cases be eliminated by polishing, while scratches that involve the working layer are impossible to eliminate.

On the CD

The companion CD contains all of the required utilities for the analysis and copying of protected CDs. Note that bypassing the protection against CD copying is not the same thing as copyright violation! The laws of many countries explicitly allow the creation of backup copies of licensed media. The PHILIPS Corporation, which is one of the inventors of CD technology, strongly opposes any deviations from the standard and insists on that protected discs including anti-copying technology should not use the "Compact Disc" logo. Legislation in many countries supports this claim. Any disc protected by a non-standard format must be marked with an unequivocal warning that, although the piece of plastic you are purchasing bears a resemblance to a CD, in reality, it is not a proper CD.

Furthermore, to develop CD protection mechanisms, the programmer must have at least a general idea about the working methods and technical tools used by his or her opponents. To master this technical arsenal at a level no lower than that of the opponent is even better. Simply speaking, it allows us to detect and reinforce the most probable targets against hacker attacks, concentrating on them the maximum available intellectual resources. This means that the developer of protection mechanisms must be inspired by the hacker psychology, and start thinking like a hacker. Thus, mastering information-protection technology assumes mastering of cracking technology. If you don't know how protection mechanisms are cracked, what their vulnerabilities are, and have no information about the hacker's arsenal, you won't be able to create a strong protection mechanism that would be both inexpensive and easy to implement.

The SRC directory contains all the source code of the demo examples used in this book.

❑ ETC — Demo examples for low-level access to CD-ROM drives
❑ RS.LIB — Libraries for low-level working with CD sectors from CloneCD and Ahead Nero and interfaces to them, with examples illustrating their practical use
❑ RS.SIMPLE — Elementary examples illustrating the principle of Reed-Solomon codes
❑ SCSI.ALT — Source code of the driver allowing execution of the IN/OUT machine commands from the application level
❑ SCSI.LIB — Tools and utilities developed by the author for working with protected CDs

Root directory has many small but useful utilities, including the Pinch of File block file copier useful for file-by-file copying of CDs containing files with incorrect lengths and starting sectors.

The README.TXT file describes the contents of the CD-ROM.

The DivX511Bundle.exe file shows video about the A-List Publsihing books. To watch this file, install Standard DivX Codec(FREE) available for free download from **http://www.divx.com/divx/**.

Index

A

Adaptec, 356
AFrame, 326
Ahead Nero, 226, 230, 266, 267, 272, 288,
   328, 338, 400
ALBA, 317, 326
Alcohol 120%, 226, 230, 240, 245, 266, 303,
   319, 324, 328, 341, 347, 357, 380, 382, 402
AMin, 326
API, 226, 378
ASec, 326
ASPI, 97, 257, 379
ASUS, 242, 303, 341
ATIP, 288, 376
Audio:
   CDs, 43, 395
   tracks, 327

B

Blind Write, 266, 273
Block file copier, 252
Blue Screen of Death, 97, 122
BSOD, 97, 122
   .EXE, 124
Bug Check codes, 125

C

C1/C2-level errors, 345
C1-decoders, 45
C2-decoders, 45
c2u, 329
Cactus Shield 2.00, 346
CalcSubChannelCRC, 267
CCD file, 308, 319, 328, 347

CD:

CD:
   unique marks, 375
   burners, 394
   file systems, 355
   measuring angles between sectors, 385
   players, 345
CD marks
   requirements, 375
CD.lock.exe, 306
CD_RAW_SECTOR_READ, 336, 337
CD-Enhanced discs, 346
CDFS, 379
   driver, 395
CD-R, 393
CD-ROM firmware, 229
CD-RW, 39, 393
   restoring, 401
CDRWin, 266, 282, 340, 402, 404
CIRC, 40
   errors, 346
Clone CD, 31, 226, 230, 232, 245, 279, 288, 303,
   319, 324, 328, 332, 337, 341, 347, 380, 400
Crash dump, 122
CRC, 17
Cross Interleaved Reed-Solomon Coder, 40
CWinThread, 118

D

Data:
   CDs, 273
   tracks, 327
DDCD media, 334
DDK, 124
Descrambling, 332
Digital playback, 329
Digital Sum Value, 27, 39, 390
Disassembler, 389

DispatchMessage, 116
Doctor Watson, 98, 99
DSV, 27, 39, 390
Dumpbin, 120
DumpChk, 131
DVD, 241

E

Easy CD Creator, 230
ECC, 22
ECMA-120, 390
ECMA-130, 19, 24, 30, 285, 336
EDC, 22
EDC/ECC, 333
EFM, 17
  words, 17
Eight to Fourteen Modulation, 17
ElbyECC.dll, 31, 332
Error Correction Code, 22
Error Detection Code, 22
ExitProcess, 115

F

F1 frame, 17, 38
F2 frame, 40
F3 frame, 45
FAR Manager, 321
FAT, 355
fc.exe, 329
Firmware, 229
  patching, 333
FPO functions, 112
Full memory dump, 123

H

HAL, 123
Hard disks, 336
Hardware Abstraction Layer, 123
HEX editor, 389
HIEW, 252, 342, 356, 369

I

i386kd, 125, 130
IDA PRO, 116

IEC 908, 22
IMAGE.CCD, 233, 266, 294
IMAGE.IMG, 233
IMAGE.SUB, 233, 344
IMATION, 389
IMG file, 319, 329
Incorrect TOC, 230
Interactive debuggers, 122
Internet, 305
IRP stack, 127
IsIdleMessage, 120
ISO 9660/Joliet, 284, 356, 395
ISO image, 401
ISO 9660, 356, 395
ISO9660.dir, 396

J

Joliet, 356

K

KAnalyze, 131
Kernel memory dump, 123

L

Lands, 27
LBA, 21, 239, 315, 345, 355
Lead-in, 46
Lead-out, 46

M

M:S:F, 315
Mac OS, 394
Memory dump, 122
Merging bits, 25
Message-handling loop, 115
MFC, 118
MFC42.DLL, 120
MFC42.LIB, 120
MFM, 229
Microsoft, 356
Microsoft Kernel Debugger, 106
Microsoft Knowledge Base, 379

Microsoft Visual Studio, 100, 106, 379
    Debugger, 106
MOD chips, 226
Modulo-2 addition, 35
MP3, 347
MS-DOS, 227, 357, 378
MSF, 21
MSI, 47
Multisession disc, 268

N

NEC, 242, 245, 277, 303, 332, 341
newtrf.dll, 267
Norton Utilities, 108
NTFS, 18
NTFS.SYS, 127

O

Orange Book, 335, 341
OVL, 118

P

P subchannel, 19
pagefile.sys, 128
Pascal, 226
PC CD-ROM, 345
PE-file, 120
PHILIPS, 40, 47, 242, 245, 347, 382
Pinch of File, 252
Pits, 27
Platform SDK, 349
PLBA, 326
    fields, 405
Plextor, 40, 328, 333, 391
PMA, 47, 48
Post-gap, 260, 336
Pre-gap, 259, 336
Professor Nimnul, 329
Protected CD copiers, 340
Protection against digital playback, 228
Protection mechanisms:
    based on physical defects, 377
    classification, 225
PTE table, 127
PumpMessage, 120

Q

Q subcode channel, 19, 230, 260, 300, 304

R

RAID array, 127
RAM, 349
RAW:
    DAO mode, 231, 350, 402
    reading, 378
READ, 274
    CD, 274, 277, 279
    HEADER, 277, 279
    SUBCHANNEL, 227, 280, 305, 313
    timing diagram, 381
    TOC, 299, 325
RealAudio, 368
Recovery Console, 128
Red Book, 22, 230, 259
Reed-Solomon:
    codes, 259, 327
    decoder, 30, 332
Reflective layer, 15
Registry Editor, 99
Romeo, 356
Roxio Easy CD Creator, 226, 347, 396
Run-in/Run-out blocks, 335
Russinovitch, Mark, 124

S

SAO mode, 231
SaveDump.exe, 130
Scrambler, 332, 390
Scrambling, 29
SEEK, 277, 279, 305
Seek_and_Q, 323, 325
SENSE INFO, 341
Soft-ice, 125
Solomon, David, 124
SPTI, 97, 257, 379
Stack
    manually unrolling, 112
Stamper-injection molding, 259
Stomp Record Now!, 230, 272, 288, 328, 334,
    335, 347, 396, 400
Stray pointers, 98

SUB file, 319
Subchannel:
    byte, 18
    data grabbing, 227
    data reading, 313

T

Table Of Contents, 47, 345, 350, 402
TAO, 261
Task Manager, 306
TDB, 261
TDK, 389
TDT, 262
TDU, 262
TEAC, 245, 277, 303, 311, 332, 341
TNO, 20, 266, 304
TOC, 47, 345, 350, 402
Track:
    At Once, 261
    Descriptor Block, 261
    Descriptor Table, 262
    Descriptor Unit, 262
Track number:
    non-standard, 322
Tracks:
    audio, 327
    data, 327

U

UNIX, 347

V

Variable capacitor, 227
Vernam cipher, 32

Virtual Memory Manager, 126
VMM, 126

W

W2K_KILL.SYS, 124
Watermark, 335
White noise, 29
WinDiff, 268
Windows 2000, 229, 329
Windows 9x, 98, 321, 379, 394
    critical error screen, 98
Windows Driver Development Kit, 124
Windows Notepad, 321
Windows NT, 98, 379, 394
    critical error screen, 98
Windows NT/2000, 321
Windows XP, 229
WMA, 347
WriteProcessMemory, 98

X

X-sector, 277, 279, 282, 347, 335
    copying, 341

Y

Yellow Book, 22, 259, 336

Z

Zip drive, 389
ZX-Spectrum, 329